HISTORICAL LETTERS

PETER LAVROV
Historical Letters

Translated with an Introduction and Notes

by

JAMES P. SCANLAN

UNIVERSITY OF CALIFORNIA PRESS

BERKELEY AND LOS ANGELES

1967

D
16.8
L 32/3

UNIVERSITY OF CALIFORNIA PRESS
BERKELEY AND LOS ANGELES, CALIFORNIA

CAMBRIDGE UNIVERSITY PRESS
LONDON, ENGLAND

TRANSLATOR'S PREFACE

PETER LAVROV occupies a position of major importance in the history of Russian thought and the history of the Russian socialist movement. His multitudinous writings, spanning the entire second half of the nineteenth century, include some of the finest products of his nation's intellectual genius in two domains—philosophy and revolutionary publicism. Through these writings his influence on both Russian opinion and Russian social reality has been great.

Yet in the English-speaking world Lavrov is almost unknown. Even in his native land his contributions are not fully acknowledged: Tsarist authorities before the Russian revolution and illiberal Marxists thereafter have conspired to limit Lavrov scholarship to a fitful if extensive body of literature, which contains to this day no complete edition of his writings, no comprehensive bibliography, no adequate biography, and no thorough study of his thought. In English-speaking countries, however, the literature is incomparably poorer. Many of Lavrov's works have been translated into other European languages—French, German, and Polish—but until excerpts from the present translation appeared in print in 1965, none of his writings was available to readers of English. And although Lavrov's thought has been treated in a number of general studies of Russian philosophy and intellectual history which exist in English translation—notably the works by Masaryk, Zenkovsky, and Venturi listed in the bibliography at the end of this volume—treatment has been limited to a modest chapter or less. Except for an excellent but unpublished doctoral dissertation by Philip Pomper (see bibliography), there is no work in the English language which presents the facts of Lavrov's biography and intellectual career in anything beyond rudimentary form.

It was to help fill this lack that the present translation of Lavrov's chief and most influential work, his *Historical Letters* (*Istoricheskiye pis'ma*) was undertaken, and that it is presented here with an introduction and other aids to further study. The introduction seeks to provide both an analysis of the content and impact of the *Historical Letters* and a more complete account of Lavrov's life and thought in general than has hitherto been available in English. Special attention has been given to Lavrov's first elaboration of his intellectual outlook in his early philosophical essays, and to its development through the *Historical Letters* to his later writings. The translation itself has been annotated wherever further elucidation or amplification seemed desirable; the notes will be found at the end of the volume. The bibliography, although by no means complete, was designed to give full publication data for Lavrov's most significant writings, particularly his theoretical works (including all editions of the *Historical Letters*), and for some of the most informative and useful secondary sources.

This translation was undertaken at the suggestion of Professor George L. Kline of Bryn Mawr College, whose services to the cause of scholarship in the fields of Russian philosophy and intellectual history are too well known to require additional comment. Professor Kline read portions of the manuscript and gave generously of his time and knowledge at every stage in its preparation. Without his help the work would never have been begun, much less completed.

I am particularly indebted to Professor Gleb Struve of the University of California, Berkeley, who painstakingly read a major portion of an early draft of this translation in close comparison with the Russian original, doing his expert best to lessen the translator's inaccuracies and stylistic infelicities. Others who deserve special thanks for their kind help in improving the manuscript are Professors Nicholas Riasanovsky and Martin Malia of the University of California, Berkeley; Professor Norman Henley of Johns Hopkins University; and Professor Richard Waidelich of San Francisco State College.

For financial assistance in the preparation of this volume I wish to thank the following institutions: the Ford Foundation, for a fellowship under which the translation was made; Goucher College, for a Danforth Fellowship and a faculty research grant which aided in carrying out the research for the introduction and in preparing the manuscript; and the Inter-University Committee on Travel Grants, which provided me with the opportunity to complete the research for the introduction and for the bibliography in the Soviet Union.

I am also indebted to the staffs of the following libraries for special help: the Julia Rogers Library of Goucher College; the University of California Library, Berkeley; the Library of Congress; the Lenin State Library, Moscow; and the Saltykov-Shchedrin State Public Library, Leningrad.

I wish to thank Quadrangle Books, Inc., Chicago, for permission to reprint the portions of this translation previously published. These portions are reprinted from *Russian Philosophy*, edited by James M. Edie, James P. Scanlan, and Mary-Barbara Zeldin, with the collaboration of George L. Kline, copyright 1965 by Quadrangle Books, Inc., Chicago.

My final and greatest debt is to my wife, whose hours of active dedication to this manuscript exceeded all reasonable bounds, qualitative as well as quantitative, and deserve far greater recognition than one ritual sentence can express.

A Note on the Translation

This is a complete translation of the so-called "Paris" edition of the *Historical Letters*, published in Geneva in 1891, which is the most comprehensive edition and the last edition prepared by Lavrov himself. The bibliography at the end of this volume contains descriptions of all editions of the work, in Russian and in other languages.

To facilitate comparison with the first collected edition of 1870, the form in which the work became best known and exerted most influence, all additions to the 1891 edition of a sentence or more in length have here been enclosed in square brackets, with the exception of those additions (a number of footnotes and the Sixteenth Letter) for which dates of composition are given by Lavrov himself. Additions or alterations within sentences have been identified if they have some substantive significance; in such cases simple additions are enclosed in square brackets, and substitutions are explained in the end notes. Passages of a sentence or more in the 1870 edition which do not appear in the 1891 edition are given in full in the end notes. Editorial comments are confined to the end notes; all footnotes are Lavrov's.

In a few cases where some ambiguity or uncertainty attaches to the translation of a Russian word or expression, the original Russian is given in transliterated form in a parenthesis following the translation.

Goucher College, October 1966   JAMES P. SCANLAN

CONTENTS

Peter Lavrov
An Intellectual Biography

THE YEAR 1870 WAS BOTH AN END and a beginning in the long career of radical socialism in Russia. For that year marked the death of Alexander Herzen, the father of Russian Populism, who first set Russian social protest on a firmly socialist foundation. It also marked the birth of Vladimir Ilyich Lenin, the messiah of Russian Marxism, who put the fruits of the intellectual and social development stemming from Herzen into ultimate and fatal practice.

But 1870 was a watershed in the history of the Russian radical movement for another reason as well. For in the same year a book appeared which is the most important single document of social protest in the Russian evolution from Herzen to Lenin—Peter Lavrov's *Historical Letters*. The author of the *Historical Letters* took over the heritage of Herzen, reworked it, gave it a new philosophical base and a strong practical focus. In so doing he helped to turn scattered protest into a nationwide force which ultimately led, in the hands of Lenin, to the most violent and sweeping social reconstruction a great nation has known in modern times—a reconstruction which proved cruelly different from that envisaged by the author of the *Historical Letters,* despite the fact that he shared many of the principles and was the first to expound some of the methods of the final transformation.

Peter Lavrov was an unlikely person to turn men's heads with radical sentiments and give new directions to a revolutionary movement. Born into the landed gentry, a colonel of artillery in the imperial army, a professor of mathematics for more than twenty years before writing the book, Lavrov was above all a scholar, even something of a pedant. His earlier writings were known for vast but dry erudition and labored analysis. As a householder he was a member of the St. Petersburg city *duma* and the provincial *zemstvo,* and his views had seemed moderate enough to arouse the ire of many progressives.

Yet his *Historical Letters* had an immediate and profound effect on the searching Russian youth of the day. Nicholas Rusanov, Lavrov's first biographer, who himself had felt the impact of the book, left this tribute to its extraordinary appeal:

Oh, you had to live in the 'seventies, in the time of the "To the People!" movement, to see around you and to feel within you the astonishing effect produced by the *Historical Letters!* Many of us—youths at the time, and others mere boys—never parted with the tattered little book; we read it and reread it until finally it wore out. It lay under our pillows, and as we read it at night hot tears of idealistic enthusiasm fell upon it—an enthusiasm that gripped us with a boundless thirst to live for noble ideas, and to die for them. And how joyously our hearts beat, in what majesty there arose before us the image of our "dear teacher"—personally unknown to us but our kinsman in thought, physically remote from us but close to us in the spirit of his teachings —who summoned us to a selfless struggle for conviction! [1]

The book became, in Rusanov's expression, the handbook and the bible of the Russian revolutionary youth of the 'seventies. And countless other memoirists, including such subsequent leaders of Russian radical opinion as George Plekhanov and Peter Kropotkin, similarly attest to the profound moral and intellectual reverberations set up in their own lives and in the lives of their contemporaries by the author of the *Historical Letters.*

Who was this scholar who moved men's hearts, and what were the ideas he preached with such powerful effect?

Early Life

Peter Lavrovich Lavrov was born in the village of Melekhova in the province of Pskov, 240 miles south of St. Petersburg, on June 2, 1823.[2] His father, Lavr Stepanovich, was a landowner who had received an exclusive education in the Cadet Corps and had risen to the rank of colonel of artillery. Wounded in 1807 in the war against France, Lavr Stepanovich settled on his estate at Melekhova and in 1811 married Yelizaveta Karlovna Handwig, of a Russified Swedish family. They had three children, of whom Peter was the youngest by six years.

Peter's father was an ardent patriot and a loyal subject who had close ties to the imperial court. The Lavrov estate was a stopping place for traveling royalty: Empress Elizabeth was a visitor, and Alexander I himself stopped at the estate in 1825, on the trip to southern Russia from which he never returned. A good friend was the notorious Count Arakcheyev, Alexander's brutal chief counsellor and organizational wizard. At the same time Lavr Stepanovich was a well-read, cultured gentleman whose cast of mind was not untouched by the belated Russian Enlightenment. Though he scrupulously observed the forms of Russian Orthodoxy, he disliked the intense religiosity of some of his wife's friends. He had a strong distaste for Freemasonry and freethinking, but his library contained the writings of Voltaire and the Encyclopedists. He was a man of taste, and the house was adorned with paintings and sculpture.

In this ordered, cultured world, with no companions near his age, Peter was brought up, in the words of one biographer, "like a girl." His father was a stern disciplinarian, and Peter showed no inclination to rebel. Forbidden to stray beyond the garden alone, he passed his childhood in solitude or among adults. He read voraciously—Russian and French from the age of five, German from the age of eight. Later he studied English. His formal education was begun at home under the direction of resident tutors, of whom one, his French and German tutor, Berget (apparently a Swiss), had a strong influence on the boy and introduced him to Schiller, Hugo, and Voltaire. Peter early desired to be a writer, and while still a boy wrote verses and dramatic scenes.

In 1837, at the age of fourteen, Peter was sent to the Artillery Academy in St. Petersburg—the same school from which the future revolutionary Michael Bakunin had graduated a few years before. After overcoming the handicaps of his hothouse upbringing, Peter acquired a large circle of friends and took an active part in student affairs. The cadets read widely, tried their hands at writing, and eagerly discussed philosophical and social issues. By the age of sixteen Lavrov had developed a world outlook which he later called "a most emphatic determinism in the form of theistic fatalism" and which he expressed in verse. At about the same time, he tells us in his autobiography, he ceased to place any significance in the ceremonies of Orthodoxy or of any other religion. In philosophy he read Victor Cousin and other French eclectics. In political and social theory, which strongly occupied some of the teachers and some of Lavrov's student friends at the Academy, he became acquainted with followers of the French Catholic socialist Buchez, and showed particular interest in their critiques of existing social institutions.

In 1842, at the age of nineteen, Lavrov graduated from the Artillery Academy and received his officer's commission. Two years later he was appointed instructor in mathematics at the Academy. In 1847 he married Antonina Khristianovna Loveyko (nee Kapger), a widow with two small children from a prominent St. Petersburg family. Between 1848 and 1855 the couple had four children of their own. Upon the death of his father in 1852 and his older brother a year later, Lavrov became sole proprietor of the family estates. The estates yielded little income, however, and to support his large family Lavrov was obliged to supplement his Academy salary by giving lessons in history and languages at private preparatory schools. Beginning in 1858 he also taught special courses in higher mathematics at the Konstantinovsky Military Academy. His strictly military service was confined to a brief period at Narva in the summer of 1855, during the Crimean war. By then a colonel, he was temporarily in command of artillery, but he saw no action.

The Russian world which the young artillery officer entered in 1842 was compounded of stern repression on the part of Nicholas I, the tsar-disciplinarian whose accession in 1825 the Decembrists had sought to prevent, and intellectual ferment on the part of the intelligentsia. Memory of the Decembrist uprising, the Polish rebellion of 1830–1831, and the swelling radical movement in western Europe urged Nicholas into thoroughgoing regimentation of the internal life of his empire, supervised by a greatly expanded secret police. The determined advocate of "Orthodoxy, Autocracy, and Nationality" was bent on repressing all manifestations of liberalism. He gave special attention to controlling education and the press, through severe censorship, strict regulation of university policies, and limitations on university enrollment.

The revolutionary outbursts in Europe in 1848 led to still greater repression in Russia. Foreign travel was further restricted. The importation of foreign literature was limited, and "objectionable" books were seized from the bookstores. University enrollments were drastically curtailed. Control of the press was perfected to the point where twelve different types of censorship were distinguished. Leading writers—Saltykov, Turgenev, Yuri Samarin, Ivan Aksakov—were placed under arrest. Dostoyevsky and other members of the socialist-minded Petrashevsky circle were exiled to Siberia.

Yet Nicholas' most vigorous efforts did not succeed in stifling thought or preventing the growth of liberal and radical convictions. Barred from expressing their sentiments in print or in overt action, members of the intelligentsia formed circles in which they could at least manifest their dissatisfaction with the existing order through discussion and debate. Whereas in the 'thirties the discussions of these circles had centered primarily on philosophical and aesthetic questions, in the 'forties they came to focus on social issues and the question of Russia's place in history. The conservative Slavophiles saw for Russia a distinctive path of social and spiritual development, grounded in the endemic institutions of Russian Orthodoxy and autocracy; their unconventional conceptions of those institutions, however, provoked serious opposition from Nicholas' establishment. Against the Slavophiles the more liberal Westernizers, led by Vissarion Belinsky and Alexander Herzen, argued that progress in Russia could come only from adopting Western democratic institutions and opening the stifling Russian air more fully to the secular, scientific breezes which blew from the West. The more radical Westernizers such as Nicholas Chernyshevsky, who carried Herzen's social critique furthest, became followers of the French utopian socialists in politics and of the "left Hegelian" Ludwig Feuerbach in philosophy.

Lavrov's intellectual development during the 'forties and early 'fifties was slow, deliberate, and decidedly Westernist—though at first of the moderate rather than the radical variety. He tells us that he read Fourier and other French socialists as a young officer, and was drawn to socialism, but at the time saw it as nothing more than a distant ideal. He wrote little during these years, but he acquired not only enormous erudition in philosophy and the sciences but also a certain reputation as a scholar and poet.

Lavrov's military teaching led him to study the history of mechanics and its applications in military technology, and more generally to extensive reading in the history of thought—

scientific, philosophical, and religious. He read the major thinkers of antiquity, including Plato and Aristotle, in translation. He made a thorough study of modern European philosophy, proceeding from the French eclectics to Kant and the entire German idealist school. Hegel interested him strongly, and he devoted much time to critical analysis of the Hegelian system. Subsequently he went on to Hegel's followers, the right-wing orthodox Hegelians as well as the disciples of the left—Bruno Bauer, Arnold Ruge, and Feuerbach. He also studied the works of modern German theologians such as Schleiermacher and August Neander. But at first the only scholarly fruits of this study were articles on military and scientific topics published in artillery journals and in a military encyclopedia.

It was chiefly poetry which served as the vehicle for Lavrov's serious convictions, particularly his liberal ethical and social views, in these last years of Nicholas' reign. Versifying came easy to him, and the praise of Polonsky, Shcherbina, and other established poets of the day convinced him that he had real poetic talent. One of his poems was published as early as 1841; most of them circulated anonymously, either orally or in manuscript. Patriotic but full of freedom-loving sentiments, the verses were well liked by the Petersburg public; some enjoyed great vogue. Lavrov writes in his autobiography that at the time he attributed great significance to poetry, particularly as a reconciling force between science and religion. A religious element is often discernible in his verses, and he tells us that he long considered the theistic outlook the most poetic, even after he had rid his own views of all vestiges of theism.

Poet and mathematician-philosopher, the mature Lavrov of the 'fifties presented a combination of attributes which his contemporaries found striking, as many attest in their memoirs. The poet Vladimir Benediktov described him thus in 1856 or 1857:

The accuracy and precision of the mathematician are reflected in his personal life by his profound integrity, by the fearlessness of his scientific thinking, by his fearlessness in professing his convictions. At the same time he does not have the arid mind of a scientist, or the brutal mind of a mathematician. On the contrary, not only is he sensitive to everything tender and beautiful, he is a poet. . . . He is capable of powerful and passionate enthusiasms, but he is accustomed to self-restraint. So strong is the spiritual element in him that sometimes I really think he has no flesh at all but brain and nerves, and those in complete enslavement to his soul.[3]

Graphic personal details were added to Benediktov's picture by Yelena Shtakenshneyder, an admirer and subsequently a staunch friend of Lavrov whose home was a gathering place for St. Petersburg writers. She describes Lavrov at the age of thirty-three, in 1857:

> Lavrov has red hair, rather large, grey-blue, myopic eyes, and a moustache which is not divided in the middle but covers his whole lip and juts out a little, so that when he reads, holding the book very close to his eyes because of his nearsightedness, the moustache touches the book. His complexion is pale, as with redheads generally, and his hands are white and pudgy as a bishop's. . . . His erudition and memory are extraordinary. . . . Benediktov can never stop talking about what an ideal son, husband, father, and brother Lavrov is. . . . He says that as a person Lavrov is faultless, while as a philosopher and mathematician he is relentless and merciless in his reasonings.[4]

Lavrov's literary career began in earnest with the change in the Russian intellectual scene which followed the death of Nicholas I and the accession of Alexander II in 1855. The new emperor at first pursued a liberal course, providing greater access to the universities, reducing controls on the press, and promising other reforms. Commissions were established to draw up plans for the prompt emancipation of the serfs—the one reform which all liberals regarded as fundamental to social health in Russia. Among the intelligentsia it was a time for rejoicing, and hopes ran high.

Lavrov shared the general optimism, which at first he continued to express in verse. In 1856 he sent some verses abroad to Herzen, along with his first prose contribution to the discussion of social questions—a letter expressing what he later called his "excessive hopes" at the accession of Alexander. He affirmed the possibility of true progress in Russia, to come about "not through dread revolution . . . but through the reconciliation of the past with the future." [5] The letter and two of the verses were printed anonymously in Herzen's miscellany, *Voices from Russia*. Other verses were printed in foreign books and journals. But it was not long before Lavrov decided that poetry was not his *métier*—a decision aided by the radical publisher and poet Nicholas Nekrasov, who called Lavrov's verses "rhymed press dispatches or editorials." With the relaxation of censorship under Alexander and a consequent increase in the number and the liberality of journals, Lavrov could turn to fuller and more scholarly development of his ideas in prose.

The liberals' optimism was short-lived, for by 1862 another wave of reaction had inundated Russian society. By that time, however, Lavrov had published a number of philosophical essays, lectures, and reviews of foreign literature which quickly won him an enthusiastic following and a high reputation as a scholar and thinker. After some essays on education and other social issues, he first drew serious attention in literary circles by two long scholarly articles on the philosophy of Hegel—"Hegelianism" and "The Practical Philosophy of Hegel"—published in 1858 and 1859. Another major article on modern German thought—"The Contemporary German Theists"—was published in 1859. There followed three works in which Lavrov shifted his emphasis from expository scholarship to philosophical statement, and developed the principles of his general world view: "The Mechanistic Theory of the World" (1859), "An Outline of the Theory of Individuality" (1859), and "What is Anthropology?" (1860). In these essays Lavrov stated in considerable wealth of detail the philosophy of "anthropologism" which was to be the basis not only of the *Historical Letters* but of his entire subsequent intellectual career.

Though Lavrov in these essays criticized the materialism dear to the radical wing of the intelligentsia, at the same time his progressive sentiments, his evident respect for science, and his elaboration of a man-centered philosophy comparable to Feuerbach's gave his views an appeal broad enough to catch even the radicals' interest. Chernyshevsky, their acknowledged spiritual leader, took Lavrov's "Outline of the Theory of Individuality" as the point of departure for his chief philosophical work, "The Anthropological Principle in Philosophy" (1860). Condemning Lavrov's "eclecticism" and regretting that Lavrov had studied "the obsolete forms of German philosophy" before becoming acquainted with "the latest German thinkers" (i.e., Feuerbach), Chernyshevsky nonetheless praised Lavrov's ability and concluded that his views were not without merit.[6] Similarly, Dmitry

Pisarev, soon to assume Chernyshevsky's mantle as chief spokes-
man for the radicals (or "Nihilists," as they came to be called),
considered Lavrov at least worthy of criticism in his influential
essay, "Nineteenth Century Scholasticism" (1861).[7]

The single chief source of Lavrov's philosophical reputation in
the 'sixties was a series of three public lectures he gave in November, 1860, published in 1861 under the general title "On the Contemporary Significance of Philosophy." These were the first
public, secular lectures on philosophy to be heard in St. Petersburg since Nicholas closed the departments of philosophy in the
universities in 1850. Lavrov's eloquent presentation of his "anthropologism," with its apotheosis of "consciousness and development," of creativity in art and in life, of social justice and human
dignity, captivated his hearers, and the lectures created an enormous impression. After the second lecture Yelena Shtakenshneyder wrote in her diary:

> This time, beyond all expectation, the hall was not only no less full
> than the first time, it was full to overflowing. . . . Auditors stood
> crowded together in all the aisles. . . . If Lavrov was successful the
> first time, then today he was doubly successful. Today he brought his
> audience to raptures, he electrified them, and they gave him not sim-
> ply applause, but a thunderous ovation.[8]

And after the final lecture she wrote: "Today it was no longer a
success but a triumph. There was no end to shouts and raptures.
Lavrov has now become a kind of hero even outside our circle." [9]

One of the fruits of Lavrov's growing reputation was an invitation from Andrey Krayevsky, editor of the influential *St. Petersburg Gazette*, to edit the philosophy section of a new multi-
volume Russian encyclopedia, the *Encyclopedic Dictionary*. Lavrov began work in 1861, and, later that year, after publication of
the first volume, the editorial board elected him chief editor, replacing Krayevsky. Lavrov himself wrote a great number of articles for the *Dictionary* on philosophical, religious, and historical
topics. Among them was one of his best brief summaries of his
own philosophical position, published in the fifth volume in 1862
under the title "The Anthropological Point of View in Philosophy."

The radical wing of the intelligentsia at first greeted the new
encyclopedia coolly. Lavrov, however, secured the collaboration
of such radicals as M. A. Antonovich and Nicholas Utin, and a

progressive bent soon became evident in the pages of the new publication. Advertised as "preaching no doctrine," the *Encyclopedic Dictionary* under Lavrov's leadership in fact mounted an attack on clericalism and "religious superstitions" and gave much attention to the Feuerbachian conceptions which Lavrov shared with the radicals. These predilections did not go unnoticed by the Russian clergy, who compared the authors with the French Encyclopedists and found in their work "the most hideous blasphemy and flagrant atheism." [10] In 1863 a religious journal pronounced an anathema against the authors of the *Dictionary* and called for their exile to Siberia. They were not brought to trial, but in the same year publication of the encyclopedia was discontinued after the sixth volume, by government order.

Nor was this the only sign of official dissatisfaction with the trend of Lavrov's intellectual development during these years of reaction. In 1861 he was denied appointment to the newly re-established chair of philosophy at St. Petersburg university, despite the fact that his candidacy was supported by the eminent scholar Professor K. D. Kavelin. Influential in securing Lavrov's rejection was the conservative censor and professor of philology A. V. Nikitenko, who argued that "it would be better for us to get along without philosophy for four years or so" (while some student is being trained abroad) rather than to appoint such an "unbridled persecutor of everything that was and is" as Lavrov.[11] In 1862 Lavrov was refused permission to give two public lectures on ethical questions. In 1863, after the *Encyclopedic Dictionary* was closed by the government, he was offered the editorship of a St. Petersburg review called the *Foreign Herald* (*Zagranichny vestnik*); this appointment, too, was officially prohibited, on the basis of a secret-police report which called Lavrov "worse than all the Chernyshevskies." Nevertheless Lavrov assumed *de facto* editorship of the journal, and this anonymous activity, along with his teaching, occupied most of his time between the end of 1863 and his arrest in 1866.[12]

To the conservatives, Lavrov's views in the early 'sixties were becoming indistinguishable from those of the Nihilist radicals. Nikitenko as early as 1860 called him "a materialist from head to toe." [13] In 1864 Nikitenko drew the following portrait of Lavrov, which illustrates, by its very distortions, the mounting tensions between Lavrov's career and the attitudes of official Russia:

We have a particular type of progressive which could not be more clearly personified than in Peter Lavrovich (Lavrov). He passionately loves mankind, and is ready to serve it everywhere and in every way. . . . As a reward for his selfless love Peter Lavrovich desires one thing: to be recognized as a great man by his contemporaries and to be honored with two or three ovations. . . .

Strictly speaking Peter Lavrovich is a philosopher because he knows German and has read in it some of the great works of Feuerbach, Moleschott, Büchner, etc. In his concern for the welfare of humanity he ceaselessly bustles about . . . striving with all his might to dispel all prejudices and to enlighten people, so that they will fully understand and will be fully convinced that man is descended from the apes, that morality and religion are chains fastened upon men by despots and priests, that *enlightened egoism* is the only moral principle, that the soul of man and the soul of a pig are perfectly identical, that "mind is a geographical designation," and so forth and so on.

Peter Lavrovich is a surprisingly mobile person. No sooner does he read some scientific or political news in a foreign journal than . . . he runs to trumpet it everywhere, wherever he is allowed to enter. He shies away from writing, partly because he is afraid of censorship and partly because he writes abominably—densely and in an involved style. He prefers the path of quiet, crawling propaganda and has a special weakness for young people and women, whom it is easier for him to stuff with all sorts of rubbish in the name of progress.

Formerly *The Bell* [Herzen's journal, *Kolokol*] was the source of all his great truths and convictions. But now that *The Bell* no longer tolls, Peter Lavrovich has become an eclectic in a particular sense—in the sense of socialism and materialism.[14]

The Philosophical System: Anthropologism

Nikitenko's comments well illustrate the view of Lavrov which prevailed in Russian officialdom, but in fact Lavrov was anything but a materialist. He did respect Feuerbach, but he developed his own "anthropologism" in conscious opposition to the philosophical views of Feuerbach's radical materialist followers in Russia. He certainly did not take the materialistic view of the human mind suggested by Nikitenko. Nor was his moral theory equiva-

lent to the "enlightened egoism" of Chernyshevsky and Pisarev.
In short, Lavrov and the radicals both drew philosophical inspiration from Feuerbach, but they developed the Feuerbachian heritage in notably distinct directions.

Like the radicals, Lavrov was steeped in the scientific spirit of
Western secular culture. But he did not accept their identification
of the scientific outlook with materialism, and in his first major
statement of his philosophical position in 1859, "The Mechanistic
Theory of the World," he undertook to show the limitations of
materialism both as a scientific theory and as a metaphysical system. Proceeding in this essay from the phenomenalistic stance he
was consistently to adopt in dealing with theoretical questions in
philosophy, Lavrov argues that materialism is *unscientific* in its
fundamental concepts, and further that there are regions of science, of the greatest importance to man, which must be *non-
materialistic* if they are to prosper.

First, the former charge. Lavrov argues that materialism's basic
notions, *matter* and *force,* are metaphysical rather than scientific
concepts. Pointing out that "since the time of Kant it has been
known that only phenomena are open to man," he contends that
matter and force are not scientific concepts because they are not
based on phenomenal evidence, on observation.[15] "Force" is simply a refuge of ignorance. "Matter," as something that stands behind phenomena, as an abstract substance, is never presented in
experience. Lavrov goes so far as to argue that their very character as general concepts makes "force" and "matter" supersensual
and thus "metaphysical" categories—to which his materialist
critics quickly retorted that Lavrov was himself displaying a
"metaphysical" interpretation of general concepts.[16] In any
event, such concepts "correspond to nothing real in observation
and experience" and hence have no place in science, Lavrov
maintains.[17]

All disputes between materialists and idealists, spiritualists, and
the like are metaphysical disputes, Lavrov contends, in which the
disputants are speaking different languages and can never understand each other. When they argue about "vital forces," ends in
nature, the connection between spiritual phenomena and physical, or the immortality of the soul, all explanations on both sides
are merely verbal. Both the materialists and the spiritualists "pose

hypotheses which are impossible to prove and very difficult to accept on faith." [18] Ultimately it is only faith, however, which can explain the acceptance of materialism as well as of spiritualism. Matter, Lavrov maintains, has become "a new idol," "a mystical being . . . endowed with all powers." [19]

The Kantian flavor of Lavrov's phenomenalistic approach and his rejection of "metaphysical" knowledge of nature is further strengthened by his explanations of the origin of metaphysical thinking. It is no accidental product of historical circumstances or individual genius, Lavrov contends, but a natural outcome of the workings of the human mind. Matter is posed as a metaphysical substance because "by a necessary law of his thinking" man always concludes that the phenomena he observes arise from "something." [20] But of course man can never prove that this inference is valid. In a more general formulation, Lavrov attributes metaphysics to a human need to believe in something extra-human, something which "can fill the emptiness of the human spirit." He quotes with approval Kant's statement that "it is just as impossible to expect that the human spirit will someday completely renounce metaphysical speculations as to expect that we would sooner not breathe at all than breathe unclean air." [21]

Lavrov's second charge against materialism is that it is inapplicable to some of the most important regions of science. There are types of phenomena, Lavrov argues, which cannot properly be studied materialistically. First, there is the entire realm of human consciousness. Phenomena of consciousness are incommensurate in every respect with sensory phenomena, and are accessible only to consciousness itself; they can only be introspected, not sensed. Materialism, Lavrov asserts, "has concealed the distinction between phenomena observed by the senses and phenomena observed by consciousness, but it has not resolved them into a higher unity, and these two types of phenomena still demand two completely different sciences." For sensory phenomena, materialism is appropriate; its efforts in that area to reduce everything to matter in motion should be continued. But the phenomena of consciousness, whatever may be their physical *source*, cannot themselves be reduced to matter in motion. Thus "for the cultivation of the field of the phenomenology of spirit there remains only the path of direct observation, by

means of consciousness and the evidence of historical remains." [22]
The science of the "phenomenology of spirit" must employ a
subjective method (as Lavrov and his followers came to call it)
—essentially the method of introspection.

The second area in which materialism is inapplicable is the
domain of *history*. Like the phenomena of consciousness, the
phenomena of what Lavrov here calls "tradition" cannot be reduced to matter in motion; they cannot be studied by methods
appropriate to sensory phenomena. In this essay Lavrov does not
detail the approach required by history (this was reserved for
later works, above all the *Historical Letters*), but he explicitly defines history as a third, distinct realm of science, on a level with
the natural sciences and the phenomenology of spirit. Its object is
"to show how man progressively became aware of himself as a
being capable of investigating the outer world through his sense
organs and the inner world through consciousness, how he discovered the laws of these worlds, how he gave embodiment to his
desires for justice and beauty . . . how old forms fought and fell
before new ideas, how mankind developed." [23]

Thus far Lavrov has considered materialism as a supposed scientific theory—more strictly, a methodology, an approach to the
study of phenomena. He has found that even in its application to
the sensory world materialism contains illicit "metaphysical" or
nonempirical elements, and that its methods are unsuited to dealing with large areas of human experience. But Lavrov has also
admitted that speculation beyond the immediate data of experience is humanly inevitable; further, he contends that over and
above the direct acquisitions of the sciences there is a need for
systematization of these additions of knowledge, and such systematization he also speaks of as the role of "metaphysics," or
simply "philosophy." If in this essay he asserts that "all philosophy is a temporary stand-in for science," at the same time he
leaves no doubt that the stand-in will long be needed; metaphysics in this sense—metaphysics as an integrating world view
—will only become unnecessary, he states, if and when investigation in the three realms of science has shown "the analogical
structure of the laws of the phenomena belonging to each of
them" and it has been possible "to reduce these laws to one common principle." [24] (Indeed a year later Lavrov ceased talking

about the ultimate demise of philosophy or "metaphysics" in this sense, and began to speak of philosophy as the general faculty of relating and integrating discrete phenomena, indispensable in the very construction of any science and in fact present in all distinctively human activity.[25]) Is it not possible that materialism, greatly limited as a methodology, has some merit as a metaphysical system, an over-all world view?

Lavrov admits that there is "something majestic in this bold and serene view of oneself and the world."[26] He denies the common charge that materialism as an outlook is harmful to personal or public morality—though subsequently he added that the materialist can make moral appraisals or express moral fervor only through self-contradiction.[27] But he finds that materialism as a theoretical world view is seriously defective. All world views, according to Lavrov, are based on principles drawn from one or more of the three areas of science, from "the natural sources of all thought: personal consciousness, the external world, and tradition." Materialists take the second source as primary and inevitably submerge the others. This, Lavrov argues, cannot be justified by the intrinsic order and relations of phenomena themselves. In the construction of an integral world view we must proceed from "the phenomena which condition the others," and to Lavrov these are clearly the phenomena of *consciousness*.[28]

For the fact is that the phenomena of consciousness are not simply on a level with the others; they are primary. Consciousness if "the chief and inescapable fact." We know of the external world only what is presented to us in consciousness. Only consciousness constructs all our theories of this world. Thus consciousness is "the basic condition of all observation, of all science, of all creation." Not that the other areas are unimportant. The ultimate task of the philosophy of the future is to provide a harmonious account of man's threefold relationship to his consciousness, to the external world, and to tradition or history. But clearly, Lavrov contends, integration must center on the conscious being, man: "Only the whole man is the true subject of philosophy."[29] And consciousness itself must be taken as the point of departure in constructing such a system, "because it conditions our knowledge of the external world and the transmission of tradition. It is the indispensable link connecting everything that is, because it is the most essential feature of everyone who thinks." [30] Thus the needed world view, Lavrov concludes in "The Mechanistic Theory of the World," is not materialism but a philosophy based firmly on the inescapable demands of human consciousness.

In effect a philosophical manifesto, Lavrov's essay on materialism enunciated all the principal theoretical themes of his mature philosophy. He affirmed a phenomenalistic positivism, but one capacious enough to include as legitimate objects of investigation not only sensory, "external" phenomena but also the nonsensory, "internal" phenomena of immediate consciousness, as well as the phenomena of history. He insisted on the distinct character of each of these three types of phenomena, with the result that history and psychology are acknowledged to be independent sciences no less important than the natural sciences. He presented the need for a "subjective method" in approaching the all-important phenomena of consciousness. Finally, he called for the elaboration of an "anthropological" world view (though not yet by that name), which would focus not merely on man but on the consciousness through which alone man views himself, his past, and his material environment.

In "The Mechanistic Theory of the World" Lavrov observed in passing that the materialist's outlook gives him little to say about questions of morality and politics. As if to show that this limitation is removed by a proper philosophical orientation, Lavrov turned to these subjects in his next work in 1859, the long essay entitled "An Outline of the Theory of Individuality." Having propounded the basic principles of his theoretical philosophy, Lavrov here proceeds to sketch in considerable detail the chief elements of his practical philosophy. His starting point is provided by the conclusions of the previous essay. On the philosophical level, the "Outline of the Theory of Individuality" is an attempt to systematize the phenomena of man's active moral life, based on the phenomena of consciousness, as the previous essay had recommended. As a "scientific" investigation of the phenomena of practical consciousness, employing the subjective method, the essay can be considered, Lavrov says, "a chapter in the phenomenology of spirit."

Lavrov makes it clear in this essay that he did not regard his practical philosophy as his own creation. He thought of himself as integrating the elements of *the* practical philosophy of the age, elements already expressed in one or another form by many thinkers before him. Among these thinkers he included Herzen and Proudhon, to whom jointly he dedicated the essay, and John Stuart Mill, whose name he frequently cites with approval.

Practical philosophy is concerned with both society and the individual, Lavrov asserts at the outset, but it must begin with the individual (*lichnost'*). The individual is prior to society and is "the only actual object of investigation." [31] But in dealing with the individual, what are we to take as our point of departure? What fact is indubitable and fundamental? As in theoretical philosophy, the starting point must be found in the realm of consciousness. Now it is with *self-consciousness* that a man begins his separate, individual existence. Self-consciousness, Lavrov concluded, must be the starting point for the theory of individuality (*teoriya lichnosti*).

But practical philosophy is interested in individual *action,* not simply in self-consciousness. What can self-consciousness tell us about the principles of human action? Analysis of self-consciousness, Lavrov contends, discloses that there is one motive which provides the fundamental explanation of all human action—the desire for *pleasure.*[32] The quest for pleasure (or the elimination of pain) is inseparably connected with self-consciousness, Lavrov argues; indeed the latter is awakened only through the experience of pleasure or pain. Striving to attain pleasure and eliminate pain is basic to all other motives and is present in all human activity. For Lavrov the entire moral life of man resides in the development of this primitive motive. All human ideals are simple or elaborate, shortsighted or enlightened developments of the striving for pleasure. Thus Lavrov agrees with Mill and the utilitarian school that at bottom all men are hedonists; but he adds that deliberate hedonism is soon transcended as man elaborates moral ideals on this hedonistic basis.

According to Lavrov man has two broad capacities for implementing the primitive pleasure motive—knowledge and creativity. In *knowledge,* in which man seeks pleasure through striving for truth, the receptivity of the human spirit prevails. In *creativity,* in which he seeks pleasure through striving for beauty, his productivity comes into play. Together, knowledge and creativity are the instruments of human development. Creativity comes to man's assistance whenever he feels a break, an absence of order. It seeks to smooth all contradictions and fulfill all lacks, the goal being harmony, wholeness, beauty. One of it chief manifestations is in the creation of ideals which inspire man to act responsibly on their behalf—ideals which transform the desire for pleasure into imperatives or "oughts" which man accepts as incumbent upon him.

At this point Lavrov comes to grips with a thorny theoretical problem. Does it make sense, he asks, to speak of posing ideals and striving to realize them through responsible action, if the "fatalistic" views now increasingly held are true? Is not true freedom of the will, denied by the contemporary spokesmen for "science" (Chernyshevsky among them), a necessary condition of responsibility and hence of morality? Lavrov proceeds to analyze this hoary problem of "free will," in a way which provides a major illustration of the force and bearing of his "anthropological point of view" and his "subjective method."

The whole difficulty, Lavrov asserts, stems from failure to distinguish between a metaphysical view of the world and a practical view in which man regards his ego as "an integral living being which is the focus of the world." [33] If we wish to know whether man is responsible before the world, before reality in general—responsible *absolutely*—theoretical freedom of the will is an important condition of morality. But in that event it is also an insoluble metaphysical problem. Both "fatalism" and its denial, as doctrines about the nature of things independent of phenomena —independent of our human consciousness of things—are unprovable.

But actually this "absolute," extra-human point of view is a thing of the past, Lavrov argues. Even if fatalism were theoretically true (which we can never know), as an outlook it could affect an individual only through its acceptance in his consciousness. But therein it would encounter another fact which it can never destroy: the individual's *consciousness* that he is free and responsible before himself and before society. "Each of us, whether he believes in fatalism or rejects it," Lavrov writes, "always acts . . . as if his actions were completely free. Freedom of the will is a great, important fact of human consciousness." [34] For *human* responsibility this consciousness of freedom, or practical freedom of the will, is sufficient. It is a scientific fact, established by the subjective method, and is completely independent of the metaphysical question of whether such freedom exists "absolutely." Thus we can "construct the laws of practical philosophy completely independently of deciding the [metaphysical] question of the existence of free will in man." [35] By taking the point of view of moral *man* and consulting his *subjective* world, we remove all significance from fatalism. Practically the question of free will is decided in the affirmative; metaphysically it is dismissed as undecidable but irrelevant.

Lavrov has here asserted, with Immanuel Kant, the autonomy of the moral consciousness, and his opposition to "metaphysics" is now seen to have two dimensions. In theoretical philosophy, it rules out metaphenomenal entities and speculations. In practical philosophy, it ensures acceptance of the phenomena of moral consciousness as primitive and valid. Man is conscious of his ability to set goals for himself, to pursue an ideal, to act in accordance with a duty he recognizes. No metaphysical speculations or extrapolations from the natural sciences can destroy this consciousness or successfully compel the individual to regard this inner experience as illusory or insignificant. "Personal responsibility (*samoobyazatel'nost'*), one's judgment of oneself," Lavrov wrote in 1860, "is inseparable from the soul of man." [36] The dictates of the moral consciousness—first and foremost the consciousness of freedom—cannot be overruled by any reasoning or any other type of experience.

When Lavrov on later occasions expressed his philosophical outlook in schematic outline, he advanced "the personal principle of freedom" as the first principle of practical philosophy. And although theoretical philosophy must include a "sceptical principle," because we cannot know whether or not phenomena are products of some extra-phenomenal "real being," in practical philosophy such a sceptical principle has no place: we are *aware* of our own free transformation of phenomena (desires, the recognition of ideals) into "the world of real being" through our action.[37] For Lavrov such awareness provides a solid foundation for practical philosophy. Describing his own philosophical procedure in another work of the period, he writes: "I have taken the fact of the consciousness of freedom, the fact of the creation of ideals, and the fact of the desire for pleasure, and on the basis of these facts I have constructed a coherent system of the moral process." [38]

With this foundation established, Lavrov proceeds in the "Outline of the Theory of Individuality" to consider the origin and character of the basic ideals man creates. Man's primitive and controlling ideal, he argues, is the ideal of personal dignity. The individual, by turning his creativity upon himself and adding to his self-consciousness a *concept* of the self, creates an ideal self, the ideal of his own dignity. Until this ideal is created, Lavrov argues, there can be no history, no development, no morality. As for the content of the ideal, it changes as man develops; but it always includes the notion that the self is worthy of *respect*. As seen by "the best representatives of the contemporary doctrine of man"—Lavrov cites Mill, Proudhon, von Humboldt, and Jules Simon—the ideal of personal dignity includes respect and "the need for self-development." [39]

Historically, personal dignity is first conceived egoistically, according to Lavrov: man ascribes to himself an absolute right to subordinate everything and everyone to himself. This egoistic principle is subsequently expanded and developed, but it never disappears or loses its position as "the basis of human morality." In its initial egoistic elaboration, the ideal of personal dignity may be expressed as a three-fold rule: "develop your body and respect it, develop your mind and respect it, develop your strength of character and respect it." [40] Lavrov finds in this formula the origin of all the various personal virtues and vices, as well as of all personal rights.

Primitive natural egoism is the source of ambition, the acquisitive drive, property. But in pursuing these drives the individual comes into contact with other egoistic individuals, similarly motivated. He finds these other individuals to be stronger, weaker, or equal in strength to himself, and in his relations with them he experiences new feelings and adds new features to the ideal of human dignity. With individuals stronger or weaker than himself, relationships such as those based on *mercy* and *selflessness* are developed. When carried to extremes these new concepts become self-contradictory or self-defeating; when restricted within proper limits, they tend to merge with a general concept of *justice*. With individuals of essentially the same power as himself, *struggle* is man's prevailing social relationship today, Lavrov finds. It, too, is self-defeating, being "based on an insufficient knowledge of life," specifically of how man gains pleasure: *informed* egoism shows man that by struggling against others he is impeding his own quest for pleasure. And here again the idea of *justice* suggests itself as a more appropriate basis for human interaction.

For Lavrov all indications point to an inner sense of justice as the key to human relationships. He argues that the sense of justice is in fact a primitive feature of human nature—as primitive, at least, as "the first developmental motive in man—that which opposes the consciousness of personal dignity to direct instantaneous motives." [41] Justice is "an inseparable feature of man," according to Lavrov; "it is born at the same time as human consciousness and human egoism." As man distinguishes himself from others like him, equal to him in power, his creative capacity forms the idea that they are equal to him in rights. As he comes to identify *himself* through the creation of the ideal of personal dignity, he likewise attributes personal dignity to those from whom he distinguishes himself. He places their dignity on a par with his, and recognizes that violation of their dignity is no different from violation of his own. Thus the idea of justice is both natural and inevitable: "From the first encounter between men of equal power it must have appeared by logical necessity in the soul of man." [42] It is the natural fruit of egoism in conflict with other egoisms.

On this basis Lavrov argues that justice is the necessary and the only firm bond among men, and the chief means man has of augmenting his otherwise insecure pleasures. All men recognize the ideal of justice, he contends, even if they often fail to carry out its demands. Some men fail through indetermination, weakness of character. On the other hand the widespread denial of justice in Europe today—in the relationship between property-owners and "proletariat," for example—proceeds chiefly from defects of knowledge. Men do not know their own best interests.

The kernel of justice is the recognition that one's own personality and the personality of another are equally entitled to respect and to the opportunity for development. *Equality of rights* is thus the watchword of justice. Lavrov proceeds to argue that the equal right of men to respect is the source of all the specific rights and duties of individuals in their relationships; indeed the very concepts of a "right" and a "duty" acquire real meaning, Lavrov maintains, only as concrete forms of this abstract concept of justice. All social virtues are forms of justice. "The moral aspiration of the human spirit in modern times," Lavrov writes, "consists in the subordination of all relationships to the principle of justice. . . . Only what is just is moral." [43]

But of course this applies only to relationships among *men*, relationships in which there is recognition of the equal rights of human personalities. In relationships between men and *things*, justice can have no application. Lavrov proceeds to apply such considerations, with potentially explosive results, to the question of property.

There is no *right* to property, Lavrov argues. Justice cannot decide disputes concerning property, because the question of the right *of the thing* to be or not to be anyone's property is undecidable. The ability to put oneself in another's place is a condition of justice, and man cannot put himself in the place of an animal or thing. From the standpoint of justice I cannot eat a human child, Lavrov asserts (apologizing for the indelicacy of the example), because the child has a right not to be eaten. But to plants or animals we have no basis for attributing (or for denying) such a right; the criterion of justice simply is not relevant. The mere fact of applying my labor to something does not give me a right of ownership; if it did, raising a child would make him my property. The appropriation by two persons of all resources existing in a given place does not give them a right to the exclusive use of these resources, to the detriment of some third person who has nothing with which to sustain himself. Proudhon was right, Lavrov concludes, when he said that "property is theft." Property is theft in the sense that it is an acquisition covered by no right.[44]

Men do have a right to development, Lavrov adds, and hence a *need* to acquire resources for development. All men equally need such resources, and clearly a problem arises when one person needs something which has been appropriated by another. But such questions must be resolved by appealing to some other principle—such as "the common good"—rather than the principle of justice, Lavrov asserts. Beyond this Lavrov does not go in this essay, but he has clearly called into question the traditional justifications of private property.

The practical conclusions of the "Outline of the Theory of Individuality" are highly general in character, but they serve to map out the broad areas which remained Lavrov's concerns throughout his long intellectual career. The ideal of justice, inseparable from the root ideal of human dignity, demands of contemporary man two things above all, Lavrov argues. First, it demands an awareness of the meaning of justice and the nature of existing social injustices. In other words it demands *knowledge*, acquired through critical thinking, through adopting "a critical attitude toward everything that exists." [45] This is Lavrov's first suggestion of the concept of the "critically thinking individual" (an expression first used in the *Historical Letters*), which came to figure so prominently in his philosophy of history and his social theory. But second, the ideal of justice demands not simply the consciousness of justice, but the embodiment of this consciousness in *action*. It demands "struggle and sacrifice for right action." [46]

The need for action—for creativity in the external world to realize the ideal created in human imagination—is strongly emphasized here as in all of Lavrov's subsequent works. Among men's duties, all of which flow from the general obligation of self-respect, he gives first place to "the duty to act." The first "sin" Lavrov mentions is "the sin of laziness." [47] For Lavrov the significance of man's intellect is undeniable; he fully agrees with the English utilitarians, for example, that intellectual pleasures are superior to physical. But in the last analysis, more important than either body or mind is *will:*

The supreme dignity of the individual does not reside in physical traits or in intellectual development. Body and mind are excellent instruments of pleasure. . . . But for actual dignity there must be *determination*, and determination belongs neither to the body, with its impulses, nor to the mind, with its reflections, but to will, which develops into character. . . . The supreme dignity of the individual consists in his character.[48]

Like Mill in *On Liberty*, Lavrov was disturbed by apathy and irresolution, which he called a "modern epidemic threatening society with the gravest dangers." [49] He pleaded for men who not only thought critically, but had a firm commitment to action. History waits for these resolute individuals:

> The recognition of the injustice of what had seemed just is the first step. . . . This recognition gradually spreads, preparing the ground for individuals who are not only conscious of the new principle, but are endowed with the determination to actualize it. These are the true heroes of humanity . . . the "salt of the earth," to use Mill's expression. They do not create or discover the new idea, but they are determined to incarnate it, determined to fight what they recognize as unjust.[50]

For Lavrov, the resolute *embodiment* of moral ideals is the all-important final focus of practical philosophy.

Lavrov's first presentation of his philosophical system as a whole, and the first in which he explicitly called it "the anthropological point of view," came in 1860 in the essay, "What Is Anthropology?" Here he defined and compared the realms of theoretical and practical philosophy, cataloging the principles we have seen developed more fully in the essays of 1859. But in practical philosophy he went beyond the previous essays to state more fully his conception of the nature and significance of human activity. In so doing he also elaborated the third branch of his "anthropological" system, the philosophy of history.

There are two separable and equally significant moments which must be distinguished in human activity, Lavrov contends in "What is Anthropology?" These are "the form in which activity is embodied" and "the content which is embodied in that form." [51] The creation of beautiful form is the realm of *aesthetic* activity; the introduction of moral content into forms is the province of *moral* activity. These two moments are separable not only theoretically but practically; an individual cannot consciously attend to both dimensions simultaneously—though Lavrov adds that a truly humane individual will be "unconsciously moral" in his aesthetic activity, and "unconsciously aesthetic" in his moral activity.

In society the distinction and interrelationship of these two moments has the greatest significance, Lavrov argues. Man's own consciousness sets before him a complex of ideals to guide his social action; as we have seen, these are the intertwined ideals of human dignity, justice, the equal right of all individuals to respect and development. Society itself is a complex of institutions or forms, more or less consciously constructed, in which these human ideals are more or less adequately realized. Often these forms are unsuited for the realization of man's ideals, and persist simply as conventional products of past activity, lacking adequate moral content. In such a case, Lavrov argues, the moral individual must bend every effort to infuse social forms with his ideals, either by introducing proper moral content into the existing forms, or by reconstructing these forms in accordance with his ideals. This progressive alteration of social forms, an activity now aesthetic, now moral, constitutes man's career in the social world:

Man creates beautiful or simply harmonious forms, into which he unconsciously inserts his moral content; harmony and beauty fortify the existence of these forms, leaving them monuments to human activity. Man embodies moral content in life, breaking up and reconstructing the forms in which he embodies it to the extent that they do not satisfy his content.[52]

It is precisely this process of the more or less conscious creation and recreation of institutions which constitutes man's *history*, according to Lavrov. Developing his conception of history from the anthropological point of view, Lavrov first emphasizes that only man has a history. In fact history is "the most essential sign which in the eyes of science distinguishes the species *homo* from other zoological species." [53] But further, like the other sciences, history must proceed from the fact of human consciousness. It can be defined as the study of man's conscious development in time. Seeking the facts of conscious development everywhere, it sees in all the diversity of historical events "the transition from a less conscious to a more conscious state." [54] In man's practical life, the visible arena of historical development, history focuses on man's growing recognition of moral ideals and his increasingly conscious creation and recreation of social institutions incorporating these ideals.

But history does not ignore the record of man's purely intellectual attainments in the realm of theoretical cognition. This, too, is a part of man's conscious career, and these attainments eventually play their role in the practical arena as well. The philosophy of history shows the progressive recognition and implementation of all the principles of the two other areas of anthropologism as a philosophical system. In Lavrov's words, the philosophy of history "includes in their process of development all the things that theoretical philosophy and practical philosophy include in the dogmatic form in which they are conceived today." [55] Theoretical philosophy derives certain conclusions from its view of man as an actual, thinking being. Practical philosophy likewise sets forth its conception of man as a consciously free, creative, and humane individual. The philosophy of history deals with the progressive development of man's *recognition* of his own characteristics and of all principles, theoretical and practical, which follow from these characteristics. Ideally the philosophy of history presents the laws of the intellectual development through which man has become convinced that he has no metaphysical access to the essence of things, that the individual is the source of all action, that the causes of this action are "inner ideals" (such as the ideals of dignity and justice) rather than "external motives and compulsions," and so on.[56]

Still, the substance of the historical process itself is for Lavrov the *actions* in which these principles of theoretical and practical philosophy are embodied in life—in which superior intellectual systems are created to replace the inferior, in which men strive more and more consciously to infuse social forms with moral ideals. Lavrov's emphasis on consciousness as the source of all distinctively human and all historical action is so great that for him all history is essentially intellectual history; men's philosophical views, whether or not they are explicitly recognized as such, are the ultimate sources of his historical action. But to *make* history these views must be expressed through the active creation and re-creation of intellectual and social forms.

The historical and activist emphasis of Lavrov's philosophy was carried to its highest point in his three public lectures on the contemporary significance of philosophy in 1860. Presenting in these lectures a somewhat popularized synthesis of anthropologism as a philosophical system, Lavrov laid heavy stress on man's responsibility to create history through his conscious, moral action. In the end he showed the intimate interconnection of action, history, and philosophy, enlarging his very conception of philosophy to incorporate the action which makes history.

In the course of history different conceptions of human good succeed one another, Lavrov asserts. At any moment some conceptions are outmoded, antidevelopmental; others are waiting their turn, and must be realized "so that society may develop." [57] The new ideals do not triumph of themselves. There must be men who have the understanding and the determination to implement them. The scientist and the artist, for example, are also men; if they are *true* men their scientific and artistic work will display their acknowledgment of progressive ideals. And when the time comes for them to act in society, "they are moral monsters if they do not cast aside their microscope and chisel and serve, by deed and life, their country or an idea." [58] Individuals move history by recognizing progressive ideals and creating events in their name.

Lavrov in these lectures sees both the discernment and the actualization of ideals as functions of "philosophy." "The highest manifestation of philosophy in life," Lavrov asserts, consists in becoming conscious of superior ideals, incorporating them as convictions, and finally "serving these convictions by word, deed, and life." [59] Practical philosophy, then, ends in history, since man's truly human, moral action makes history. Indeed philosophy in general merges with history, since all man's knowledge looks toward creative action as its goal. Lavrov's final definition of philosophy in the third lecture makes explicit this connection between philosophy and the action which makes history: "Philosophy," he states, "is the understanding of everything that exists as a unity *and the embodiment of this understanding in artistic form and in moral action. It is the process of identifying thought, form, and action.*" [60] The history which such action creates is the goal and the visible capstone of all philosophy.

Such is the philosophy of anthropologism developed by Lavrov in his early essays. Like Comte, Lavrov began with a positivistic critique of metaphysics; but he did not end with the rejection, historically characteristic of positivism, of man's subjective world, his moral ideals, or synthetic philosophizing. Lavrov based his positivism on the phenomena of the human consciousness in all its realms, and he gave the same validity to subjective phenomena as to the phenomena of the external world. He placed history and introspective psychology on a level with the natural sciences as lawful areas of scientific investigation. He accepted moral phenomena as validating human freedom and responsibility, so as to legitimize man's quest for moral ideals. He broadened the scope of philosophy itself to include not only the synoptic work of integration in man's intellectual world but also the practical expression of man's moral ideals in historical action. In the end, then, Lavrov's anthropologism is a far cry from the positivism of Comte and his followers. It is a moralistic, activistic positivism which calls on the philospher to make history.

The intellectual influences which formed this outlook were many, as Lavrov himself acknowledged. In his autobiography he traced the philosophical descent of anthropologism from the ancient Greek philosopher Protagoras and the sceptics of the Second Academy through Immanuel Kant, Ludwig Feuerbach, and the neo-Kantians, particularly Albert Lange. Nor should the influence of J. S. Mill and Proudhon be overlooked, to name only thinkers most frequently and most favorably cited by Lavrov himself. In this light it is easy to understand the charge of eclecticism leveled against Lavrov, first by his critics of the 'sixties, subsequently by Plekhanov, and today by many Soviet philosophers.

But if eclecticism is taken to mean either a merely external combination of essentially incoherent elements, or a mélange of views which, though consistent, are drawn indiscriminately from many thinkers and display no guiding character, Lavrov's anthropologism can hardly be accused of eclecticism. His outlook, whatever its other difficulties, forms a coherent system focusing on the data of human consciousness and looking toward moral action. Further, its formation shows the clear predominance of some intellectual influences over others—influences which gave definite direction to Lavrov's philosophical system. Rusanov narrows these influences to three when he speaks of "the interesting combination which grew up in Lavrov's mind of Kant's subjectivism, Feuerbach's anthropologism, and Proudhon's theory of human individuality." [61] Lavrov did draw from all three, but his debt to Proudhon does not extend beyond certain features of his conceptions of individuality and justice. In his fundamental philosophical approach, Lavrov was above all a Feuerbachian who, even before the German thinkers of his day, returned to Kant.

Lavrov derived his positivism not from Comte but from Kant. While he mentioned Comte as early as 1859 in his "Outline of the Theory of Individuality," he did not become seriously acquainted with Comte's writings until the late 'sixties.[62] His own positivistic doctrines are expounded, as we have seen, with explicit reference to Kant. Again, Lavrov's affirmation of the autonomy of the moral consciousness, the basis of his practical philosophy, follows the Kantian inspiration in establishing a moral world, independent of the physical, in which man's moral values gain legitimate and elevated status. Lavrov even connected with Kant his own emphasis on the social embodiment of moral impulses: the Kantian doctrine, he wrote, "sought to elaborate a strictly scientific and at the same time exalted theory of moral duty, and laid it down as a sociological task that social forms should be determined by the moral demands of the individual." [63]

Most important, the whole tenor of Lavrov's anthropologism is Kantian: it consists above all in a Kantian insistence that man's thinking inevitably starts from himself and is molded by inescapable features of the human mind and outlook, by what Lavrov calls "the demands of human consciousness." Just as Kant insisted that man of necessity looks at things from the point of view set by his own mental economy, shaping the contents of knowledge to the forms of his sensory and intellectual apprehension, so Lavrov regarded man as (the image is Gustav Shpet's) a lens gathering everything in the prism of consciousness.[64] Man inevitably views the objects of his attention in ways determined by his subjective characteristics as a thinker. Lavrov sees consciousness as "the chief and inescapable fact" in all areas of thought because, like Kant, he proceeds philosophically through reflective analysis of the conditions imposed on thought by the nature of the thinker.

Lavrov's Kantianized anthropologism provided his fellow Russians with a system of ideas significantly different from that of the other Russian Feuerbachians. A broader outlook than theirs, it made a place for everything they had emphasized and provided more. When Chernyshevsky called man "a complex chemical compound," Lavrov admitted that this is a valid approach from the point of view of the natural sciences; but he insisted that the other regions of science must treat man differently. When Chernyshevsky said that man's will is causally determined, Lavrov answered that "metaphysically" this may well be so; but he added that practically this makes no difference to man, who in his action inevitably conceives of himself as free. When Chernyshevsky proclaimed that men are egoistic and strive solely for their own pleasure, Lavrov agreed—and proceeded to outline the process by which the primitive striving for personal pleasure is transformed into ideals of human dignity and justice which have implications quite different from the undeveloped egoistic hedonism on which they are based.

Lavrov and Chernyshevsky agreed that the "anthropological point of view" takes the integral psycho-physical human individual as its incontestable datum. But Chernyshevsky's anthropologism was a reductionistic, deterministic outlook which centered attention on man's physical, material properties. Lavrov's anthropologism took its departure from human consciousness and creative action, and consequently emphasized not the natural sciences but ethics and history. It stressed the autonomous moral individual, man the actor and creator. It is true, Lavrov asserts, that man is formed by the natural world around him; but in the last analysis man is more a principle than a consequence. In creating his scientific theories, acting in the outer world, and perpetually reordering his inner world, "man is the source of nature, the source of history, the source of his own consciousness." [65]

Politics and Exile

Lavrov tells us in his autobiography that the need for political and social overturn in Russia was evident to him from the very beginning of his literary career. Certainly his philosophical views just examined, with their emphasis on deliberate social change, had a direct if unexpressed application to the Russian society of his day. When Lavrov in his early works spoke of the need for "breaking up and reconstructing" social forms and for "eternal struggle against the created in the name of the creating," he gave no indication that he meant to exclude the possibility of revolution in his own society. His words were at least reformist, and his silences could be interpreted as revolutionary.

Still, Lavrov's published works of the time gave no precise clues to the direction or the extent of his protest against the Russian social system. Censorship would have prevented him from preaching socialism, all the more revolutionary socialism, even if he had been prepared to do so. What he did say, the radicals found too moderate. On the other hand conservatives like Nikitenko charged him with socialism, and the government soon found him a radical dangerous enough to banish.

For the charge of socialism there was a certain amount of evidence, even in Lavrov's published works. His clear admiration for the French socialists could be viewed as subscription to their radical socioeconomic doctrines—though actually Lavrov seemed more attracted to their psychological and moral views. More significant, perhaps, were Lavrov's scattered references to the plight of labor and the unjust dominance of propertied classes over unpropertied in contemporary society. As early as 1856, in his published letter to Herzen, Lavrov had expressed the fear that emancipation of the serfs would be rendered nugatory if the former serfs were not protected against future exploitation by officials and by their wealthier fellows. Anticapital, prolabor sentiments were vented in Lavrov's essays when he spoke of "the aristocracy of property and the proletariat of the masses," and when he juxtaposed "cannibalism, slavery, the exploitation of the proletariat by the factory owners, the poor by the rich, the weak by the strong." [66] Clearest of all was Lavrov's discussion of property in his "Outline of the Theory of Individuality," where his agreement with Proudhon amounted to a critique of the institution of private property.

As for considering Lavrov a dangerous revolutionary, there was, of course, little foundation in his early published works. Beyond his general references to "breaking up" outmoded social forms and such statements as "we Russians have no social traditions which contain the potentiality for broad development" [67] there is nothing to indicate that Lavrov before 1861 harbored any thoughts of violent revolt in his homeland. A government agent who was present at Lavrov's three lectures on philosophy in 1860 reported that Lavrov "permitted himself various sharp expressions directed against the supreme authority and the existing order," [68] but these amounted to nothing more than one or two deprecatory references to "patriarchalism" and use of the radical leader Insarov in Turgenev's novel *On the Eve* as an example of how readers can be inspired by a fictional character.

Only in private did Lavrov express his radical convictions more clearly, and only his closest friends knew the depths of his revolutionary hopes. To Yelena Shtakenshneyder, the Lavrov of 1860 was "the apostle of a new faith—the faith of destruction." "His dream was revolution," she reports, and she sums up his message in these words: "Destroy! The entire existing order of life must be destroyed. The state, the church, the family—all this must fall and disappear, and every honorable man is duty-bound to contribute to their downfall with all his efforts." [69] Still, before 1861 there is no evidence to show that Lavrov himself took any overt steps to implement these convictions, or advocated direct revolutionary action. He states in his autobiography that at the time he found "no ground for social revolution or even for political action apart from the slow preparation of minds." [70] His "socialist ideal" was already well established, he asserts; but finding its realization impossible in the present, he devoted himself to promoting understanding and appreciation of the ideal.

Contrast this with the summary of Lavrov's activity from 1861 to 1866 in a secret Third Section report compiled shortly before Lavrov's arrest: "Lavrov, at every convenient opportunity, has not only expressed his revolutionary mode of thought but has taken an active part in all intrigues directed against the government." [71] However exaggerated, this account does point to a change which occurred in Lavrov's career around 1861. While still ostensibly promoting "the slow preparation of minds," Lavrov found himself drawn more into the social arena. From 1861 on he took an increasingly active part in the promotion of radical causes and moved closer to the political position of Chernyshevsky and his followers.

The early 'sixties were a time of renewed ferment in Russian society. By 1860 it had become clear to the radicals and the less sanguine liberals that Alexander's vaunted administrative, juridical, and educational reforms were by no means fulfilling the hopes for social betterment which their prospect had aroused.

When emancipation came in 1861, its economic terms were such as to ensure the *de facto* subjugation of the serfs, in most cases, for decades to come. There were peasant uprisings in the countryside, followed by student disturbances in the cities. The government responded to the student agitation by imposing new regulations on the universities in May, 1861, limiting the enrollment of needy students and instituting a police regime to control student activities. The new regulations provoked still greater agitation. Many students were injured and arrested in demonstrations, and the universities of St. Petersburg, Moscow, and Kazan were temporarily closed by administrative order.

Lavrov writes in his autobiography that he advised against participation in these disturbances, but at the same time he could not remain aloof in the face of what he viewed as persecution of the students by the government. He openly supported the students in the public press, was active in raising funds for them, and at times took a sympathetic part in student meetings. At the height of the agitation he joined the students in one St. Petersburg demonstration, defying police orders to stand aside. It was at this time that Lavrov's activities first attracted the serious attention of the secret police, and a file was opened in his name in Third Section headquarters.

Further repressive measures against education and the press followed in 1862. Some of the leading radical writers were arrested. Pisarev received a four-year prison sentence. Chernyshevsky, arrested in 1862, was banished to Siberia in 1864. The Polish rebellion of 1863 goaded the government to further controls, and the severity with which the rebellion was suppressed inflamed the radicals and liberals. Alexander's reforms continued throughout the 'sixties, but the dissidents were no longer interested in the emperor's administrative and judicial contrivances. They were preparing to take matters into their own hands.

In 1861 or 1862 Lavrov made his first contact with the revolutionary underground, through the secret society "Land and Liberty" (*Zemlya i volya*). Lavrov wrote later that his participation in the society was "so insignificant that it is not worth talking about," but there is evidence that in 1862 and 1863 he took part in formulating the society's proclamations concerning emancipation of the peasants and the Polish rebellion, and that the society's St. Petersburg committee held meetings in Lavrov's apartment.[72] In 1863 Lavrov took part in forming a "Working Women's Society," but he nominated so many women "of the most extreme political convictions" (as the secret police reported) that the aristocratic ladies in charge declined his further help; his obvious aim, affirmed a police agent, was revolutionary propaganda.[73] Similarly propagandistic, according to Nikitenko, were the lectures which Lavrov gave privately in 1864, in which he aimed at (in Nikitenko's words) "transforming young women and girls into Nihilists." [74] At about the same time Lavrov helped to establish a cooperative workshop for impoverished St. Petersburg seamstresses. In 1865 he used his seat in the new St. Petersburg *zemstvo* to speak out against the government's repressive measures. In the same year he led an unsuccessful fight to raise money to aid the banished Chernyshevsky and secure a review of his case by the authorities.

All these activities, as well as others less significant, were dutifully noted by the secret police in a list of Lavrov's "illegal activities." A note for April 20, 1863—during Lavrov's involvement with "Land and Liberty'"—reads: "Today Colonel P. L. Lavrov, who is strongly suspected of revolutionary intrigues, has been placed under particularly strict surveillance." [75] Lavrov came to be regarded by the authorities as one of the leading troublemakers. Prince Ol'denburgsky included him among the "five or six instigators" whose arrest, the Prince held, could quell all traces of revolution.[76] Yet the police found no conclusive evidence on which to charge Lavrov, and he remained at liberty. In 1865 he took his ailing wife abroad for four months for medical treatment; she died early in 1866, after their return to St. Petersburg.

Lavrov's fate was sealed by Dmitry Karakozov's attempt to assassinate Alexander II on April 4, 1866. An immediate reign of terror was instituted under the infamous Count Muravyov. The fact that Lavrov had been associated since 1865 in a publishing *artel* with two acquaintances of Karakozov was the immediate ground for action against him. His quarters were searched, and on April 25, 1865, he was arrested. Seized among his belongings were a few verses critical of Nicholas I and Alexander II, and some letters which showed his acquaintance with Chernyshevsky, the revolutionary poet M. L. Mikhailov, Nicholas Utin, who had been a member of "Land and Liberty," and the bookseller N. L. Tiblen, who had had dealings with the exiled Herzen. Also seized were the proof sheets of a short unpublished article entitled "Little by Little," written about 1863, in which Lavrov's radical sentiments were expressed in the clearest fashion yet: criticizing the "gradualists" who worked for one isolated reform at a time, he called for concerted and comprehensive social overhaul.

Lavrov's arrest came as a shock to the Petersburg public. Even the secret police reported that "many people are very displeased by the arrest of Lavrov, saying that he sought only to corrupt the youth intellectually." [77] Further, no evidence was found directly linking Lavrov with any revolutionary activity or group. Nonetheless he was brought before a military court in August, 1865, and was pronounced guilty on a variety of charges, including "disrespect" for Nicholas I and Alexander II, "sympathy and intimacy with persons known to the government for their criminal inclinations," and finally an intention to propagate "pernicious ideas" in the press.[78] The court imposed a prison sentence, which was subsequently altered by higher authority: Lavrov was dismissed from the service and was banished for life to "one of the inner provinces" under police surveillance.

The "inner province" selected was distant Vologda, to which Lavrov was removed in February, 1866, after nine months' imprisonment in St. Petersburg. He was first settled in the small town of Tot'ma, some 670 kilometers east of St. Petersburg. In 1868 he was transferred to the town of Vologda, the provincial capital, and a few months later to tiny Kadnikov, where he remained, the hamlet's only political exile, until his escape abroad in 1870.

Even in this harsh age of Russian imperial despotism, banishment was by no means extinction. Despite security measures Lavrov found it possible to continue his active intellectual life during these years, writing and even publishing in a number of St. Petersburg journals. His writings were forwarded through the police, and although they could not be published under his own name, his pseudonyms—particularly "P. Mirtov"—soon became common knowledge. Both the public and the government were well aware of Lavrov's continued literary activity.

Nor did Lavrov lack opportunities for contacts with other

political dissidents in the Vologda region. In Tot'ma he met the Polish revolutionary Anna Chaplitskaya (whose common-law husband he soon became) and the exiled writer D. K. Girs, banished for a speech he made at Pisarev's funeral, as well as a number of St. Petersburg students transported to the provinces for their part in the university disturbances. In the provincial capital when Lavrov arrived were still other, more prominent exiles, including the radical writers V. V. Bervi-Flerovsky, then at work on his major book, *The Condition of the Working Class in Russia*, and N. V. Shelgunov, Chernyshevsky's colleague with whom Lavrov was already acquainted. From Kadnikov Lavrov was able to make clandestine excursions to visit his friends in other towns, and even in Kadnikov he was in touch with the radical element of the local population, particularly students from the Vologda seminary.

The local radicals, Lavrov found, were intoxicated with the ideas of Pisarev. Chernyshevsky had been effectively silenced after 1863; but Pisarev, in prison in St. Petersburg, had continued to publish, and his brilliant apotheosis of "rational egoism" soon won him a large and dedicated following. It was not, however, a following devoted to vigorous social action. Under Pisarev's spell the Nihilists began to turn inward: they put their faith more and more in individual self-cultivation, particularly through immersion in the natural sciences, the materialists' grand panacea for the ills of mankind. One of Pisarev's heroes was Bazarov, the solitary, frog-dissecting Nihilist of Turgenev's novel, *Fathers and Sons*. By the mid-'sixties the Pisarevites were sufficiently numerous and vocal to constitute what Bakunin called a "new school of lonely, melancholy self-development in science and life, independent of the people and apart from all political and social-revolutionary action." [79] By the time of Lavrov's arrival the school had spread even to remote Vologda, though there it was anything but melancholy: the "progressive inhabitants" of Vologda, wrote one contemporary observer, "had gone mad over the works of Pisarev." [80]

To Lavrov this intellectual atmosphere was profoundly disturbing. If he was drawing closer to the Nihilist radicals in the severity of his opposition to the existing order, he remained no less opposed to their materialism, their increasing withdrawal from the social arena, and what he considered their dangerous disregard of moral ideals and the whole realm of history. Lavrov sought a turn from the natural sciences to the pressing problems of moral and social life. In exile he continued his scholarly investigations into such problems, hoping to promote greater interest in the study of moral and historical man through such articles as "Some Thoughts on the History of Thought" (published in 1867), "Civilizations and Savage Tribes" (1869), and "Modern Doctrines of Morality and the History of Morality" (1870).

But Lavrov was well aware that scholarly disquisitions alone cannot conquer a reigning orthodoxy. Consequently he early conceived the idea of writing a more popular work in which, free from the paraphernalia of scholarship (which were in any event difficult to muster in Vologda), he could elaborate with greater familiarity and force both his opposition to Pisarev and his own social program, on the philosophical foundation already developed in his early essays. Years before, in 1856, Lavrov had begun a series of articles on separate but related themes entitled "Letters on Various Contemporary Questions," but censorship cut the project short after only two letters had been published. Reviving the old format for his present purpose, Lavrov in 1867 began work on his *Historical Letters*. Their publication commenced in *Week* (*Nedelya*), a St. Petersburg review, with the first issue for 1868. This series was more successful, and was published in its entirety, in fifteen installments, by mid-1869.

Lavrov himself was not entirely happy with the series. His scholarly soul rebelled against the popularization the letters required, and among his writer friends he minimized their significance. To the congratulations of a fellow exile in 1868 he replied that the letters were "not really a serious work, but *feuilletons* I write in my spare time." When in 1870 the letters were first published together as a separate book, Lavrov was still inclined to disown them. "The *Historical Letters*," he complained, "could ruin my reputation as a scholar." [81]

There were others who had serious misgivings about publishing the *Historical Letters*, though their reasons were quite different from Lavrov's. To many members of the editorial board of *Week* —including, as Lavrov says in the preface to the second edition, "outstanding representatives of our progressive literature"—the letters were not sufficiently popularized. One of the critics was Nicholas Mikhailovsky, subsequently regarded as the coleader, with Lavrov, of the Russian Populists; despite his sympathy with Lavrov's intellectual position, Mikhailovsky agreed with his editorial colleagues that the letters were too dry for the majority of journal readers. Only at the insistence of Yevgeniya Konradi, the woman who had founded *Week* and to whom Lavrov refers in the preface as a "good personal friend," was publication of the letters begun and continued.[82]

But most disturbed of all were the St. Petersburg censors. The letters attracted the government's attention with their first appearance in *Week* early in 1868. One of the reasons for a "first warning" addressed to the journal later that year was that in its pages "there was systematically developed a doctrine of . . . struggle against the existing social order, as for example in the articles 'Historical Letters' printed in Nos. 16 and previous." [83] But despite continued scrutiny and further critical reports by the censors, the series was allowed to run to its completion. The authorities concluded that they had no firm grounds for judicial proceedings since "the author's discourse has the character of a general historical discussion and can be applied to any European power." [84]

Shortly after the work was published in book form without preliminary censorship in 1870, it was again brought before the St. Petersburg censorship committee. The censor Skuratov found it to be a "philosophical work which cannot count upon a wide circle of readers," but felt impelled to warn that it could be "a source of considerable harm" among students. The committee agreed that the book harbored "evil intentions" and referred it to the Central Press Board. Board member F. P. Yelenev subjected the book to a scathing attack, concluding that "in general, all the principles of moral, social, and political corruption have found an ardent extoller and advocate in the author of this book. Contrariwise, all the truths on which morality, society, and the state are founded are denied or ridiculed by him." However, Yelenev continued, the author manages to escape providing grounds for prosecution by "the use of that conventional terminology which, while it is completely clear to a certain class of readers, nevertheless escapes from coming directly under any article of the Criminal Code." Hence the Board concluded reluctantly and not without a note of exasperation that it would be "inconvenient" to bring proceedings against the book, until such time as the courts would cease confining themselves to "the casuistical bringing of certain thoughts and expressions under the articles of the Code" and would proceed to "fathom the inner meaning of the whole book and weigh the author's aim and the influence which the work must have on the class of readers for which it is intended" [85]—a refinement in censorship proceedings reserved for a later day in Russian history.

Thus despite the misgivings of author, publisher, and government, in 1870 the *Historical Letters* of a certain P. Mirtov, whom everyone knew to be the celebrated political exile Peter Lavrovich Lavrov, became widely available in Russia to spread their "false doctrines concerning the religious, moral, and political foundations on which every social order is based." [86] And spread them they did, until the book became the bible of Russian Populism and a leading force in the Russian revolutionary movement.

The Argument of the Historical Letters

Russian Populism (*narodnichestvo,* from *narod,* "people") was an amorphous social movement which traced its origin to the socialist writings of Alexander Herzen. It reached a peak in the mid-1870's with the "To the People!" movement, in which thousands of idealistic young Russians took to the countryside, more or less spontaneously, to live with "the people" and bring them the saving message of socialism. The efforts of these young zealots proved somewhat premature; "the people" showed surprising resistance to socialist teachings, and in many cases handed over their would-be benefactors to the authorities. Many of these early Populists (*narodniki*) lived on into the twentieth century, and with their intellectual progeny were active in more successful revolutions. But as a recognizable movement Populism was dead before the end of the nineteenth century, when leadership of the Russian revolutionary movement passed from the Populists to the Marxists. Lenin's literary career began with polemics against the Populists in 1893 and 1894.

As a set of doctrines Russian Populism was a form of radical agrarian socialism centering on the institution of the Russian *obshchina,* or peasant village commune. To the Populists the *obshchina,* with its existing traditions of collective ownership and collective responsibility, provided Russia with a "special path" to socialism, not open to the industralized nations of the West: in Russia, they argued, the nucleus of a socialist society already existed, and hence the socialist revolution could be successful in Russia *before* the development of industrial capitalism with its multiform evils. The Populists looked to the peasantry as the wellspring of revolution, and saw the social order of the future as a highly decentralized federation of communes.

With Populism both as a movement and as a set of doctrines the name of Peter Lavrov is firmly linked. To S. V. Utechin, not Herzen but Lavrov is "the real father of Populism," since the most significant feature joining all the Populists is their common adherence to Lavrov's social philosophy.[87] Isaiah Berlin writes that Lavrov and Mikhailovsky, who also wrote a number of influential Populist works in the late 'sixties and 'seventies, represent "the deepest strain of all, the very center of the Populist outlook." [88] If Herzen was its prophet and the *obshchina* its god, Lavrov was at least one of the chief apostles of Populism.

Hence it may seem surprising that in the *Historical Letters,* the "bible of Populism" which inspired the young *narodniki,* there is only one fleeting mention of the *obshchina*—a hypothetical reference in the Thirteenth Letter to "the world as a collection of separate, autonomous communes (*obshchiny*)." * Beyond this there is not a single reference to the doctrines of agrarian socialism. Indeed there is not a single reference to socialism of any sort, agrarian or otherwise, in the original volume of 1870. Specific mentions of socialism were incorporated only in the second edition, in 1891. Censorship, of course, would have prevented explicit advocacy of socialism in the first edition, printed in the Russian empire; but Lavrov made little attempt in the *Historical Letters* even to suggest the distinctive economic and political platform of Populism.

The fact is that in his chief and most influential work, Lavrov presented a side of Populism which is not captured by or confined to the *obshchina* and agrarian socialism. More than a social

* P. 249, below.

movement or a set of doctrines, Russian Populism was first and foremost a moral phenomenon, the release of a particular sort of moral enthusiasm. In the *Historical Letters* Lavrov helped to provide the initial burst of passion for that release; more important, he provided the philosophical principles which not only allowed but demanded it. By bringing his "anthropological point of view" to bear on problems of history and society, Lavrov defined the ethical core of Populism, the value foundation on which its economic and political reconstruction was to be based. And although he also sketched the character of this reconstruction in broad outline, its detailed depiction was reserved for later works, particularly his writings for the journal *Forward!* (*Vperyod!*), beginning in 1873.

The moral burden of Lavrov's argument in the *Historical Letters* lay in the concept of a *debt*—a debt to "the people" incurred by the privileged minority. Lavrov told his cultivated readers that they owed their cultivation to the suffering majority who supported them, and he made them believe it and want urgently to do something about it. The theme of responsibility to the masses whose toil created the material conditions for the flowering of the minority was not new in Russian social thought. It had haunted the more sensitive members of the gentry ever since the assault on their conscience in the late eighteenth century by Alexander Radishchev, the acknowledged founder of the Russian radical tradition. But recently, in the works of the Nihilists, this theme had been neglected in favor of another strain detectable in the radical tradition since Radishchev's day—the idea of self-interest. The very concept of a debt was alien to the outlook of Chernyshevsky and Pisarev; Chernyshevsky, indeed, had explicitly argued that the actions of one man can never obligate another, since the first was acting, like all men, from purely egoistic motives.[89] Lavrov, on the other hand, presented an intellectual outlook which revolved precisely around the idea of repaying a debt. He not only restated the theme, he made it dominant. And he orchestrated it convincingly for a new generation of the intelligentsia whose membership went well beyond the bounds of the old "repentant gentry."

The notion of repaying a debt implies action in relation to others, or in other words action in a social context. It implies rec-

ognition of a principle of moral obligation: a *debt* is something
that *ought* to be repaid. And it implies consideration of a past in
which the debt was incurred and a present and future in which it
must be repaid. Lavrov convinced his readers, then, that they
could not ignore the temporal movement of history; that in dealing with history they could not avoid recognizing certain moral
principles; and that having recognized these moral principles they
could not remain aloof from social action. History, morality, and
social action are the leading motifs of the *Historical Letters*.

Lavrov's case for history is a direct if implicit deduction from
the principles stated in his earlier philosophical essays. He does
not deny the value of the natural sciences; but in keeping with his
"anthropological point of view" he finds that man's fundamental
problems are not scientific but "subjective," problems of human
consciousness. To the solution of these problems, the contributions of the natural sciences are merely accessory. The chemist
and the physiologist, for example, may give us much essential
information concerning food and nutrition; but in the last analysis, Lavrov asserts, "food is important not as the object of nutritional processes but as the product which eliminates the conscious
pain of hunger." Moreover the natural scientist would never undertake his investigations were it not for the conscious satisfaction
they provide him. Now it is history, Lavrov argues, that deals
directly with these basic phenomena of consciousness: man as a
conscious agent is precisely the subject of history. History presents us with a temporal record of the very thoughts, feelings,
and ideals that give substance and meaning to the other sciences.
Lavrov's moral is clear, and it is entirely consistent with the central role accorded history in his philosophical works of 1860: of
all the sciences, history has first claim to the attention of everyone
seriously interested in the problems of mankind.

The linking of history with morality is also effected by Lavrov
through the use of notions developed in his earlier philosophical
writings, above all through what came to be called the "subjective method." Without using that term, Lavrov in the *Historical
Letters* nonetheless extends the method to history, in such a way
as to make the historian's work inseparable from moral demands.

In his early discussions of the subjective method, particularly in
"The Mechanistic Theory of the World," Lavrov had viewed it

simply as an introspective approach to psychic phenomena, applicable in the realm he called "phenomenology of spirit"—a domain distinct from history. It is necessary, he had held, because psychic phenomena are not open to the sensory methods of the natural sciences. But at the same time he had also found the distinctive phenomena of history inaccessible to sensory investigation. Now in the *Historical Letters* he makes it clear that the chief data of history, too, are psychic phenomena, and consequently that they, too, must be approached subjectively. Direct introspection, obviously, will not do; but Lavrov seems to envisage the historian as operating through a kind of referred or sympathetic introspection. For in Lavrov's view the historian, himself a conscious being, must (and inevitably does) take as his focus of attention the conscious needs and aspirations which move men, their desires and their moral objectives. He must bring into his own consciousness the subjective, moral motives of the actors in the drama of history, and must dispose all other data of history around these subjective facts. Only thus, Lavrov contends, can the historian form the perspective necessary to understand the drama itself.

But in the study of history Lavrov finds still a further dimension of subjectivity, requiring a further extension of the subjective method. The historian, in forming his historical perspective, Lavrov maintains, cannot avoid bringing into play *his own* moral ideals. Like his subjects he is a moral creature, and in studying their ideals he cannot avoid *judging* them. His own moral judgments, indeed, form the capstone of his perspectival system: ultimately, what is "important" in history means what is *morally* important to the historian from the standpoint of his own value system. This is the basis, of course, for Lavrov's insistence that we inevitably look for *progress* in history: we view historical events as furthering (or as hindering) the realization of our ideal. From the anthropological point of view we cannot avoid imposing our own value framework upon history, cannot avoid seeking progress in the march of historical events. Thus in history, the subjective method as Lavrov understands it inevitably includes evaluation.

The genuine inevitability of treating history in this way may, of course, be questioned; but Lavrov did not pursue this issue in the

Historical Letters. He was more concerned with another possible criticism of his argument: in what sense can such an evaluational approach be considered (in his word) "scientific"? Is it not hopelessly relativistic, dependent upon the pet fancy of every observer? Lavrov had considered this question explicitly in a critique of Comte's positivism published in 1868, at the same time the letters were appearing serially in *Week.* In this work, "The Problems of Positivism and Their Solution," he had argued that the subjective method is not restricted to phenomena which are the unique property of one individual subject. Swedenborg's visions could not, of course, serve as the foundation of "scientific" (universally valid) theories, since they are not publicly verifiable. But, Lavrov continues, "the subjective method can be utilized *scientifically* to establish truth by means of induction or deduction, provided only that a significant number of observers, critically developed and capable of scientific observation, can, each separately, perceive analogous phenomena." [90] Undaunted by the confusion this statement introduces into the distinction between "subjective" and "objective" methods, Lavrov applies these observations to ethics, where he finds that ends and purposes, the chief subjective categories of moral behavior, are "accessible to all individuals." Ends and purposes are found only in conscious awareness, but all individuals may be aware of them; hence "these phenomena compel us to use the subjective method and at the same time permit us to do so fully scientifically." [91] Now Lavrov had already argued, in his earlier writings in practical philosophy, that man's moral consciousness, properly developed, discloses to all men uniform ideals of justice, human dignity, and the equal rights of all individuals to self-development. It is on this basis that Lavrov can affirm in the *Historical Letters* that "the unity of moral ideals may be regarded as a thesis no less convincing than the unity of scientific truths," and that the over-all goal of *individual development* which he proclaims in the Third Letter defines the moral perspective within which *every* cultivated and progressive thinker will view history.

Having persuaded the would-be historian that it is legitimate to adopt a moralistic point of view, and that furthermore this "subjective" approach can disclose a common ideal which gives universal validity to his point of view, Lavrov has no difficulty establishing the crucial concept of the debt. For in effect he has placed the reader as a moral agent securely within history. The student of history cannot extricate himself factually or morally from the processes he is studying, cannot deny that his goal as a cultivated being is also the goal of history. Consequently he cannot deny his own *responsibility* for the course taken by this moral drama in which he himself is an interested actor. In the past, Lavrov argues, progress toward the goal of individual development has been effected to a very slight extent, and it has been restricted largely to the fortunate minority who have attained some degree of moral and intellectual cultivation. To make possible this cultivation for a minority, the majority has worked and suffered. Twenty years before, Alexander Herzen had pointed out that inequality of condition is an initial requisite for social progress: "those who are better off can develop at the expense of the others." [92] Lavrov takes up this idea of Herzen's, but he finds that the cost has been excessive. The minority has hitherto taken no pains to diminish or to alleviate the sufferings which made its own advance possible, or to spread the cultivation it has acquired. Elementary considerations of justice require that the privileged minority now repay the majority for its sacrifices. Such in essence is the simple moral appeal addressed by Lavrov to his fellow members of the Russian intelligentsia.

History and morality are major topics of the *Historical Letters,* but Lavrov's ultimate concern is the social action required to pay the debt, and it is in this area that the book makes its furthest and most substantial advances over his previous writings. In the earlier essays, as we have seen, Lavrov had stressed man's "duty to act," his responsibility to embody in external reality the moral ideal created in his imagination. In the *Historical Letters* he first spells out in some detail the type of action he envisages and the general directions it must take. The social program which thus begins to emerge in the *Historical Letters* speaks for itself; but some of the distinctive features of social action as Lavrov views it deserve special comment.

For Lavrov action must be directed, of course, not to Pisarevian "self-improvement" but to the material transformation of the social order. In fact genuine self-improvement is impossible without social betterment, he argues, since in the last analysis the interests of the individual are identical with the interests of society. To Lavrov repayment of the debt by bringing progress to society at large is demanded on selfish as well as on moral grounds.

Society at large, however, can by no means initiate progressive social action. The creation of progress is reserved by Lavrov to those individuals, first mentioned in his "Outline of the Theory of Individuality," to whom intellectual cultivation has given "a critical attitude toward everything that exists." In the *Historical Letters* he christens them "critically thinking individuals," the title by which they became renowned in the Russian radical movement. It is they more than any others, Lavrov maintains, who have incurred the debt. But more than that, it is only they who have both the vision and the opportunity to move society forward. Expanding on the view of history which he had sketched in "What Is Anthropology?" Lavrov argues that a society's "culture" (its established pattern of social relationships) is transformed into "civilization" (a more highly rationalized system of institutions, more appropriate to human needs) only through the operation of critical thought. All historical change consists in this transformation. Hence the critically thinking individuals who discern the shortcomings of existing institutions are the real movers of history. They alone are both sufficiently cultivated and sufficiently free from material concerns to promote the cause of progress successfully; a member of the masses who strove to be an agent of progress would, Lavrov contends, soon "die of hunger or sacrifice his human dignity." This strain of intellectual elitism is a persistent feature of Lavrov's social doctrine, though it must be qualified to be properly understood. Lavrov makes it clear in the *Historical Letters*, as he had in the "Outline of the Theory of Individuality," that intellect is powerless without moral determination; it will be noted that beginning in the Seventh Letter he often refers not simply to "critically thinking" but to "critically thinking and determined" individuals (*kriticheski myslyashchiye i energicheski zhelayushchiye lichnosti*—literally, "critically thinking and energetically desiring individuals"). Moreover, Lavrov's cultivated minority is an open, not a closed elite: Lavrov seeks to add to its ranks through the educative force of his own discussions in the *Historical Letters,* and his ultimate goal is to provide every member of society with the opportunity to become a critical thinker.

Critically thinking individuals move history, but they will not move it most effectively, Lavrov argues, until they have learned to organize. Powerful forces support the status quo; for any decisive victory over them, the intellectual elite must form itself into a cohesive, fighting party. Lavrov's Eighth Letter, in which these points are elaborated, was the first extended discussion of revolutionary party formation to appear in the Russian press. Nicholas Ogaryov, Herzen's collaborator, had already gone further, spelling out the strategy and tactics of revolutionary secret societies in a number of privately circulated papers writen in London in the late 'fifties and early 'sixties. Lavrov could not be as explicit or as precise. Nonetheless he was able to draw in bold outline the picture later detailed and implemented so effectively by Lenin and the Bolsheviks. The party, Lavrov explained, must be a monolithic, militant organism; the independence of those who join it "must vanish in the common direction of thought and the common plan of action"; it must direct its full force against its enemies, "fighting as one man, with all its resources"; and it must consider all those who disagree with it as enemies. In this way the *Historical Letters* first brought home to Russians in the homeland, on a broad scale, the problems and the promise of disciplined party action.

Lavrov's most specific indications of the social program to be followed by the organized elite, contained chiefly in the Ninth to the Fourteenth letters, are guided by a notion which Lavrov, for once, shared with Chernyshevsky, and indeed with the entire socialist camp—the idea that social institutions must be grounded in the natural needs of man. In the *Historical Letters* Lavrov expounded this principle more fully and explicitly than any of his Russian contemporaries, and used it as the basis for criticizing what in the Tenth Letter he calls the "false idealization" of existing institutions, whereby institutions which in fact pervert natural needs or disallow their full satisfaction are rationalized by privileged defenders of the status quo. Lavrov finds that existing institutions are entirely inadequate to the proper expression of the sexual impulse, for example; appropriate institutions would provide for the equality of women and would make marriage "a free

moral union to which all external compulsion or control is alien"
—that is, would provide the parties greater freedom in contracting and in dissolving the marital bond. Similarly, man's need for
economic security is scarcely met, Lavrov argues, by a society in
which "a minority of hereditary proprietors is surrounded by a
majority of slaves, hirelings, and beggars." To Lavrov "a new
time" (in the second edition he said "socialism") will bring institutions which provide all men with the material necessities and
comforts of life. And the same principle underlies Lavrov's contention in the Thirteenth Letter that the institution of the state,
although necessary given man's present low level of cultivation,
must ultimately be abandoned. For the state, in Lavrov's view,
corresponds to no real need of mankind; all genuine human needs
are more fully satisfiable through other social means. Consequently the state will be eliminated as soon as men learn rationally to
employ other institutions to fulfill the needs for which they are
ideally suited.

But if the satisfaction of particular human needs is the key to
the structure of particular social institutions for Lavrov, the final
criterion of all social action remains the moral demand to extend
individual development. Moral criteria are clearly evident not
only in the premises but at every stage of Lavrov's argument. The
unusual doctrine of contract he expounds in the Twelfth Letter
—the aspect of Lavrov's argument which the censor Skuratov
found "the strangest and most false of all" [93]—stems from his desire to preserve what he considers to be the moral basis of
contract, to prevent "the transformation of the moral principle of
contract into a formal principle of law." National patriotism is
made subservient to moral demands in the Eleventh Letter: it is
justifiable, Lavrov contends, only in those cases where a nation is
genuinely serving the cause of truth and justice. Even questions
of national unification and independence, discussed in the Fourteenth Letter, are treated by Lavrov without concession to the
principles of *Realpolitik* but with complete attention to the ethical goals of social organization. Lavrov's own argument is a
model of the consistently moralistic orientation he hoped to
foster, an attitude which would convince at least a few readers, as
he put it in the final letter, that it is they "who must repay, with

their thought, life, and action, their share of the enormous accumulated cost of progress."

The *Historical Letters* found such readers, and not simply a few but thousands. Already in 1868 and 1869, when the letters were appearing serially in *Week*, they had a certain influence in youth circles.[94] After the collected edition was published in 1870, Lavrov's teachings spread rapidly through the broad Russian empire, despite the fact that in 1871 the book was banned on the strength of a new law prohibiting the publication of works by emigrants. It continued to circulate illegally in lithographed form and in laboriously hand-copied excerpts, carrying Lavrov's message from one student group to another.

Typical was its reception in the town of Kherson, in the southern Ukraine. A nucleus of radical sentiment was created there, as in many provincial towns, by the imperial government itself: to prevent disorder in the centers, young troublemakers were dispatched to the provinces. Andrey Franzholi, subsequently a member of the terrorist "People's Will" society, was sent to Kherson for his participation in student disturbances in St. Petersburg. Exiled leaders such as Franzholi soon gathered sympathetic local youths around them, often forming "study circles" which concentrated on the reading and discussion of radical works. A. O. Lukashevich, a student in Kherson at the time and later a participant in the "To the People!" movement, recalls the attitudes and activities of one such group in 1871–1872:

Many young people yearned to leave Russia, which was so stifling, for some free country—Switzerland, or, still better, America. But our circle rejected this temptation—"on principle," of course. . . . The views of the members soon became revolutionary-Populistic. . . . At crowded meetings, attended by outsiders as well as the members of our circle, we read aloud and discussed the works of Lassalle, the articles of Dobrolyubov, and the *Historical Letters* of Mirtov [Lavrov]. The latter book, which quickly became a special sort of gospel among the young people, placed before us very vividly the thesis—which stirred us profoundly—of the *irredeemable debt to the people* owed by the Russian intelligentsia.[95]

Before the appearance of the *Historical Letters* the young Russian followers of Pisarev and imitators of Bazarov whom Lavrov was above all addressing were committed to social change, but their scientism and "enlightened egoism" had diverted their energies into other channels. With a moral appeal, Lavrov redirected their attention to the problems of suffering humanity. The change of outlook was in many cases dramatic, as Rusanov testifies:

At one time we had been attracted to Pisarev, who told us of the great utility of the natural sciences in making a "thinking realist" of man. We were all preparing to become such "thinking realists": we wished to live in the name of our own "cultivated egoism," rejecting all authority and making our goal a free and happy life for ourselves and for those who shared our ideas.

And suddenly [Lavrov's] little book tells us that there are other things besides the natural sciences. That the anatomy of frogs by itself doesn't take one very far. That there are other subjects of human importance. There is history. There is social progress. There are the people, the hungry masses worn down by labor, the working people who themselves support the whole edifice of civilization solely to make it possible for us to study frogs and all the other sciences. There is, finally, our irredeemable debt to the people, to the great army of toilers.

One can imagine what a hurricane of new thoughts and new feelings swept into our souls! How ashamed we were of our miserable bourgeois plans for a happy personal life! To the devil with "rational egoism" and "thinking realism," to the devil with all these frogs and other objects of science, which had made us forget about the people! Henceforth our lives must belong wholly to the masses, and only by dedicating all our strength to the triumph of social justice could we appear anything but fraudulent bankrupts before our country and before all mankind.[96]

Clearly this change of heart was not so much a conversion as a rededication, with renewed energy, to the permanent humanitarianism of the Russian radical tradition—the tradition of Radishchev, Herzen, and Belinsky. To the troubled young rebels of Russia, Lavrov offered a path through a tangle of conflicting inclinations. Before they read the *Historical Letters* their own deep sentiments and unformulated ideals fought against the lure of the Pisarevian Nihilism they professed. At heart they were undecided between the attractions of the natural sciences and a gnawing need to correct the ills of society; between a concern for their own cultivation, which kept them aloof from politics, and a recognition that tormenting political realities were the central fact of their existence; between an egocentric individualism which separated them from "the people" and a craving to be the friends and benefactors of these same people; between a "realistic," scientific disdain for moralizing and a burning awareness of the immorality and injustice of their surroundings; between an abstract materialism and a guilty conscience. In these acoustics, Lavrov's message was heard so clearly by the rebels because it both resolved their ambivalence and articulated their inmost ideals. At the crossroads between cloistered scientific theorizing and a commitment to social action, Lavrov supplied them with a unique amalgam—a *theory of action,* "scientifically" respectable and morally compelling. This was the intellectual resolution which, in the early 1870's, inspired so many readers of the *Historical Letters* and freed their energies for an idealistic fight for progress.

Later Life and Thought

After completing the *Historical Letters* Lavrov himself stood at a crossroads. Not surprisingly he, too, chose the path of action—though he was to follow it somewhat ambivalently. Early in 1870 he succeeded in escaping from his forced Russian exile and made his way to western Europe, where he began to play an active role in the international socialist movement.[97]

Invited to Paris by Alexander Herzen, Lavrov arrived in March, 1870, to find Herzen dead and France in a crisis, soon to crystallize in the fall of the Second Empire and the agonies of the Franco-Prussian war. Lavrov's reputation as a scholar and social radical made up for the loss of his distinguished patron, and he was quickly drawn into the heat of French intellectual life. He was elected a member of the Anthropological Society of Paris; later he accepted an invitation from the celebrated French surgeon Paul Broca, the father of modern anthropology, to join the editorial board of the *Revue d'Anthropologie* when it was founded. More important for the evolution of Lavrov's social views, he met many members of Marx's International Workingmen's Association, formed a few years before in London. Among them was the revolutionary leader Louis-Eugène Varlin, who in the autumn of 1870 led Lavrov to join the Paris section of the International. In the heady radical atmosphere on the eve of the Paris Commune, Lavrov's attitudes shifted rapidly and decisively to the left. In the words of Rusanov, "from a political radical sympathetic to the noble ideas of socialism, Lavrov became a confirmed socialist revolutionary." [98]

During the siege of Paris, Lavrov served the republican government as an artillery adviser and a hospital orderly. When the Paris Commune was proclaimed in March, 1871, he greeted it enthusiastically and offered to help the new government establish an educational program. But the communards were preoccupied with the heavy exigencies of defense. As their situation worsened, Lavrov set out in May, 1871, with Varlin's approval, to seek outside help. He journeyed first to Brussels and then to London, in an attempt to arrange military support through the General Council of the International. Accounts of the General Council's resources and influence proved exaggerated, however, and in any event the fate of the Commune was by this time sealed by events in Paris. The only significant result of Lavrov's mission was a personal one: in London he met Karl Marx and Friedrich Engels, with whom he was to remain in lifelong (but mutually reserved) communication.

Lavrov's first contact with the Russian revolutionary movement came in March, 1872, when a delegation from the homeland traveled to Paris to bring the renowned author of the *Historical Letters* a proposal first broached to him in Russia by members of a Populist propagandist group known as the Chaikovsky circle: that he edit a Russian socialist journal abroad. Occupied with an anticipated second edition of the *Historical Letters* as well as with other writings, Lavrov put off his decision. In the autumn of 1872 he moved to Zurich, where there was a large colony of Russian political exiles and students, and shortly thereafter he accepted the proposal. Thus was founded *Forward!*, after Herzen's *Bell* the best known and most respected Russian *émigré* journal. Its publication marked the most active period in Lavrov's life as a revolutionary publicist.

The first issue appeared in Zurich in the summer of 1873. The journal's goal, Lavrov wrote, was "the supremacy of the people," which could be achieved only through "popular uprising." Lavrov pledged the journal to an unrelenting fight on two fronts—the campaign of "science against religion," and the campaign of "the worker against the classes which are exploiting him." [99] By "the worker" Lavrov and his editorial colleagues meant, of course, not the industrial proletarian, still uncommon in Russia, but the peasant, the rural worker who preserved the traditions of the *obshchina* and the *artel*. "Our social revolution must come not from the cities, but from the villages," Lavrov wrote in *Forward!*[100] The revolution was to be not fundamentally political ("constitutional parties" were scorned) but economic: its task was to destroy the existing socioeconomic order and create a loosely federative society of autonomous communes. Against religion and for agrarian communism, the journal's leaders recognized, Lavrov wrote, that the central task of the day is "the subordination of the interests of all other classes to the interests of the peasantry; establishment of the autonomous *secular commune* as the fundamental element of the Russian state and social system." [101]

While *Forward!* received the eager support of a broad segment of the Russian revolutionary youth, its policies did not attract the Russian revolutionaries universally. Promised backing from "radical writers" in the homeland largely failed to materialize—though a liberal like the novelist Ivan Turgenev sent financial help. A more serious defection was that of the fire-breathing Bakuninists, who formed an active and highly vocal minority in the Russian colony in Zurich. Initially the Bakuninists were counted on for support and their collaboration was enlisted, but before the first issue of *Forward!* had appeared, organizational questions caused a serious split. Dissatisfied with Lavrov's "gradualism," the Bakuninists broke with Lavrov and his followers, set up their own journal, and launched a furious campaign against the Lavrovists which included physical violence as well as more scholarly modes of attack. Lavrov's associates took to closing his shutters at night to protect him from the bullet of some Bakuninist assassin.

The Bakuninists found Russia quite ready for bloody revolution, and favored immediate revolutionary agitation—direct incitement of the people to rise and smash the state machinery. Lavrov on the other hand preached the need for preliminary "preparation of minds," a school for revolution in which the ground could be prepared for favorable results from revolutionary violence. The

Bakuninists, Lavrov had said as early as 1871, "are in a hurry, as if it is simply a matter of political revolution." [102] He favored going to the people not to incite them to revolt, but to propagandize and organize. Where the Bakuninists focused their attention on the sleeping might of the "revolutionary masses," which needed only to be stirred up, Lavrov pinned his hopes on further and broader recruitment to the "critically thinking" revolutionary elite.

A final blow suffered by the Lavrovists had also fallen before the first issue of *Forward!* appeared: in June, 1873, Alexander II had ordered home the many women students in Zurich, among whom were some of Lavrov's staunchest supporters. The Russian colony thus depleted, Lavrov resolved to move the press to London. The move was effected in March, 1874, after the second issue; a third issue was published in London later that year. Beginning in January, 1875, the journal was transformed from an irregular miscellany into a semimonthly review. It carried international labor news and pieces by correspondents in Russian cities as well as theoretical and polemical articles on socialism. Smuggled into the homeland in considerable quantities, the journal met with great success—as did the books and brochures also published by the *Forward!* press.

Many of Lavrov's most influential writings date from his editorship of *Forward!* Widely read was his "Chronicle of the Worker's Movement," one of the journal's regular features. His articles on the famine in the Russian province of Samara in 1873 were read aloud in student circles in the homeland, like the *Historical Letters* before them, with powerful effect. A popularized exposition of socialist doctrine entitled "To Whom Does the Future Belong?" published in *Forward!* in 1874, was reprinted frequently both in Russia and abroad. Lavrov's lengthy work *The Element of the State in Future Society*, published in 1876, developed and updated his views of the state first expounded in the *Historical Letters*. Perhaps the most widely known of all Lavrov's writings was an inspirational verse—"Arise, working people!" began its refrain—which he published in *Forward!* for July 1, 1875, under the title "The New Song." Set to music and called "The Workers' Marseillaise," the song won great popularity in the revolutionary movement. It remained a favorite of Russian revolutionaries in the twentieth century.

Lavrov's journalistic work brought him the satisfaction of engagement in the revolutionary struggle, but it left him little time for the scholarly study which always competed strongly for his attentions with revolutionary activism. Furthermore he found himself more and more at odds with his associates on the journal. Though still accused of "gradualism," Lavrov had never been as much a gradualist as the followers he attracted, and as work on *Forward!* progressed their differences became more marked. Accordingly in December, 1876, Lavrov resigned his editorship to devote himself to "more scholarly work" (as he explained it), thereby proclaiming as well his ideological independence from the increasingly pedantic and moderate "Lavrovists" to whom he had given his name.

In May, 1877, Lavrov moved back to Paris, and from that time until 1882 he had little contact with the Russian revolutionary movement. Except for some collaboration with French socialists and a half-hearted attempt to form a small secret organization, his energies were devoted to writing and lecturing. He lectured on socialist theory and the history of thought, chiefly to Russian students in Paris. His writings of the period include an account of the Paris Commune which has been called "one of the most important pieces on the Commune in European literature," [103] as well as a great many articles on leading thinkers of the time, including Darwin, Schopenhauer, and Carlyle. It was also during this period that he wrote his long essay, "The Theory and Practice of Progress," first published in 1881 and later included in the second edition of the *Historical Letters*.

With the formation by Populist extremists of the terrorist "People's Will" party (*Narodnaya volya*) in Russia in 1879, Lavrov's revolutionary convictions were put to a severe test. At first he viewed terrorist tactics as a mistake, and argued against them publicly. Yet he rejected a proposal to edit a journal directed against the People's Will. Some time after the assassination of Alexander II in 1881, Lavrov came over to the side of the People's Will, though not without a difficult inner struggle. "I am not a member of the People's Will," he told friends, "but I am a true ally of that party." [104] Somewhat later he wrote in favor of terrorist tactics. Turning again to the active preparation for revolution, Lavrov took part in forming a Paris section of the "Red Cross of the People's Will," an organization devoted to aiding political prisoners in Russia.

Banished from France in February, 1882, for this renewed revolutionary activity, Lavrov took refuge in London. By now the patriarch of the Russian socialists abroad, and with his reputation enhanced by his banishment from France, Lavrov found himself once more waited upon by a delegation from the homeland. Again he was invited to edit a revolutionary journal—this time by the Executive Committee of the People's Will. Lavrov accepted, and after contriving in May, 1882, to move back to Paris—despite the fact that the official decree of banishment was never rescinded— he set to work making arrangements for the new publication, to be called *Herald of the People's Will* (*Vestnik narodnoy voli*). The first issue appeared in November, 1883, under the co-editorship of Lavrov and L. A. Tikhomirov. Militantly preaching revolutionary socialism, the journal remained in publication for three years. Lavrov's chief contribution was, as he put it, to stress "the theoretical explanation of the socialistic principles" behind revolutionary activity, lest the terrorist struggle against autocracy lose sight of the economic struggle against capital.[105] Less inspired in its content than *Forward!*, the *Herald* was not as successful with the public.

After 1886 Lavrov played a role in many socialist activities, including the formation of the Second International in Paris in 1889. But increasingly his time was spent in individual pursuit of the scholarly and publicistic aims which, in shifting proportions, had guided his career ever since the *Historical Letters*. Revered by radicals of all shades, Lavrov continued his work as a propagandist of socialism and educator of "critically thinking individuals." He lectured regularly to workers' societies, groups of Polish socialists in Paris (a Polish translation of the *Historical Letters* was published in 1885), and Russian student organizations. Despite his age and his scholarly preoccupations, Lavrov's moralistic preaching of socialism was in no way diminished in passion, and in these last years of the nineteenth century still another generation of Russian youth fell under his spell. Some suggestion of his influence in these years is provided by this description by a Russian *émigré* physician, a *fin de siècle* sceptic who happened into one of Lavrov's evening lectures:

This remarkable old man possesses surprising powers of inspiration. The very sight of him arouses civic feelings, and what he says acts as a specific on the sick conscience of the Russian intelligentsia. I am an incorrigible indifferentist myself and don't believe in anything; but I shall never forget this evening. And for more impressionable souls, who believe in mankind—especially for the youth—this archimandrite of Russian revolution is positively dangerous. He can inspire to the most heroic sacrifices, to the most desperate undertakings.[106]

Lavrov wrote topical pieces for many journals, French and German as well as Russian-language journals published in Geneva and New York. But most of his time and attention went to more scholarly writing, which continued with unabated vigor until his death in Paris on February 6 (N.S.), 1900. In addition to further work in preparing the second edition of the *Historical Letters,* which appeared finally in Geneva in 1891, he collaborated with other People's Will veterans in a series of works entitled "Materials for the History of the Russian Social Revolutionary Movement"; Lavrov's chief contribution was *The Populist Propagandists from 1873 to 1878,* published in two volumes in 1895 and 1896.

Most important among Lavrov's late works, however, were his studies in the history of thought—the field he always viewed as the locus of his chief scholarly contributions. As early as 1867 he had written his essay "Some Thoughts on the History of Thought." This was followed by a series of articles published together in 1875 under the title "An Essay in the History of Thought." Now in his late years Lavrov found more time to pursue this interest, and he published a number of major studies. Chief among them were *The Problems of Understanding History,* which appeared in 1898, and the monumental *Essay in the History of Thought in Modern Times,* published serially over the years 1888 to 1894. The more than fifteen hundred pages of the latter work were designed merely as the first volume of a contemplated *magnum opus* which, however, was never completed.[107] Another major work of almost one thousand pages, *Paramount*

Moments in the History of Thought, was published posthumously in 1903.

Lavrov's intellectual development after the first edition of the *Historical Letters* can best be characterized as a limited evolution toward Marxism. All the changes in his views were such as to bring him closer to the doctrines of Marx and Engels. But the evolution was incomplete—some would say unsuccessful—since in fact Lavrov stopped far short of accepting the cardinal tenets of Marxism at face value.

Ambiguities in Lavrov's own expressed attitude toward the impact of Marxism on his views, coupled with ambiguities in those views themselves, have made it difficult to assess precisely the shift in Lavrov's orientation. Lavrov himself states in his autobiography, written in the third person in 1885, that in economics he "regarded himself a disciple of Marx ever since he became acquainted with his theory" [108]—that is, since the early 'seventies. Furthermore we know from Rusanov's testimony that Lavrov, as editor of the *Herald of the People's Will* in the 'eighties, refused to allow criticisms of Marx's and Engels' views to appear on the pages of the journal.[109] Such facts, coupled with the undeniable evidence of Marxist elements in Lavrov's own writings after 1870 have led some commentators, even in the Soviet period, to regard Lavrov as a Marxist pioneer. To Yuri Steklov, for example, Lavrovism was "the original Russian Marxism." [110]

At the same time Plekhanov and other Russian Marxists have categorically rejected this characterization. For Plekhanov a great gulf separates Russian Marxism from the "Russian socialism" which Lavrov represented. "Lavrov and his followers," wrote the Soviet scholar M. Ostrogorsky in 1932, "were never even bad Marxists." [111] In the contemporary Soviet interpretation, Lavrov is labeled a "subjective idealist" hostile to the basic principles of Marxism. And finally we have Lavrov's own testimony, from the same autobiography, that after he had elaborated his outlook in his early philosophical essays (long before he became acquainted with Marxism) he had found it "neither necessary nor possible to change it in any material point." [112]

In what ways, then, *did* Lavrov's views change? His writings after 1870 clearly testify to a number of shifts, of which two stand out above all. To each of these major shifts Lavrov himself attributed considerable significance, and each shows the distinct influence of Marx and the other men of the International. They are the acceptance by Lavrov of a form of economic determinism, and his whole-hearted adoption of the concept of the class struggle.

Lavrov's new emphasis on the primacy of economic factors in society is clearly displayed in his revisions of the *Historical Letters* for the second edition. In the original edition Lavrov had held out some hope for political resolution of the social problem. Now he ridicules any attempt at social reform which is not fundamentally economic in character: "A constitutional state," he writes, "is no longer conceivable apart from the victory of labor in its struggle against capital." * The state, he argues, must realize its "complete dependence upon the economic forces which govern the forms of social development." Thus in seeking to realize justice, freedom, and equality in society we must be concerned not with "better juridical relationships," but with the establishment of "a sounder economic order." * * Going further, as if in criticism of his own previous emphasis on intellectual factors in history, Lavrov in the added Sixteenth Letter dismisses the notion that "ideas rule the world," maintaining that the establishment of a sounder world view and the extension of "rational education" in society are not the key to social reconstruction. The progressive movement of history can proceed only through the impulse of "vital interests," he contends—and man's basic vital interests are economic. Failure to recognize "the supremacy of economic interests over other interests in the social order" is one of the chief hindrances to progress, he argues.

The second major element of Marxism adopted by Lavrov—the concept of the class struggle—also receives clear expression in his post-1870 works. Lavrov came to agree with Marx that the capitalist economic order generates a radical class antagonism between the owners and the users of the means of production. Lavrov himself describes this conception as a critical alteration of the social theory he presented in the original *Historical Letters*. He long believed, he writes in his autobiography, that there was a

* See Lavrov's footnote on p. 233, below.
* * P. 296, below.

fundamental harmony of interests between "the individual of the ruling class and the majority of the subject class"—a harmony masked by ignorance, but discoverable simply through the intelligent calculation of personal advantage on the part of all members of society. This assumption, he now confesses, was "one of the gravest of errors." His acquaintance with the International, he says, convinced him of "the existence of an irreconcilable conflict of class interests," and consequently he came to believe with the Marxists that only the radical reconstruction of social institutions could produce a genuine harmony of interests in society.[113]

This change is the reason for Lavrov's whole-hearted espousement of revolutionary socialism in the 1870's, and it is reflected not only in his other writings after 1870 but in many revisions in the *Historical Letters* for the second edition. The long footnote added to the Third Letter is an example: rejecting as absurd, for present-day society, his earlier assertion that "justice is identical with the pursuit of personal interest," he speaks of existing society as a "war of all against all" in which competition must be replaced by "social solidarity." In the Thirteenth Letter, an earlier reference to "the antagonism of social parties" is changed to "the antagonism of economic classes," and a passage is added distinguishing between "particular abuses" in society and the over-all evil of the class struggle, "which becomes more and more acute as it is waged more consciously."

These concessions to economic determinism and the class struggle constitute the chief evidence for regarding Lavrov as a convert to Marxism in social philosophy. Beyond these shifts, however, it is safe to say that Lavrov took no further significant steps in assimilating the philosophy of Marx and Engels. On the contrary, all the evidence of Lavrov's later writings testifies that on other major issues he consistently failed to follow the Marxist lead. More important, even the elements of Marxism which Lavrov did accept received at his hands a peculiarly non-Marxian interpretation.

In questions of political organization, for example, Lavrov remained on the Bakuninist side of Marx. Although he carefully avoided the extremes of Bakuninist anarchism and recognized the need to utilize the coercive machinery of the state in the transitional period to the good society, he was by no means as far from anarchism as was Marx. He was much more wary of the state, even as a temporary weapon. "In using this weapon," he wrote in the revised Thirteenth Letter, "those who fight for progress must remember that it has its peculiarities, which oblige the agent of progress to treat it with extreme caution. . . . Strengthening the authority of the state can, by the very nature of this authority, be detrimental to social progress the moment it goes a little beyond what is absolutely necessary in the case at hand." Like Bakunin, Lavrov had a horror of centralized authority, no matter in whose hands it was vested. He envisaged the world of the future not as a permanently centralized communal system but as a collection of autonomous communes among which loose and provisional federations are formed as exigencies dictate.

To the much debated question of whether the socialist revolution could be effected in Russia before the full-blown development of capitalism, answered decisively in the negative by the Marxists, Lavrov refused to give an explicit reply. Calling the question "merely speculative," Lavrov maintained that it is always the practical duty of the socialist to support any genuinely socialist party "by all the means at his disposal," striving "to eliminate, as far as possible, the obstacles to the success of socialism, such as the political forms which support capitalism"—thus tacitly assuming, it would seem, that the revolution *can* proceed without the complete development of capitalism.[114]

But all such particular deviations from Marxist dogma are secondary to what is clearly the central feature of Lavrov's failure to carry Marxist concepts further in the adjustment of his world view—his underlying conception of history. The *Historical Letters* were written from the standpoint of an individualistic, intellectualistic, non-necessitarian conception of history. The evidence of Lavrov's later writings shows that throughout his long flirtation with Marxism, Lavrov continued to employ this conception as the focal point of his view of human action and social progress. Lavrov did *not* in fact abandon the view that "ideas rule the world," for at the same time and in the same works as he is preaching economic determinism and drawing out the ineluctible necessities of the class struggle, he is still exhorting the critically thinking individual to reconstruct his environment through embodying his ideas in action.

In the added Sixteenth Letter Lavrov's accommodation to economic determinism and the class struggle does not prevent him from reasserting, in perfect agreement with the original *Historical Letters,* that the task of the history of civilization is "to show how the critical thought of individuals has remade the culture of societies by striving to invest their civilizations with greater truth and justice." In the autobiography of 1885 he still asserts that "the basic point of departure for philosophical theorizing is man"—not matter or the factors of economic production —and that it is above all human consciousness that the theorist must consult in erecting his systems. And he asserts further that every human thought and action presupposes not only an objective world of phenomena linked by laws of causality but also "the possibility that we can establish goals and choose means in accordance with criteria of what is most agreeable, most useful, most proper." [115]

Such is the libertarian, possibilistic, "subjective" orientation to which Lavrov invariably returned. If, as Rusanov points out, Lavrov in his vast *Essay in the History of Thought in Modern Times* seems at times to suggest that individual consciousness is a subjective illusion, epiphenomenal on "the fatal processes of evolution, determined in human society by 'the process of production,' " [116] the impression is soon dispelled by the extravagant glorification of "conscious individuals" which characterizes the same work, serving to remind us of Lavrov's long-standing philosophical tenet that however "objectively necessary" may *seem* the events in which his action plays a part, the human subject can never seriously adopt the necessitarian view. And if, in another of his last works, *The Problems of Understanding History,* Lavrov ever asserts that consciousness is *not* the guiding force of social life, he is speaking only of primitive, prehistorical society, founded on the rule of custom, and adds that as society progresses the role of conscious elements increases.[117] And in the same work he reasserts the necessity of employing the subjective method in the study of history, and of approaching human phenomena as if causal determinism does not hold.[118]

Does this mean that Lavrov must be convicted of a fundamental contradiction between the Marxist elements in his later outlook and the philosophical freight he brought with him from the

past and refused to jettison? [119] Between a newly adopted economic determinism and a repeated insistence that consciousness
rules the world? Between his claim to have become a disciple of
Marx and at the same time to have no need to modify his own
philosophical principles? Contradictions will be found here only
if we fail to see that Lavrov's Marxist elements did not supplant
but merely supplemented his former principles. These elements
were adopted by Lavrov in a distinctive form, limited and conditioned by his enduring "anthropological" outlook.

For Lavrov, "economic determinism" may be said to operate
within the objective order of social facts. But for the Lavrov of
1890 as well as the Lavrov of 1860, the subjective human consciousness which both studies and acts within the social order is
not itself determined by any "laws" which may be discovered in
that order, and the critical thinker retains his ability to modify
the social order through his own free choice and activity. The
"primacy of economic factors" means to Lavrov simply that it is
economic factors which critically thinking individuals must attend
to and alter if they wish to improve society, since these factors are
basic *within the determinate order of objective social facts.* The
conscious individual stands always outside this order, raised
above it by his very consciousness; he scrutinizes society, comes
to understand it, alters it through his own conscious efforts which
flow ultimately from his perception of compelling moral ideals.
For him there is no causal necessity in any process which involves
human action; what might seem to be a historical necessity from
an objective point of view, is for him nothing more than a possibility which must be realized by the vigorous action of conscious
individuals.

Lavrov adroitly summarized the situation in one of his last
works, written in 1897. Referring to various conceptions of history, he shows both his acceptance of Marxist concepts and his
"subjective," activistic interpretation of them:

A better conception of history has revealed that the struggle of interests in the past has consisted, in essence, in the struggle of classes,
which has led inevitably to the modern struggle of capital and labor,
and in this phase of the struggle has definitely pointed out the possibility of the cessation of this struggle of interests along with the disap-
pearance of class divisions.

But this same better understanding of the course of the historical process leads to the conviction that the *possibility* just indicated can be turned into an *actuality* only through the energetic initiative of the intelligentsia, for whom what is *understood* as *historically inevitable* has been transformed, in the sphere of acts of the *will*, into a personal, obligatory ideal, into a moral conviction, implacably demanding from the cultivated person actions, struggle, and sacrifices.[120]

From Lavrov's "anthropological point of view," history still awaits the conscious moral individual, however primary may be the economic factors within the objective order of facts with which the individual must deal.

Similarly the "class struggle" is knowable by individual thought and eliminable through the joint action of individuals. For Lavrov the concept of class is fundamental to an understanding of the *objective social order as it exists* around the individual. But the *subjective* individual is still the fundamental unit of philosophical thought in all its branches. The concept "class" acquires no higher metaphysical, epistemological, ethical, or, in the last analysis, even historical significance for Lavrov. It is the individual who discerns classes and their struggle; who, as an individual, poses ideals which demand the elimination of class struggle; who joins with other individuals to undertake the action which will realize these ideals.

Finally, it is the development of individuals which progress in history serves. The virtue of socialism for Lavrov was that it would free human individuality, perfect the conscious development of man. Of all the Russian socialists, Lavrov most ardently emphasized the view that socialism is not simply a matter of economics or an automatic outcome of class relationships but is rather a moral task, to be fulfilled through individual effort and for the sake of individual development.

Thus in the last analysis Marxist concepts form only a moment in Lavrov's thorough-going philosophy of the critically thinking individual. Its intellectual core, which Lavrov never recanted, was brilliantly summarized by the Russian philosopher Gustav Shpet—who, incidentally, paid with his life in a Soviet prison camp in 1937 for his own critical thinking. For Lavrov, Shpet writes,

man with his consciousness is the initial demand and problem of philosophy; the morally conscious and critically thinking individual is the solution of this problem. The human, free, creative historical process is the actualization or realization of conscious individuality as an ideal; and the subjective method, with its acknowledgment of the moral nature of this process and its conscious personal equation in the establishment of its nature, is the criterion for determining the stage of realization of the ideal. Thus philosophical theory passes over into the philosophy of life—the philosophy of the ideal—therefrom to draw new force for the justification of the theoretical principle. And thus the beginning and the end of Lavrov's philosophy are joined in one living ring—in man, through man, and for man: *human consciousness, the conscious act, the active individual.*[121]

Understandably, the best remembered of Lavrov's writings is the work in which this integral philosophy of the critically thinking individual was presented with the greatest moral and social impact—the *Historical Letters.*

THE HISTORICAL LETTERS

More than twenty years have passed since the first edition of this book appeared—twenty years, moreover, which have been momentous for our native land.

Then the teachings of Chernyshevsky and Herzen were still fresh in men's minds. The satire of Shchedrin was increasingly capturing the realm of what were not yet "forgotten words." [1] Disputes raged between the partisans of Pisarev's brilliant articles, with their exaltation of the natural sciences in theory and of individualism in life, and the nascent Populists, for whom all else was overshadowed by the need for social struggle occasioned by the introduction of the newly emancipated Russian peasants into historical life. At the time one could have only a vague presentiment—but certainly could not foresee—that in three years, among the scattered circles of Russian youth occupied chiefly with self-education, there would resound the fiery call "to the people!" under a banner having as its shining motto the theoretical doctrine of Marx and Lassalle along with the practical demand to "live the simple life."

Since that time Russian society has outlived this age of the selfless crusaders of socialism. It has outlived the intoxicating burst of liberalism with which the acquittal of Vera Zasulich was greeted in all of Russia.[2] It has outlived yet another brief but terrible episode: at the beginning of the 'eighties a small group of young people succeeded in fusing the old revolutionary tradition of the Decembrists of the 'twenties with the ideological tradition of the Russian intelligentsia, which throughout the whole long and stifling reign of Nicholas had preached the principles of humanism and human dignity. Now these principles were hatched from their liberal larvae and unfolded their wings as mature social issues, vitalized by the historical struggle of classes. "The People's Will" (*Narodnaya volya*), heedless of the sacrifices its supporters had to make, took up an unrelenting fight against Russian absolutism in the name of the economic and political emancipation of the Russian people. But the Russian liberals, natural enemies of absolutism who had cultivated the tradition of ideological struggle in the past, showed that they had not yet grown up to the political determination of their Decembrist grandfathers to defend their ideas in action.

Russian society has paid a heavy price for its mistakes. The Russian social-revolutionary movement has carved an indelible mark for the present and for the future on the history of our native land, but its temporary suppression is a symptom of an agonizing social disease. An age of demoralization has set in. The weary and the disillusioned have begun to drop from the ranks of the selfless fighters for the future of Russia. To the names of some of these fighters of yesterday it has been necessary to add "apostate," "turncoat," and "traitor." Along with the mortal remains of Saltykov and Chernyshevsky, of Yeliseyev and Shelgunov, Russian literature has buried the "forgotten words" of these seemingly final representatives of ideological struggle.[3] Those who have remained on the literary scene are solitary and dispirited. The literary "youth" of the 'eighties have begun manifestly to repudiate the traditions of Belinsky and Dobrolyubov.[4] "Leading" writers have begun to accept advocates of vague idealistic metaphysics and defenders of more or less heretical Christian theology as their comrades-in-arms. The preaching of "nonresistance to evil" has acquired a considerable following. Place hunters and indifferentists have begun to speak up loudly and boldly among Russian students. The timeservers are no longer ashamed of their compromises, which go farther and farther.

Everyone in Russia who is alive, everyone who is filled with the determination to fight intellectual corruption, social indifferentism, the archaic institutions of Russian absolutism, and capitalistic exploitation in the entire civilized world—everyone who has preserved the great ideological tradition of the Russian intelligentsia and who has come to understand the still more mighty practical tasks of scientific socialism—is forced to return to the cautious, conspiratorial work of underground groups. He must guard himself not only against police agents both open and secret but against the cowardly bewilderment of society. Besides shunning possible betrayers, he must shun the demoralized comrades of yesterday, who try to drown their moral depersonalization in vodka and amorous adventures; and he must shun as well the new representatives of the youth, who have lost the very desire to fight, and to die if necessary, for their ideological convictions and their political and social aims.

And now, after these twenty years in the life of our society, publishers are found for a book which appeared in 1870, the material for which was provided by articles in a journal published at the end of the 'sixties.

Should the author agree to prepare a new edition, and what form could a new edition take for it to be of any interest? Since this book appeared, the problems which confronted the Russian writer and reader in the sphere of thought to which it belongs have been either reformulated or replaced by others. The reader of the early 'seventies himself has changed, while the new generation, given the different forms its life has taken during this period, differs considerably from its predecessors. For both, in all likelihood, something different would be desirable.

The new reader has good reason to wonder whether it was necessary to republish a work which endeavored to reflect the problems of Russian life and thought as they arose at the end of the 'sixties. If it was necessary to return to this subject, should not the author have redone the work completely and given the reader something which conforms more to the present state of Russian thought and life, to the author's present attitude toward them, and to the circumstance, finally, that the second edition is appearing abroad rather than under the conditions which were and are imposed upon every writer and publisher within the boundaries of the Russian empire? Or if there really were a need among Russian readers for a new edition—while the book, reflecting an age of Russian evolution long outlived, would now demand complete reworking—should it not have been published without any alterations, in the same form in which it appeared in 1870, when the two copies which reached the author in Paris arrived on the very eve of the day when the German army, surrounding the city, cut him off for several months from communication with all the rest of the world, including Russia?

Since the author did agree to prepare a second edition of his work and at the same time decided neither to revise it completely nor to reprint the edition of 1870 without any alterations, he feels obliged to offer his new readers some explanation.

Books have their own fate, as the Latin saying goes, and this fate, in many cases, is very dimly foreseen—if it is foreseen at all —by authors at the time they commence their work. The *Historical Letters* first appeared in the journal *Week* (*Nedelya*), which at the end of the 'sixties was under the direction of a woman who was a good personal friend of their author and who promoted their publication at a time when, to the best of his knowledge, publishing them encountered the censure of many outstanding representatives of our progressive literature.* The object at the time was not a unified book but a series of separate articles on questions having, on the whole, a certain analogy.

The author composed his letters in a remote town in the province of Vologda, and had good reason to fear that the series might be interrupted at any moment and that the editors, "due to circumstances beyond their control," might ask him to switch to subjects of another sort. The questions taken up in the separate letters were by no means always those the author considered most important in themselves; sometimes they were the questions which at the moment most exercised the press. The author would have assigned each question quite a different place and weight had he supposed from the very beginning that a more or less integral and finished book would result, and had he foreseen that the Russian youth would give this book the attention it managed to arouse. Such attention was all the more unexpected since the author himself well knew, and only too often had heard from his more candid friends, that his rather abstract and ponderous style is not particularly attractive to most readers.

As the series proceeded it took on greater unity even apart from the author's conscious intention by centering on two or three chief questions, and in the author's mind it was deliberately developed into a work which could at least set definite questions before the reader, whether well or poorly, and propose definite answers to them. When the series was concluded, the author learned in his Vologda exile that here and there it had found attentive and sympathetic readers; that its publication as a book might enjoy a certain success; and that many thought such a book would answer the needs of the readers of that era. The author busied himself with reworking the letters into a more consistent whole, as he has explained in the preface to the first edition; and

* See the introduction, p. 38, above.—TRANS.

thus from the separate articles in *Week* at the end of the 'sixties came the book, which appeared in September, 1870.

Since he was not in Russia and had very little contact with the mother country, the author could not follow fully the progress and circulation of the book or the impression it produced. Nothing but a few criticisms reached him. He published replies and elucidations provoked by these criticisms in the journal *Knowledge* (*Znaniye*), and in part did the same in the journal *Annals of the Fatherland* (*Otechestvennyye zapiski*), in an article on Mr. Mikhailovsky's formula of progress.[5]

In March, 1872, the author was asked to prepare a second edition of the book for publication in Russia. He gladly undertook this task, utilizing the suggestions contained in the critical articles which had reached him and incorporating in his corrections and additions more or less extensive excerpts from the articles in *Knowledge* and in *Annals of the Fatherland* just mentioned. This second edition, while considerably supplemented and revised, still aimed simply at elucidating the problems of progress for Russian readers in the manner which the author considered feasible at the end of the 'sixties and the beginning of the 'seventies. The manuscript was completely prepared for the press; it was sent off to Russia, and apparently even the printing was begun. It turned out, however, that this new edition could not be published: it was banned. And at the same time, or shortly thereafter, the first edition, too, was removed from circulation by administrative order.

Ten years passed. The author learned that the book had become a rarity; that quite contrary to his expectations it had managed to acquire a certain significance among the Russian youth; that the questions it raised were of lively interest to them; that in the distant homeland the book had had many sympathetic, friendly readers. But for that very reason the author gave no thought then to a new edition. It seemed to him that his work of the late 'sixties could no longer be adequate; that Russian thought had grown more mature; that broader and clearer horizons had opened up before Russian life; that by this time the Russian reader who was truly alive needed something that not merely prepared him for a time of social struggle but defined the tasks of that struggle more precisely; that the heightening of spirit and the vigorous social agitation going on in our homeland in the late 'seventies and early 'eighties demanded all in all a completely new work, which would pose questions in a much more determinate and integral manner.

An opportunity arose for the author to publish articles in a new journal, *Word* (*Slovo*). He decided in 1881 to replace the *Historical Letters* of 1870 with a new work, in which the same problems would be explored from the standpoint at which he considered it possible to place the Russian reader at that time. The article entitled "The Theory and Practice of Progress," which has been incorporated in the present edition as the Sixteenth Letter, was to have been the first of this sort. But it remained the only one: *Word* was banned.*

Ten more years passed, and last year the author received the proposal to republish the *Historical Letters*. An attempt has been made above to characterize in a few lines the sad state of Russian thought and life at present in comparison with the end of the 'sixties, and all the more with the beginning of the 'eighties. The author of the *Historical Letters* is not at all certain that there are now many readers whom he might call friends in the homeland he left long ago. He does not even know whether there is in Russia a sufficient number of readers interested in the questions which he continues to regard as among the most important for the cultivated human being in general and, perhaps, for the cultivated Russian in particular.

Thus he did not deem it necessary to propose to the new publishers that he replace the *Historical Letters* (which have almost disappeared from circulation in printed form and circulate here and there in Russia only in lithographed copies) with a new work on the same questions, as he had intended in 1881. Nor did he see a sufficient reason for refusing the publishers. But he considered it permissible to take as the basis for the new edition not the text of 1870 but the revised and supplemented manuscript which had been completely prepared for the press and, it seems, even partly run off in 1872. To this edition, intended for publication in Russia but never put on sale, belong all the major additions and alterations which the reader will find here.

---

* To the best of my knowledge, however, my article was in no way responsible.

But in sending his work to be printed outside the territory in which Russian press control operates, the author found no need to retain in his presentation the circumlocutions and qualifications which are unavoidable in every work published within that territory and were unavoidable in the 1870 and 1872 manuscripts of the *Historical Letters*. In all such cases the 1891 edition employs more definite, precise, and straightforward expressions. The author has also taken this opportunity to indicate what his contemplated work of 1881 on these same questions might have been, by adding to the previous letters of 1870 a new Letter, the Sixteenth, which consists of the article from *Word* revised in like fashion. Almost all the remaining minor alterations and additions which the author felt it necessary to make in this new edition are marked with the year in which they were made.

Thus, what the reader of this new edition of the *Historical Letters* actually has before him is the proposed edition of 1872, in a form in which at that time it could only have appeared abroad, with the addition of one article of 1881, and with minor revisions and notes of 1890–91, which are almost everywhere identified.

In 1870, when the author gave his work to the press in book form, he had no idea how it would be greeted by the Russian public. It was greeted with greater sympathy than he expected— with greater sympathy, perhaps, than a work with many faults deserved. The author then found readers who were friends. He is deeply grateful to these friends for the pleasant moments which the knowledge of their sympathy afforded him. And now once again the author does not know whether many of these friends of the 'seventies retain their sympathy for this work. Still less does he know how readers of the new generation will receive it, either in general or in the form in which it now appears. It is difficult for him to follow the real mood of the Russian public from Paris.

In any event he sends greetings to the readers who are sympathetic with him in his distant homeland, however few or many they may be. As for those who are not sympathetic, let this book remind them of the questions which aroused the interest of readers twenty years ago as questions of vital importance. And as for those who in scattered groups have dedicated themselves to the same untiring struggle for the future of Russia which their predecessors waged with both ideological and vital weapons, and who are continuing this struggle with the weapons most suitable at the moment—they need, not a reminder of the irretrievable past, but rather the ability to unite into one historic force, a clear understanding of the new tasks confronting cultivated Russian people, and the selfless determination to fulfill these tasks.

Paris, 29/17 October, 1891

In offering readers this collected and revised edition of the letters which previously appeared in *Week*, I think it is not out of place to preface it with a brief explanation.

When I began sending off these letters I was not at all confident that the editors of a journal would find it feasible to carry a systematic series of studies on the questions here examined. Remoteness from the capital prevented me from following the course of events and from seeing to what extent I had succeeded in arousing readers' interest. A periodical must constantly keep in mind the aim of being read. Several times while these letters were appearing I had reason to fear that I should have to discontinue them, and only when the whole series had been printed was I assured that it would form a more or less coherent whole for the readers of the journal. Furthermore I well know that journal readers seldom have the patience to follow the development of a rather abstract train of thought if it is begun in one number and stretched out over several, so that its conclusion is separated from its beginning by an entire year. All this prompted me to give each letter a more finished form than would be necessary for a connected series of studies, and for this reason the series as a whole suffered from the point of view of both coherence and completeness. And my own thinking, too, applied only intermittently to the work, made it overly disjointed.

Thus in revising these letters it has been necessary to point out their connection in some instances, to explain the order of dependence among the separate studies, to develop certain points more fully, and to do a certain amount of rearranging so that the reader might more readily comprehend the whole. Such purely formal alteration is what chiefly distinguishes this edition from the *Historical Letters* in their original form. I venture to hope that the new form, with greater coherence of the parts and elucidation of the basic ideas, will make my work at least somewhat more worthy of the reader's attention.

I should like very much to have made improvements of greater substance in the work, but in this connection our Russian critics have given me no assistance. In neither the literary monthlies, nor the daily newspapers, nor the serious historical journals, nor the partisan journals of various persuasions—as far as I have managed to see these publications, at least—have I encountered a critique, refutation, correction, or suggestion which would lead me to an idea that demands more precision or fuller development, or would indicate that at some point I had overlooked an important aspect of a subject or at another mistaken an illusion for a vitally important fact. Perhaps I have not succeeded in arousing the interest of readers and critics sufficiently with these letters; perhaps critics have found the ideas expressed here too elementary for their attention; finally, it is possible, too, that the publications I should need are precisely those which have not reached me. Be that as it may, in this respect I was left to my own resources and to the few fragmentary individual comments which reached me.

The latter centered particularly on one fault: that the work is abstract, dry, difficult to read. Unfortunately, this fault lies partly in the subject itself; but I own nonetheless that it pertains also to my mode of exposition. In the present edition I have attempted to correct this in places by bringing in examples, but it was not my intention to write a new work. I wished only to offer readers the former work in a somewhat superior form. Too great an assortment of examples might, it seems to me, somewhat impair the coherent development of the thought. The latter has remained completely without alteration, and only here and there has a more precise expression replaced the original.

While I did not wish to change the general title of my work, I did, however, deem it unnecessary to retain certain forms of epistolary style I previously employed.

I am entirely unaware of the extent to which my letters have been read or ignored by the readers of *Week*. Perhaps critics will find them little worthy of their attention even now. I have stated in the final letter that I myself am conscious of the many faults of this work, especially in comparison with the importance of the subject. I give my readers what I have, as best I can.

[*Kadnikov, 1869*]

The Natural Sciences and History

IF THE READER IS INTERESTED in the trend of contemporary thought, two of its provinces will immediately assert their own claims to his attention: the natural sciences and history. Which of them is more relevant to contemporary life?

This question is not as easy to answer as it might seem at first glance. I know that natural scientists and the majority of thinking readers will decide it in favor of the natural sciences without a moment's hesitation; and indeed, how easy it is to demonstrate that the natural sciences thrust themselves into man's life at every moment—that he cannot turn around, glance at something, breathe, or think without a whole series of laws of mechanics, physics, chemistry, physiology, and psychology coming into play! By comparison, what is history? A pastime of idle curiosity. One may spend a lifetime in the most useful private or public pursuits without ever even needing to recall that once Hellenism penetrated Asiatic tribes with the troops of Alexander the Great, or that the Codes, Pandects, Novels, and the like which are the foundation of the modern juridical systems of Europe were compiled during the age of the world's most despotic rulers, or that there were ages of feudalism and chivalry when the most coarse and animal motives coexisted comfortably with a rapturous mysticism. Turning to the history of our native land, let us ask whether there are many useful applications to the life of modern man in a knowledge of the heroic *byliny* or *Russkaya pravda*, in the barbarous *oprichnina* of Ivan the Terrible, or even in the Petrine struggle of European against Old Muscovite forms of life.[1] All this has passed irretrievably. New questions, succeeding the old, demanding all of modern man's reflection and concern, leave for the past nothing but *interest*—the interest of more or less dramatic pictures, of a more or less clear embodiment of common human ideas. Thus it would seem that there can be no

79

comparison between a kind of knowledge which conditions every element of our lives and another kind which expounds upon subjects that are merely *interesting*—between the daily bread of thought and the pleasant dessert.

The natural sciences are the foundation of rational life—this is indisputable. Without a clear understanding of their demands and fundamental laws, man is blind and deaf to his most ordinary needs as well as to his loftiest aims. Strictly speaking, in the modern world a man who is a total stranger to the natural sciences has not the slightest right to be called an educated person.

But once this point of view is accepted the question arises, what is most relevant to man's vital interests? Questions of cellular reproduction, the transformation of species, spectrum analysis, and double stars? Or the laws of the growth of human knowledge, the clash of the principle of social utility with the principle of justice, the conflict between national unification and the unity of all mankind, the bearing of the economic interests of the starving masses on the intellectual interests of the more prosperous minority, and the connection between social evolution and the form of the political system? When the question is put in this way, hardly anyone but a Philistine of learning (they, however, are quite numerous) will refuse to acknowledge that the latter questions are more relevant to man, more important to him, more intimately connected with his everyday life than the former.

In fact, strictly speaking they alone are relevant and important. The former questions are so only insofar as they lead to a better understanding of the latter and facilitate their resolution.

No one questions the usefulness of literacy or denies that it is absolutely indispensable for human development, but literacy hardly has advocates so obtuse as to attribute to it some sort of independent, magical force. Scarcely anyone will say that the actual processes of reading and writing are important to man in themselves; they are important only as *aids* to assimilating the ideas man can acquire through reading and communicate through writing. A man who gets nothing from his reading is in no way superior to an illiterate. To call someone "illiterate" is to say that he lacks the basic requisite of education, but literacy in itself is by no means the goal—it is only a means.

The natural sciences play what would seem to be the same role in the over-all system of human education. They are simply the *literacy of thought;* developed thought employs this literacy in solving problems that are purely human, and it is these latter problems that constitute the essence of human development. It is not enough to read a book; one must understand it. Similarly, for a cultivated human being it is not enough to understand the fundamental laws of physics and physiology, to be interested in experiments on albumen or in Kepler's laws. For such a person albumen is not simply a chemical compound, but a basic constituent of the food of millions of people. Kepler's laws are not simply abstract formulas of planetary motion, but acquisitions of the human spirit in its progress toward a general philosophical understanding of the immutability of natural laws and their independence of every sort of [divine] arbitrariness.

We come, then, to the very antithesis of what was said above concerning the comparative importance for practical life of the principles of the natural sciences and the principles of history. A chemical experiment on albumen or the mathematical expression of Kepler's laws is a mere curiosity. The economic significance of albumen or the philosophical significance of the immutability of astronomical laws is vitally important. Knowledge of the outer world provides us with absolutely indispensable material, to which we must appeal in solving all the problems which occupy mankind; but the problems for the sake of which we appeal to this material are problems not of the outer but of the inner world, problems of human *consciousness.* Food is important not as the object of nutritional processes but as the product which eliminates the *conscious* pain of hunger. Philosophical ideas are important not as manifestations of the evolution of spirit in its logical abstractness but as the logical forms through which man becomes *conscious* of his own dignity as higher or lower, of the aims of his own existence as broader or narrower; they are important as forms of protest against the present in the name of a desire for a better and more just social order, or as forms of satisfaction with the present.

Many thinkers have noted the intellectual progress man made in coming to see himself as only one among the countless products of the laws of the external world in their unchanging application, whereas formerly he had pictured himself as the center of all existence—in making the transition, in other words, from a subjective to an objective view of himself and of nature. True, this was extremely important progress, without which science would have been impossible and the development of mankind inconceivable; but it was only the first step. A second step inevitably followed: the study of the unchanging laws of the external world *in its objectivity* in order to attain the sort of human condition which would be recognized subjectively as the best and most just. And at this point the great law divined by Hegel, which seems to apply in so many spheres of human consciousness, was borne out: a third step, apparently a return to the first, in fact resolved the contradiction between the first and the second.[2] Man again became the center of the entire world, but this time the center of the world not as it exists in itself, but as it is comprehended by man, conquered by his thought, and turned toward his aims.

Now this is precisely the point of view of history. The natural sciences give man, who is himself a scarcely noticeable part of the world, an account of the world's laws; they inventory the products of mechanical, physical, chemical, physiological, and psychical processes; they find among the products of the latter processes, throughout the entire animal kingdom, a consciousness of pain and pleasure; and they find, in the part of this kingdom closest to mankind, a consciousness of the possibility of setting up goals and striving to achieve them. This fact of natural science is the sole foundation of the biographies of the individual creatures within the animal world and the histories of its separate groups. History as a science takes this fact as given, and shows the reader how history as the life-process of mankind has resulted from man's aspiration to eliminate what he regarded as pain and to attain what he regarded as pleasure. It shows what modifications took place at the same time in the concepts associated with the words "pleasure" and "pain" and in the classification and hierarchy of pleasures and pains, and what sorts of philosophical ideas and practical social institutions these modifications engendered. It shows by what logical process the aspiration for betterment and justice gave rise to protest and conservatism, to reaction and progress. It shows what connection existed in each age between man's perception of the world—in the form of religious belief, science, a philosophical idea—and the practical theories of betterment and justice embodied in the acts of individuals, in forms of society, and in people's living conditions.

Thus the historian's work is not the negation but the necessary supplementation of the work of the natural scientist. The historian who scorns the natural scientist does not understand history; he wants to build a house without a foundation, he praises education while denying the need for literacy. The natural scientist who scorns the historian simply demonstrates the narrowness and immaturity of his thinking; he is unwilling to see, or is incapable of seeing, that setting up goals and striving to achieve them are facts of human nature just as inescapable and natural as respiration, the circulation of the blood, or metabolism. Goals may be petty or exalted, strivings pitiful or laudable, actions irrational or expedient; but goals, strivings, and actions always have existed and always will exist, and consequently they are no less legitimate objects of study than the colors of the spectrum, chemical elements, or the species and varieties of the plant and animal kingdoms. The natural scientist who restricts himself to the outer world either does not wish to see or cannot see that for man the entire outer world is simply the material of pleasure, pain, desire, and action, and that the most highly specialized scientist studies the outer world not as something external but as something knowable, something which affords *him*, the scientist, pleasure in coming to know it, prompts his activities, enters into his vital processes. The natural scientist who disdains history imagines that foundations are not meant to be built upon, and that man's whole development should be confined to literacy.

Here it may be objected that the natural sciences have two undeniable advantages over history which permit the natural scientist to take a somewhat condescending view of the scientific merits of the historian's work. First, the natural sciences have developed exact methods, obtained incontestable results, and built up a fund of immutable laws which are constantly being confirmed and which allow us to make predictions. As for history, it is still doubtful whether it has discovered even a single law which is properly its own; it has produced nothing but elegant *pictures*, and with respect to accuracy of predictions it is on a level with forecasting the weather. Second and more important, the contemporary quest for betterment and justice draws its material almost exclusively from the data of the natural sciences, whether the question is one of achieving a clear understanding of the goal, making the right choice of means, or giving the proper direction to actions. History, again, offers very little material of any use, both because of its vagueness as to the significance of past events —which can provide equally good arguments for diametrically opposed theories of life—and also because conditions change radically with the passage of time, so that the application to the present of findings drawn from rather remote events is extremely difficult even when these findings are precise. Given this inferiority from the standpoint of both theoretical science and practical utility, can the historian's work be placed on a level with the natural scientist's?

[To understand the question here posed we must agree on the scope we assign to the term "natural science." I have no intention of making a strict classification of the sciences here, with all the controversial questions that involves. It goes without saying that history, as a natural process, could be brought within the sphere of the natural sciences, and then the very opposition examined above would not hold. In all that follows I shall understand by the term "natural science" two sorts of sciences: *phenomenological* sciences, which investigate the laws of recurring phenomena and processes, and *morphological* sciences, which study the distribution (*raspredeleniye*) of the objects and forms which condition observed processes and phenomena, the aim of these latter sciences being to reduce all observed forms and arrangements of forms to moments in genetic processes. The morphological sciences aside, I may say that to the class of phenomenological sciences I should assign geometry, mechanics, the physico-chemical sciences, biology, psychology, ethics, and sociology. Taking the term "natural science" in the sense just indicated, I shall turn to the question posed above.]

There is no question that the methods of investigation employed in mechanics, physics, chemistry, physiology, and the theory of sensation in psychology are both self-sufficient and scientific. But as soon as we come to the theory of ideas or concepts in the individual person and to personal ethics such scientific methods are employed very little. As for social science (sociology)—that is, the theory of the processes and products of social evolution—here [almost] all of the physicist's, chemist's and physiologist's tools are inapplicable. This important part of natural science, the part most relevant to man, rests upon laws of the foregoing regions of natural science as given data, but it finds its own laws in a different way. How? Where do phenomenology of mind and sociology get their material? From biographies of individuals and from history. To the extent that the work of the historian and the biographer is unscientific, the conclusions of the psychologist in the broadest part of his domain cannot be scientific, nor can the work of the ethicist or sociologist in their scientific spheres; in other words, to that extent natural science must be considered unscientific in the areas having the greatest human relevance.

Scientific advance comes about here through the mutual assistance of both fields of knowledge. From superficial observation of biographical and historical facts come rough truths of psychology, ethics, and sociology. These rough truths permit a more intelligent observation of the facts of biography and history, which in turn leads to more exact truths, permitting further improvement in historical observation, and so on. Improved tools make a better product, and a better product allows further improvement in the tools, promoting in turn a still greater improvement in the product.

History provides material which is absolutely essential to natural science in its proper sense; only as guided by historical work can the natural scientist understand the processes and products of the intellectual, moral, and social life of man. A chemist may consider his speciality more scientific than history and may scorn the latter's material. But a man who takes the term "natural science" to mean the science of all natural processes and products has no right to set this science above history, and he is obliged to recognize the close interdependence of the two fields.

The foregoing resolves the question of practical utility. If psychology and sociology are subject to continual improvement through an improved understanding of historical facts, then the study of history is absolutely necessary in order to understand the laws of personal and social life. These laws rest as much on historical data as on the data of mechanics, chemistry, and physiology. The fact that historical data are less precise should entail not the elimination of historical study but, on the contrary, its broader dissemination, since historical specialists are not so far beyond the mass of readers with respect to the precision of their conclusions as chemists and physiologists are.

To cope with the vital contemporary problems of betterment and justice the reader must understand the findings of the phenomenology of mind and sociology, but the required understanding is not achieved by accepting on faith the opinions of this or that school of economists, politicians, or moralists. Confronted with their disputes, the conscientious reader must turn to a study of the very data on which their conclusions have been built; at the same time he must consider the genesis of each school, seeking to understand its teachings by looking both to their filiation and to the state of affairs at the time the school arose; finally, he must study the events which influenced the development of the school. But all this, with the exception of the data provided by the basic sciences, belongs to history. Whoever neglects the study of history is displaying either his indifference to the most important interests of the individual and of society, or his readiness to accept on trust whatever ideology happens to catch his eye first.

Thus the question presented at the outset—Which is more relevant to contemporary life, the natural sciences or history?—can be answered, I think, in the following way: The basic natural sciences are the absolutely indispensable groundwork of contemporary life, but the interest they have for it is rather remote. The higher natural sciences—those which make a comprehensive study of the processes and products of individual and social life —are exactly on a level with history from the standpoint of both theoretical scientific character and practical utility; no doubt they are connected with questions more vital for man than is history, but a serious study of them is absolutely impossible without a study of history, and the reader can comprehend them only to the extent that he has comprehended history.

Therefore it is in the interests of contemporary thought to explore historical questions, especially those closely connected with problems of sociology. In these letters I shall examine general questions of history, investigating the factors which make for social progress and the significance of the word "progress" for various aspects of social life. Of necessity sociological questions will be intertwined with the historical, especially since the two fields of knowledge have the closest interdependence, as we have seen. This will, of course, impart to the present discussion a more general, somewhat abstract character. The reader is presented not with pictures of events, but with inferences and the juxtaposition of events of different periods.

Tales from history are plentiful, and perhaps I shall manage to proceed to them later. But, though the facts of history remain, man's understanding alters their meaning; each period, setting out to interpret the past, reads into it its own topical concerns and its own present stage of development. Thus for each age historical questions become a linking of the present with the past. I do not force my views upon the reader, but offer him my understanding of things, my view of how the past is reflected in the present, and the present in the past.

SECOND LETTER

The Historical Process

LET US TURN to the other sense of the word "history." *

In the First Letter we discussed history as a field of human knowledge; now we shall examine it as the process which forms the object of study for history as a field of knowledge. History as a process, as a phenomenon among other phenomena, should have and in fact does have its own distinguishing features. What are they? In the eyes of a thinking person, what distinguishes the historical phenomenon from the fall of a stone, the fermentation

---

* (1889) Significant changes of detail would be required to make this letter fully consistent with the point of view which now seems to me more correct. Readers who are interested in these questions may compare this letter with the Introduction to my Essay in the History of Thought in Modern Times (No. 1, Geneva, 1888). Here I limit myself almost exclusively to changes prepared for the press in 1872.

of a decomposing liquid, the digestive process, or the various phenomena of life which can be observed in an aquarium?

My question may seem strange, since it will immediately occur to every reader to say that the historical process is the work of men, nations, mankind in general, and that this suffices to distinguish it from all other processes. But this is not quite the case. In the first place, geologists, with some justification, speak of the history of the earth, and theoretical astronomers of the history of the universe. In the second place, by no means everything in the lives of men or nations enters into the process of historical life. The day-to-day activities of the most important figures in history include much that the most painstaking biographer has never recorded and never will record, just as there are thousands of individuals whose entire lives from their first breath to their last offer nothing of interest to an investigator. In studying the life of societies, the historian does not record phenomena which repeat themselves year after year with mathematical regularity; he notes only what changes.

Many historians single out certain nations and races from the whole mass of mankind, calling them historical, and leave the rest of mankind to ethnography, anthropology, linguistics—in short, to any science you please except history. And in *one* respect they are right. The questions science asks and the modes of thinking it employs in dealing with the life of these peoples perfectly parallel those with which a zoologist approaches a given species of birds or ants. The zoologist describes the animals' anatomical features, their habits, their methods of building nests or anthills, their struggles with other animals, and so on. The same questions arise for the ethnographer. True, the functions of a human being are more complex and there is more to be described. The linguist learns not only the mode of expression but the *meaning* of words in a language; but the zoologist, too, would be delighted to learn from his birds the significance of this or that sound modulation if only he could. The anthropologist records knowledge, handicrafts, implements, myths, customs; nevertheless his task is the same as the zoologist's: to set down the given facts *just as they are*. The anthropologist's subjects are more interesting to us, since when we study people we also sympathize with them, but this should not deceive us as to the scientific significance of the method applied. The anthropologist is *simply* a natural scientist who has taken man as his subject. He describes only what *is*.

But I said that historians who divide nations and races into historical and nonhistorical are right in *one* respect. Actually there is another consideration, which casts some doubt on the propriety of this division. There hardly exists an island so wretched that its inhabitants would be described in identical terms by two travelers coming a hundred years apart; during the intervening period these inhabitants would have *changed*. Such change is so common that science is fully justified in assuming it even in areas where no information about it exists, and that is why an anthropologist always supplements his analysis of a tribe with further indications, more or less hypothetical, of how the tribe's culture arose and how it has changed in the course of time. But such questions the historian, with some justification, considers part of his own province.

[In our time it is even possible to speak of the history of the entire organic world, since from the point of view of transformism each organic form makes sense only as a moment in the over-all system of organic genesis. In this case, however, the genesis of forms is itself still only a scientific explanation, not an observed fact. Science is confronted simply with an array of organic forms which are to be classified, and each particular case becomes an object of interest only as it has a bearing on the investigation of the over-all process.] [1] The particular case is nothing more than an instrument of research. The emergence of a particular form under a certain set of conditions interests the scientist only as it relates to his study of the laws of dependence between particular environmental conditions and the forms which arise under them. Besides, the changes in organic forms which have been most fully investigated are changes in plants and animals under human influence, and this is already part of the history of man himself.

To be sure, within the sphere of zoology there are phenomena which are [to a considerable degree] analogous to those the historian studies—specifically, the phenomena of evolution and change in the social patterns of animals. At present we can only conclude that changes of this sort must have occurred, did occur, and are occurring, but the zoologist has not yet succeeded in observing a single such change as it actually takes place. [It is highly probable that all social (*kul'turnyye*) animals *had* something analogous to history, or at least that with time there was a series of changes in their form of society. For example, it is very likely that the present social organization of bees sprang from a simpler organization. Among vertebrates changes of habits have been observed, chiefly in regard to adaptation to new environmental conditions. But the "history" of bees, like the "history" of all invertebrates with complex societies, lies beyond the bounds of scientific observation. As for the changes observed in the habits of vertebrates under the influence of new environmental conditions, they are no more facts of history than are the changes in dwelling construction, clothing, or even food which inevitably result in colonies of human migrants establishing themselves under new climatic conditions.] The zoologists' world, as *science* presents it, is a world of invariably recurring phenomena. Thus it is still merely speculative to apply the analogy of human history to animals; in fact history is confined to man.

In all other processes the investigator seeks a law covering a phenomenon in all its repetitions; only in the historical process does interest attach not to a law of a recurring phenomenon but to the actual change which has taken place, in itself. The contours of a particular crystal interest only the layman; the mineralogist traces the irregular, distorted shapes to invariable types which follow strict geometrical laws. For an anatomist a particular anomaly is only an occasion for establishing a law which will show the limits of deviation for the normal structure of this or that organ. But the phenomena of human life, individual or collective, have a dual interest.

Caspar Hauser suddenly appeared on the streets of Nuremberg, and five years later was stabbed to death.* Kepler dis-

---

* A friend has pointed out to me that very few people today, particularly among Russian readers, remember Caspar Hauser or know what kind of person he was. This is quite true and it might be better to use another example, but I prefer to amend matters with a note.

In 1828 a young man in peasant dress was encountered on a street in Nuremberg, bearing a note which explained that he was a foundling, born October 7, 1812, and that he had been taught to read and write. The strangeness of his manner led to an investigation. It was discovered that in his entire life he had seen only one human being, the man who had raised him. He had eaten nothing but bread and water, had lived in a dungeon,

covered the laws of planetary motion. The North American civil
war called forth a dreadful loss of life and money in America and
was echoed by an economic crisis in Europe. What do we study
in these events?

To the psychologist Caspar Hauser is interesting as a rare instance of a person who entered society as an adult and who is
thus a better subject than other individuals for the investigation
of certain *general laws* of psychic phenomena. To the biographer
and the historian Caspar Hauser is a singular phenomenon of a
particular period, the product of a strange complex of circumstances, encountered *once,* owing to which this mysterious creature was isolated from all social relationships until the age of sev-
enteen, and five years later perished at the hands of a murderer.
When Anselm Feuerbach assumed him to be the last representative of the House of Zähringen, he was investigating not a recurring but a *unique* historical phenomenon.

Similarly, for the logician the train of thought which led Kepler
to his discoveries is nothing but an instance of *general laws* of
scientific thinking; Mill and Whewell could argue whether it con-

and had not even come to know his master until shortly before his release.
Prior to that, if Hauser's word can be accepted as true, this unknown person
had changed his food and clothing while he was asleep (probably by giving him a sedative in his food, which was also responsible for the nervous
disorder—the facial and bodily convulsions—noted in Hauser).

At first the unfortunate young man became an object of idle town curiosity and crude experiments, and he suffered a good deal. Later many
outstanding people took an interest in him, especially Anselm Feuerbach
(the eminent jurist, father of the philosopher). As a rare instance of a
child who had grown up outside society, Caspar presented a subject for
interesting psychological investigations. But still more interest was aroused
by the question of his origin. All investigations proved futile. In 1828
Feuerbach, who published a special work on Caspar, sent a secret note
(since published) to the Queen of Bavaria (a member of the House of
Baden), in which he argued that Caspar was probably the last representative of the male line of the House of Baden-Zähringen; he reasoned that
the Grand Duke Charles Frederick's morganatic wife, a descendant of the
family of Geyer von Geyersberg, had removed the boy in order to give
the throne to her son, Leopold; and he explained Caspar's release by the
death of his ambitious persecutor in 1824.

In 1829 an unknown person attempted to kill Caspar. Feuerbach died on
May 29, 1833. On December 17 of the same year, Caspar Hauser was
stabbed to death. The murderer was not apprehended, and Caspar's origin
remains unknown. (1889. In the light of recent research it appears most
likely that the affair of Caspar Hauser had no political significance. But I
consider it better to leave the original text unaltered.) [2]

stitutes a model of true induction. For the historian, however, Kepler's discoveries constitute an event which happened *once* and which cannot possibly be repeated, because it was conditioned by an extremely complex conjunction of circumstances, including previous scientific discoveries, the stage of social development at the beginning of the seventeenth century, the peculiarities of events in Germany at the time, and still more the peculiarities of Kepler's biography. But as soon as this event took place it became an element in a new intellectual development, which again cannot be repeated because it is the outcome of an interweaving of scientific, philosophical, religious, political, economic, and fortuitous biographical elements.

In the cluster of phenomena connected with the North American civil war, the sociologist in like fashion will find a number of instances of *general laws* pertaining to various spheres of social life. The historian will view this cluster in its complexity as a phenomenon apart, which was observed *once,* and which, precisely in its wholeness and complexity, does not admit of repetition.

To the extent that historical phenomena provide material for establishing immutable laws—laws of psychic phenomena in the individual, of economic phenomena in a group of individuals, of the inevitable succession of political institutions or ideal aspirations in nations—to this extent they are of interest to psychology, to sociology, to the phenomenology of mind, individual or social —in short, to one of the departments of natural science in its application to man. But for the historian, historical phenomena are not instances of immutable laws, but characteristic features of a change that happened once.

Opposition to the foregoing may arise from two standpoints. Historical theorists will say that I do not understand the demands of history as a science. They will maintain that history, like all sciences, seeks unchanging laws; that the facts of historical progress are important to the historian only to the extent that they help him to understand the general law of this process, while in themselves they are unimportant; that to attach importance to facts is to turn history into that motley kaleidoscope of tragic or comic scenes which for mediocre historians still constitutes the ideal of history. At the same time there are readers who will find, not without justification, that I am repeating an idea long hackneyed—that only man has a history and that in history events do not repeat themselves but constantly present new combinations.

To the latter I may remark that I do not pretend my idea is novel. Sometimes even old ideas are worth recalling, and I wished to recall this one precisely because some confusion of ideas has arisen of late concerning the meaning of the term "*historical* law." Many of Buckle's followers, for example, say that he discovered laws of history. It is not my object here to deny or to affirm the accuracy of Buckle's discoveries, but in any event they have nothing to do with laws of *history*. Buckle simply established, with the *help* of history, certain laws of sociology; that is, aided by historical instances, he determined how the prevalence of this or that element affects the development of society in general, and how it *always will affect it,* if this prevalence recurs. This is by no means a law of the historical process as the establishment of such a law was understood by Vico, Bossuet, Hegel, Comte, and Buchez.

With regard to the historical theorists, I believe that they will agree with me on two points. The first is that all the attempts of thinkers such as Vico to reduce history to a process of recurring phenomena have proved highly unsuccessful as soon as it has come to comparing two periods in detail; and consequently that history is a process in which the historian must determine, at each moment of the process, the consecutive connection of phenomena which are presented to him in a particular complex *once only.* The second point is that a law of the historical sequence as a whole still remains to be found. This being the case, let us look for such a law.

[What is a *law of history?* Our first task is to understand the very meaning of the question. In the two sorts of natural sciences mentioned above the word "law" has very different meanings. In the phenomenological sciences, a law of phenomena formulates the conditions under which phenomena repeat themselves in a certain order. Since in history phenomena do not repeat themselves, this sense of the word is quite inapplicable to history. In the morphological sciences, the same word has an entirely different meaning: here it expresses the actual distribution of forms and objects into more or less tightly coherent groups. For example, the word "law" is encountered in this sense in stellar astronomy when the astronomer is concerned with a law of the distribution of stars in the firmament, and in biological taxonomy when biologists speak of a law of the distribution of organisms. In this sense the word "law" is applicable to history, too, since it could designate the grouping of events in time.

[But what does it mean to *discover* or to *understand* a law of some sort of distribution of forms? To answer this question we need only consider the one morphological science in which the distribution of forms is quite clear to us—the morphology of individual organisms. We *understand* both the normal and the abnormal anatomical structure of an organism when, with the help of embryology and the theory of evolution, we have traced the genesis of tissues, organs, and organ systems from the elementary cell of the unfertilized ovum through all the phases of embryo, foetus, newborn organism, to the stage which we observe. We understand the distribution of anatomical forms because we see it as simply one moment in the whole series of successive distributions which is determined by the process of organic development, which is nothing but a complex of mechanical, physico-chemical, and biological phenomena.

[In another morphological science our knowledge is not so advanced nor our understanding so clear, but what we do understand, we understand in exactly the same way. I have in mind geology. The distribution of formations, types of rock, and minerals is understandable only as a vestige of the earth's history, as a result of the origin of the globe, that is, as one member of the series of products wrought by the continuous operation of mechanical and physico-chemical laws within the bounds of our planet.

[In the other morphological sciences, understanding the laws of distribution would again be nothing but explaining the *genesis* of forms, if only we could know it. Until the latter condition is fulfilled we can gradually, by careful observation, come to *learn* the laws of distribution, as purely empirical laws, but we cannot *understand* them. Thus with more powerful telescopes new groups of stars appear in the sky, and the law of the distribution of stars is modified or further confirmed; with an increase in factual knowledge in the morphology of organisms, the law of their classification becomes more determinate.[3] But we cannot say that we *understand* the law of the distribution of stars until we know the *genetic* process of the world's matter in sufficient detail and can trace the observed groups of stars to phases of this process.

[In astronomy this has not even been attempted, and for that reason the distribution of constellations is to this day merely an object of empirical description rather than scientific understanding. With regard to the distribution of organisms, the period of scientific understanding began with the first attempts to discover the genesis of the organic world as a whole. Darwin's theory permitted an enormous step in this direction, and today we can study the law of the classification of organisms in a fully scientific manner: to understand this law means to reduce organic forms to their genetic connection.

[In both of these cases the distribution at first seems disorderly, almost arbitrary; it very easily arouses in the mind of primitive man the idea of a capricious being who scattered stars across the sky and toyed, as it were, with a strange variety of organic forms. Scientific understanding sees unchanging phenomenological laws at work in the genesis of this distribution, with phenomena constantly being repeated; but at the same time the phenomenological laws, operating within a certain environment, give rise to ever newer distributions of matter in cosmic space and ever newer distributions of organic forms on the earth's surface. The morphology of matter should include the law of the successive changes in the distribution of matter, both in space (mechanically) and according to differences in its composition (chemically). The morphology of organisms, as Haeckel understands it, has already set itself the task of discovering the law of the successive changes in the distribution of organisms, on the basis of eternal biological laws.

[On the analogy of these sciences, it is easy to infer what it means to find a law of history and to understand it scientifically. In history we have the advantage that the genesis is given as a fact from the very beginning; as in the other fields, however, the superficial observer at first sees only a series of heterogeneous events, similar to the disorderly distribution of constellations and nebulae or the diversity of organic forms; but again as in the other fields, in history classification according to genetic connection and according to the *importance* of the events begins very quickly.

[In understanding the connection of phenomena, just as in understanding the distribution of forms, objects, or events, the first step always consists in distinguishing the more important from the less important. In the phenomenological sciences this is easy: what is repeated in unchanging connection is more important, because here there is a law; what pertains to chance variation is of little importance, and is merely kept in mind for possible future consideration. Probably no investigator has found *absolutely* identical angles of light refraction for the same refracting medium, or received *absolutely* identical results in a chemical analysis; but discounting chance deviations in the experiment, he has revealed under them an invariable law of a recurring phenomenon. This is the *only* important thing.

[What determines the importance of a fact in the morphological sciences? As we have seen above, in these sciences understanding a law of the distribution of forms coincides with understanding the continuous action of the phenomenological laws which condition the *genesis* of the distribution. Evidently, then, the most important thing here will be the element which promotes a better understanding of the law of the distribution of forms—the phenomenological element.

[Astronomers distinguish the solar system from other groups because the bodies which compose it are linked by mechanical phenomena coming under the law of gravitation; systems of double or triple stars are isolated in the same way. Similarly, in descriptive chemistry we relate potassium and sodium, or chlorine and iodine, on the basis of similarities in their chemical action; we relate minerals on the basis of similarities in their chemical composition and crystallographic features. Thus laws of the phenomenological sciences determine what is more important and what is less important in the distributions studied by the morphological sciences. For a particular distribution this distinction can be made only by taking into account all phenomenological laws which operate in the situation, especially those which have the greatest influence on the distribution itself and on its genesis.

[What phenomenological laws have an influence on the distribution and the genesis of events in human history? Laws of mechanics, chemistry, biology, psychology, ethics, and sociology —that is, laws of *all* phenomenological sciences; consequently, it is both necessary and in accordance with the demands of science to take them all into account. Which of these laws are especially important for an understanding of history? Here we must take into account the characteristics of the being who is the sole instrument and the sole subject of history—man. It is not special electrical phenomena that distinguish the electric eel from its zoological group, just as particular chemical products do not determine the classification of plants; in both cases, biological phenomena supply the most important indices. Similarly, in all sciences pertaining to man the criterion of relative importance should be applied in accordance with the characteristic features of man—features which in this case are inevitably fixed by a *subjective* evaluation, since the investigator is himself a man and cannot for a moment detach himself from the processes which *he regards* as characteristic.

[It is possible (even probable) that consciousness is a very minor phenomenon in the over-all order of the world. Yet *for man* it has such surpassing importance that he will always first and foremost divide his own actions and the actions of those like him into *conscious* and *unconscious,* and regard these two groups in different lights. Conscious psychic processes, conscious activity in accordance with conviction or opposed to it, conscious participation in social life, conscious struggle in the ranks of this or that political party, with an eye to this or that historical revolution— for man such activities have and always will have a significance completely different from that of mechanical actions performed under the same circumstances. It follows that conscious influences should take first place in the ordering of historical events, to the same extent that they do in human consciousness itself.

[From the standpoint of consciousness, what elements have primary influence on the genesis of events? Human needs and inclinations. How are these needs and inclinations classified, as they bear on the individual's consciousness? They can be divided into three groups.

[Some needs and inclinations flow *unconsciously* from the physical and psychical structure of man, as something inescapable, and are recognized by him only when they constitute a ready-made element of his activity.

[Others come to the individual just as unconsciously from his *social* environment or from ancestors in the form of habits, traditions, customs, established laws and political arrangements—in general, as *cultural forms*. These cultural needs and inclinations are also apprehended as ready-made, as something *given* for the individual, though not completely inescapable; it is assumed that they had some meaning at the time the cultural forms originated, and scholars search for this meaning and make conjectures about it. But for each individual, living in a particular age under particular cultural forms, they are something external, independent of his consciousness.

[Finally, needs and inclinations of the third group are fully *conscious* and seem to each individual to arise in him apart from any external constraint, as free and independent products of his consciousness. This is the province, first of all, of activity based upon the conscious calculation of interest—the individual's egoistic interests and the interests of those dear to him. Second, and still more important for historical progress, it is the province of the need for what is best; of the aspiration to extend human knowledge and to set oneself a higher goal; of the need to alter everything given from without to conform with one's own desire, one's own understanding, and one's own moral ideal; of the aspiration to rebuild the world of thought according to the demands of truth, and the real world according to the demands of justice. Subsequently, scientific investigation persuades man that even these needs and inclinations do not develop in him freely and independently but arise through the intricate influence of his environment and the peculiarities of his personal development. But although he is convinced of this *objectively*, man can never eliminate the subjective illusion which is present in his consciousness and which establishes, for him, an enormous difference between activity for which *he* sets the goal and selects the means, critically analyzing the merits of each, and activity which is mechanical, impulsive, or habitual, in which he recognizes himself as an instrument of something given from without.

[The three groups indicated have been distinguished from one another on the basis of the phenomenological process which is

most important to man in all sciences treating of him. Consequently these groups have been established *scientifically,* and
their significance for the classification of historical events flows of
necessity from their relationship to the conscious process. The
most highly conscious needs and inclinations should have predominant importance for the history of man, by the very nature of
this history, just as they inevitably have predominant importance
for the historian as a human being, by virtue of his personal characteristics. Purposeful conscious activity provides, by its very
posing of the question, the central thread around which the other
varieties of human activity are grouped, just as the various goals
toward which a man strives are arranged in a hierarchy in accordance with his greatest personal interest (for the majority of
people) or with his conception of moral value (for the most cultivated people).

[The scientific character of the theory results here from the
concurrence of two processes which are equally subjective, but of
which one takes place in the mind of the historian while the other
comes from observation of historical individuals and groups. The
law of the course of historical events becomes, on this view, a determinate object of investigation. The historian must find, for
each age, the intellectual and moral aims which the most cultivated individuals of that age recognized as paramount, as the
truth and the moral ideal. He must discover the conditions which
gave rise to this outlook, the critical and uncritical thought processes which developed it, and the ways in which it was subsequently modified. He must arrange in their historical and logical
sequence the different outlooks which thus arose. He must dispose around them, as causes and effects, as helps and hindrances,
as instances and exceptions, all the other events of human history.
Then from a kaleidoscope of heterogeneous events the historian
passes of necessity to a law of the historical sequence.

[In such an investigation all the chief objects and tools of research belong to the subjective world. Subjective are the various
goals which individuals and groups of individuals pursued in the
given age. Subjective is the outlook in accordance with which
these goals were appraised by their contemporaries. And subjective is the criterion which the historian applies to the different
outlooks of the age so as to select from them what he considers

central and paramount, and to the whole series of outlooks so as
to determine the course of progress in human history, to identify
progressive and retrogressive periods and their causes and effects,
and to show his contemporaries what is possible and desirable at
the present moment. But the sources of the subjectivity in these
cases are different, and the means of eliminating the errors which
might result from the use of this method are also different.

[The subjectivity of particular goals and of their moral evaluation in a given age is a fact, quite unavoidable and scientific,
which should be observed and investigated in all its aspects. To
avoid error here the historian must simply study the individuals'
cultural surroundings and stage of development in the particular
age with the utmost thoroughness and care. He is gathering facts
as in any other science, and his personal views have or should
have an extremely small role in establishing these facts. If he
ascribes to Sesostris or Tamerlane the intricate diplomatic calcu-
lations of Louis XIV or Bismarck, he simply does not know his
period. If he reads Hegel's dialectic into the thought of Heraclitus, again he has not sufficiently mastered the difference between two periods.[4] If he gives predominant significance in history to custom and tradition, state expansion, or international
strife, he has not become clear as to the characteristic features of
human nature as man himself conceives it. In all these cases, the
best means of eliminating error is to make scientific information
accurate, broad, and comprehensive.

[But objective appraisal of the different world views of a given
age or of the theory of historical progress which the historian
formulates is quite a different matter. Here the most precise
erudition cannot eliminate error if the author sets up a false ideal.
Here is reflected the historian's personal, individual development,
and only through concern for his own development can he find
the way to make his conception more correct.][5] Consciously or
unconsciously, a man applies the level of moral development
which he himself has attained to the entire history of mankind.
One person seeks in the life of mankind only that which furthers
the formation or destruction of powerful states. Another follows
primarily the conflicts and the rise and fall of nations. A third
tries to convince himself and others that the victors always had
more right on their side than the vanquished. A fourth is inter-

ested in facts to the extent that they have implemented this or that idea which he accepts as an absolute good for mankind. They all judge history subjectively, according to their view of moral ideals. Indeed they cannot judge it otherwise.

The reader must not suppose that the historian can acquire an objective criterion for judging the importance of events by considering the number of persons an event affects. For Augustine or Bossuet, events which influenced the inhabitants of tiny Palestine were incomparably more important than the campaigns of Genghis Khan or Alexander the Great. Similarly the modern historian would, I believe, consider the conquest of the vast Chinese empire by the Mongols less significant than the struggle of a few mountain cantons of Switzerland against the Habsburgs. [Of course the criterion of the greater number of persons can be applied even here if one considers not only the individuals immediately affected by the events but the succeeding generations whose life and thought were influenced by these events. But in such cases the historian or thinker is very often laboring under an illusion. What he considers paramount by virtue of his own subjective moral outlook seems to him to have exerted greater indirect influence on the future fate of a more considerable portion of mankind. One author will find in the intellectual culture of modern Europe the predominant influence of sermons once heard in Galilee, and will maintain that the influence of the Greek philosophical schools has been insignificant by comparison; another historian will maintain the exact opposite with equal determination.]

Thus, willy-nilly, a man is bound to evaluate the historical process subjectively: that is, having acquired, in accordance with his level of moral development, one or another moral ideal, he is bound to put all the facts of history into perspective according to whether they have promoted or opposed this ideal, and to give primary historical importance to those facts in which this promotion or opposition is most vividly exhibited.

But here two further significant circumstances present themselves. First, from this standpoint all phenomena become identified as beneficial or harmful, as morally good or evil. Second, in the historical perspective set by our moral ideal we stand at the end of the historical process; the entire past is related to our ideal as a series of preparatory steps which lead inevitably to a definite end. Consequently, we see history as a struggle between a beneficent principle and a harmful principle, where the former—in unchanging form or through gradual development—has finally reached the point at which it is for us the supreme human good.

[Not that the beneficent principle was in fact bound to triumph without fail, or that each successive period necessarily drew nearer to our moral ideal. No, many observers are perfectly aware of the fact that epochs of retrogression are quite common in history; others are only too willing to complain of the predominance of evil in this "vale of tears" and of the corruption of modern generations; still others frankly maintain that a better future for mankind is impossible. Nevertheless, when these people begin to survey historical events they inevitably arrange the entire past in perspective according to what they consider *best*. The only events which stand out are those which have furthered the development of their ideal, or have most hindered its realization.

[If the thinker believes that his moral ideal is actually realized now or will be realized in the future, he will arrange the whole of history around the events which paved the way for this realization. If he transfers his ideal to a mythical region beyond the grave, then history is simply a preparation for the creed that entails beatitude in a future world. If he renounces all possibility of realizing his ideal, it remains the highest inner conviction which history has produced in the mind of man, and again all past events, important and unimportant, are displayed before him as the preparation for this moral conviction, which is unrealized now and unrealizable in the actual future, but has been realized in the sphere of human consciousness as the pinnacle of human development.

[This approach of historical facts to a real or ideal best of which we are conscious, this evolution of our moral ideal in the past life of mankind, is for everyone the *only* meaning of history, the only *law* of the historical ordering of events, the law of *progress*—whether we consider the progress to be in fact continuous or subject to fluctuation, whether we believe in its actual realization or only its realization in consciousness.]

Thus we inevitably see *progress* in the course of history. If we support a principle which is triumphing in our time, we regard our age as the crown of all those which preceded it. If our sympathies belong to a principle which is clearly on the wane, we believe that our age is critical, transitional, or pathological, and that after it will come an age in which our ideal will triumph [either in the real world, or in a mythical future world, or in the consciousness of the highest representatives of mankind.] Those who have believed that the end of the world was imminent—and the world seemed to them full of evil—believed that beatitude for the righteous was sure to follow. Those who have accepted the idea of a primitive state of perfection have advanced from the very next step to a theory of progress. Even the proponents of the cyclical theory of history (which, however, we shall not develop here) have unwittingly submitted to this general law of human thinking. By the inevitable necessity of this thinking, *for man* the historical process is always more or less clearly and consistently a struggle for progress, [a real or ideal development of progressive aspirations and progressive understanding,] [6] and only those phenomena were historical, in the strict sense of this word, which affected this progress.

I know that a great many people will find my conception of the word "progress" distasteful. All those who wish to endow history with the same objective impartiality which characterizes the processes of nature will be indignant because I make progress depend upon the personal views of the investigator. All those who believe in the absolute infallibility of their own moral outlook would like to convince themselves that the elements of the historical process which are most closely connected with the principles of their outlook are more important not only *for them* but *in themselves.*

But really it is time for thinking people to learn one very simple thing: that distinctions between the important and the unimportant, the beneficial and the harmful, the good and the bad are distinctions which exist only *for man;* they are quite alien to nature and to things in themselves. While man of necessity applies to everything his human (anthropological) way of looking at things, by an equally inescapable necessity things in their totality follow processes which have nothing to do with the human point of view.

For man general laws rather than individual facts are important because he understands things only by generalizing them; but science with its general laws of phenomena is characteristic only of *man*, while outside man there is nothing but simultaneous and successive concatenations of facts, so minute and fractional that man can scarcely even apprehend them in all their particularity. *For man* some of the thoughts, feelings, and deeds of a person (or a group of persons) are marked out from the unbroken thread of life's commonplaces and allotted to biographies and histories as being paramount, having ideal significance, historical importance—but this selection is made only by *man* himself. Unconscious natural processes produce the idea of universal gravitation and the idea of popular solidarity, just as they produce a hair on a beetle's leg or the shopkeeper's desire to extract an extra penny from his customer. Garibaldi, [Varlin,] and others like them are, for nature, exactly the same sort of nineteenth-century specimens of the human race as any senator of Napoleon III, any small-town German burgher or any of the self-satisfied nonentities who strut along the Nevsky Prospekt.[7] On scientific grounds the impartial investigator has no right to transfer his moral judgment concerning the significance of a general law, a genius, or a hero from the realm of *human* understanding and desire to the realm of unconscious and passionless nature.

I must comment here on the conceptions of progress of two outstanding thinkers who *seem* to disagree with the foregoing definition.

"Progress," says Proudhon (*Philosophie du progrès,* 24), "is the affirmation of universal movement and consequently the negation of every immutable formula . . . applied to any being whatever; of every inviolable order, not excepting the order of the universe itself; of every subject or object, empirical or transcendental, which does not change." [8] This seems to be a completely objective point of view, which sacrifices personal convictions on the altar of universal change.

But read on and you will find that for this great thinker progress, in any area you choose, is a synonym for the combined ideas of freedom, individuality, and justice; that is, he calls progress those changes which lead to the *best* understanding of things, to the *highest* moral ideal of the individual and of society, as this ideal has been worked out by *him,* Proudhon. An absolute

good existed for Proudhon just as one has existed and will exist for
every cultivated person; for Proudhon it was named truth, freedom, and justice, and this absolute became the aim and essence
of progress, with a subjective compulsion comparable to that of
the millennium for the chiliasts.

Furthermore, in another place—namely, in the ninth essay of
his great work, *On Justice in the Revolution and in the Church*—
Proudhon himself stated a different conception of progress,
[which in many respects approaches the one expressed in my letters. He says (ed. 1868, Brussels, III, 224 ff): "Progress is more
than movement, and one has not in the least proved that a thing
is progressing when he has shown that it is moving"; he does not
see progress in "crises determined *a priori* and in a certain order
by the necessity of our constitution," or in "the series of physico-
social transitions which do not depend on man's will." For him
"progress is the same as justice and freedom considered (1) in
their movement through time, (2) in their action on the faculties
which obey them and which they modify in proportion to their
progressive movement." Proudhon even demands from "a complete and true theory of progress," among other things, proof that
in progress there is nothing fatalistic. Later on he says (III, 270)
that "we inevitably believe in progress."]

Spencer writes (*Collected Works*, I, 2): "Rightly to understand
progress, we must inquire what is the nature of these changes,
considered apart from our interests. . . . Leaving out of sight
concomitants and beneficial consequences, let us ask what Progress is in itself." He then calls the transition from the homo-
geneous to the heterogeneous "organic progress," and argues that
it is the law of all progress. Up to this point we seem to be looking at the phenomenon completely objectively.

But read carefully how Spencer actually approaches his work,
and you will see that he is proceeding from a completely subjective point of view. He takes as *given* such everyday conceptions
of progress as increase in population, increase in the quantity of
material products and improvement in their quality, increase in
the number of facts known and laws understood—in short, increase in everything which directly or indirectly promotes human
happiness. He simply finds that these conceptions are *vague,* that
they contain the *shadow* of progress but not progress itself. He

wants to understand precisely *these* changes, to discover the *nature* of precisely this process, and he believes that he has found it in differentiation, on the analogy of organic development, which he chooses to call *progress.*

But does organic development contain the characteristic feature of the phenomena from which the author borrowed the conception of progress? It is highly doubtful. Increase in population and increase in material and intellectual wealth have in common the fact that we see in them something *better,* more desirable, more in accordance with what we *demand* of the individual and of mankind. But how is a newborn animal better than the embryo or the egg from which it sprang? And why is a grown animal better than one newly born? If we may speak of *progress* in the development of an animal, then it is equally correct to speak also of *ends* in nature, of the desires of plants, or of the government of the solar system. Moreover, it would be interesting to know whether Spencer himself would call it progress if, in the transition from homogeneity to heterogeneity in human society, differentiation reached the point where each person spoke a different language and had his own notions of the true, the just, and the beautiful.

Spencer's idea is in general correct, since experience has shown that in a great number of cases the approach of the individual and of society to *his,* Spencer's, moral ideal did proceed through differentiation; but this conception does not, by itself, embrace all the phenomena of progress, nor does it even consistently rule out things which are completely at variance with progress viewed as the working out of the particular moral ideal. And even in those instances where the idea is correct, it merely indicates the *cause* of progress, while progress itself still lies in the thinker's subjective view of what is better or worse for the individual or for mankind.

[We may note that as early as the first edition of his *First Principles* Spencer recognized the inaccuracy of using the term "progress" too extensively and in the majority of cases substituted for it the term "evolution," for which he gave this formula: "Evolution is a change from an indefinite, incoherent homogeneity, to a definite, coherent heterogeneity; through continous differentiations and integrations" (*Collected Works,* VII, 233). This formula is less open to objection, partly because of its genuine breadth and partly because of its imperfect clarity, which allows it to encompass extremely diverse cases which hardly fit its direct sense. However, since this is a formula of *evolution* rather than *progress*, it is not directly pertinent to the question being examined here.]

Thus I believe that the two thinkers I have taken by way of example disagree with the foregoing views on progress only verbally, and that essentially they stand, like everyone else, on the ground determined by the nature of human thinking. They create some moral ideal or borrow one from others, and they see in the events of history a struggle for this supreme good and a movement toward it. And everyone proceeds in just this way.

THIRD LETTER

The Extent of Human Progress

EVERYTHING I HAVE SAID in the foregoing letter demands, of course, that I give the reader a definite statement of what exactly I take the goal of human progress to be. This I shall do. [First, however, I should like to dispose of one objection which seems to destroy the scientific character of my entire discussion at its very foundation.

[I may be told that if history can be understood only as the science of progress, whereas progress is in itself nothing more than a subjective view of events from the standpoint of our moral ideal, then history can be scientific only if it is possible to work out scientifically the moral ideal which mankind *must of necessity* affirm as the one scientific truth. If this inference is admitted (and I admit it), it may be objected (and has been objected) that men's moral ideals have hitherto been extremely diverse, and by their very nature as purely subjective phenomena must always remain diverse.[1] It will be said that we are here in the province not of science but of faith; that just as one man's faith is not binding on another, no more is anyone bound by another's moral ideals; that everyone has a perfect right to cultivate his *own* moral ideal, since there is no criterion of scientific truth for purely subjective opinions. Consequently, neither an evaluation of progress nor even an understanding of progress can be developed scientifically. Consequently, it is absolutely impossible to have a scientific theory of progress, a scientific interpretation of history, or even to reach agreement on these matters.

[I cannot consider these objections well-founded, and I shall dwell on them for a moment.

[If we base our conclusions on the diversity which exists and always has existed among men, we shall have to reject not only the unity of moral ideals but also the unity of scientific truth. Of the 1,400 million persons who constitute mankind, the vast majority not only lack the slightest smattering of scientific information —they have not developed even the rudiments of a scientific outlook, have not traversed the initial stages of anthropological development. Whole tribes of men cannot conceive of numbers of any great size and have no abstract terms. Fetishism, belief in charms and fortune-telling, and belief in miracles prevail not only among savages and in the illiterate classes of the European population, but constantly arise in the so-called civilized minority. Must we conclude from this that science does not exist as an absolute truth *for man?* Must we regard the findings of European scientists as mental phenomena having no more right to be affirmed than ghost stories and prophetic dreams? Yet if the state of affairs we presently observe continues in the world, the individuals who think scientifically will always be overwhelmingly outnumbered by the mass of those who believe in ghosts and prophetic dreams.

[I believe that the unity of moral ideals may be regarded as a thesis no less convincing than the unity of scientific truths. Anyone may, if he wishes, reject *both* on the grounds that both require special cultivation on the part of individuals and that for the majority *neither* has existed in the past just as it does not exist now. But persons for whom the science of the intellectually cultivated minority is the *one, binding* truth scarcely have the right to reject the ideals of the morally cultivated minority as something purely individual.

[The findings of science are not attained all at once but come about through the elaboration of ideas and the critical investigation of facts. The mind must be prepared by practice before it can have the capacity to understand and to assimilate scientific truth. That is why the majority of people remain outside the scientific movement to this day, and why a great number of people who are acquainted with the findings of critical scientific thought repeat these findings only on faith, as they might repeat an account of a miraculous event.

[To the scientific investigator a fact becomes scientific when it has passed a series of methodical tests: freedom from contradiction, agreement with observation, admission of only those hypotheses which have analogies in reality, elimination of all hypotheses which are unnecessary or are not open to experiment —such are the demands on every new theoretical construction which lays claim to join the ranks of scientific truths. These demands are not easily fulfilled, and for this reason the history of human knowledge represents a long series of errors, out of which gradually, bit by bit, exact science has developed.

[The demand of freedom from contradiction was one powerful cause of delay in the growth of knowledge, because a new proposition had to be compared with what was felt to be indisputable truth, and the comparison could be fruitful only when the points of comparison were themselves established critically. Specialized science had to be developed out of the general mass of philosophical speculations; the truths of the simpler sciences had to become the groundwork for more complex sciences. Thus it is small wonder that certain scientific theses were rejected and are rejected to this day, by men of the most powerful intellect, on the ground that they contradict *apparent* truths.

[The demand of agreement with observation posed a task no less arduous: men had to *learn to observe,* and this is not easy. The greatest minds of antiquity and eminent modern scientists have left us much evidence of the most flagrant errors of observation, and controversies about the accuracy of an observation made in one case or another continue to this day.

[We shall not enlarge upon the difficulty of framing proper hypotheses: for the advancement of science it is just as impossible to do without them as it is difficult to indicate the limit beyond

which a scientific hypothesis becomes a metaphysical speculation.
There are examples of this daily in the most widely circulated
works and among the most respected scientists.

[All these difficulties explain the slow growth of scientific understanding, and they should convince the critically thinking
investigator that there is no reason whatever for believing that
strictly scientific thinking cannot be extended to fields which are
presently as much under the sway of a disorderly chaos of opinion as the basic areas of natural science were in antiquity. The
ancient world worked out an understanding of logical-deductive,
mathematical and geometrical truth; but to this day there are
people who try to square the circle. The seventeenth century established the method for verifying truths in the objective phenomenological sciences; but to this day specialists advance opposing experiments on heterogenesis which lead to contradictory
conclusions. The significance of psychological observation is still a
matter of dispute. Sociology has only recently begun to establish
some of its theses. In all these fields, people with different opinions still oppose one another, stubbornly denying the scientific
legitimacy of their opponents' views and unable to agree on what
observations are indisputable, what hypotheses are permissible,
and where contradictions exist and where they do not.

[Yet in all these fields investigators are seeking a scientific,
common, indisputable truth; the majority of critically minded
people everywhere assume that this truth exists and that it can
and should be sought. Why, then, assume eternal contradiction in
the sphere of moral ideals? Why put the man who lives by instinct
and momentary inclination on a level with the man who attempts to analyze moral phenomena and discover their laws?
Why infer from the *present* disputes among those who think
about moral questions that scientific results will never be attained
in this area? Judging by Aristotle's theory of motion—unquestionably the product of a great mind—we might reject the possibility
that dynamics would ever exist.

[Thus it is not impossible to work out scientifically the moral
ideal which, as mankind develops, will inevitably become the
binding truth for an ever-widening circle of persons. At the same
time it proves possible to develop a scientific understanding of
progress and construct history as a science.

[In any event, in the absence of convincing proofs of the impossibility of using scientific methods in the field of morals, for everyone who is not indifferent to the questions which are paramount for mankind it is permissible and apparently obligatory to strive to elaborate critically the most rational moral ideal, and to construct the science of progress—history—on the basis of this ideal. Accordingly I venture to set down, as a foundation for the entire subsequent discussion, a definite indication of my view of human progress.]

The physical, intellectual, and moral development of the individual; the incorporation of truth and justice in social institutions —here is a brief formula embracing, I believe, everything which may be considered progress. And I may add that I view nothing in this formula as my personal property: it is present, more or less clearly and fully expressed, in the minds of all thinkers of recent centuries, and in our time it is becoming a truism, repeated even by those whose actions are inconsistent with it and who desire something quite different.

[I believe that the concepts contained in this formula are entirely determinate, and that for anyone who takes them seriously they do not admit of varying interpretations. If I am mistaken, then in any event it is the task of ethics rather than the theory of progress to define these concepts, to prove the propositions contained in the formula, and to develop the formula in detail. Just as truths of chemistry need not be proved in a treatise on physiology, so it is unnecessary to elaborate truths of ethics when the question is one of their application to the historical process.] I believe that the proposed formula, for all its brevity, is open to extensive development, and that by developing it we can obtain a complete theory of both individual and social morality. Here I am taking the formula as a basis for what follows, and I shall proceed directly to the investigation of some of the conditions necessary for the realization of progress in the sense indicated.

The *physical* development of the individual is possible only when he has acquired a certain minimum of hygienic and material comforts. Short of this minimum pain, illness, and constant anxiety are far more likely than any sort of development, and the latter becomes the property of exceptional individuals only. All others are doomed to degeneration in a continual struggle for existence, with no hope of improving their lot.

The *intellectual* development of the individual has a firm foun-

dation only when the individual has cultivated the need for a
critical view of everything which presents itself to him, the conviction that the laws which govern phenomena are unalterable,
and the realization that in its consequences justice is identical
with the pursuit of personal interest.*

The *moral* development of the individual is likely to occur only

---

* To prevent misunderstanding I find it necessary to explain these last
words, which it was impossible to elucidate properly in a book published
in the Russian empire.

In present-day society, pervaded by universal competition, the identification of justice with personal interest seems absurd. Actually the people
who now enjoy the advantages of civilization can enjoy them only by
acquiring wealth and increasing it. But the capitalistic process of acquiring
wealth is by its very nature a process of shortchanging the worker, of dishonest speculation on the exchange, of merchandizing one's mental capacities and one's political and social influence. The most inveterate sophist
will hardly call this process *just,* but he will maintain that an individual's
intellectual development is still very low if he is seeking a way to reconcile
his personal interest with justice. The sophist will advance a different
thesis: life is a struggle, and true intellectual development consists in being
sufficiently well-armed for continual victory in this struggle.

Formerly this view was countered by pointing to the pangs of remorse
one would feel, the danger of being defeated in the constant struggle and
having no one to lean on in the hour of need, the social scorn and hatred
one might incur, and so on. All these arguments are easily destroyed by the
contemporary theorists of earthly pleasures: Remorse is an affair of habit,
and it is very easy to steel yourself against it when you are convinced that
you are acquiring wealth *legally,* and that there is no judge who can bring
your action under an article of the criminal code. If the vast majority is
competing on a legal basis for the acquisition of wealth and an increase in
pleasures, then this majority feels no scorn or hatred for the clever victor
but admires him, respects him, strives to imitate him and learn from him. As
for chances of defeat in the constant struggle—in the first place, wealth of
sufficient proportions is insurance against them to a large degree, and in the
second place a person's life is short, and the point is simply to provide for
enjoying life while it lasts.

Thus it must be admitted that in the present social order personal interest
not only is not identical with justice, it directly contradicts it. To maximize
his pleasures an individual today must stifle the very idea of justice within
him; he must bend all his critical ability to exploiting everything and everyone around him, so as to provide himself with the greatest share of pleasures
at their expense; and he must remember that if he yields for a moment to
considerations of justice or even to a feeling of sincere affection, he himself
will become an object of exploitation for those around him. The employer
must keep the worker down or the worker will rob him. The head of the
family must keep a watchful eye on his wife and children or they will cheat
him. The government must have an Argus-eyed police or others will seize its
power. Amass wealth, but be on your guard: a friend will make a sacrifice for
you only when he can count on a high rate of return; the kiss a mistress gives

when the social environment permits and encourages the development of independent convictions in individuals; when individuals have the opportunity to defend their different convictions, and by the same token are constrained to respect the freedom of conviction of others; and when the individual recognizes that his dignity resides in his convictions, and that respect of another's dignity is respect of his own.

The incorporation of truth and justice in social institutions presupposes, first of all, the opportunity for scientists and thinkers to advance propositions which they regard as expressions of truth and justice. It presupposes, further, a certain minimum of general education in society, which will permit the majority to understand these propositions and to evaluate the arguments adduced to support them. It presupposes, finally, social institutions which

you is a purchased kiss. War is everywhere, and weapons must be ready against everyone and at every moment.

Thus, *either* the identification of justice with personal interest is absurd, *or* the present social order is a pathological one. If the reader finds that the latter is untrue and that everything is as it should be, let him close this book: it is not written for him. But then certain questions arise: Has the reader cultivated the need for a critical view of his whole environment? Has he become imbued with the conviction that a society founded on a war of all against all is, by an immutable law, a society which no legality and no police can bind together, that it is a rotting society, and one which demands radical reform?

If the reader is instinctively or consciously revolted by this social order which is fatally predestined to mutual distrust and mutual exploitation, if he has discerned beneath the glitter of modern culture the existence of pathological processes which are inseparable from this order given its present foundations, then the need for a critical view of his environment should lead him to another set of questions: Are we to treat the morbid symptoms exhibited by this social order, or seek the source of the disease and take action against it? If its source lies in the very foundations of modern social life, does not radical alteration of men's economic, political, and social relationships demand also another formulation of the very principle of these relationships? In rebuilding the pathological social order into a healthy one, must we not take as our foundation not the war of all against all, not universal competition, but the closest possible and broadest possible *solidarity* among individuals? Can a society be sound and strong if there is no solidarity among its members? And what is social solidarity if not the consciousness that personal interest coincides with social interest, that personal dignity is maintained only by upholding the dignity of all who share in this solidarity?

And if this is the conclusion to which the need for a critical view of one's environment must lead, how does it differ from the conclusion presented in the text, that in a *healthy* community justice is identical in its consequences with the pursuit of personal interest? (1889)

will permit of change as soon as it appears that they have ceased to embody truth and justice.

[Only when the physical development of the individual is possible, his intellectual development firmly grounded, and his moral development likely, only when social organization provides for sufficient freedom of speech, a sufficient minimum of secondary education, and sufficient openness to change in social institutions—only then may the progress of society as a whole be considered more or less assured. Only then may we say that all the conditions of progress are present, so that only external catastrophes can stop it. Until all these conditions have been fulfilled, progress can only be accidental and partial, and cannot be guaranteed even for the most immediate future; until then we may always expect an age of stagnation or reaction after an age of apparent advance. Under the most disadvantageous conditions for society as a whole, favorable circumstances may place some individual in a position to develop far beyond the level of his environment. These favorable circumstances may exist even for a group of individuals. But they remain nonetheless an ephemeral phenomenon, while society as a whole is left to stagnation or reaction. The law of large numbers will never be slow to demonstrate, with relentless rigor, what little historical significance there is in the development of a small group of individuals under exceptional circumstances. A majority must be placed in a position where its development is possible, likely, and firmly grounded before we may say that society is progressing.]

While I counted on the reader's unquestioning acceptance of the brief formula of progress set forth above, I am not nearly so confident that he will accept the conditions of progress I have enumerated. But this is the common fate of formulas. A great many people will assent to them so long as they are not explained; as soon as explanation begins, these people who have subscribed to one and the same formula begin to realize that they did not understand one another entirely. To me these conditions seem necessary, and I leave it to anyone who disagrees with me, but retains the formula, to supply other conditions.

But having supplied *these* conditions, I shall venture to ask the reader whether we have any right today to speak of the progress of *humanity*. Can we say that the *elementary* conditions of progress have been fulfilled for a majority of the 1,400 millions who today constitute mankind? That even *some* of these conditions have been fulfilled? And for what portion of these 1,400 millions? And can we reflect without a certain horror on the *cost*, to the wretched millions of the generations which have perished, of realizing progress for the handful of individuals whom the historian may deem representatives of civilization?

I should consider it an insult to the reader if I doubted for a moment how he will answer the question of whether the elementary conditions of progress have been fulfilled. Only one answer is possible: the conditions of progress have not *all* been fulfilled for a single person, and *none* of them has been fulfilled for the majority. [Only isolated individuals or small groups have sometimes, here and there, found themselves in sufficiently favorable circumstances to win some sort of progress for themselves and to pass on the tradition of fighting for betterment to other small groups, to whom fate also has given a somewhat more advantageous position.] Everywhere and always, individuals who have made progress of some sort have had to combat innumerable obstacles and waste the greater part of their strength and lives in this fight, simply to uphold their right to physical and intellectual cultivation. Only under particularly favorable circumstances have they succeeded. Only in exceptional situations have individuals not had to struggle for existence, so that time and energy could go to the fight to increase pleasures. Still more exceptional was the situation of those who could profit to such an extent by the struggles of others on their behalf that they could strive for the moral pleasure of consciously cultivating humane principles and embodying them in social institutions. And in all these cases the struggle itself demanded so large a portion of their strength and life that extremely little of either was left for actually realizing its goal.

Thus it is small wonder if mankind, even in its most privileged segment, has achieved so little. Indeed it is surprising that under such unfavorable conditions a portion of mankind has nevertheless achieved something which can properly be called, not the realization, but perhaps the preparation for true progress. But then how small is this portion which has succeeded? And what has it cost the rest?

Mankind has advanced farthest in regard to the conditions of the *physical* development of the individual. Yet even in this re-spect how negligible still is the number of people for whom the *necessary* minimum of hygienic and material comforts has been provided! What an insignificant minority of mankind's 1,400 mil-lions enjoy adequate and wholesome food, have clothing and housing which satisfy the basic requirements of health, and can get medical care in case of illness and social care in case of famine or sudden misfortune! What an immense majority spend almost all their lives in ceaseless concern for their daily bread, in an unremitting struggle for their wretched existence, and still cannot always sustain themselves!

Consider the tribes which this struggle still keeps in a state that differs in almost no respect from that of other species of animals. Consider the victims of famine and epidemics in the numerous tribes which are deprived of all the aids of rational culture. Con-sider that mass of people in the heart of civilized Europe who are condemned to fight all their lives for tomorrow's scrap of bread. Recall the frightful accounts of the living conditions of workers in the most *advanced* countries of Europe. Note how the figures in the mortality tables correspond to a rise of a few percent in the price of bread, and how the life expectancies of the poor man and the rich man differ. Remember how meager are the earnings of the vast majority of Europe's inhabitants.

When these figures appear before you in all their terrifying reality, you may wonder what portion of mankind actually enjoys those vital comforts, those necessary conditions of physical devel-opment for man, which contemporary culture produces in its fac-tories, medical schools, and charity committees. How great is the *practical* significance of human science and human philanthropy in our time for the life of the majority of people, for their devel-opment? Yet it must be confessed that the increase in the material comforts of life in Europe is striking, and that, unquestionably, the number of individuals who have an opportunity to enjoy the comforts of wholesome food and housing, medical care in the event of illness, and police protection in an emergency, has in-creased greatly in recent centuries. In this small portion of man-kind which is protected from the gravest need, all human civiliza-tion now resides.

Mankind has made far, far less progress toward fulfilling the

conditions of intellectual development. There is no use even talking about the development of a critical outlook, about an understanding of the immutability of natural laws and of the utilitarian
conception of justice, for the vast number of people who must
still defend their own existence against constant danger. But even
the minority which is more or less protected from these grave
cares contains only the most negligible number of individuals
who have become accustomed to think critically, who have
learned the meaning of the term "law of phenomena," and who
clearly understand their own interest. Too much ridicule and in-
dignation have been heaped on instances of the sway of fashion,
custom, tradition, and authority of every description in the civilized minority for it to be necessary for me to enlarge upon this
subject or to repeat a truth which has been repeated a thousand
times—that people who have cultivated the habit of thinking
critically *in general* are remarkably rare.

Somewhat less rare, though still by no means numerous, are
people who have become accustomed to take a general view of
phenomena in some single, more or less extensive field. Outside
this field, they are just as prone to the meaningless repetition of
others' opinions as the whole remaining majority of mankind.

As for a conception of the unalterability of the laws governing
phenomena, this may be expected only in the small group of persons who have studied science seriously. Even among this group
however, by no means all who preach the unalterability of natural laws can be regarded as having actually assimilated this principle. Epidemics inspired by the latest magicians—mesmerists,
exorcisers, spiritualists—have provided long lists of enthusiastic
victims, and among these victims, unfortunately, men of science
are encountered. Even apart from these epidemics, men of
science—especially in moments of vital danger, emotional shock,
and so on—have turned time and again to charms and incantations (in their current [Christian] form, of course), which shows
how weak is their belief in the unchanging course of phenomena
and in the impossibility of deflecting the processes of nature from
their inevitable fulfillment. Is it any wonder, then, that [Chris-
tian] charms and incantations play their role in the elegant culture of Europe in the nineteenth century just as effectively as
[others do] among our contemporaries in the wilds of Africa, or

did among our ancestors thousands of years ago? The science of nature has captured little ground from the world of the miraculous; in everyday life the culture of our time represents a motley mixture of rational and superstitious procedures, and belief in the miraculous is ready to awaken in the majority of the *educated* classes at the first convenient opportunity.

I shall not even venture to raise the question of the development of an understanding of the utilitarian view of justice. [In the present social order, universal competition leads to a direct denial of the utilitarian conception of just conduct, and an idea which contradicts the prevailing trend of thought cannot be expected to grow. One can only marvel at how man's healthy instincts, despite the prevailing and growing competition, still compel people to respect the fictions of justice. Almost everyone, down to the most unscrupulous and omnivorous exploiter, desires to *appear* just—and not simply to others but very often to himself as well. This shows unwitting recognition of the truth of the conception advanced above, even in the midst of a system based on the denial of that conception. But it goes without saying that] [2] at present the number of people who have made this conception their own, in theory and in practice, is utterly insignificant.

The conditions of intellectual progress, however limited even among the minority which is sheltered from the immediate struggle for existence, are nevertheless being fulfilled at least in part. There is a small group of people who have cultivated the habit of thinking critically, if only in a particular field of knowledge. The unalterability of the laws of phenomena is acknowledged in theory by the majority of scientists, even if it plays a very small part in their personal convictions. It is only the utilitarian conception of justice that is acknowledged very little even in theory.

But what are we to say of the *moral* development of the individual? Since we may speak of convictions only among people who have developed a capacity to think critically, the conditions of moral development exist only for this small group. But only a part of this group lives in countries where the law protects rather than penalizes personal conviction. Only a small part of this part lives in a social order which does not view independence of conviction as a moral vice, does not attempt to eradicate it from childhood on by an education which instills submission to custom, does not persecute it in every possible way, as an impropriety harmful to public order. Of the individuals in this scarcely noticeable fraction of mankind which is the most fortunately situated with respect to the conditions of moral development, only a small number, when they have developed a conviction, remain tolerant of the convictions of others, and a still smaller number add the recognition that man's dignity resides in his convictions. Judge by this, then, for what an infinitesimal portion of mankind moral progress is possible in each generation! And in moral progress each generation repeats the same work, since strength and independence of conviction, as well as the willingness to stand up for it, are not inherited by one individual from another but are developed by each independently.

Progress in the moral realm is simply a matter of the number of individuals who have acquired strong and independent convictions. Given the small number for whom such convictions are at all *possible*, there is no way to determine whether such progress exists or not. It might be supposed that it is taking place as a consequence of the geographical expansion of territories in which the law protects freedom of thought, but on the other hand better means of administrative supervision are restraining it more than ever before in places where there is repressive legislation in this regard. Thus the answer must be left to the future. For the present the question is not even particularly important, since the portion of mankind to which it applies is so small. I may add that Buckle, in denying moral progress in mankind, had in mind something quite different.

Let us turn to the conditions necessary for the incorporation of truth and justice in social institutions. The first condition—the opportunity to express scientific conclusions and philosophical convictions—has been fulfilled, more or less, in a fairly appreciable part of Europe and America, and this is the most effective progress that has been made in human history.[3] [Even here, however, considerable discomfort seems inevitable for people whose opinions are too marked: the fate of Ludwig Feuerbach in Germany, of the earlier Rochefort, of Maroteau, and of Humbert in France, and even in England the difficulties Bradlaugh encountered in entering Parliament, indicate that in this direction, too, there still remains much ground for progress to win.]

But the second condition—a sufficient minimum of public education—has been fulfilled, as we have seen, only for the inconsiderable minority which is secured against the most stubborn struggle for existence and is accustomed to think critically. All other members of society are either overwhelmed by their daily cares or accustomed to follow authority.

The third condition—the opportunity to discuss and alter outmoded social institutions—[would seem to be fulfilled wherever a constitution legitimizes constituent and legislative assemblies. In our day, however, hopes for these legal organs of public opinion have grown very dim. Do they faithfully represent and *can* they represent *public* opinion—the opinion of the majority of the adult population of a country? We have seen that the conditions of physical development are very inadequately satisfied for the majority of people, and the conditions of intellectual and moral development for almost all. In such a case, can we assume that any sort of constituent or legislative assembly will express actual public opinion in its debates and decisions?] [4]

A grinding concern for their daily bread makes it absolutely impossible for the vast majority to participate in legislation, given the complicated forms which have been imparted to it; and in most cases the existing social order places obstacles of every description in the way of even the few individuals within this majority who by chance have had an opportunity to develop intellectually. For these reasons existing social institutions are created and changed by the representatives of the protected minority only. Since this minority is very little developed critically, and least of all with respect to an understanding of the utilitarian conception of justice, a just judgment on their part is accidental; the general rule is judgment and decision on the basis of the exclusive, selfish interests of the minority which circumstances have placed at the head of the legislative machine.

Depending upon its knowledge and its understanding or misunderstanding of its own interests, the minority more or less fully embodies these interests in legislation. [But legislation thus becomes, at best, an attempt to satisfy a minimum of the masses' demands so as to avert revolutionary outbursts. For the most part the ruling classes or governing minority embody in legislation the same social conflict which prompts those who possess capital to

view the masses only as objects of economic exploitation for their
own enrichment, and prompts those who share in the government
to view them only as objects of police supervision and punitive
measures.] [5]

Not only the interests of the minority hinder the improvement
of social institutions: accepted customs and time-honored traditions hinder it still more. In the eyes of a considerable number of
persons in the most advanced societies, only a few political institutions and some minor economic institutions have ever been
open to discussion and change. Everything else remains an inviolable sanctity, even for many of those who are harmed to some
extent by these inviolable sanctities, and all the more for those
who do not feel their burden. There was a time when not a single
political speaker in a free republic could so much as mention the
abolition of slavery. There was a time when toleration of men of
another faith was a topic which could lead to the stake. Even in
our time, in the parliaments of Europe and America, while one
may calmly discuss tariffs and loans, radical consideration of the
distribution of wealth is impossible. Debates about the responsibility of ministers are allowed, but the substitution of one dynasty
for another [or the transition from a monarchical to a republican
form of government can come about only through revolution.] [6]
The economic side of family relationships comes under review,
but the essence of these relationships remains untouched.[7]

In many cases it cannot be said that discussing these sanctities
is directly prohibited by law or will expose the transgressor to a
definite penalty. An opinion might be expressed, if a critically
thinking and courageous individual were to be found among the
legislators. But custom and tradition will not permit a majority of
the legislators or a considerable portion of society to discuss the
grounds of the opinion, even privately. The opinion will be rejected, not after it has been heard out and acknowledged, and not
because its opponents believe that the arguments supporting it
are weak or that it would infringe upon their interests, but simply
because in their eyes such an opinion *is not to be discussed.*

Given the lack of critical development in the protected minority which supplies the legislators, and given the fact that the interests of this minority are less harmed by the inviolable sanctities, the latter remain virtually sacred even long after they have

lost their inviolability in the domain of thought, and after the vast majority have felt their oppressive weight but have not yet recognized the need to alter them. [Dissatisfaction mounts. Suffering increases. There are local outbursts, which are easily crushed. The government and the ruling classes resort to palliatives and half-measures to relieve the sufferings that are too obvious to ignore, and to a reduction in police supervision and punitive measures.] When the critically thinking minority repeats its demands for reform, it encounters insurmountable obstacles. Everything remains as it was, until the belief that these institutions are worthless (accepted on faith, of course) spreads to a fairly large number of people, [and until the malcontents realize that the path of peaceful reform is closed to the society.] Then the obsolete institutions are destroyed—but now not by peaceful legislative reforms but by violent revolution.[8]

[In the course of history revolution generally proves to be, in fact, a far more common instrument of social progress than radical reform in legislation by peaceful means. Governments, of course, always strive to avert revolutions, and even to the opposition parties demanding reform revolutions are almost always thoroughly undesirable. But the lack of intellectual and moral development in the ruling and governing individuals and groups usually leads in such cases to an unavoidable and bloody clash. The evils of revolutions are well-known to all. The enormous quantity of suffering they engender, for the very masses who are overwhelmed by daily cares, makes them always highly regrettable instruments of historical progress. But since progress is usually impossible through any other means when serious social discomforts exist, and since sometimes even plain calculation proves that if the existing order is preserved the chronic sufferings of the masses may far exceed all the sufferings likely to result from revolution, the most peaceable but sincere reformers are compelled to become revolutionaries. The evils unavoidable in this situation can be mitigated only by rational discussion of the *real* changes to which the revolution should lead: we too often see history confining itself to the replacement of one ruling group by another, while the masses, to improve whose lot the sincere revolutionaries fight, and by whose power revolutions are effected, gain very little by the overturn.]

When we see the slight extent to which the conditions of human progress have been fulfilled, we shall, of course, cease to be astonished that in all ages there exists a mournful chorus of writers who repeat bitter complaints about the miseries of mankind and lament the fragility of the so-called historical civilizations. Just as in our time the vast majority of mankind is condemned to unceasing physical toil, which dulls the mind and the moral sense, and to the likelihood of dying from starvation or an epidemic, so this has always been the lot of the majority. For the eternally toiling human machine, often starving and always worried about tomorrow, things are no better now than they were in other ages. For him there is no progress. The culture towering above him with its palaces, parliaments, temples, academies, and studios, means very little to him.

[In a former day the inviolability of ancient custom and the sanctity of a common religion linked him with the ruling minority. Later he believed that patriarchal chiefs—the distant sovereigns—were concerned about his welfare. Still later he pinned his hopes on "people's" ministers and on the "radical" orators in parliaments and mass meetings, hearing them speak ardently about "the people." But history swept away these illusions one after the other, and civilizations with all their glitter have ever remained means of enjoyment for the minority while the majority continued to suffer.

[Yet every society is confronted again and again with the fact that it is necessary, for the stability of civilization, to establish a solidarity of interests and convictions, a bond between the ruling classes and the majority.] [9] If such a bond does not exist between the needy masses and the civilized minority, the minority's civilization is always precarious. A clash with an alien conqueror, the preaching of a new religion, or a short-lived outburst of the hungry masses can annihilate the most brilliant culture in the shortest time, for all its apparent material, intellectual, and moral preeminence. The only way for a civilization to be more durable is constantly to link its existence with the material, intellectual, and moral interests of the needy majority, extending to more and more individuals the benefits of the material comforts of life, the edifying effect of science, the consciousness of personal dignity, and the magnetic influence of social institutions embodying

greater justice. Only by distributing more uniformly the accumulated capital of prosperity and of intellectual and moral cultivation can the civilized minority make it likely that its own cultivation will endure.

The ancient Oriental kingdoms, like the kingdoms of Mexico,
Peru, and probably that anonymous society which left palaces
and temples in the forests of Palenque, were swept away with
their whole civilizations by the first social storm. This was not a
series of accidents, but a perfectly natural product of the form of
these civilizations. When a theocracy monopolized intellectual
development, when a small circle of hereditary proprietors or
men with access to the royal court monopolized material comforts
and cultural advances, when the palaces for one man and the
temples for a few were products of the endless toil of the vast
majority, when this majority expected neither significant improvement in its way of life from preservation of the indigenous
social institutions nor significant harm from submission to an
alien conqueror—what, then, could truly bind this majority to a
civilization which was for it simply a curious spectacle, remote
and useless?

The alien conqueror came and lightly skimmed the shallow
stratum of the civilized minority from the summit of society. The
splendid palaces and temples of Nineveh were deserted; they
crumbled and were reclaimed by the forest—to rise in Babylon.
Then Babylon fell—to send labor and capital to Susa and
Persepolis. The majority lost nothing but a gaudy spectacle. It
toiled uselessly for the Sennacheribs as it had for the Nebuchad-
nezzars; it was as little bound by interests or by intellectual life to
Amasis as it had been to Darius; it perished mechanically in the
armies of Cyrus as it had in the armies of Croesus. The profound
injustice in the distribution of the prerequisites of physical, intellectual, and moral development lent an extreme instability to all
these civilizations.

The same phenomenon was repeated with the fall of the Greco-
Roman world. Here, however, civilization was more widely
disseminated and its institutions were somewhat more just. For
this reason the classical civilization was also more stable, and it
did not succumb so easily to the pressure of external and internal
destructive forces. Thus its traces in the history of mankind are

deeper and more numerous. To this civilization were linked the economic interests of a large number of citizens and the intellectual interests of all those who had freed themselves from their most burdensome cares and could move to one of the urban centers of thought and political life. Degrading personal despotism was replaced by an idealized despotism of government and law. The monopoly on intellectual development disappeared with the theocracy. Exact science, independent philosophical thought, and the conscious participation of the citizen in the body politic extended the fulfillment of the conditions of physical, intellectual, and moral development.

Yet beneath the stratum of free citizens was an incomparably larger class of slaves, to whom all manual labor was assigned and who were in no way linked with the political life of the citizens. Beyond the walls of the sovereign towns extended territories subject to arbitrary rule and exploitation, and cut off from the scientific and philosophical cultivation of the centers. The educative influence of scientific and philosophical thought in the centers was weak, and instead of extending the circle of the learned, the philosophers posted bans on their academy doors prohibiting the unlearned from entering. Greek thought rose rapidly to a great height, but all the more isolated at that height stood the scientists, whom the society could not understand, and the philosophers, who were strangers to the interests of everyday life.

The inevitable retribution was not long in coming. The numerous citizens, who had failed to link their interests with the interests of the artisan-slaves and the dependent territories, were unable to defend the freedom of their towns against external force. In a prolonged struggle the urban population, custodians of the tradition of civic virtue, became intermingled with the newly arrived majority alien to this tradition, and the centers of ancient political life lost their living significance. The small number of scientists and advanced thinkers, who had failed to connect their thinking with the thought of a considerable number of people through education, were unable to defend the rights and methods of critical inquiry against the fetishism of the masses and the intellectual indolence and inconsistency of the prosperous minority. In the unrest that accompanied the Diadochi and the Roman conquest, the critically thinking minority was swamped by the

majority who knew nothing of critical inquiry. The need for absurd creeds stifled the need for creeds which were well reasoned,
just as the need for material security stifled the need for civic life.
The Hellenic ideal of the just life was replaced by the Roman
ideal of legal form. The circle of urban exploiters narrowed first
into a circle of the consuls of a single town which exploited the
world, and then into the retinue of a single man who ruled the
world.

When the external enemies of ancient Rome came to sack it, it
crumbled beneath their fingers, because there was no one to defend the imperial treasury with its onerous yoke. When the new
[Christian] wonder workers confronted the descendants of Aristotle, Archimedes, and Epicurus with the demand to think the
unthinkable, critical inquiry grew silent, science was buried, and
philosophy went into bondage, because their representatives were
isolated or themselves had succumbed to the influence of the
masses to whom intellectual interests were foreign. The insufficient justice of ancient civilization had sapped its strength,
despite its remarkable advances in comparison with earlier forms
of life and thought.

And the civilization of modern Europe can count upon its own
strength only to the extent that the material, intellectual, and
moral interests of the minority which represents it are linked economically with the majority's well-being, educationally with its
thinking, and vitally with the conviction of a majority of individuals that their dignity is bound up with the existing civilization.
[Whoever finds that these conditions have not been fulfilled in the
present social order, that in it reigns not solidarity but social discord, must of necessity seek ways of converting this pathological
condition into a healthy one, into a more just order in which
solidarity is established among the interests of the various social
groups.] The civilization most just in its distribution is also the
most long-lived.

But a civilization sometimes buys longevity at the price of its
capacity to develop. If geographical conditions somehow protect
a civilization from without, it can defend itself against internal
dangers by preventing the development of individuals who think
critically; they are by no means so numerous that it would be impossible to crush them whenever they appeared. For some races

of men, who adhere more tenaciously than others to habits and
old ways, and perhaps even in virtue of their brain structure are
less inclined toward critical development, there will ultimately be
formed, after a number of generations, a fixed cast of mind which
will be repeated as invariably as the structure of beehives and
termites' nests. Then the society may have palace revolutions,
bloody wars, dynastic changes, even the growth of a voluminous
literature—but its civilization does not change, and its *historical*
life ceases. China is a familiar enough example of such stagnation. But it should not be thought that the most superior races
have been completely delivered from the danger of stagnation.
Byzantium went rather far in that direction. Muscovy was inclin-
ing toward it. And even more advanced forms of state can
petrify.

Thus two dangers continually threaten every civilization. If it is
confined to an excessively small and exclusive minority, it is in
danger of vanishing. If it will not permit the critically thinking
individuals who vivify it to develop among the civilized minority,
it is in danger of stagnating.

[Inadequate satisfaction of its most fundamental conditions has
prevented progress from ever becoming a firm appurtenance of
any civilization, protecting it from halts and shocks, from reactions and revolutions. Stagnation has threatened and still threatens every civilization. If examples of this are scarce in history, it is
only because not even a tendency toward stagnation could eliminate the causes of instability in the social order; external enemies
and internal diseases did not give the society time to become an
ant heap. Thus the *likelihood* of stable progress in mankind has
never existed.

[Despite unfavorable conditions, however, the improbable has
happened. Here and there, for a scarcely noticeable minority of
mankind, the science of progress—history—has managed to accumulate a certain amount of material. Here and there individuals and groups of individuals have succeded in developing
physically, intellectually, and morally, have succeeded in acquiring a number of truths, in realizing in the life of small groups a
little more justice, and in bequeathing to future generations the
resources for a successful fight for progress.

[If the conditions of *social* progress have nowhere been fulfilled (that is, the conditions necessary for unimpeded and stable progress in a particular society), the conditions for progressive action on the part of separate individuals have frequently been present: a critical attitude toward contemporary culture, strong conviction and the determination to implement it, whatever the dangers. On the whole these latter conditions have been fulfilled less rarely than one might think, considering the complete absence of the conditions for *social* progress. The intellectual development of an individual, unsubstantial as it may have been, has in some cases allowed him to reach the point of criticizing the existing order, and even at times of recognizing the coincidence of justice with the personal interest of a cultivated individual. Moral development, however *unlikely* under the existing social order, has nonetheless been displayed in the most backward environments. Under the most trying circumstances thinkers have expressed their theories of truth and justice and met with sympathy and understanding from those around them. Forms of social life stubbornly opposed to progress have more than once collapsed under revolutionary outbursts, if they did not yield to the pressure of intellectual development.[10]

[Under the most hostile conditions progress has proved *possible*. It has actually taken place. When the results achieved in one locality disappeared as instability destroyed its civilization, their tradition usually survived elsewhere, took root, and again won a little ground for history.

[But mankind has never been able, at the cost of every sacrifice and the entire historical struggle, to win adequate conditions of *stable* progressive development. And at the same time it must be remembered that these are simply the *conditions* of progress, while its *goals* make demands far, far more extensive. We can see this most readily if we compare each of the basic conditions of stable social progress mentioned above with the ultimate goal to which it corresponds.

[A minimum of hygienic and material comforts—this is the necessary condition of progress; secure employment, with the comforts of life available to all—this is the ultimate goal corresponding to that condition. The need for a critical outlook, the conviction that the laws of nature are unalterable, an understanding of the identity of justice with personal interest—these are the conditions of intellectual development; systematic science and a just social order—this is its ultimate goal. A social environment favorable to independent convictions and an understanding of the moral significance of convictions—this is the condition of moral progress; the development of reasonable, clear, firm convictions and their embodiment in action—this is its goal. Freedom of thought and speech, a minimum of general education, social institutions which are *open* to progress—these are the conditions of progressive social organization; the maximum possible development of each individual, social institutions which are the *result* of the progress to which each is open—this is the goal of social progress.

[In relation to these goals the conditions mentioned above represent a very low level of social development. Yet they have never been satisfied anywhere. As for the true goals of progress, they strike the majority of thinkers as nothing short of utopian. But despite this, despite the total absence of the conditions of stable progress, history has taken place among mankind and progress has come about.

[But what a staggering price mankind has paid for it!]

FOURTH LETTER

The Cost of Progress

IN THE COURSE OF ITS LONG EXISTENCE humanity has produced a few men of genius whom historians proudly call its representatives or heroes. So that these heroes could act, so that they could even *arise* in the societies which have been blessed by their appearance, there had to be a small group of people who were consciously striving to cultivate their human dignity, extend their knowledge, clarify their thoughts, strengthen their character, and establish a more commodious social order. So that this small group could be formed, there had to appear, in the midst of a majority struggling hourly for its existence, a minority secured against life's gravest cares. So that this flower of humanity, these sole representatives of civilization, could be produced by a majority which is obliged to fight for its daily bread, for shelter, and for clothing, this majority had to maintain its own existence. And that was by no means as easy as it may seem at first glance.

In the initial struggle for existence against his fellow animals, man fared badly. He lacks the powerful natural weapons of attack and defense possessed by other species, which have established themselves in the midst of enemies thanks to just such weapons. In physical combat the stronger animals devoured him. He lacks organs for climbing, jumping, flying, or swimming which would facilitate his escape from danger, while other, weaker species no doubt owe their preservation to just such organs. Man must *learn* everything, adapt himself to everything; otherwise he perishes. According to some writers, man's young are a helpless burden to the parents for one-fifth of their lives, on the average, whereas for other species this period never exceeds one-twentieth. Even assuming that for primitive man this difference was not so great, it still could not have been in man's favor. All in all, it was extremely difficult for man to maintain his existence in the midst of the animal kingdom.

One organ as it gradually developed *was* able to give man the victory in this struggle, replacing and outweighing the advantages of all other species. This was the organ of *thought*. A countless multitude of two-legged creatures must have perished in the hopeless struggle against their brute enemies before the fortunate individuals appeared who could think better than these enemies, individuals who could invent means of protecting their existence. They succeeded in defending themselves at the price of the destruction of all the rest, and this original, entirely natural aristocracy among bipeds created mankind. Inherited ability, or a gift for imitation, conveyed the inventions of these primitive geniuses to the small minority placed in the conditions most favorable for imitating them. The existence of mankind was secured.

If previously man had fought with man as with any other animal, to take food from him or to devour him, now the conflict which was important for the future was limited to struggle among men. Here the odds were more equal, and for that reason the struggle was bound to be more stubborn and prolonged. Any advance in bodily skill, in the use of offensive or defensive weapons, or in the imitation of the first brute teachers, any invention which succeeded for an individual, brought about the death of many individuals. Abandoned infants perished; pregnant women and women who had just given birth perished; the weaker, the less skillful, the less inventive, the less wary, the less imitative perished. The infant survived whose sturdy constitution permitted him to get along without care sooner, or whose fortunate situation allowed him to enjoy care longer; the most capable in body and mind survived; the most fortunate of those equally capable survived. He was better nourished; he slept more soundly, he knew more, he had time to *consider* his actions more fully. These fortunate individuals constituted a second aristocracy among the breeds of men who were able to maintain their existence at the price of exterminating all their brothers.

The first and greatest step in the moral development of mankind must have been [1] [a firm union of individuals for common defense and for common labor. Man derived the first, most ancient family from his zoological state: it was organized around the mother, who fed her children for such a long period. Developing further, men became acquainted, after the example of predatory animals and certain monkeys, with another type of association—the temporary band for attack or defense. But the first comprehensive and purely human union, which arose on the foundation of the primitive maternal family, was the matriarchal clan. Forged by man in the hard struggle for existence, this was a firm union which was grounded in a common cause and to which personal egoism was subordinated.

[The general result of investigations of the matriarchal clan by a number of modern scholars shows us a tightly knit group with wives, children, and property in common as the most ancient and all but universal purely human form of social life. This was the first firm *bond* among men—a bond still based on the blind rule of custom, but one through which man acquired for the future the chance to calculate lines of actions, the chance to plan his life. This was the individual's first lesson in how much he gains in the struggle for existence by joining an association to which he sacrifices his exclusive egoism but from which he gains an enormous increase in strength, benefits by the common experience and the common thinking of all members, and inherits the traditions of a long line of generations. It was from this basic human union that subsequently were developed the patriarchal clan, the patriarchal family, various forms of family unions, and finally tribes and nations.

[In the struggle against these kinship associations all weaker groups were bound to perish, unless they, too, formed unions of one sort or another.] In the presence of these united forces, all individuals who did not in good time hit upon union of some sort, or for some reason did not adopt this invention, disappeared without a chance of defending themselves. The destructive strife among the kinship associations must have been all the more cruel, the greater were the forces at the combatants' disposal, the greater became the economic needs of the human groups as they consolidated, and the more implacably, therefore, they competed with one another for the meager means of satisfying these needs. At the price of this extermination of the majority, man bought the *possibility* of continued cultural progress; by transmitting it from one generation to another, he bought the habits of community and of personal attachment, the traditions of knowledge and belief.

The strife continued among the clans, [tribes, and nations when subsequently the forms of association became more complex. There developed different forms of property—communal, clan, family, tribe, private. There developed classes, castes, political relationships—and slavery.] As long as it was only a matter of the struggle for existence, vanquished opponents were ruthlessly destroyed. But the first lesson in the use of another's life for one's own *convenience* could not have been wasted. The desire to increase their own pleasure prompted men to reflect: Isn't it sometimes more profitable *not* to kill the defeated opponent? Isn't it more profitable for the victor to devote himself exclusively to cultivating his bodily and mental skills, charging another with the labor of producing necessities?

The prehistoric geniuses who hit upon this utilitarian principle thereby laid down the foundation for respect for another's life and respect for one's own dignity. By the same token they [unwittingly] imposed upon themselves and upon their descendants the duty and the moral ideal of physical and intellectual development, culture, and science. They provided themselves and their posterity with *leisure* for progress. They created progress among mankind, as the fortunate geniuses who preceded them had created mankind among the brutes, had created human [societies and] races in the struggle between human individuals [and semi-animal groups,] had created the *possibility* of future progress.

But this progress for a small minority was purchased at the price of enslaving the majority, depriving it of the chance to acquire those same bodily and mental skills which constituted the dignity of the representatives of civilization. [While the minority were cultivating both their minds and their bodies, while these bodies were being developed in a comprehensive fashion in military activities—varied, temporary, accompanied by leisure and rest—the majority were condemned to monotonous, exhausting, and continual non-military work for the benefit of others. The majority had no leisure for intellectual pursuits, they were inferior to their leaders in skills, and thus they remained incapable of using their enormous strength to win themselves the right to cultivation and a truly human life.]

Recognition of the great importance of culture and science, as forces and as pleasures, led, of course, to the desire to monopolize them. The minority of the wellborn, the learned, and the developing were segregated from all the rest by direct compulsion, social organization, legal punishment, religious awe, and customary tradition instilled from the cradle. At the price of the others' tireless labor and struggle for existence, the few could choose the better women for themselves, beget better offspring, nourish and rear them better. They could take time to observe, to reflect, to calculate—without having to worry about food, shelter, and the simplest comforts. They could seek truth, deliberate about justice, search for technical improvements and a better social order. They could cultivate a passionate love for truth and justice, a willingness to sacrifice their lives and their well-being for them, and a determination to preach the truth and put justice into practice.

The preaching of truth and justice spread from the convinced and understanding few to a small circle of people for whom cultivation was a pleasure. In this circle it found ready adherents, who were joined by believers from the protected minority. From time to time, through force or persuasion, the teachings of truth and justice were incorporated in law and custom. As the cultivated individuals, from an inner need, strove to realize justice in action and to disseminate truth, so the reasoning minority, for its own good, found it better to share a *portion* of the comforts of life with the majority and to expand somewhat the circle of the learned. I have already said that the stability of civilization hinges upon recognition of the need for such expansion.

But understanding was disseminated slowly. Petty calculation always induced them to give other people as few of the comforts of life as possible, and to restrict as much as possible the sphere of knowledge available to others. Reluctance to think induced them to see in all the new demands of the day something inimical to social order, something criminal and sinful, and for that reason the monopolizers of knowledge for the most part opposed the progress of knowledge by every means. [They chained their learning to traditional theories and authoritarian dogmas, fused it with sacred legend and supernatural revelation, and by so doing tried to render it inaccessible to further critical investigation. Subsequently, when learning was secularized and could no longer shelter its monopolizers under a screen of mystic sanctity, there arose coteries of official scholars with their distinctive mandarin buttons and their grandiloquent diplomas as Doctors, Professors, and Academicians. They, too, tried to save themselves further intellectual labor by carefully keeping their coteries tightly closed, by expelling from them and stifling the new forces which advanced the banner of scientific criticism too boldly. The monopolizers tried to make the *official* science a matter of custom and tradition, as the *sacred* science had been before. *Recognized* learning became too often an enemy of criticism and of scientific progress.]

The feebleness of this progress inevitably gave rise to a poor understanding of human dignity and the forms of justice. Hence the prolonged instability of civilizations. Hence also their constant tendency toward stagnation. Hence, finally, the extreme insignificance of human progress (mentioned in the previous letter), despite the fact that for a few great men in the course of thousands of years, and for the progress of a scarcely noticeable minority, there have been paid billions of lives, oceans of blood, incalculable sufferings, and the endless toil of generations.

Mankind has paid dearly so that a few thinkers sitting in their studies could discuss its progress. It has paid dearly for a few little colleges where it has trained its teachers—who to this day, however, have brought it little benefit. If one were to count the educated minority of our time and the number of people who have perished in the past in the struggle for its existence, and estimate the labor of the long line of generations who have toiled solely to sustain their lives and allow others to develop, and if one were to calculate how many human lives have been lost and what a wealth of labor has been spent for each individual now living a *somewhat* human life—if one were to do all this, no doubt some of our contemporaries would be horrified at the thought of the capital in blood and labor which has been lavished on their cultivation. What serves to soothe their sensitive consciences is that such a calculation is impossible.

Perhaps what ought to be horrifying, however, is not that the progress of the minority has been costly, but that it has been *so* costly and that for this price *so* little has been achieved. If the minority had troubled itself sooner and more diligently with disseminating the development achieved in the sphere of culture and thought, the quantity of wasted lives and labor would not be so great; the debt incurred by each of us would be smaller, and would not increase so enormously with each generation.

We have no power over the laws of natural necessity, and for this reason a reasonable person should accept them, limit himself to calm investigation of them, and as far as possible make use of them for his own ends. We have no power even over history; the past simply gives us facts, which [at times] may help us to improve the future. We are responsible for the sins of our fathers only to the extent that we continue these sins and profit by them, without attempting to rectify their consequences. We have power to some degree only over the future, since our thoughts and our actions are the material out of which the whole content of future truth and justice is created. Each generation is answerable to posterity only for what it *could have* done but did not do.

Thus in light of the verdict of posterity we, too, shall have to answer certain questions: How much of the evil contained in the process to which we give the high-sounding title of "historical progress" is unavoidable and natural? To what extent did our ancestors—who provided us, the civilized minority, with the chance to enjoy the advantages of this progress—needlessly increase and prolong the sufferings and toil of the majority which has never enjoyed the advantages of progress? In what instances may the responsibility for this evil fall also upon us, in the eyes of future generations?

The law of struggle for existence is so universal in the animal world that we have not the slightest ground for blaming primitive men when this law was applied among them, too, so long as a sense of mutual solidarity and the need for truth and justice had not awakened among them. Since a sense of solidarity could hardly have awakened so long as men, mutually exterminating one another, had not reached the point of substituting exploitation for murder, we must regard the whole long period of strife among individuals, [bands, clans, tribes, and nations] as simply a zoological fact.

As for the growth of knowledge and the development of a conception of right and duty, one can scarcely imagine it as at first anything but a process occurring in the few who were placed in particularly favorable circumstances—that is, in individuals who had leisure, the best food, and the best education at the expense of other individuals who furnished the former with these advantages through an increase in their labor, if not at the price of their own lives or considerable suffering. Before one can be taught, one must have teachers. The majority can develop only through the action upon it of a more cultivated minority. Thus, either mankind had to remain undeveloped, or the majority at first had to carry the more fortunate minority on its shoulders, work for it, suffer and die for it. This, too, would seem to be a law of nature.

Given this law, it remains for us either to say that we want no part of a development bought at such a price, or to regard this, too, as an anthropological fact. But since I have already included comprehensive development in the very formula of progress at the beginning of the previous letter, to repudiate development in general would be to fall into a contradiction. Let us, then, accept the fact that for his development it was necessary for man to provide himself, at a very, very high price, with the teachers' college and the more cultivated minority, so that the science and the diversified practical experience, the thinking and the techniques which accumulate at these centers would gradually spread to a greater and greater number of people.

The necessary, natural evil in progress is confined to the foregoing, and beyond the bounds of these laws begins the responsibility of human generations, more particularly of the civilized minority. All the blood which has been shed in history beyond the immediate struggle for existence, in the period of more or less clear recognition of man's right to life, is blood criminally shed and lying within the responsibility of the generation which shed it. Every civilized minority which was unwilling to be *civilizing*, in the broadest sense of this word, bears the responsibility for all the sufferings of its contemporaries and of posterity which it *could have* eliminated, had it not confined itself to the role of representative and custodian of civilization but assumed also the role of its motive force.

If from this standpoint we assess the panorama of history down to our own day, we shall no doubt have to acknowledge that every generation in history has shed rivers of blood even without having the justification of the struggle for existence, and that in almost all times and places the minority, while priding itself on its civilization, has done extremely little to disseminate it. A few individuals have troubled themselves with broadening the sphere of learning among men; a still smaller number, with strengthening thought and searching for more just forms of society; as for members of the civilized minority who have endeavored to convert such forms into fact, they are encountered in very small number.

Many brilliant civilizations have paid with their own destruction for this inability to link the interest of a greater number of individuals with their existence. In all civilizations without exception, the majority of those who have enjoyed the comforts of culture have never given a thought to all those who did not and could not enjoy them, much less to the price at which the acquired comforts of life and thought had been purchased.

There has always been quite a number of people, however, who at each stage of civilization have considered that stage the

limit of social development and have indignantly rebelled against
any critical attitude toward it, against any attempt to spread the
blessings of civilization to a greater number of persons, to diminish the toil and the suffering of the majority who do not enjoy it,
and to introduce more truth into thought and more justice into
social institutions. [These apostles of stagnation are terrified at the
thought that all history is an inexorable steeplechase in pursuit of
the better, where everyone who has lagged behind promptly
drops out of the circle of historical figures, disappears into the
mob of anonymous, dumbfounded spectators, and perishes in
animal insignificance.[2] Those incapable of such a race persuade
the others to stop also, to rest, to enjoy peace and quiet—as if this
were possible for a man who wishes to remain a man.] The apostles of stagnation have very rarely succeeded in erecting a complete barrier to social progress, but they have often succeeded in
retarding it and in increasing the sufferings of the majority.

In view of this, we must admit that the benefits of modern
civilization have been purchased not only with *unavoidable* evil
but moreover with an enormous quantity of absolutely *needless*
evil, the responsibility for which rests with preceding generations
of the civilized minority—partly because of its lack of concern,
and partly because of its direct opposition to every civilizing
endeavor. This evil in the past we can no longer correct. The
suffering generations of the majority have perished, their labor
unrelieved. The present civilized minority is profiting by their toil
and sufferings. More than that: it is profiting by the sufferings
and toil of a vast number of its contemporaries, and can contribute to an increase in the toil and sufferings of their grandchil-
dren.

Since for this last circumstance we have borne and shall bear
the moral responsibility before posterity, historical investigation
of the cost of the progress which has been made leads to the next
practical question: what resources does the present generation
have for lessening its responsibility? If living representatives of
the different levels of development were to ask themselves: what
must we do so as not to answer to posterity for the fresh sufferings of mankind? and if they all *clearly understood their tasks,*
the answers would, of course, be diverse.

A member of the majority who are fighting daily for physical existence, as their ancestors did in the earliest periods of the life of mankind, would say to himself: Fight, to the best of your knowledge and ability! Defend the right to life for yourself and for those you love! This was the law of your fathers, and your plight is no better than theirs. This is the only law for you, too.

A more unfortunate member of this same majority, in whom civilization has aroused a sense of his own human dignity but has gone no further, would say to himself: Fight, to the best of your knowledge and ability! Defend your own dignity and the dignity of others! Die for it, if necessary!

A member of the civilized minority who desires only to augment and ensure his own pleasure, but is inclined to seek it more in the sphere of material comforts than in the intellectual sphere, would say to himself: [You can find pleasure only in a society where some degree of solidarity reigns. Oppose, then, in yourself and in others, whatever is incompatible with this solidarity. You, too, suffer from the discord of contemporary society, when you realize that this discord is a social disease. Reduce, then, your own suffering by striving to improve the lot of the majority: what you sacrifice in present benefits with this aim will return to you in the knowledge that you have alleviated in some small measure the disease of society—a disease which brings suffering to you, too. So consult your own *true* interest: reduce the suffering around you and in yourself. This is what benefits you most.] [3]

A member of a small group within the minority, who finds pleasure in his own development, in the search for truth, and in the realization of justice, would say to himself: Each of the material comforts I enjoy, each thought which I have had the leisure to acquire or to develop, has been bought with the blood, suffering, or toil of millions. I cannot correct the past, and however high the cost of my cultivation I cannot repudiate it: it constitutes the very ideal which arouses me to action. Only a weak and uncultivated person collapses under his responsibilities and flees from evil to the Thebaid or to the grave. Evil must be corrected as much as possible, and this can be done only in life. Evil must be corrected *vitally*.[4] I shall relieve myself of responsibility for the bloody cost of my own development if I utilize this same development to diminish evil in the present and in the future. If I am a cultivated person I am obliged to do this, but for me this obligation is very light, since it coincides exactly with what constitutes pleasure for me: by seeking and disseminating greater truth, by coming to understand what social order is most just and striving to realize it, I am increasing my own pleasure and at the same time doing everything I can for the suffering majority in the present and in the future. And so my task is limited to one simple rule: live according to the ideal which you yourself have set up as the ideal of a *cultivated* man.

This would all be so easy and simple if every individual understood his task, but the trouble is precisely that very few understand it. The foregoing rules are followed only by a portion of those in the first category and by a few in the other categories. The remaining portion of those who are struggling for their physical existence do not defend themselves with sufficient energy—not because they lack the knowledge or ability to do so, but through lack of determination, through apathy. The majority of persons in the second category sacrifice their dignity for their daily bread and are abased in their own eyes—without, for all that, gaining the chance to escape from their predicament. The majority of persons in the third category fail to understand their own [true] interest; they follow routine and do not know how [to counteract, even in small measure, the social malady which brings suffering to each individual and consequently to themselves as well: that is, while they seek to avoid suffering, they do not know how to lessen in themselves the sufferings which flow from social discord.] [5] As for the majority of persons in the last category, either they set up idols in place of truth and justice, or they limit themselves to truth and justice in thought but not in life, or they do not want to see what an insignificant minority enjoy the advantages of the progress of civilization.

And the cost of this progress keeps mounting.

The Action of Individuals

MY LAST TWO LETTERS LEAD ultimately to one and the same conclusion. A society is threatened with stagnation if it stifles critically thinking individuals; a society's civilization, whatever its
merits, is threatened with destruction if it becomes the exclusive
property of a small minority. Consequently, however limited the
progress of mankind, what progress there is depends exclusively
upon the critically thinking individuals. Without them, it is absolutely impossible; without their firm desire to disseminate it, it is
extremely precarious. Since these individuals ordinarily assume
that they are entitled to be considered cultivated, and since it is
precisely for *their* cultivation that the terrible price discussed in
the last letter has been paid, it is upon them that the moral duty
to repay the cost of this progress is incumbent. This repayment,
as we have seen, consists in the greatest possible extension of
material comforts and of intellectual and moral development to
the majority, and in the introduction of scientific understanding
and of justice into social institutions.

Let us, then, consider for a moment these individuals who are
the sole instruments of human progress. Whatever its characteristics may be, it depends upon them. It will not spring from the
earth, like a weed. It will not propagate itself from germs wafted
in the air, like infusoria in a decomposing liquid. It will not suddenly appear among men as a result of the mystical ideas which
were discussed so much forty years ago and which many still discuss even now.[1] Its seed is in fact an idea, but not an idea mysti-
cally present in mankind: it is conceived and developed in the
brain of an individual, passes from there into the brains of other
individuals, grows qualitatively with the increase in the intellectual and moral stature of these individuals and quantitatively
with the increase in their number, and becomes a social force
when these individuals recognize their unity of thought and re-

solve upon united action; it triumphs when the individuals imbued with it have introduced it into social institutions.

If a person who talks about his love of progress is not willing to reflect critically on the conditions for its realization, then in reality he has never desired progress, and has never even been capable of desiring it sincerely. If a person who recognizes the conditions of progress waits passively for it to realize itself without any effort on his part, then he is the worst enemy of progress, the most detestable obstacle in its path. All those who complain about the corruption of the times, about the worthlessness of men, about stagnation and reaction, should be asked: and *you* yourselves, you with eyes among the blind, you who are healthy among the sick, what have *you* done to promote progress?

To this question most of them plead weakness, lack of talent, a limited sphere of influence, hostile circumstances, a hostile environment, hostile people, and so on. "How can we be important figures?" they say; "we haven't been sufficiently educated, we don't have the ability to write journal articles, the Lord did not endow us with prophetic eloquence, our positions (if we even have any) are insignificant, grandfather didn't leave us any capital, and what we can earn is barely enough to keep us from starving. If we had these things—capital, important positions, and talent—then we would prove our worth."

I am not referring to those who fight all their lives for a scrap of bread. I mentioned them in the last letter, and no accusation falls upon them. If progress has passed them by without allowing them to develop at all, then they are nothing but its victims. If intellectual development has brushed them, if an awareness of what is best has kindled in them a hatred of falsehood and evil, while circumstances have crushed every manifestation of this awareness and have confined their lives to preoccupation with their daily bread; if at the same time they have nevertheless preserved their human dignity, then by their example and by their existence they remain the most vigorous promoters of progress. In historical importance, the greatest figures in history are insignificant compared with these invisible heroes of humanity who have not performed a single striking deed. If the latter did not exist, the former could never have carried out a single one of their undertakings. The visible heroes fight for what is best, and often

even perish in the struggle; but at the same time, despite unfavorable circumstances, the invisible heroes sustain in society the
tradition of human dignity and the consciousness of what is best.
And when one of the great figures in a hundred succeeds in
putting his ideas into practice he suddenly finds around him a
group of stalwart men, hardened by toil and steadfast in their
convictions, who cheerfully offer him their hands. It is from these
invisible heroes that the ground for reform is created at every
great historic moment. They preserve within themselves the
whole potential of the future. In a society without them all historical progress would cease at once. Morally, the subsequent life
of such a society would differ in no respect from the life of other
social animals.

But these vigorous figures contain only the *potentiality* of
progress. Its actualization never is or can be their task, for a very
simple reason: each of them who set about bringing progress into
being would soon die of hunger or sacrifice his human dignity, in
either case vanishing from the progressive ranks. The actualization of progress belongs to those who have freed themselves from
their most oppressive concerns for their daily bread. But of these
latter, *anyone* who thinks critically can bring progress into being
among men.

Yes, anyone. Please do not say that you lack talent and learning. Neither special talent nor great learning is needed here. If
your talent and learning sufficed to give you a critical attitude
toward what exists around you and to make you aware of the
need for progress, then they will suffice to put this criticism and
this knowledge into practice. But do not miss a single opportunity which life actually presents. Suppose that your activity is
trifling: all substances consist of immeasurably small particles;
the most enormous forces are composed of infinitely small impulses. Neither you nor anyone else can estimate the quantity of
good your action will produce: it depends upon a thousand
different circumstances, upon a multitude of coincidences impossible to foresee. The best intentions have often had appalling
consequences, just as actions which at first glance seem unimportant have had countless ramifications.

But we can expect, with some degree of assurance, that by im-
parting the same direction to a whole series of actions we shall

obtain only a few contrary results, while at least some of the actions will coincide with conditions favorable to appreciable results in the direction intended. We, perhaps, shall never witness these results, but certainly they *will exist,* if we have done everything in our power. The farmer, having cultivated the soil and sown his seeds, knows that many of the seeds will die and that he can never completely protect the cornfield against cattle damage, crop failure, and nocturnal marauders; but even after a crop failure he returns to the field with another handful of seeds, expecting a future harvest. If everyone who thinks critically will constantly and actively strive for what is best, then however insignificant the sphere of his activity, however circumscribed the arena of his life, he will be an influential motive force of progress and will repay his share of the terrible cost of his development.

But is it true that some spheres of activity are important and others trivial? What fields entitle people to a monopoly on progressiveness? Does the man of letters really have such a monopoly? Does the artist? The scientist?

Look at this progressive litterateur, who writes so splendidly about the common good and still more artfully exploits his brothers, or by his own behavior delivers to his adversaries for desecration the ideas his writing seems to serve. And this is not to mention the various "dark legions" for whom literature is an instrument of the most appalling depreciation of thought and human dignity, an instrument of stagnation and social corruption.

Look at this progressive artist, who sings the praises of free speech though he is by no means averse to taking part in the institutions of censorship, and who, outside his studio, has never given a thought to what distinguishes an evil deed from a good one.[2] And this is not to mention all those—their name is legion—who have simply used some modest stepstool of poetic, musical, pictorial, sculptural, or architectural creations to climb their way to pensions, decorations, high ranks, and huge mansions.

Look at this progressive professor, who is prepared to fashion from his erudition artillery for whatever movement you please, depending upon the circumstances. And furthermore how numerous are the soulless arguing and experimenting automatons who spend their whole lives observing processes of chemical substitution and decomposition, cell growth and muscle contraction, the declensions and conjugations of Greek words, sound mutations in Sanskrit and Zend, and the distinctive features of the household utensils used in the days of Alexander Nevsky and Ivan the Terrible. These human appliances have never given a thought to the fact that their intellect and learning is a power paid for by the sufferings of generations—a power for which they, too, must pay. It has never occurred to them that this power imposes upon them a duty, and that argumentation and experimentation can reduce a man to the level of a spider, just as they can lift the scientist to the highest level of human dignity attainable in his time.

Neither literature, nor art, nor science constitutes salvation from immoral indifferentism. In themselves they neither contain nor create progress. They only provide the tools for it. They accumulate the force for it. But the only man of letters, artist, or scientist who is actually serving progress is one who has done everything he could to use the power he has acquired to disseminate and strengthen the civilization of his time; who has fought against evil; who has embodied his artistic ideals, scientific truths, philosophical ideas, and literary aspirations in works which pulsate with the full life of his time and in actions which are in strict accord with the dimensions of his power. He who has done less; he who through selfish calculation has stopped halfway; he who is so concerned with the beautiful head of a bacchante or interesting observations on infusoria or a vain controversy with a literary rival that he has forgotten the enormous quantity of evil and ignorance which must be combatted—such a person can be anything you please: a sensitive artist, an outstanding scientist, a brilliant writer; but he has struck his name from the roll of the conscious agents of historical progress. In moral significance, as a human being, he is inferior to the mediocre scribbler who all his life tirelessly repeats, to equally mediocre readers, old truths about the struggle against evil and ignorance. He is inferior to the half-educated teacher who ardently hammers half-understood knowledge into the heads of backward boys. These persons have done everything they knew how, everything they could; nothing more can be asked of them. If, out of hundreds of readers, one or two are a little more talented and a little more impressionable, and apply in life the truths they learned from the scribbler, then there was progress. If the teacher's ardor kindled, even in a small number of pupils, a desire to think and work a little on their own, a thirst for knowledge and for labor, again there was progress. And I am not saying how immeasurably inferior—for all their artistic talent, for all their scholarship, and for all their literary renown—are the aforementioned gentlemen in comparison with the completely invisible agents of progress discussed above, who preserve within themselves all potentiality of progress for the future.

I shall be told that I am unjust to both art and science. A beautiful work, even one which has not been given meaning by the artist himself, is nevertheless an augmentation of mankind's capital for development. Not to mention the other effects of art, it is ordinarily only through the beautiful that man rises from the world of petty triviality to the realm of truth and justice. A work of beauty sharpens attention, increases sensitivity, and consequently is in itself an instrument of progress, independent of the thought which animated the artist.

Similarly, every new known fact, however trifling and insignificant for vital contemporary problems, is an augmentation of the capital of human thought. Only by classifying and studying all the creatures of nature as they really are can man acquire the chance to classify and study them with respect to human welfare, according to their usefulness and harmfulness to the majority.

Today the addition of two or three previously unobserved beetles to his collection momentarily delights the entomologist. Later, however, the study of one of these beetles will give the technician a new means of reducing the price of some useful product, and thus in part also a means of increasing the material comforts of the majority. Later still, another of these beetles will become the starting point for a scientist's investigation into the laws [according to which the human race, too, has evolved from its zoological state, whence it inevitably conveys many regrettable survivals into its history; laws which show man that it is only by fighting for his own development that he can cultivate, along with the inevitable animal elements of his nature, that other element which has allowed him to be an agent of progress.] [3]

Today the linguist enthusiastically records some peculiarity of verb conjugation in an ancient language. Tomorrow this peculiarity will link several hitherto disparate languages. Later, this link will clarify a number of prehistoric myths. And suddenly it has become possible to trace the influence of these myths on the teachings of the Christian churches; [4] the majority's system of ideas has become more intelligible to the minority; and consequently it has become easier to find resources for progressive action that contributes to man's development.

Thus it will be said that in their works art and science are instruments of progress, regardless of the attitude and aim of the artist and the scientist, even against their wishes. Provided the work of art is truly artistic, provided the scientist's discovery is truly scientific—they already pertain to progress.

I had no intention of saying that art and science are not *instruments* of progress, that an artistic work and a scientific discovery, as *facts*, do not serve progress. Unquestionably, however, metals locked in the earth and silk being manufactured by a silk worm are also instruments of progress, facts which serve it.

The artist who has art alone in mind and has never thought about its humane influence can be a very great aesthetic force. What he produces may be beautiful; his influence may be vast and even highly beneficial. But in moral dignity his power is not superior to the power, admittedly enormous, which has scattered deposits of copper ore across the earth and imprisoned iron in swamps and lakes—and no one will question the usefulness of metals for human civilization. Aesthetic power, in itself, is a power in no way moral. It becomes a moral, civilizing, progressive force, independent of the artist, only in the brain of one who, inspired by a beautiful work, has been led to do good; in one who has become better, more sensitive, more cultivated, more vigorous, more active under the influence of an impression received from an artist's work—just as metal became a civilizing force only in the brain of him who devised the first useful implement from it. The artist, as an artist, is on a level with any mighty physical or organic process which has no humane significance. Both sound and the circulation of the blood serve as springs of thought, of desire for the good, and of determination to act, but they are neither thought, nor good, nor determination.

For the artist *himself* to be a civilizing force, he must *himself* put humanity into his works. He must cultivate within himself the source of progress and the determination to bring progress into being. He must set to work imbued with progressive ideas. And then, in creating, without doing violence to himself he will be a conscious historical agent, because for him, too, the demand for truth and justice will keep shining through the ideal of beauty which he is pursuing. He will not forget the fight against evil which is binding upon everyone, and all the more upon him since he is a repository of greater natural power.

The same may be said for the scientist. The accumulation of knowledge, in itself, has no greater moral significance than the accumulation of beeswax in a hive. But beeswax becomes an instrument of civilization in the hands of the beekeeper or the chemist. They are much indebted to the bees, take very good care of them, and realize that without the bees there would be no beeswax. Nevertheless bees are not human beings; they cannot be called moral agents of civilization, and their secretion of beeswax in accordance with an inner need is only the *material* of progress. The entomologist collecting beetles and the linguist recording conjugations, if they do so only for the inner pleasure they derive from contemplating a collection of beetles or knowing that a verb is conjugated thus and so, are not at all inferior—but on the other hand not superior, either—to the bee secreting his little lump of wax. If the lump falls into the hands of a pharmacist who turns it into a medicinal dressing, or into the hands of a chemist who with its help discovers a new general law, the lump will be part of the material of civilization. If it melts uselessly in the sun, the bee's labor is lost to progress. But in neither case did the bee have anything to do with the matter. The bee satisfied its need, transformed food into a lump of wax, carried the lump into its hive, as it is his nature to do, and then flew off for more food. Similarly, a known fact, too, becomes a tool of civilization in two ways only: first, in the brain of one who employs it in technology or in a general theory; second, in the brain of the same person who produces the scientific fact, if he does so not for the pleasure of contemplating it, like a new lump of wax, but with premeditated aim, as material, having in mind some technical application or some scientific and philosophical generalization.

Science and art are powerful instruments of progress. But, as I have already said at the beginning of this letter, progress is actualized only within individuals. Only individuals can be its motive forces. And in this regard the artist and the scientist, as individuals, not only can fail to be mighty motive forces of progress—they can, despite their talent and learning, stand completely aside from the march of progress, on a level with an unconscious metal or an animal, from which no one even expects morality. Other, *true* human beings, perhaps less talented and less learned, can humanize the material accumulated by the great artists and the great toilers of science, but they will humanize these labors through *their own* understanding. *They* will introduce these labors into historical progress.

I have purposely dwelled on science and art—the most potent elements of civilization—in order to show that even these spheres do not in themselves constitute progress; that further, neither talent nor learning in itself makes a person a motive force of progress; that in this regard it is possible to do more with less talent and learning, if you will do everything you can. Yes, I repeat: everyone who thinks critically and is determined to convert his ideas into reality can be a motive force of progress.

SIXTH LETTER

Culture and Thought

LET US SUPPOSE THAT AN INDIVIDUAL who thinks critically has become conscious of the fact that he can promote, and is obligated to promote, the progress of humanity. How, in the name of this consciousness, is he obliged to act in order to become a true agent of progress?

First of all, of course, he must look critically at *himself*—at his knowledge and his capacities. A field in which he lacks knowledge must either be studied or set aside. A task for which he lacks the capacity had best be avoided until he has acquired sufficient capacity to accomplish it. Not that an entire area of activity should thus be closed to anyone—but a person turning to this area must clearly pose and answer this question: what *precisely* can I accomplish here, given my knowledge and capacities? Only when this question has been answered can one reasonably set oneself some life task.

But in proceeding to this task the individual is confronted with several doctrines which seem mutually contradictory, and perhaps the reader who is familiar with Louis Blanc's well-known views on *individualism* and *sociality* [or *fraternity*], noting the great significance which I attach to the individual in history, has suspected the author of these letters of leaning toward individualism in just the sense attributed to that word by the [once] celebrated French socialist. I shall not dwell on this question at length, because I consider it a question more of words than of substance.

[Louis Blanc says that "individualism, considering man apart from society, . . . gives him an exaggerated sense of his rights without pointing out to him his duties, leaves him to his own devices, and in place of any government proclaims *laissez-faire*."* Later he says that individualism "leads to oppression through anarchy." Concerning "fraternity" we find in Louis Blanc more sonorous phrases than well-defined concepts, but from the ambition ascribed to that principle—"someday to organize society, which is the work of man, on the model of the human body, which is the work of God"—it is clear that, under the rule of the principle of fraternity, the individual is considered by Blanc to be just as subordinate to society as a particular unconscious organ of the human body is subordinate to the conscious human ego.] Individualism, as Louis Blanc understands it, is the urge to *subordinate* the general welfare to the personal, selfish interests of individuals. Sociality, from his point of view, is inclined to *absorb* the individual, in his particularity, into the interests of society.

But an individual only subordinates the interests of society to his own interests when he views society and himself as two principles which are *equally real* and have competing interests. Similarly, absorption of the individual by society can occur only given the idea that society can achieve its ends not in individuals but in something else. But these are both illusions. Society apart from individuals has no real content. The interests of the individual, clearly understood, demand that he strive to fulfill the common

Hist. de la révol. francaise, Paris, 1847; I, 9–10.

interests; social goals can be achieved exclusively in individuals. Thus a true social theory requires not the subordination of the social element to the individual and not the absorption of the individual by society but the *fusion* of social and particular interests. The individual must cultivate an understanding of *social* interests, which are also *his* interests. He must direct his activity toward bringing truth and justice into social institutions, because this is not some kind of abstract aspiration but is *his* most intimate personal interest. At this level individualism becomes the realization of the general welfare through individual strivings—but the general welfare simply cannot be realized in any other way. Sociality becomes the realization of individual goals within social life—but they simply cannot be realized in any other context.

Thus the individual's life task, if he is a critically thinking individual, does not set his interests against the interests of society. But perhaps it may be thought that each of these two complementary conditions of progress can be fulfilled separately. The development of the individual and the incorporation by him of truth and justice in social institutions can be mentally distinguished, and a problem arises which different thinkers have resolved in different ways. The questions which arise are these: Should a man labor chiefly for his own development, taking personal perfection as his goal regardless of the social institutions which surround him, and participating in social life only to the extent that its institutions fully satisfy his demands? Or should he direct his activity primarily toward producing, from the given social institutions, the best possible results now and in the future, even if the institutions within which he must act are extremely unsatisfactory and his activity is negligible?

Each solution, taken as exclusive, leads to the perversion of the individual and his activity. In creating his own moral ideals, the individual can never take into account all the historical circumstances of a society's life in all its fullness and variety, and thus his ideals always will and must be far in advance of the historical actuality. Consequently, in the majority of cases the individual would have reason to withdraw from social activity. The more highly developed and perfect he is, the sooner he would be obliged to do so, and to sit, idly and with futile irony, watching things take their regular course—that is, watching persons of in-

ferior moral cultivation direct them. Such self-perfection would
be tantamount to social indifferentism.

But it would also be self-contradictory. An individual who is
capable of indifferently disregarding social evil when he *could*, if
only in part, alleviate it, is incapable of cultivating in himself
anything more than *seeming* strength of thought, a scholastic and
utterly useless set of high-sounding maxims, or a mystical self-
exaltation divorced from everything real. Besides, if the individual's environment has allowed *him* to develop to the point of taking a critical attitude toward everything around him, then this
environment is not yet absolutely evil. Another can develop in it,
and a third, provided they are presented with the same conditions
—provided the most oppressive, stifling institutions within this
environment are overcome. Something better is possible in it, and
if the individual fails to see this, it means that he has not cultivated *himself* sufficiently, but only *thinks* himself cultivated.

In adapting oneself fully to given social institutions, however, it
is easy to pass imperceptibly to complete submission to them. In
contenting oneself with ever-diminishing returns from one's activity, one may finally be content with no returns at all. Then the
public figure descends to the highly unenviable level of the squir-
rel running circles on a treadwheel or the tribune delivering a
fiery speech in an empty chamber. Having given up the demand
for a personal dignity which consists in refusing to descend beneath a certain level in his activity, the individual not only renounces self-perfection, he also renounces the capacity to judge
whether he brings society benefit or harm, whether his life in society is productive or parasitic.

The two conditions stated above are inseparably bound together. The individual cannot develop in a comprehensive manner except through critical examination of reality. Critical examination of the real world—nature—shows man the absolute limits
of his own and others' action, the inescapable laws against which
it is absurd to rebel. Critical examination of past reality—history
—permits him to assess the terrain on which he and all his contemporaries inevitably stand, a terrain which admits of reworking, but only on the condition that it is taken into account *just as
it is*. Critical examination of social reality teaches man to distinguish people with an independent yearning for progress from

people who live by the ideas of others and from proponents of reaction, teaches him to distinguish major evil from minor, and today's problem from the problem which may be postponed until tomorrow. Critical examination of his real self permits man to weigh his abilities and to determine his course of action without self-disparagement and without arrogance. But all these forms of criticism are nothing other than the development of one's own individuality. At the same time, they are impossible or illusory unless the individual takes the most vital part in the problems and discomforts of society, unless his critical inquiry is simply a prelude to useful action.

On the other hand, social action has human significance only when the individual is cultivating himself, only when he is constantly surveying himself, his capacities, his knowledge, his convictions, and his skill and determination in defending these convictions. In action, capacities are exercised and increased; experience of life and of life's problems increases knowledge; through struggle, conviction and the capacity to defend it are strengthened. The sense of taking a part in social affairs is in itself a factor which heightens and engenders development. As an individual can develop normally only in interaction with social life, so fruitful social action can take place only when the individuals who participate in it are cultivating themselves.

This very fact establishes a limit which the individual cannot overstep in taking part in social life without abandoning his dignity. Where there is still a chance to revitalize and raise the level of social interests, where there is still hope of humanizing the mechanism of life, awakening thought, strengthening conviction, and arousing hatred and aversion toward customary evil—there the individual can and must take his stand with the agents of social progress. But suppose he has found that vulgar banality has spun a web around him which it is not within the power of a single individual to break. Suppose that, while a man needs the cooperation of others in order to act, these others live as parasites on the body of society, without ever giving a thought to its needs. Suppose that red tape, formalism, and servility have crushed within officialdom every thought of the welfare of the state. Suppose that the military man, in his concern for straight ranks and correct tempo at drills and parades, has completely forgotten that he is a human being and a citizen. Suppose that the social assembly is deaf to everything but personal animosity, personal connections, and ant-heap interests. Suppose that evil is increasing in society, while cowardice and baseness ignore it or slavishly applaud it. Then there is nothing for the rational, conscientious, but powerless individual to do but step aside from this slough—when he can. His powers being insufficient to halt social evil even in the smallest degree, he can at least refrain from using them to prolong and increase it.

Surrounded by social stupefaction, he will join with those invisible custodians of the tradition of progress of whom I spoke in the previous letter. Perhaps a moment will come when he *can* take part in social life. If it does not come, he will transmit to the next generation the tradition of truth and justice which for him existed only in the realm of consciousness, and which he could not actualize or did not know how to actualize. In such a case, even the fact that he did not bow to the universal evil, did not become its tool, constitutes a service. Someone else, with better understanding, with greater energy and greater ability, perhaps would have found a way to be a positive agent of progress even here—would have found a way to fight, and if he did not triumph would at least have given others an example of struggle. Not all have equal powers. Sometimes even those who, having developed in a particular age under particular conditions, can *avoid* the universal evil, can adopt a critical attitude toward it and shield themselves from it in their private lives, are exceptional individuals.

But the moment it becomes possible to act, the moment there are signs of struggle and life in society, a cultivated person has no right to shun the fight. However distasteful it may be to seek a road amid pools of filth, a road must be sought. However exhausting it may be to push one's way through crowds of semihuman creatures to find the one or two in a hundred who can be awakened to new life, the latter must be found.

One can see in advance that there will be many failures. In the majority of cases even the people who *seem* open to fresh ideas will yield to cowardice or petty motives, will chase after a fat sop, or will sacrifice action for a high-sounding word. Many will lag behind; many will be routed; a still greater number will abandon the banner through personal differences, sometimes in the very thick of battle. [Men who have preached progressive ideas and the need to fight relentlessly for them, once they have seen these ideas at work in their harsh real setting, will be frightened by the very thing that was so beautiful, mild, and inoffensive on paper. They will repudiate their past and their former brothers in thought and followers, and will become ludicrous and solitary maunderers, colorless and cowardly nonentities. There will be those, too, who openly and brazenly betray their own past for the sake of personal interests.] The very odds of the struggle will change, and when the ranks of the defenders of progress seem most impenetrable and most invincible, it may suddenly appear that this is an illusion—that crushing two or three of the leading figures is sufficient to make these pseudo knights of progress take to hiding, betray the banner, or renounce it.

All this is, of course, highly repugnant and shocking. But if the champions of progress had only to triumph, their task would be far too easy. To succeed in the struggle it is necessary to operate within the environment provided for every historical process in the present. One must arm oneself with the weapons most convenient in *this* environment and most suitable for precisely the kind of fight confronting one in the present. Only he who knows himself to be powerless has the right to step aside. He who feels or imagines that he has strength has no moral right to waste it in a petty, private sphere of activity when there is any chance of broadening this sphere. The cultivated person, in proportion to the broadening of his own cultivation, must compensate mankind for the still greater sum which it has spent on that cultivation. Thus he is morally obliged to choose as broad a sphere of social activity as is open to him.

Hence it becomes necessary to determine which elements, in the complex system of society, constitute the *ground* to be acted upon and which constitute *instruments* of action. Where is the more or less tinseled but in itself dead form, and where is the living strength?

Needs give rise to the processes of the organic world, the growth of vegetation, the reproduction of animals. They constitute one of the most important topics of physiology, human psychology, and sociology, and they also constitute the inescapable starting point for the explanation of every historical phenomenon. [Wherever there is an act of will, there is a need at the basis of the act; thus all the elements of historical phenomena can be reduced to the various needs of individuals.] Needs are facts common to all men, but the diversity in the physiological and psychological characteristics of individuals has as its consequence a diversity in the inclinations which needs generate. [Here one can already point to a distinction beween two classes of needs.

[Some needs, common to all living beings, give rise to unconscious or barely conscious reflex action and to the elementary techniques of adaptation to the environment. They produce the various instincts of the animal world. In human society they give rise to all the actions we call *habits;* to everything in the life of man that belongs to tradition; to everything he does mechanically, giving no consideration or very little consideration to why he acts *thus* and not otherwise; to everything for which he can give only some such explanation as: "I am used to this," or "that is how it is done," "it has always been done that way," "it is accepted," and so on. I have already said that these physiological and habitual needs unite all the classes of the animal world, and do not in any way distinguish man from other vertebrates or from invertebrates. In fact the latter subkingdom presents the most striking examples of their manifestation—namely, the societies of ants, bees, and other creatures closely related to them.]

These needs constitute the most solid, if it may be so expressed, and the most naturalistic element in the life of societies. They provide the unalterable economic and statistical laws and the reciprocal determination between the physical conditions of a country and its civilization which underlie human history. They give rise to the first technology and hence to the first science. It is under their influence that human beings, [like other animals,] are first drawn together.[1] Social life, issuing from this source, is already a *cultured* life; and man, inconceivable without needs, is by the same token inconceivable without some sort of culture. Just as do certain of his fellows from the world of insects and vertebrates, man belongs to the class of cultured animals.

[With the first individualized inclinations a second group of needs makes its appearance in the organic world—needs which are more complex, more diverse, and less common. They are observed in anything like determinate form only in the higher classes of vertebrates (among birds and mammals), and even here they are developed fully only in certain families, genera, and species. They are expressed in *choice* which seems to be voluntary, in various feelings of attachment and aversion which cannot be reduced to a need shared by all, in the variability of inclinations, which range under quite similar circumstances from complete indifference to an uncontrollable passion which makes the individual forget self-preservation, drowns out all other needs, generates sometimes completely reckless and sometimes cunningly calculated action, and manifests itself in man as heroism or as crime.

[This second group of *affective* needs plays a large role in the private biographies of individuals but a very negligible one in the over-all history of mankind. The brevity of the life of individuals prevents them, even when they occupy very influential positions, from leaving any very appreciable traces of their affective states in the life of society—especially since affective states by their very nature vary from individual to individual, and, for the most part, in the diversity of the affective states of coexisting individuals these influences cancel out.

[Physiological and habitual needs would reduce every culture to the perpetually repeated forms of the beehive or the ant heap. Affective needs would give rise to personal dramas, but could not create history. History takes place only under the influence of the work of *thought*. It is engendered by yet a new type of needs, observed only in man, and there only in the small groups of individuals for whom the sufferings of generations have produced exceptional cultivation. These are the progressive, historical needs, the needs of *development*.]

The first technology and the first calculation of utility are already products of *thought*, and the culture of societies becomes diversified as their thought develops. Under the influence of its operation needs multiply and inclinations change; [calculation gives rise to a series of expedient actions which push immediate inclinations aside. The inclinations themselves, in the form of desires and passions, become the springs of activity calculated to provide the best satisfaction of the desire. Finally there comes a moment when the critical work of thought is directed not to the *satisfaction* of an immediate inclination but to the inclination itself. Then thought compares inclinations and arranges them in order of the *worth* they prove to have when examined critically. On the other hand, thought itself becomes a favored objective and arouses a desire; the satisfaction of this desire becomes a new, purely human, higher need. The actual cultivation of thought—thought as an absorbing goal, as the sought-for truth, as a desirable moral good—becomes a need for a cultivated individual.

[Under the unceasing work of critical thought, on behalf of *development* in general as the end, all] needs and inclinations are arranged in various perspectives, as better and worse inclinations, as higher and lower needs. There arises a need for truth and justice, independent of utility.[2] The beginnings of science and art are created. There arises a need to set ideals of life for oneself and to realize them through a moral life. Man becomes capable of resisting his inclinations and needs and of giving himself up whole-heartedly to an idea, a notion, a life goal—sometimes to an illusion—sacrificing everything to them, and [often] without it even occurring to him to submit them to critical examination.[3] As soon as thought's work on the cultural terrain has leavened social life with the demands of science, art, and morality, then culture has been transformed into civilization and human history has begun.

The results of the intellectual labors of one generation are not confined to the sphere of thought for succeeding generations. They become habits of life, social traditions. For people who have received them in this form their origin is a matter of indifference; the most profound thought, repeated habitually or in accordance with tradition, is no higher phenomenon for mankind than the customary actions of the beaver and the bee are for beavers and bees. The invention of the first ax and the first baked clay pot was an enormous labor of [elementary technical] thought, but today man uses axes and baked clay no more consciously than a bird builds its nest. The first Protestants, shunning the gaudy pomp of the Catholic churches and gathering around their preachers, were acting under the influence of fully conscious thought; but their present-day descendants, for the most part, go to one church rather than another for the Sunday sermon simply

because their fathers and grandfathers went to the same church
and heard the very same sermons, just as a migrating stork lights
on the same roof it lighted on the year before.

The same phenomenon is repeated even in the highest region
of human thought. Today's teachers and students repeat the ideas
of Archimedes on the laws of equilibrium and the lever, the ideas
of Newton on universal gravitation, the ideas of Proust on the law
of chemical proportions, the ideas of Adam Smith on the law of
supply and demand. But far more often this is done in accordance with the pedagogical tradition that things have been
taught this way, are being taught this way, and must be taught
this way, rather than in accordance with a living, spontaneous intellectual need which inevitably leads man at a given moment to
a given question and calls for precisely this answer and no other.
Presumably beavers, too, fell trees, bark them, float them, and
erect their dams and lodges in consequence of a similar pedagogical and technological tradition.

Generally speaking the ancestors' contribution to civilization, in
the form of customs and traditions, is nothing but a [zoological,]
cultural element in the life of the descendants. This second-order
[customary] culture must be operated upon critically by the
thought of the new generation so that society will not sink into
stagnation—so that among the customs and traditions which it
has inherited it will discern those which present an opportunity
for the further work of thought on the path of truth, beauty, and
justice, will discard the rest as obsolete, and will create a new civilization—a new system of culture, revitalized by the work of
thought.

And in each generation the same process is repeated. From nature and from history man receives a complex of needs and inclinations which are in large measure determined by cultural customs and traditions. He satisfies these needs and inclinations
through the ordinary usages of life and through inherited social
institutions, craftsmanship, and routine technology. All this constitutes his culture, or the zoological element in the life of mankind.

But among the inherited customs of every civilization is the
custom of critical inquiry—and it is this which gives rise to the
humane element in history—[to the *need for development*, and,

in the light of this need,] to the *work of thought*. Scientific criticism introduces more truth into world views; moral criticism extends the application of science and justice in life; aesthetic criticism promotes a fuller grasp of truth and justice, gives life more harmony and culture more humane refinement. To the extent that culture principles prevail in a society and the work of thought is stifled, to that extent the society, however brilliant its culture, is approaching the social order of ants and wasps; it is nothing more than a difference in degree, a difference in the form of the needs and inclinations. To the extent that the work of thought—the critical attitude toward one's culture—is vigorous in a society, to that extent the society is more humane and further distinguishes itself from the world of the lower animals, even if the strife engendered by the work of thought—by the critical examination of what exists—has melancholy scenes as its specific consequence, [has recourse to the weapons of social or intellectual revolution, and disturbs the public order and tranquillity.] [4]

Very often it is only through temporary agitation and disorder, [only through revolution,] that one can buy a better guarantee of order and tranquillity for the majority in the future. When Thrasybulus and the Athenian exiles appeared in Athens to stir up their native land against the oligarchy of the Thirty Tyrants, of course they created agitation and disorder. When the humanists of the fifteenth century and the realists of the eighteenth century waged war upon the scholastics, they created extraordinary agitation in the schools and terrible disorder in minds. When the English colonies of North America detached themselves from the mother country, it was an out-and-out rebellion. When Garibaldi and his thousand landed on the shores of Sicily, no respect for order was in evidence. When Darwin overthrew the idol of fixed species, he upset botanical and zoological classifications and destroyed their foundation. But, for the freedom of Athens, for modern European science, for the political ideal of the North American republic, for the overthrow of the Neapolitan Bourbons, and for a majestic generalization of the evolution of the organic world, a certain disorder and agitation were a price well worth paying.

A society's culture is the environment which history has provided for the work of thought, and this environment determines what is *possible* for that work in a given age just as inevitably as the immutable laws of nature set its limits in all ages. Thought is the only factor which *humanizes* social culture. The history of thought, conditioned by culture, in connection with the history of culture as it changes under the influence of thought—this is the entire history of civilization. The only events which can enter into the rational history of mankind are those which elucidate the history of culture and thought in their interaction.

Needs and inclinations are given by nature or engendered by culture, and they give rise to social institutions. To introduce truth and justice into these social institutions is the task of thought. What *nature* has contributed to social institutions, thought cannot alter and must simply take into account. Thought cannot relieve man of the need for food and air, cannot abolish sexual attraction, cannot arrange things so that children will not exist along with adults, cannot change the process of its own dissemination in such a way that the individual will cease to be its necessary organ. But everything which *culture* has introduced into social institutions is subject to the critical examination of thought. In the work of thought culture must be taken into account as the historically given environment, but not as an unalterable law. If we compare the cultures of different ages we can easily observe the extent to which the most basic elements of culture are liable to alteration. Nevertheless, for those who lived during the age of the ascendancy of a given culture this culture formed the environment within which each individual had to act, with no chance of exchanging this environment for a different one. Natural needs and inclinations, under the influence of the critical activity of thought, must forge for themselves social institutions which contain the greatest quantity of truth and justice that the given status of the culture will permit.

Thus, before us is the specific task of progress: *culture* must be reworked by *thought*. Before us, too, is the specific and the only real agent of progress: the individual who defines his abilities and the work which he can do. Thought is real only in the individual. Culture is real in social institutions. Consequently the *individual* with his capacities and demands stands face to face with *social institutions*.

Individuals and Social Institutions

LET US SUPPOSE THAT THE INDIVIDUAL has resolved the most momentous of his vital questions: he has weighed his capacities and defined his task.

Before him are various social institutions. There may be cases in which these institutions, by their nature and breadth, are in conformity with his convictions concerning truth and justice. Then he is indeed fortunate: he may act within these institutions without struggling against them and without being confined by them. He is fortunate—but in this case he has no reason to consider himself an *agent* of progress. As a critically thinking individual he is in no way superior, as far as his usefulness is concerned, to other individuals who do not think critically. All of them are borne on the tide of progress, and obey its movement. He simply has a better *awareness* of what is happening.

But this is a tale of Scheherazade! Where and when have all social institutions satisfied the demands of science and justice, even in a very limited way? If an individual sees nothing but goodness, happiness, and rationality everywhere around him, he may be sure that there is much he has not thought out critically, much he has overlooked through inattention or a congenital moral myopia. He lacks the determination or the capacity to become in full measure a critically thinking individual.

He who thinks critically persists in seeking not the pleasure of contemplating existing good, but the limits beyond which this good ends and evil begins, as hostile opposition to progress or as banality and routine. Let all those who have not cultivated their individuality take pleasure in fine company, insofar as this company is fine; in the various cozy nooks of social life, insofar as these nooks are cozy; in life's various gay revels, insofar as these revels are gay. People who are not individuals cannot do otherwise: for them independent struggle is impossible.

But a man who thinks critically explores the depths of the thoughts and actions of fine people, to find out where each ceases to be fine and to appraise him by reference to his faults and virtues considered together. One may boldly be shown his weaknesses, in the hope that he himself will see them, understand them, and correct them. Another, who is weary and dispirited, may be encouraged and given new energy for further and more rapid advance. A third, who is straying from the path, may be redirected to his former course of action. A fourth, who is incapable of ridding himself of what partially debilitates him but who directs all his remaining energy to the promotion of progress, may be forgiven his weaknesses on the strength of his deeds. A fifth may resolutely be unmasked and his shallowness or opposition to progress exposed. But all this requires study, *especially* study of the evil in a man, his weaknesses as well as his strengths, his shallow sides still more than his shining virtues.

Similarly, critical thinking rests only for a moment in the cozy nooks and quiet sanctuaries of life. A dutiful wife and affectionate children, a secure existence and a prominent position, unimpeachable accounts and a stainless conscience, the vast erudition and renown of the scholar, the unquestionable talent of the artist plus a good fee for his creations—all this is fine, all these things are good, but this is all merely the *mechanism* of a cultured human life. Within this gay protective shell with its eternal bustle a man may spend his entire life not as a human being but as a reasoning ant, contributing only to the repetition, year after year and generation after generation, of fathers and mothers begetting children, capitalists spending their profits, officials turning over their duties to other officials, scholars writing dissertations, and artists titillating aesthetic tastes.

A human ant heap becomes a society of human beings only when critical thought, with its relentless inquiries, begins to disturb the tranquil bliss or sleepy routine of the cozy nooks. Faithful couple, do you really love each other sincerely, humanly, consciously? Are you really *cultivating* your children rather than simply begetting them? Successful speculator, have you really earned your capital and your position? Honored official, have you really worked for the good of society? Scholar with your many publications, have you really advanced science? Artist, have you really created aesthetic works for the present day? Do all these artistic forms in which you drape yourself, in which as something sacred you take refuge, on which you feed, and in the elaboration of which your whole life has been spent—do these forms, as they are and in what you have made them, really have rational human content? Do not truth and justice require them to be *different?* Must they not be combatted in order to be revitalized? Are they not idols, in which you worship your own conventionality, your own fear of thinking, your own egoism, in the narrow meaning of this word? Must not these idols be cast down, to be replaced by what is truly sacred?

But here I sense objections arising from all sides. What! An individual—a solitary, insignificant, powerless individual— presumes to criticize social institutions forged by the history of nations, by the history of mankind! An individual thinks he has the right and the power to overthrow as idols what all the rest of society considers sacred! That is *criminal,* because as against the mass the individual has no rights. It is *pernicious,* because the happiness of the mass of people who are satisfied with social insti- tutions is more important than the sufferings of the individual who rejects them as evil. It is *absurd,* because the long line of generations which have produced the existing social institutions is in sum more intelligent than any separate individual. It is *foolish,* because the individual is powerless before society and its history. Let us examine these objections in turn.

First, as to rights. Either there is no progress, or it is the incor- poration in social institutions of a consciousness of falsehood and injustice. I find truth and justice in institutions which are different from those now existing, I point to the falsehood and injustice in what exists, and I wish to combat this falsehood and injustice of which I am aware. Where is the right which denies *my* right to do this? In other living individuals? But let them prove to me that I am mistaken; let them argue against me; let them fight me— that is *their* right, which I am not disputing. But *I,* too, have the right to prove to them that they are mistaken, to argue against them and to fight them. In society as a whole? But that is an ab- straction, and an abstraction has absolutely no rights as against me, a real being; and in its real content it resolves itself into indi- viduals who have no greater rights than I. In history? But again the entire real content of history consists in the actions of individuals. Of these individuals some are dead, and as against me, a living being, the dead have no rights. The others are living and have no more rights than I. Thus no one can deprive me of the *right* to fight for truth and justice, unless *I* deprive myself of it in view of the *harm* which may issue from my activity; in view of mistrust of my personal *reason* as against the historical reason of society; or in view of my *impotence* as against the enormous power of organized society. The individual has already won the first point; three remain.

What *harm* can come from my showing society the falsehood and injustice in its institutions and striving to actualize truth and justice? If I speak and no one listens, if my actions are unsuccessful, it is I alone who suffers. If I am heeded, and society is organized with greater truth and justice, this is not harm but benefit, because truth and justice in social institutions is the condition of the greatest pleasure for individuals and the extension of pleasure to the greatest number of individuals.

Of course, if one part of society heeds me and sides with me while another opposes me, a struggle will commence which for a time will disturb the tranquillity of all those who have been enjoying the comforts of the social order. Some will no longer find pleasure because they are haunted now by the knowledge that their pleasure is a function of unjust social institutions. Others will no longer find pleasure because they are hampered by their enemies, and still more by the fear that their prosperity is about to end. I do not deny that this is an unpleasant situation for all who enjoy the comforts of a given civilization. But can it unconditionally be called harmful? Hardly. In the preceding letter a few examples were given of the beneficial consequences which sometimes flow from introducing a certain disorder into established life. I have already said in the Third and Fourth letters that up till now only a very small minority have enjoyed the comforts of progress; that for the development of this minority a price has been paid which proved impossible even to calculate; that this price can be repaid only by striving to disseminate truth and embody greater justice in society. If this is so, then to fight for such embodiment not only is not harmful—it is the only way to make the existing civilization more durable.

The majority have suffered in all ages; thus pain is not something unprecedented in mankind. We must simply strive to make the pain less useless for history, and what sort of pain could be more useful than that which leads to the incarnation of truth and justice? In the first place, if the fortunate persons who enjoy the comforts of the existing civilization pay for this enjoyment with a certain amount of pain, they are not thereby repaying even a small portion of what preceding millions have endured for them. In the second place, if we are calculating harm, we must remember that history does not end with the present generation but that other generations will follow, and that the absolute quantity of harm brought by any action is measured by the sum of the increments of evil which follow from this action for the entire future. If I succeed in actually promoting the embodiment of greater truth and justice in social institutions, the quantity of evil will be diminished for the long line of succeeding generations which will profit by the amount of good thus introduced into life. If I decline to do this, their pain will increase—although in contemporary society (or to be more exact, in the minority which enjoys the comforts of the contemporary social order) there will be somewhat less pain. But as a matter of fact even this is questionable, since to the extent that there is less truth and justice in society there is more pain in it for some and an abasement of dignity for others.

Thus on one side there is indisputable harm for a more or less long line of generations; on the other, a doubtful advantage for the present generation. Can there really be any question as to which side should gain the decision? And is there really anything objectionable in it? Suppose a few people have come to realize that an institution which yesterday they accepted as just is not in fact just, and that no cultivated person can take pleasure in it. Can this unpleasant consciousness of error be an evil? Suppose a social ant heap has taken the first step toward becoming a human society. Can the humanization of men be an evil?

Thus the value of fighting for truth and justice is in any case unquestionable, provided it is a matter of genuine truth and justice and provided success is possible. I acknowledge the harmfulness of struggling, and consequently can forfeit the right to struggle, only when I doubt my *understanding* of truth and justice or am convinced that I am *powerless* to realize my convictions.

The individual has gained two points; let us turn to the third. Let us see to what extent the struggle of an individual against social institutions can be considered *absurd*.

An individual, after critically analyzing his knowledge and his intellectual abilities, has supplemented his knowledge in a particular field, has directed his thinking to this field, and has arrived at a definite conviction. This conviction proves to conflict with some historically produced institution. Thereupon he is told: resign yourself, because opposing you are the national spirit, the experience of the human race, the reason in history. Are these arguments sufficient ground for the individual to renounce his conviction as *absurd?*

What is the national spirit? To a series of generations living under the influence of a certain environment, the physical features of this environment have imparted an *inevitable* natural basis of nationality. The small minority within this nation who have lived historically have created for it a culture, which has been disseminated in varying degrees and forms to the different strata of the people, and, in all its diversity, has come to constitute national custom and tradition. From time to time individuals have appeared who were in a position to influence the minority, and through them the majority as well. These individuals have introduced new thought into the old cultural forms or have altered certain cultural forms in the name of a new culture—sometimes, indeed, have effected these alterations on the basis of new thought. At each moment in its history, a nation's life is the product of these three elements: natural necessity, historical custom, and individual thought. Their combination has formed and now forms the national spirit. In this combination, only what is physically and climatically conditioned is inevitable. All the rest is custom, constantly changing under the influence of the thought and actions of individuals.

If individuals think and act little, custom remains unaltered through a long line of generations; the culture retains its characteristic features; the civilization sinks further and further into stagnation; the national spirit assumes more and more determinate forms, which can be described almost as one describes the ways of animals. If, on the other hand, individuals are active, and if their thinking is not restricted to the narrow circle of the minority but tends to penetrate to the majority as well, then customs scarcely have time to become established; the culture changes rapidly in the minority and the changes spread somewhat more slowly to the majority; the civilization is more in danger of becoming unstable than of ossifying. It is then extremely difficult to define the national spirit, and for the most part the writers who discuss it fail to understand one another. As a result of the more rapid cultural changes in the minority and their slower diffusion in the majority, several strata of historical, customary culture are no doubt present in a society, on a common foundation of natural necessity. According to his own level of development, a writer assigns the national spirit to the stratum which most appeals to him, and sees the true history of the nation in one or another model age.

Ask the French: where is the model France, which expresses the true national spirit? [After the fall of all the monarchies (whether legitimate, elective, or usurped by force), after the shameful fall of Caesarism, after so many attempts at republics, which were drowned in blood or sold out by their official defenders who betrayed them—after all this you will still find in literature, in society, and in the present sovereign chamber representatives of all parties, who will argue that the *true* France and the true national spirit were embodied in the history of precisely that period whose tradition they are sustaining.] One will point to the *ancien régime* and Louis XIV with his [ardent Catholicism, his] Racines and Boileaus; another to 1789 with its "rights of man"; a third to Robespierre [or to Babeuf]; a fourth to the Little Corporal; a fifth to the tumultuous period of parliamentarianism under Louis Phillippe; a sixth [is not ashamed even now to point] to the age of "tranquillity, [riches,] and glory" under the aegis of the Second Empire; and there are even those who go back to Saint Louis and the Inquisition. And all will advance arguments to prove that *this* is the age of the *true* national spirit of France.

Ask our fellow countrymen: where is the true national spirit of Russia? Some will point to the Moscow of Ivan the Terrible with its *Stoglav* and *Domostroy;* some to Novgorod with its *veche* bell; some to Vladimir I and the mythical Svyatogor; or else they will begin to enumerate Peter the Great, Catherine the Great, and Speransky with his reforms.[1] Some will stop at 1854, some at 1861, some at 1863, [some even at 1889].[2] And all will argue; all will contend that here is captured, divined, embodied in myth, in mode of life, in ukase, or in lay the true Russian national spirit.

Which of them is right? Where did the development of the Russian national spirit stop? At the prehistoric Slavic way of life? At the level of Byzantine culture? At the level of Petrine civilization and bureaucracy? Or can this spirit, while retaining its identity, continue to accommodate newer and newer elements?

If some think not, then permit another individual, given the variety of opinions, to take the latter view and to act in accordance with this conviction. Permit him to think that the spirit of a nation has a somewhat greater capacity to assimilate new elements than have the animal species of oxen and hyenas. Amid the endless variety of conceptions of the national spirit—or, more exactly, conceptions of what is truest and most just for a particular nation—permit the critically thinking individual to express and implement *his* opinion about truth and justice, in the hope that it, too, can become an element in the national spirit, to the same extent as the multitude of forces which have become part of it previously. Why should the author of the *Domostroy* have more right than I to express the national spirit? Why can one decree introduce a new vital element into this spirit while another cannot?

The only judge of this is the critical investigation of history, of the national spirit, of truth, of justice. But this critical investigation can and does take place only in the individual. It is on behalf of the national spirit itself—but a humanly developing rather than a zoologically invariant spirit—that the individual must subject the national spirit to critical examination, must discern what within it is an element of natural necessity, to what extent the cultural elements within it are unchangeable at the moment, and which among them can be reworked from the standpoint of a more exact truth and a broader conception of justice. The national spirit in a given age is the spirit of the critically thinking individuals of that age, who understand the history of the nation and desire to introduce into its present as much truth and justice as possible.

Similarly, "the experience of the human race" is nothing but the understanding of its history by these same critically thinking and determined (*energicheski zhelayushchiye*) individuals.

As for "the reason in history," it is no more than a word, a vision for dreamers, or a bugbear for cowards if this reason is anything other than the following formula: the majority have always submitted to necessity; the minority have always sought to enjoy themselves; a few individuals have desired to understand truth and justice and to translate them into reality. The individual who clearly understands the past and is determined to implement truth and justice is, by his very nature, the rightful judge of the true experience of the human race and the rightful interpreter of the true reason in history.

And thus, if a man has found within himself a clear understanding of the past and an active desire for truth and justice, he cannot and must not renounce, in the face of the historical institutions of society, the convictions which he has developed, for *reason, utility,* and *right* are on his side. He must only weigh his *strength* for the impending struggle, conserve the strength he has, increase it as much as he can, judge what is possible and attainable, calculate his actions, and then decide. And thus only one point remains.

For an individual to struggle against social institutions protected by custom, tradition, law, social organization, physical force, and a moral halo is said to be *foolish.* What can one individual accomplish against a mass of men firmly united, when many of them are just as strong separately as this solitary, struggling individual?

But how has history proceeded? Who has moved it? Solitary, struggling individuals. How have they accomplished this? They have had to become and did become a *force.* Consequently, the fourth point requires a more complex answer. In the face of social institutions the individual is indeed powerless, but his struggle against them is only foolish if he cannot become a force. But history shows that it is *possible* for him to become a force, and that moreover this is the *only* way in which progress has been brought about in history. Thus we must pose and answer this question: *how* can feeble individuals transform themselves into a social force?

The Growing Social Force

"THE VOICE OF ONE MAN IS THE VOICE OF NO ONE," says an ancient proverb, and the individual who confronts society with a critique of social institutions and a desire to infuse them with justice is, of course, as a powerless unit, insignificant. Yet such individuals, by becoming a force which sets society in motion, have created history. How have they accomplished this?

First of all, it must be acknowledged that if the person in question is really a critically thinking individual, he is never alone. In what does his critique of social institutions consist? In the fact that he has come to understand the inadequacies of these institutions, their lack of justice for the present day, more clearly and more profoundly than others. But if this is so, then a great number of individuals will be suffering and groaning, writhing and perishing under the burden of these institutions. They, as individuals whose thinking is not sufficiently critical, do not understand *why* they are so miserable. But if they were told, they could understand; and those who do will understand just as well as he who first expressed the thought—perhaps even better, because they may have suffered the truth of this thought much more fully and comprehensively than has its original proclaimer.

Thus in order not to be completely alone, a person taking up the fight against social institutions has only to express his ideas in such a way that they will be understood: if they are true, he will not be alone. He will have comrades, men who share his ideas [among the people whose thinking is the most fresh and receptive]. They are unknown to him. They are scattered and unknown to one another. They feel alone and powerless before the evil which is crushing them. Perhaps when the ideas explaining this evil reached them they became more wretched still. But they are everywhere, and the truer and more just the ideas, the more of them there are. This is a force which is invisible, intangible, not yet manifested in action. But it is already a force.

For this force to be manifested in action, an example is needed. For the individual to feel that he is not alone he must know that someone else not only understands how wretched he is, and why, but furthermore is taking action against the evil. Not words alone but deeds are needed. Vigorous, fanatical men are needed, who will risk everything and are prepared to sacrifice everything. Martyrs are needed, whose legend will far outgrow their true worth and their actual service. Energy they never had will be attributed to them; the best ideas and the best sentiments of their followers will be put into their mouths. For the multitude they will become unattainable, impossible ideals. But on the other hand their legend will inspire thousands with the energy needed for the fight. The words they never uttered will be repeated—at first only half-understood, then understood better and better. The ideas which never animated the original ideal historical figure will be embodied in the work of succeeding generations as if inspired by him.

The number of those who perish is not important: legend will always multiply it to the limits of possibility. And history shows that the conservators of social institutions, with commendable selflessness, have themselves always supplied slaughtered champions for the multitude to worship, in sufficient numbers for those who oppose some social institution to be able to compile a long martyrology.

In this phase of the struggle the critically thinking individuals already have before them an actual force, but it is a disordered one. For the most part it is expended futilely, on empty trifles which first strike the eye. Men perish over the symptoms of evil, while its essence remains intact. Suffering does not diminish but perhaps even increases, because as the struggle intensifies the animosity of the antagonists grows. Dissension and division arise among the crusaders themselves, because the more ardently they fight the more jealously they watch one another. For all their energy and sacrifices, the results are trifling. The force has shown itself, but it is spent in vain. Nevertheless it is now a force which has become conscious of itself.

So that the force will not be spent in vain, it must be organized. The critically thinking, determined individuals must be determined not only to fight but to win; to this end it is necessary to understand not only the goal toward which one is striving but also the means by which it can be attained. If the struggle has been in earnest, those who are combatting outmoded social institutions will include not only individuals who are fighting in the name of their own suffering, which they have come to understand only through the words and thoughts of others, but also individuals who have thought through the state of affairs critically. They must seek each other out; they must unite, [and bring order and harmony to the disorderly elements of the historical force which has arisen].[1] Then the force will be organized; its action can be focused on a given point, concentrated for a given purpose. Its task is then purely technical: to do the most work with the least expenditure of strength. The time for unconscious suffering and dreams has passed; the time for heroes and fanatical martyrs, for the squandering of strength and for futile sacrifices, has also passed. The time has come for cool, conscious workmen, calculated strokes, rigorous thinking, and unswerving, patient action.[2]

This is the most difficult phase. The first two follow a natural course of development. Suffering engenders thought in an individual; the thought is expressed and disseminated; the suffering becomes conscious; here and there individuals with greater energy burst upon the scene; martyrs appear; their destruction augments the energy; the energy intensifies the struggle. All these things arise in inevitable succession, one after the other, like any phenomenon of nature. There are no ages in which this phenomenon is not repeated on a larger or smaller scale, and indeed at times it has attained extremely vast proportions.

But of all the parties which have fought for truth and justice against outmoded institutions, very few have triumphed. The rest have perished, or have disintegrated or ossified; they have disappeared and their time has passed irretrievably, while a new time called forth new protests and produced new parties. Victory escaped them simply because, having traversed the first two phases by natural paths, they did not know how to create the third for themselves, since it is not self-creating. It must be thought out in all its particulars: in its causes and its consequences, its ends and its means. It must be willed and willed resolutely, despite hundreds of personal discomforts, despite exhausting drudgery which in most cases goes unnoticed and unappreciated. One must prepare, sustain, and guard it with all one's strength, enduring failures patiently and taking advantage of every circumstance without losing sight of anyone or anything.

This is the phase which is humanly thought out and deliberately created, and which it is desirable to traverse as rapidly as possible, because as long as it continues the parties are exposed in the highest degree to the dangers threatening every living creature, which we have already discussed in referring to the progress of civilization: the danger of disintegrating in consequence of a fragile bond, and the danger of ossifying in the stagnation of a narrow ambition. For parties these dangers are strongest in this phase precisely because it is only in this phase that a party lives the life of an organism: all the diverse organs are directed to a common activity. Only to an organism do disintegration and ossification threaten destruction. Before this phase individuals obeyed their impulses, and impulses are stable because they proceed directly from circumstances. Now individuals must submit to thought, which is stable only when it is clear; but the most diverse impulses constantly threaten the clarity of thought.

Let us see, then, in what the chief difficulties of this phase consist, because only by overcoming these difficulties do individuals become a real organic force in society in the fight for truth and justice.

Because critically thinking individuals, who must join together to organize the party, are more capable and vigorous than other men, they possess a more marked individuality.[3] They have worked out their *own* mode of thinking, and thus to adopt another's point of view and submit to it is more difficult for them than for others. They have cultivated independence of action, and thus to force themselves to act in a way which they think is not entirely best is more difficult for them than for someone else. They have been able to defend their independence in the midst of social routine more successfully than others, and thus it is easiest for them to act in isolation. Yet it is precisely these people, who think and act independently and are accustomed to moral solitude, who now must come together, unite, think together, act together, and organize something strong and single, but strong as a collective force, and single as an abstract unity. Their own individuality, which they have protected from the smothering influ-

ence of routine—the individuality to which they have become so
accustomed and which they value so highly—must vanish in the
common direction of thought and the common plan of action.
They create an organism, but they reduce themselves to organs
within it. And they do so voluntarily.

All this is very difficult. There is constant danger of disunity
and discord among these vigorous individuals. Now, however,
discord has a significance completely different from that of the
preceding phase. There, where individual action prevails, in the
period of propaganda by example and individual energy, the circumstances on which the energy is spent is not particularly important: if only the energy exists there will be a hero, who can be
placed on a pedestal and whose name and example can inspire
men to new deeds. Two enemies who have wasted their strength
in a futile contest can stand side by side in the pantheon of posterity, like Voltaire and Rousseau. But now disunity is death; it
means renouncing the victory of the common cause and the future of the party.

And so, independent individuals join together with the firm
intention of yielding some of their customary views and renouncing some of their customary actions, if only their most intimate
and profound convictions may in time triumph. All the power of
their thinking is again directed to a critical examination of their
own hearts and their own actions, but now not with the aim of
determining whether some idea or practice is really just and true,
but to answer the following question: Is this particular point
really linked so inseparably with the essence of my aspirations
and convictions that I cannot renounce it without injuring my
own dignity, without sacrificing everything most dear to me? So
inseparably that I could not renounce it even if it meant a chance
for my ideas to triumph, since if I renounced this point they
would triumph in name only, while the names would conceal
something so distorted and debased that I would not recognize
my ideas in it? Only after coming to a full understanding of how
far concessions can go and where betrayal of the cause begins,
can the individuals who join together in this common cause organize a strong and vigorous party.

If they come together determined not to yield an inch, there is
no use coming together. For them no common cause exists. Each

will be ready to turn the others into tools of his own system of thought, in the total form in which this system has developed within him, including everything both essential and incidental in his convictions and customs. But coming together to reduce one another to moral slavery constitutes not the organization of a party, but an attempt to convert everything into a mechanism serving the motives and aims of a single individual.

Each individual must separate the essential from the customary in his opinions. Each must enter the association determined to sacrifice the customary, though it be very dear, for the sake of the essential. Each must consider himself an organ of the overall organism. He is not a lifeless instrument, not an insensate mechanism, but he is nevertheless *only* an organ. He has his own nature and his own functions, but he is subordinate to the unity of the whole. This is a condition, and a necessary condition, of the life of an organism. It is a condition of harmonious action, a condition of victory.

But if discord is disastrous, if concessions with respect to what is *customary* are necessary, and if individuals must submit to the common cause—concessions on what is *essential* would be just as disastrous, and it is just as necessary that the party members remain *thinking* individuals without being transformed into machines to serve another's ideas. He who has yielded on what is essential to his convictions has no serious convictions at all. He serves not a cause he has understood, reflected upon, and desired to promote, but a meaningless word, an empty sound. To be sure, victory is impossible without firm alliance, without unity of action; and of course victory is desired by all who fight. But victory *in itself* cannot be the goal of the thinking person. Victory must have some inherent meaning. It is not *who* has won but *what* has won that is important. It is the triumphant idea that is important. And if through compromises the idea has lost all content, then the party has lost its meaning: it has no cause, and the dispute is simply one of personal predominance.

Then the champions of truth and justice are in no way distinguished from the routine defenders of the social order they are combatting. On their banners are inscribed words which once denoted truth and justice, but now denote nothing. They will repeat these sonorous words a thousand times. The youth will trust them, and will invest in these words their minds, their souls, and their lives. And then the youth will lose faith in their leaders and their banners; renegades will drag through the mud what yesterday was sacred; reactionaries will ridicule these banners that are defiled by the very men who bear them. And the great, immortal words will await new champions, who can restore meaning to them and put them into action. As for the old party which sacrificed everything for victory, it may not even win; and in any event it will ossify in its empty stagnation.

Thus, organization of a party is necessary for victory, but for the party to be a living organism it is equally necessary that the organs be vital and that they be subordinated to the whole. Parties must be composed of thinking, confirmed, and vigorous allies. These allies must clearly understand why they have joined together; they must strongly value their independent convictions; they must be determined to do everything they can for the triumph of these convictions. Only under these conditions can they hope to escape both dangers which threaten them: dissolution and stagnation.

Let us suppose these conditions have been fulfilled. Critically thinking, determined individuals have joined together and organized a party. But it is evident, from the very conditions under which such organization can take place, that there will be extremely few men, even among critically thinking individuals, who fully satisfy the requirements the party's organizers must lay down. [Nevertheless these few have, in the first place, *potential* allies among other critically thinking individuals, and, in the second place, *inevitable* allies in the masses who have not developed to the point of thinking critically but who are suffering from the same social disorder which the party is being organized to eliminate.

[Let us first discuss the former. They are, as has been said, people who think critically, members of the intelligentsia, but in the given case they lack something which is needed to become organizers of a strong party.] Some, for all their strength of intellect, have not come to the conclusion that victory is possible only through organization, but have remained at the standpoint of the solitary heroes of the previous phase. Others have arrived at this conclusion, but have not brought themselves to sacrifice their personal pride and customary mode of action for the common cause. Those in a third group have not sufficiently succeeded in separating the inessential from the essential. Those in a fourth group, on the other hand, from a passionate desire for victory, are prepared to submit *completely*, to sacrifice the essential, to become mechanical instruments; and they reproach those who are unable to do this. And still other categories will be found.

Obviously, those who have organized a party to fight for truth and justice, given their small number, must above all augment their strength with all the resources which are scattered about them and are capable of becoming part of the organization. What is important here is not so much the quantity as the quality of the participants, their independence of thought and energy of will. Particularly important are those who can become independent, vigorous centers of influence, bearing the life of the new organism farther and farther. Thus particularly important are the first three categories of persons who have not yet joined the movement. To the first it is necessary to explain the practical importance of the cause, and to the third its theoretical essence; the second must simply be attracted to it. All of them can in the future be very useful members; all are *potential* allies, and an understanding of the common interest must compel us to view them as such. Indeed this point of view determines the activity of the nascent party with respect to all elements, both those which have already become part of it and those which may become part of it subsequently.

[But a social party is not a party of arm-chair scholars. It is fighting for truth and justice in concrete form. It has in view a definite evil existing in society. If the evil is real, then a great many people are suffering from it, feeling its whole enormity, but understanding clearly neither its causes nor the means of combatting it. These are the invisible heroes of whom I spoke above, and who make progress possible. They are the real foundation of the nascent party. The latter is, in fact, being organized precisely because it knows of the existence of a great number of individuals who are *bound* to welcome its demands, who are *bound* to stretch out their hands to it, precisely because they are suffering from the evil against which it has arisen. It is quite possible that these suffering masses, these invisible custodians of a better future, will not at once recognize their allies, will distrust them, and will be unable to see that the struggle now beginning on the ground of cultivated critical thought is the same struggle which they themselves instinctively demand on the basis of unenlightened inclinations and beliefs. This means nothing. The party must nonetheless be organized with a view to union with these social forces—a union which is inevitable, if not today then tomorrow. Unrecognized and misunderstood at first, the advocates of struggle for a better future should keep in mind, in all their words and actions, these not merely potential but inevitable allies.

[Thus the party is organized. Its nucleus is a small number of highly developed, deliberate, vigorous people, for whom critical thinking is inseparable from action. Around them are members of the intelligentsia who are less highly developed. But the party's real foundation is its inevitable allies, the social groups suffering from the evil which the party has been organized to combat.]

The distinction which has been established between the essential and the inessential in personal beliefs determines both the freedom of action within the party and what the party will tolerate from without. However widely its members may differ on points considered inessential, they are nonetheless useful and inevitable party allies for the future.

All members of the party—actual and potential—are under its protection. Every thinking person who has entered the party organism becomes a natural defense attorney not only of those who already belong to it but of those who may enter it tomorrow. An attorney should not distort his client's case; he simply brings out everything which actually speaks to his client's advantage, and is silent about everything which might injure him. This silence is not a lie, because the opposing parties, too, have their attorneys, who do not and should not spare their opponents. An attorney who manifestly distorts the truth simply harms thereby both his cause and his own prestige as an intelligent and conscientious attorney. But an attorney who gives his opponents their best arguments is no attorney at all. The mutual bar of its members is the party's most powerful bond and its most vigorous means of counteracting opponents. It is also one of the best means for an organized party to attract persons who have not yet joined it. Just as unity of thought and unity of aim make up the party's inner strength, so the mutual bar of its members makes up its outer strength.

Beyond the bounds of the inessential, the freedom of action of the party's members and its tolerance of those outside it ceases. If any member oversteps these bounds, he is no longer a member of the party, but its enemy. If anyone outside the party disagrees with it on essential issues, he, too, is its enemy. Against these enemies the party directs and must direct the whole force of its organization, fighting as one man, with all its resources, concentrating its blows.

Just as each member of the party is a natural defense attorney of his actual and potential allies, so too he is a natural prosecutor of all his avowed enemies. Distorting the truth is not required in this case, either: that is by no means a duty of the conscientious prosecutor. What is required is attention to the opponents' actual offences and exhibition of all the incriminating circumstances. To defend the accused is the task of defense attorneys. An overly petty accusation aids the case of the accused and damages the prosecutor's prestige in the eyes of the attentive public, just as a manifestly prejudiced defense on the part of an attorney exerts an influence contrary to his own desire. But to lose sight of the opponents' mistakes, to give them the means of concealing their offences, is completely inconsistent with the task of the party man. Intent and steadfast struggle against its enemies is a manifestation of the party's life, just as unity of thought is the foundation of this life and the mutual bar of its members is the party's bond.

Thus grows the social force, proceeding from the solitary, weak individual to include, first, the sympathy of other individuals, then their unorganized cooperation, until finally a party is organized which imparts unity and direction to the fight. At this point, of course, the party encounters other parties, and the question of victory becomes a question of numbers and tactics. Where is the greatest strength? Where are the individuals with the most intelligence, the best understanding, the greatest energy and skill? Which party is best organized? Which is most successful in taking advantage of circumstances, in defending its own men and overcoming its enemies? Now it is organized forces that are contend-

ing, and the interest of history is focused on the principles inscribed upon their banners.

"There is nothing new here; I already knew this," the reader
will say.

If you already knew it, fine. There is no use searching history
for tales and fantasies, but in history one may learn what was,
what is, and what will be. The struggle of the individual against
social institutions and the struggle of parties within societies is as
old as the earliest social organization in history. I wished simply
to remind the reader of ancient truths concerning what is needed
for the struggle of weak individuals against the enormous power
of social institutions; what is needed for the operation of intellect
on cultural customs and traditions; what is needed for the triumph of the parties of progress; and what is needed for the vital
development of civilizations.

Individuals who have developed the capacity to think critically
have by the same token acquired the right to be agents of progress, the right to fight against outmoded social institutions. This
fight is both useful and reasonable. Individuals, however, are only
potential agents of progress. They will become its actual agents
only when they are *able* to carry on the fight, when they can become, from insignificant units, a collective *force*, an organ of
thought. Only one road leads to this goal, and the indisputable
evidence of history points it out.

NINTH LETTER

The Banners of Social Parties

IN THE LAST FEW LETTERS I have set forth my view that all social
progress depends of necessity upon the action of individuals; that
only individuals can make a civilization durable and at the same
time save it from stagnation; that individuals have both the right

and the capacity to criticize the social institutions within which they live; and that the struggle for the new against the old, for the growing against the dying, leads of necessity to the formation of parties under the banners of various ideas, and to conflict among these parties in the name of these ideas.

But in this conflict how are we to know who is fighting for the past and the moribund, and who stands for the living and the growing?

The question may seem strange, because in practice it seems extremely easy to determine whether a party is preaching ideas which were in vogue years, decades, or a century ago, or ideas of the very latest stamp, which in an earlier age would have been rejected with derision, fright, or horror. The latest intellectual fashion, the latest article in an influential journal, the latest sermon of a favorite preacher—here is what is living and growing; on the other hand the party whose ranks, voluntarily or involuntarily, have grown thin—here is the party of reaction.

This is the easiest method; it is followed by all human sheep with the most dim-witted consistency, and by all unprincipled phrasemongers with the most amazing resourcefulness. The likelihood of advancement, the likelihood of feasting at the social banquet for the man who joins the ranks of one or another party—this is what they call striving forward, following the times.

If they should be right, then the word "progress" is devoid of meaning and history is a kind of meteorological table on which we may register rainy days and clear days, days when the wind is from the southwest or the northeast, but where it is very difficult to go beyond statistical figures. Then, too, as far as I am concerned there would be no reason to write the letters I am now writing, since social meteorology interests me as little as physical. Rain and drought follow a simple sequence only in exceptional cases and exceptional lands. We live in a zone of changeable weather. It is rather hard for us to predict the direction of the wind tomorrow on the basis of its direction yesterday and the day before; we suffer from changes in the weather, but we do not understand them. Provide yourself, if you wish to and can, with galoshes and umbrellas, warm clothing, and houses with tight-shutting windows; but would you think of investigating the connection between today's rain and the rain which fell last Thursday? In the present state of our knowledge, that would be thankless work in physical meteorology as well as in political. Science goes no further than providing weather stations for the people who are most exposed to danger, and no further than warning them of an approaching hurricane a few hours before it strikes.

Unfortunately I cannot accept such an easy method of distinguishing progressives from reactionaries as the one I have indicated above. Having set forth the requirements of progress at the beginning of the Third Letter, to be consistent I am obliged to assume that these requirements also determine the differences between parties. A defeated party may be a party of progress. A little-read book, written, ten, fifty, or a hundred years ago, may contain more in the way of vital historical elements than the latest journal article. Yesterday's fashion may be inspired by a better instinct for the future than today's. Yes, surprising as it may seem, I prefer our journals of 1861 to the journals of 1867 [or even 1890]. I prefer Kant to Schelling, Voltaire to Cousin, and I find in Lucian many more of the vital elements of progress than in Katkov.[1]

This will, of course, shock some progressives, who think of themselves as keeping daily abreast of the most fashionable trend. It will bring a contemptuous smile to the lips of those ever-tranquil souls for whom "follow the leader" seems like a childish pastime. It may gladden the hearts of the obtuse worshipers of Byzantium and the *Domostroy,* who will imagine that from this point of view they, too, may prove to be true progressives. I grant them all leave to be shocked, amused, and gratified.

If we accept the view that progress consists in the development of the individual and the incorporation of truth and justice in social institutions, the question raised above concerning the marks of progressive and reactionary parties becomes much more difficult to answer. For the unfortunate fact is that no external distinguishing marks are to be found. In the whole vocabulary of human civilization there is no word which would unconditionally, in all times and places, appear only on the banners of progressives or only on the banners of reactionaries. The greatest ideas —the ideas which in the majority of cases have been, for the best segment of the thinking public, the most life-giving principles of society—have in some periods of history served as lures to swell the ranks of parties which were obstructing mankind's development. And in some ages the most reactionary principles have become instruments of progress.

To elucidate this let us consider separately those ideas which we can call *general principles* of personal and social life and those other ideas which correspond to *particular institutions* of social life. These two sorts of ideas, in various combinations, ordinarily serve as the banners for contending parties in those cases where the parties are in fact pursuing selfish, calculated ends as well as in the cases where they fanatically believe that their followers, and they alone, are the spokesmen for absolute truth and justice. Each of these two groups of ideas may become either a source of development or an instrument of stagnation. In reality each has been alternately one and the other, but the causes of this phenomenon are different for each group.

The general principles—development, freedom, reason, and the like—have suffered this fate simply because of their broad meaning, which has left them always extremely unclear to the majority and made it possible for some to repeat them without any definite meaning and for others to use them as tools for the most petty and reactionary ends.

The word *development* has been taken in a fatalistic sense, as an inevitability to be viewed not only as an existing fact but as a legitimate principle demanding intellectual recognition and moral admiration in all its manifestations. For those who make a fetish of historical process, the pathological cells of a social cancer are just as much elements of true human development as the healthy cells of the social nerves and muscles. But it is otherwise for the person in whose eyes history has human meaning: he knows that pathological cells and healthy cells are the equally necessary and natural consequences of past processes, but that only the latter produce development, while the former are elements of destruction and death. The first type of development (if we are to call it that) must be opposed as much as possible, now and in the future. The second type of development (which alone, properly speaking, has the right to this designation in history) must be promoted.

The meaningless use of the word *freedom* is so familiar to everyone who has given any thought to history that it seems

needless to discuss it. Freedom for the strong to oppress the
weak, freedom for the poor to die of hunger, freedom for parents
to pervert the physical, intellectual, and moral capacities of their
children—these are some of the more notorious forms of this
principle.

In the name of *reason* people have become absorbed in con-
templation of the Absolute, rejecting the critical examination of
fact. They have regarded what exists as rational, rejecting the
critical examination of social institutions.

Justice has been identified with legality, even if it were the law
of Draco. *Truth* has meant mystical propositions inaccessible to
the understanding and requiring only blind repetition. *Virtue* has
been found in the sacrifice of the superior person to the inferior
and of real good to imaginary; [it has meant not the struggle
against evil, but nonresistance to evil]. The discharge of *duty* has
been seen in spying and in barbarity, in a Jesuit seminarian in-
forming against a comrade, in the extermination of whole peoples
such as the Midianites, the Amalekites, and the Ammonites, in
breaking one's word to someone of another faith, in the auto-da-
fé of the Inquisition, and in the Massacre of Saint Bartholomew.
Sanctity in life has been found in denying individual development, in denying real truth and human justice, in the senseless
self-torture of the fakir, in the brutish existence of the hermit, [in
the madness of the saint,] in faith in the inconceivable, in the
persecution of non-believers [and those who believe otherwise].

In a word—all the worst, most animal, antisocial, degrading,
antihuman sides of man have found defenders under the guise of
development, freedom, reason, virtue, duty, and sanctity.

Only critical thought—unremitting, implacable critical thought
—has been able to save the individual from being enticed by a
high-sounding word into a camp completely at variance with his
desires, his instincts, his entire nature. In such a case general
principles have been the most common lure, and very often two
contending parties which are essentially antithetical have proclaimed themselves defenders of one and the same great principle. All sectarians have called themselves true believers and the
members of other churches heathens. All philosophers have
maintained that the true, rational conception of things is found
only in their own systems. To all appearances both Caesar and

Cato stood for the welfare of Rome. Both the slave owners and
the opponents of slavery demanded justice. Thinking people were
obliged to ask: For which party does the great word have real
meaning? Was not the demand for freedom (as with the French
clergy) only a demand for the right to oppress others? [2] Was
not the appeal to justice (as with the landowners who favored
serfdom, the slave owners, [and the capitalists]) only a desire to
legitimize an immoral fact of history even after its immorality had
already been recognized?

While the general principles can serve as banners for opposing
parties by virtue of their excessively broad meaning, one would
think that this could not be the case for particular social institutions. It would seem that the family, law, the nation, the state, the
church, a scientific, economic, or artistic association has a definite
objective which is not particularly difficult to understand, and
consequently that it is not difficult to say whether one or another
of these institutions is a vivifying, progressive element or a dead-
ening, reactionary one.

Unfortunately this is by no means true, but for a reason quite
different from that which sometimes transforms the great general
principles into high-sounding phrases. The general principles,
precisely because of their generality, acquire definite meaning
only when there is clear awareness of the real content which has
been given them. Particular social institutions, however, precisely
because of their particularity, are in themselves neither progressive nor reactionary: they all potentially have a progressive influence on individuals, just as they all can serve as the most oppressive obstacle in the path of individual development.

The historical significance of each institution is determined by
the complex of circumstances under which it exists in a given
period and by the complex of all the social institutions existing in
that period. At any given time the conditions of social growth are
inevitably advancing some particular institution to the forefront
as an instrument of progress, and in this period society can develop only on the condition that all other social institutions are
subordinated to the one guiding institution. But conditions
change: what yesterday was the predominant, fundamental requirement becomes today only *one* among many requirements of
the individual and of society. Forms of social organization which

yesterday were subordinate today demand equal rights, and to-morrow predominance. Society must advance to a new complex of institutions if it wishes to remain progressive. An institution which yesterday prevailed and for the ascendancy of which yesterday's progressives rightfully fought, today is obliged to yield its priority, and whoever defends it is a reactionary. New complexes of institutions will in turn have their day, after which they must be replaced by newer ones.

He who worships some temporary combination of social institutions like a fetish, of necessity risks becoming an accomplice of reaction, because there is no single combination which can satisfy the demands of progress once and for all. For a thinking person social institutions should be nothing more than the light and changeable vestments of history, having no independent significance and deriving their meaning only from the extent to which these institutions, in the given combination, correspond to the demands of the given age—correspond, namely, to the free development of individuals, to the greatest justice in their relationships, to the broadest possible participation of the individual in the benefits of civilization, to the strengthening of these benefits, and to the elimination of the danger of stagnation.

[The kinship bond among men, which gave rise to the clan and the family, has apparently changed its progressive significance more than once.

[It is difficult to form a clear conception of the form of society inhabited by the primate who was man's predecessor or even by primitive man, whose traces archeologists would sooner divine than observe in the Tertiary strata of the earth's crust. But this zoological form of society must have been a backward social form compared with the clan organized around the mother—the union (discussed in the Fourth Letter above) which present-day social embryologists, with mounting credibility, resurrect before our imagination as the first purely human union. This matriarchal clan yielded almost everywhere to the patriarchal clan, and subsequently to the patriarchal family which the latter engendered.

[For us the progressive significance of the conflict between these two forms is by now completely obscure. Perhaps—even probably—the victory of the patriarchal clan was a victory of the egoistic principle over the social, as a consequence of the somewhat greater security of human groups and a certain mitigation of the struggle for existence, so that it became easier for the selfish passions to attain their separate ends. But perhaps the individual critical outlook of a minority more advantageously situated and having greater leisure could not have developed without the transition through the patriarchal form, with the exceptional position it gave to the patriarchs and the well-born. Perhaps, in fact, there was for mankind an age in which the patriarchate was the cardinal progressive principle of association —an age in which the economic, the political, the religious, and to some extent the scientific requirements of mankind were best met by a system in which the patriarch had absolute sway over his descendants and there was the firmest hierarchical connection between generations.

[However, let us leave aside the question—now very difficult to answer—of whether the patriarchal mode of life was progressive in comparison with the matriarchal period. Let us include under the term "kinship bond" all forms of primitive union in which the common cause was inseparably connected with kinship relations within the union. Under this concept, then, will be included the matriarchal clan with wives and children in common; the patriarchal family, which the tradition of the Semites has preserved for us and which Greco-Roman legislation developed into a further form; various transitional forms having the institution of polyandry; and other more exceptional forms which have been preserved here and there in the human race. In all these forms the kinship association, as the first association which united people and led them to create a firm union for mutual defense, was a basic progressive principle.

[Even then, of course, this principle led to the despotism of custom, xenophobia, petty genealogical pride, superstitious trafficking with deceased ancestors, tribal hostility—all of which brought much suffering. Yet by comparison this form either reduced suffering in society to a minimum, or at least created the only opportunity for thought to work toward truth and justice more extensively in the future, and thus also for the reduction of suffering in future generations as a result of this intellectual labor. In any event, it must be said that in that period the kinship system was progressive.] [3] However great the mutual slaughter among tribes in a blood feud, [perhaps] fewer perished in this slaughter than when individuals did not have the protection of the kinship bond. However oppressively [custom weighed on separate individuals, and, subsequently, however unceremoniously] the patriarch exploited the labor and the lives of the members of his tribe, the unity of action in a tribe [bound together by ancestral custom or by the authority of the patriarch] made it possible for the tribe to protect more of its members from starvation and other perils than could have been protected by the uncoordinated activity of these individuals themselves. However inhumanely the members of these groups treated outsiders—enslaving, exterminating, or devouring them —nevertheless in the kinship association man was inculcated with the idea that he should defend the life, the well-being, and the dignity not only of his own person, and not only of those personally dear to him, but also of others linked with him ideally in that they have the same rights and the same responsibilities as he—in that in their well-being resides his dignity as well, and in that an offense against them is an offense against him.

As soon as law came to the individual's protection, the bloody vendetta became a pernicious social practice, and from a progressive element was transformed into a reactionary one. As soon as free economic association provided the individual with greater security and more benefits than the kinship and communal group, defense of the economic principle of the kinship association also took on a reactionary character.[4] As soon as the idea developed in man that the dignity of *every* human being is bound up with his own dignity, that an offense against *any* human being is also an offense against him, then the idea that common descent constitutes a preeminent bond among men became an obstacle in the path of civilization.

In the next era of the life of mankind *law* became the prevailing principle and, rightfully, a progressive one. It secured the life of the weak against the arbitrary will of the strong. By securing contracts it gave the community the opportunity for free and extensive economic development. It was one of the most powerful instruments for cultivating in men a conception of their moral equality, a conception of human dignity apart from every accidental circumstance of birth, property, and the like.

But even law was not always, and is not always, a progressive principle. In another letter I shall examine further the tendency toward stagnation which inevitably develops along with the strengthening of the formal element of law in society. Here I shall content myself simply with a few indications.

Law always means the letter of the law. Social life, in its unceasing organic development, inevitably branches out into categories incomparably more diverse than a legislator can foresee, and rapidly outgrows the conditions under which even the most conscientious legislator penned his formula. He who wishes to squeeze all the diversity of life into the established formulas of the code, at any price, will not be an agent of progress. He who sides with an obsolete law in the face of new historical needs is a reactionary. Of course in almost every society which is at all well-constructed it is possible to repeal obsolete laws. But sometimes the selfish interests of the government or of an influential minority preserve the formal existence of a law which is inimical to all the natural aspirations of social consciousness.[5] [If the dreadful war of 1870 had not completely sapped the foundations of the second Bonapartist empire, this empire might long have continued to stand over France as a legal form; yet the number of its true supporters was so small that it did not find *a single* defender on September 4, even though the government which succeeded it was not notable for its political, intellectual, or moral virtues.*

[In such cases] the letter of the law remains in the code and [sometimes] even finds vigorous and interested defenders; but justice, life, and progress are not in it. Then, however correct are the public prosecutor's demands from a legal point of view, justice is on the side of the jurors who pronounce, against the evidence: not guilty. Then, however legal are the actions of the executioner in placing the criminal on the wheel, or of the police in protecting the instruments of torture, progress is on the side of the lawless mob which snatches the martyr from the executioner's hands and destroys the shameful instruments. However legally the Senate decreed that Caesar Augustus Domitian was a god

---

* And with respect to present-day Russia, despite the universal discontent aroused by the government of Alexander III, it is difficult to say how long this government with its outrageous institutions may continue to exist if all classes which are its victims do not organize an opposition as vigorous as, but broader than, that which socialists have thus far been able to mount. (1890)

and that sacrifices were to be made to his statue, history is surely
on the side of the tattered preacher who said: no, Domitian is not
a god and the sacrifices should not be made. However correct was
Gessler's demand that his cap be saluted, history is surely on the
side of the half-mythical archer who instead of saluting Gessler's
cap dealt him a mortal blow.*

In the age of the last Caesars and the first barbarian kings, the
Church as a social institution rightfully acquired ruling significance, and all elements of society were subordinated to it. When
the Roman treasury on the one hand and barbarian plundering
on the other were depriving the majority of all means of subsistence, when neither ancient law nor new social needs were
strong enough to protect the individual, then the bishop, in the
name of a binding spiritual authority, became an agent of social
progress. His concern was one-sided, but nevertheless it was a
concern for the suffering people. His court was irregular, but
nevertheless it was a certain approximation to justice. He could
on occasion publicly censure an outrageous action even on the
part of the emperor, whom no one could try. Through fear of the
torments of hell and the vengeance of the saints he could halt, at
least at times, the predatory outbursts of the barbarians, whom
nothing had been able to stop. However barbarous were the regulations of Cassianus and Benedict, under the existing conditions
they provided the only chance of preserving the tradition of
learning, or simply of literacy and elementary culture. Consequently, these were positive elements of progress for western
Europe in this period.

Before very long, however, such a conception of the social significance of bishops and monasteries became a reactionary principle in the West. The rudest tribal court became more just than
the ecclesiastical court in civil affairs. All the abuses of feudalism,
of the central state administration, and of purely formal law were
nothing compared with the abuses flowing from interference by
the Catholic hierarchy in the affairs of society. The idea of the
Church as a hierarchical element independent of the state became a reactionary idea. The domination of the other depart-

* I retain without alteration the text published in Russia twenty years
ago. The reader himself may make the application to present-day Russia.
(1890)

ments of learning by theologians became a highly pernicious obstacle to development. The hierarchical system was an aid to progress only where it became not the guiding force in society but one element in the fight for other guiding principles—for nationality, for the dissemination of the culture of higher races among lower, and so on.

Let us take another example, which I mentioned also in the Fifth Letter. Science as a process of discovery is, of course, an element of progress. But in a particular case a scientific association, as a social institution, may well retard the development of society at a time when all its available energies should be directed to questions of life, when any member of society who is indifferent to these questions is its enemy, and when no one has the right to consider himself an agent of progress if he regards the transient polemics of journalists, the noisy debate of mass meetings, and the bloody clash of parties with Olympian disdain.

At such moments, if the scientific association understands its own human significance it gives its labors a direction which corresponds to the needs of society; or its members, postponing their investigations on new forms of infusoria, the style of Clovis' garments, or the conjugation of Celtic verbs, devote their abilities, their time, and their lives to questions of life. Then the creator of a new branch of geometry, Monge, spends whole days in the workshops, lives on dry bread, and writes instructions for the workers. Then two men who shared in the creation of scientific chemistry, Berthollet and Fourcroy, devote themselves to procuring saltpeter for gunpowder and training men taken from the plow. Then the creator of comparative philology, Wilhelm von Humboldt, bends all the power of his intellect to the regeneration of Prussia. The astronomer Arago sits on the council of the founders of the Second Republic. The father of cellular pathology, Virchow, thunders against Bismarck in the Reichstag.

But the scientific association may also act in another way. Priding itself on the celestial calm of its arm-chair inquiries, it may use its influence to spread indifference to the sufferings of the masses or deference to the official *status quo,* or at least it may regard participation in the fleeting controversies of the day as beneath its dignity. In such a case all the scientific merit of its labors will not save it from the inevitable condemnation of history. The scientific association which propagates indifference to the questions of life in the name of science—an ill-understood science, of course—and which shuns participation in them will be an agent of reaction, not an agent of progress.

For now we shall content ourselves with these examples. They all prove the same thing: that the principle of development has not been, [and is not now,] the absolute property of any one of the social institutions which have been considered, but that each of them may become, to a greater or lesser degree, an effective instrument of progress in a particular age and under particular circumstances. Those who defend any of them absolutely and under all circumstances are preaching an absolutely reactionary principle, for the same institution or even the same combination of institutions cannot prevail under all circumstances with benefit to mankind. Institutions must rule by turns and yield to one another if history is to follow its proper course.

But at a particular moment in history how are we to know where progress lies? Which party is its representative? Great words are inscribed upon all the banners. All parties preach principles which, under certain conditions, have been or will be motive forces of progress. This principle is good, but so is that. How, then, are we to choose?

An uninformed, unthinking person who is prepared to follow the authority of someone else cannot choose without erring. No word has had an exclusive right to progress; progress has never been squeezed into a single institutional frame. Behind the word, look for its content. Study the conditions of the day and the given social institution. Make yourself a person of learning and conviction. This is indispensable. Only one's own understanding, one's own conviction, one's own determination make an individual an individual, and apart from the individual there are no great principles, there are no progressive institutions, there is no progress whatever. What is important is not the banner, and not the word inscribed upon it, but the thought of him who bears it.

In order to discern this thought more readily, one must come to understand the process by means of which people sometimes conceal the foulest things under great words.

Idealization

PART OF THE WORLD and a slave of nature, man has never liked to acknowledge his slavery. Submitting constantly to irrational impulses and fortuitous circumstances, he has never liked to call his motives frankly irrational or his action a product of accidental influences. In the inmost depths of his soul there is an urge to conceal from himself his dependence upon the immutable laws of unconscious matter and [to embellish somehow in his own eyes] the inconstancy and inconsistency of his actions. This he has done through idealization.

It works as follows. I have performed an act, good or evil, on the spur of the moment—without even giving a thought to whether it is good or evil. After the act has been performed, there is an appraisal. If in my opinion the act is good, I am gratified. But if I were to admit to myself that I have performed a good act without even considering its value, I should not gain much credit in my own eyes. Perhaps I *had* considered it, but do not remember. But now I remember: actually, I *had* quickly grasped that it was good, and the rapidity of my reflection increases my merit still further; I am both a good man and one who grasps things quickly.

Let us assume, however, that I am endowed with a sufficiently good memory so as not to make a mistake on that score. Very well. I have performed a good act without reflecting upon it, without calculating, but through an inner, natural inclination. This means that my nature is so permeated with goodness that I can perform good acts without even having to recognize, intellectually, how valuable they are. I am a good man not through intellectual cultivation but by nature. I am, then, one of those men who are exclusively good.

Or else still another method is followed, which is effective given religious modes of thought.[1] I did not perform the good act of my own volition: it was inspired in me from on high, by a deity, who directs the will and the actions of men without the mediation of their conscious reflection. God chose me as His instrument to carry out the divine purpose of effecting this good act. The seeming humility of this last method conceals still greater self-glorification than the methods previously examined.

In each of these cases, from a completely unthinking act which through its consequences has accidentally turned out to be good, idealization has drawn the conclusion that I am a very good man and remarkably quick of comprehension, or that I am exclusively good by my very nature, or that I am a person chosen by God for good acts.

When the act is evil the methods of idealization are somewhat different, but they fall into the same categories. First, the last method works here too, without alteration: I did not perform the act of my own volition, but was the instrument of God's wrath and judgment. God selected me for an act which only *seems* evil to feeble human reason; the Supreme Reason judges differently, and if it has decided that the person chosen is to perform this act, then in reality the act is not evil. The rationalist will speak not of God but of a higher law which guides events and draws good consequences from evil actions; of a higher harmony of all that exists, where the acts of individuals are the particular notes which grate upon the ear if we hear them separately, but which are necessary for the over-all harmony. It turns out that the evil deed, as a necessary element in the universal harmony, is by no means evil and had to be performed; while I, from being the perpetrator of an evil deed, have become a valuable participant in the universal concert.

But the method which people employ most readily is the method of a supposed higher consideration. Taken in itself the act is, let us say, evil. But memory quickly produces a long list of *great principles* and tries them on my act, and if any of them even remotely fits, imagination suggests that I had in mind precisely that principle in performing my act. I have quarreled with a friend and killed him in a duel: I was defending the great principle of honor. I have seduced a woman and thrown her and the child into the street with no means of subsistence: I was following the great principle of freedom of attachments. I have concluded a contract with peasants which is disadvantageous to them, and have through lawsuits reduced them to penury: I was acting in the name of the great principle of legality. I have informed against a conspirator: I was upholding the great principle of the state.[2] In a time of trial for literature, out of personal spite I trample in the mud the last remaining ideological organs of my own party: I am a champion of the great principle of independent opinion and the purity of literary manners. There is scarcely any foul act which it is absolutely impossible to bring under one of the great principles. It seems that from a higher point of view my act not only is not evil, it is good. Once again an unthinking act, despite the fact that its consequences have shown it to be harmful, has made me out to be a defender of great principles, a valuable participant in the universal harmony, the chosen instrument of a higher will.

[The domain of idealization is very vast. In all aspects of its development it is based upon the urge to impart, in man's imagination, a conscious character to unconscious and semi-conscious actions, and to elevate conscious actions from a more elementary level to a higher one. At the same time, however, we must discriminate between, first, cases of idealization which are *inevitable* since they are determined by the very nature of human thinking; second, the vast province of that *false* idealization against which the work of critical inquiry must be directed in the name of truth and justice; and finally, the few cases of *true* idealization, where this same critical inquiry must defend the real and rightful needs of men against those who would deny them.

[The only idealization which is absolutely inevitable for man is the notion of *free will*, in virtue of which he cannot in any way rid himself of the subjective conviction that he voluntarily sets goals for himself and chooses means of achieving them. However convincingly objective *knowledge* demonstrates to man that all his "voluntary" actions and thoughts are nothing but necessary consequences of an antecedent series of events—external and internal, physical and psychic—the subjective *consciousness* that these actions and thoughts are voluntary remains a constant, inescapable illusion, even in the very process of demonstrating the universal determinism which rules both in the external world and in the spirit of man.

[What is inevitable must of necessity be accepted. In the realm of human activity this involuntary idealization of one's motives becomes a fruitful basis of vast provinces of human intellectual labor, both scientific and philosophical. Quite independently of the extent to which the ends man sets himself and the means he chooses to achieve them are *in fact* real or illusory, these ends and means arrange themselves in his mind into a definite hierarchy of *better* and *worse*.

[But scientific criticism sets to work establishing the *correct* hierarchy among them. An indisputable truth is set against a probable hypothesis, a faulty argument, an invention of fantasy, a contradictory concept. The ineffective means is distinguished from the effective, the harmful from the beneficial. The moral motive is distinguished from the whole mass of irrational, fortuitous, passionate, and selfish motives. To the province of those motives, thoughts, and actions in which man himself cannot discover the traces of a conscious will, he opposes the province of his other motives, thoughts, and actions, concerning which he cannot rid himself of the idea that he willed them, that he is responsible for them, and that other people similarly consider him to have this responsibility—however subject all of this is, equally with the former province, to the universal determinism.

[By a process as inevitable for the human mind as the objective laws which rule in nature, the fundamental inner idealization of the voluntary establishment of goals and the voluntary selection of means sets before every individual a hierarchy of morally better and morally worse goals, leaving him only the ability to determine critically whether it is necessary in this critical examination to refashion the hierarchy and to regard something *else* as better and worse. The decision of the will and the choice of one or another action as a result of this decision prove always to be inevitable, but ethical criticism can credit this choice with a higher or lower significance and can charge the individual with responsibility for this choice in his own eyes and in the eyes of others who share the same convictions.] [3] This makes it possible to compare the province of theoretical *knowledge* with the province of moral *consciousness*, and in the later province to take one's departure from the primary subjective *fact* of free will *for oneself*, independently of the theoretical significance of this fact. [4]

It provides a solid foundation for practical philosophy, and has permitted me in these letters to speak to the reader of the moral duty of the individual, of the moral need for individuals to fight against moribund social institutions, of moral ideals and of the historical progress which flows from them.[5]

If the principle of personal responsibility [for everything a man regards as a manifestation of his will] must be recognized as an inevitable idealization, and for that reason cannot be eliminated, it is the only idealization entitled to this privilege. Everything avoidable should be admitted only on the basis of critical examination.

Proceeding to the phenomena of idealization with this demand in mind, we may remark how extensively idealization has applied its method of rationalizing unconscious processes. Far from confining itself to man, it has endeavored to anthropomorphize and rationalize the entire world. Observation points to three groups of idealizations stemming from man's desire to read consciousness and rationality into all phenomena, or at least into the majority of them. First, he has imagined phenomena to be the *actions* of supernatural, otherworldly persons [—spirits and gods—] endowed with consciousness, reason, and will. Second he has imagined phenomena to be *manifestations* of the indivisible conscious and rational essence of the world. [But the most ancient of all, going back to primitive times in the life of the human race, is the third method of idealizing the world: the objects of the external world, in almost all its provinces, have been regarded as *beings* endowed with consciousness, reason, and will, or as the abode of such beings, and the phenomena of the world have been seen as the deliberate actions of these beings.

[Science has pronounced the world of spirits and gods an invention of fantasy. It has pronounced the "world spirit," the "absolute spirit," and the "absolute will" inventions of metaphysics. But it has had to devote more study to the question, still not decided in all its particulars, of to what objects in the external world consciousness, reason, and will must be attributed and in what degree. For a long period prehistoric man was disposed to apply the notion of a conscious life, similar to human consciousness, to almost all objects.] [6] Subsequently, critical inquiry narrowed the circle of conscious objects more and more. There was an attempt to attribute psychical processes to man only, but later it proved necessary to extend them also to many animals, in a different degree. [Presently there is a tendency among some investigators to assume consciousness both at a very early stage in the development of organisms and, further, in nearly every substance, peopling, as it were, even the atoms of gases with thinking "homunculi."]

On the other hand, even in man critical inquiry has revealed a long series of gradations in the rationality of actions. It has found in him a set of purely mechanical, unconscious phenomena. Next —another set of phenomena, in which the lowest animal impulses become conscious, but operate with an irresistible force and without reflection playing any role. Then a third set, in which thought follows a routine course as if mechanically, though it cannot be said that consciousness or reflection are absent here or that the rapidity of the action prevents it from being appraised; nevertheless the judgment of one's personal responsibility comes only later, after the act is mostly or entirely completed. Still further on we encounter a highly complex set of actions performed under the influence of powerful emotions and passions; here both reflection and the judgment of one's own moral responsibility are generally present, but the force of the emotion or passion prevails to the point where the person submits to it despite reflection and moral demands. Only beyond this group do we find the domain of actions in which a man is a reflecting and fully responsible being.

There are men who pass the greater part of their lives without performing any action which can be regarded as belonging to this last group. Much the greatest number of human actions must be attributed to the third group, that is, to actions performed under the influence of routine, habit, and tradition—as all the social animals perform their actions, which are often rather complex. The judgment of responsibility here, as we have said, comes during the action itself, or upon its completion, and sometimes does not come at all. The level of a man's vital development is determined by the proportion of actions of the last, fully conscious sort among all his actions.

From the foregoing it is evident that the attempt to find a rational motive for an accomplished action cannot be regarded as a

process which is always rational, and that in human actions
mechanical or animal motives are at work more often than the
strictly human. Just as it is essential for the criminologist to bear
this in mind in considering sentences and framing criminal law,
so too it is essential for the historian and the man of social action
to bear it in mind. It is essential for a critical approach to past
and present human actions and to men's tendencies to idealize
their own actions and the actions of others by seeking rational
motives for them, and essential, finally, so that there will be no
errors of calculation in the pursuit of practical objectives.

However limited is the sphere of human actions which may be
called rational, the tendency toward the idealization which sup-
poses actions to be rational is very widespread, and consequently
the majority of people desire to represent all their mechanical,
routine, and impulsive actions as rational. Some practice this
idealization with complete sincerity, but others do so only to elevate their own egos in the eyes of others or to achieve selfish
ends. Lack of knowledge and intellectual resourcefulness, however, prevents a significant number of people from doing this
unaided. Then they are delighted when others will do it for them,
and they willingly attach themselves to such people, who allow
them to pass off their stupidity as deliberation, their animal impulses as moral and political principles, their conventionalism as
conservative theory, their cowardice as devotion to the state, their
baseness as heroism, their cupidity as service to law, their personal vexation as a crusade against falsehood.

This is what furnishes the parties which inscribe great words
upon their banners with the greatest number of adherents.
Whenever such banners are raised there are people who need
them to screen the petty content of their own activity with high-
sounding words. Thus the calculating proclaimers of great
principles—under the protection of which the leaders aim to implement the selfish interests of their own class or circle—generally
gather a party of followers more readily, or this party becomes
more numerous, the easier it is to use the new banner to conceal
the mechanical, animal, conventional, and impulsive inclinations
of individuals. In this case what makes it all the easier to effect the
idealization is that each of the high-sounding words has been in
fact a slogan of a progressive party, a formula of progress, more

than once in the course of history. Consequently in such periods poetry and philosophy, custom and tradition have quite sincerely and rightfully surrounded it with the halo of greatness. The false idealizers have only to point to these panegyrists, notoriously sincere and gifted, and draw from the arsenal which the latter have set up the weapons they need for their own ends.

In view of this phenomenon, critical inquiry must address itself still more rigorously to the high-sounding words inscribed upon party banners, and examine still more carefully the extent to which idealization of the degrading or legitimate impulses of the individual is concealed under them.

In the last letter I distinguished two groups of great ideas, corresponding to general principles and particular social institutions. The same distinction may be made here. As for the general principles, criticism's method of exposing false idealization is extremely simple: all that is needed is to determine in what sense the parties are employing the words "reason," "freedom," "the common good," "justice," and so on, and to see how far the meaning attributed to all these words corresponds in the given case to their true progressive significance. Of course this is possible only when critical inquiry itself has already clarified the true significance of these words.

For particular social institutions the task is more complex. I have already stated in the Sixth Letter that social institutions are the product of natural needs and inclinations. To the extent that these needs and inclinations are natural, to that extent, but no further, the institutions produced by them are legitimate. In history, however, an institution which is a product of one need has often proved suitable, for lack of something better, for satisfying other needs as well. As a result such an institution has been turned into an organ with the most diverse functions, and in this form—by being subjected to true and false idealization—it has been proclaimed as a party banner, as a highly important instrument of progress.

In such a case the task of critical thought is twofold. First, it must identify the real ambitions concealed behind the words inscribed upon the party's banners. Second, it must discover the natural, and consequently the legitimate, need which called into existence the institution which the party proclaims as its fundamental principle. Through the former procedure, critical thought destroys the false idealization of those who advance an institution —which may in itself be worthy of respect—in defense of ambitions that have nothing in common with it. Through the latter, critical thought combats both those who have made a fetish of a high-sounding word without understanding its meaning, and those other false idealizers who *deny* the legitimacy of a need that is entirely natural, and in so doing give rise either to a perversion of human nature or, more commonly, to hypocrisy.

The latter task has a positive as well as a negative side. By revealing a natural need or a natural inclination at the basis of a given social institution, critical thought thereby recognizes the legitimacy of these bases and demands the construction of social institutions on a foundation of *sincerity* of feeling—on a foundation of sincere regard to the needs and inclinations inherent in the nature of man. This realization in social institutions of moral ideals which are rooted in the very nature of man is a legitimate and truly human idealization of man's natural needs, in opposition to their *false* idealization in the guise of historically generated cultural institutions that in no way correspond to them.

[This truly human idealization is fully scientific, because the element of subjective opinion is present in it only to the extent that it is completely inevitable in any investigation of psychic phenomena. A need is a real psychic fact, the particular features of which must simply be studied as fully as possible. Once a need has been established as natural it must be satisfied within the limits of its healthy operation, and social institutions must be sought which will best satisfy it. I may be mistaken in my definition of the natural need which underlies a particular social institution. I may be mistaken as to the consequences which in my view necessarily flow from a sincere regard for this need. A more expert investigator may uncover new sides to the latter, and consequently construct a more correct theory of the corresponding social institutions. But the possibility of errors and their successive elimination in no way destroys the scientific character of the over-all method. Tracing social institutions to the needs which generate them, a sincere regard (that is, a straightforward regard, one free from irrelevant considerations) for these needs on the part of the investigator, the demand to adapt social institutions to them—nothing here requires any personal arbitrariness, dogmatic blindness, or work of creative fantasy. The investigation can be carried out strictly methodically, with all sources of personal error eliminated. Consequently it is scientific, and its result—a theory of social institutions as they *ought to be* on the basis of clearly understood human needs—is a product of true and scientific idealization in accordance with need.] [7]

Thus every need admits of a legitimate and truly human idealization appropriate to it, just as we may reject only what has been introduced into it by culture. This is the limit of thought's relationship to it. By denying a law of nature we shall not abolish it, but shall only call forth a more pathological manifestation of the law, while hypocrisy prevails in the social institution. False idealization cannot make the slightest change in a law of nature. It only introduces falsehood into social institutions, which always makes it possible for the more cunning and less moral person to oppress the less cunning and more moral.

But it is precisely this falsehood and injustice, introduced into social institutions by petty egoistic interests under the screen of false idealization, that generates constant irritation and makes [existing] social institutions precarious. The only way to make them more durable is to introduce real vitality into them—to replace their false idealization by true. This is what chiefly constitutes the work of thought on cultural institutions, in which the advance of civilization consists.

As the reader can see, in this process there is, properly speaking, nothing negative, destructive, or revolutionary. Thought strives constantly to make social institutions more durable by discovering their true bases in genuine human needs; through studying these needs, it fortifies social institutions with science and justice. What thought's critical inquiry rejects is exactly the element that is making social institutions unstable. What it destroys is precisely what threatens to destroy civilization. It strives to prevent revolution, not to provoke it.

Turning to the most elementary human need, the need for food, we find false idealization even here in the form of an artificial, culturally developed need for costly delicacies and in the form of the illusory benefit of free meals for the poor, which promotes parasitism. At the same time the false idealization of asceticism, by denying that every man should have his fill, has led naturally to [absurd forms of fasting, to the equally] absurd accumulation of precious metals in the temples of gods, where no one needs these treasures, and to the transformation of centers of asceticism into sanctuaries of immorality and ignorance. To both these false idealizations science opposes the recognition that the need for food is natural and legitimate, plus a theory of its satisfaction based upon physiology and sociology. If science idealizes the need for food it idealizes it correctly, by indicating how much food a given individual needs and how much he can appropriate without violating distributive justice, and by developing techniques of culinary art for the wholesome, economical, and appetizing preparation of the required amount of food.

What can be said about the elementary need for food applies still better to all other needs. For all social institutions, progress has always consisted in the more strict identification of the natural needs which have engendered them, in a more sincere regard to these needs, in dispelling the illusions connected with them, and in idealizing them only in the manner indicated by the very nature of the need. Let us examine the principal institutions one by one.

[The first firm human union, the maternal clan, of necessity embraced all social functions and attempted to satisfy at once all needs of the individual. The same state of affairs continued after the maternal clan became the paternal clan and produced patriarchal families.] [8] Poverty of cultural development obliged this social form to satisfy at once the need to rear the new generation, the need of individuals for economic security, the need to defend them from outside enemies, the need to protect one member of the family from violence at the hands of another, the need to increase knowledge, and the need for creative activity. The heads of the [clan or of the patriarchal] family were at once instructors of the children, all-round craftsmen, statesmen, judges, custodians of traditions both theoretical and practical, lyric poets in prayer, epic poets in myth, actors in the cult rituals—and all this simply because kinship ties gave them a certain position in their tribe.[9]

Custom and tradition invested the family bond in its complex [patriarchal] form with poetic fascination, the majesty of a sacred union, the armor of law, the fetters of public opinion. At the same time, asceticism not only rejected the existing cultural forms of the family, it regarded the sexual impulse as a desecration of human dignity and preached abstention from sexual relations.

As a result of false idealization of the family, the power of the head of the family came to be frightfully abused, marriage was transformed into sale and purchase, and the subordination of children to parents became slavery. There appeared in the family a depravity, under a mask of decorum, which surpassed all the excesses of open depravity. The family reached the point of destroying every truly human relationship within it. It gave free rein to nothing but hypocrisy and the debasement of the individual.

Similarly, the ascetics who preached abstention from sexual relations could not destroy the sexual impulse without resorting to the radical measures of eunuchism. Here again there were only two outcomes: either the perversion of human nature, or a hypocrisy which concealed a still more refined attachment to what openly was denied. The majority of the sectarian fanatics who embarked upon this path ended by perverting man's physical organism. Others—the Shakers for example—apparently succeeded in perverting men psychically in this regard. Wherever fanaticism ceased to operate hypocrisy began to reign, and beneath the angelic garb of monks and nuns who had renounced all things carnal there often were concealed still more numerous animal motives than among laymen.[10] Celebrated trials have shown that the so-called sanctuaries of purity became in fact arenas of orgies which explored not only all levels of natural need but ventured very far into the realm of impulses which modern Europe has come to regard as unnatural. At times the mystical negation of sexual impulses has even been reconciled, in the rapturous ecstasies of some sectarians, with the artificial excitation of these very impulses. In all these cases we see that asceticism has engendered false drives in groups of people whose specific purpose it has been to deny or to pervert a fundamental impulse of human nature and who have prided themselves upon so doing.

In history the progress of the [clan and the] family took three paths, of which the chief was the gradual withdrawal from the head of the [patriarchal] family of those powers with which he had to be invested only when culture was very undeveloped. [First of all the kinship tie based upon unexamined custom gave way to other social ties, in which individual thought was active in the form of calculation, feeling, or conviction.] Critical thinking produced the industrial system of the division of labor—at first according to hereditary caste succession, later according to personal inclination. It produced the political system of state protection of individuals against external enemies, along with varied participation of the subjects [or citizens] in the government. It produced the juridical system of courts which are less involved in the interests of the accused.[11] It produced a system of methodical preparation for scientific work, independent of the authority of the heads of the [clan or] family. It produced standards of art which made artistic activity the property of especially gifted individuals only. And it produced (and is still producing) a system for the education of the younger generation by only those adults who have been properly prepared for this task both intellectually and morally.

As the powers of the head of the [patriarchal] family were reduced in number, thought also had a better cultural basis for combatting false idealization in this sphere. Eulogy of the family was countered by satire. Skepticism and cynical attacks shook its sanctity. Law began to protect the members of the family against the despotism of the head, and permitted divorce. Public opinion sought other ideals. Parallel with this, critical thought combatted, on grounds of science and justice, the asceticism which denied the sexual impulse completely. Physiology proved that asceticism is unnatural. Political economy proved that it is ruinous to society. History proved that its legends are fantastic and that it has failed to live up to its own ideal.

In replacing these false ideals which paled under the light of critical thought, the true idealization of the sexual impulse took precisely the path mentioned above: the demand for sincerity. As a physiological impulse, it was an undeniable natural fact. As a free choice, it became a fact for thought to work upon. Since ancient times this choice has been idealized aesthetically, as a choice made in the name of an attraction to beauty. The progress of idealization consisted simply in the fact that, in conformity with the work of thought, beauty or attractiveness was transformed into merely an *occasion* for choice, while intellectual and moral worth became its true foundation.

The idealization of love has been celebrated—independently of the family tie and in spite of asceticism—for almost as long as traces of the human word have been preserved. But it has always had something of a false ring when, along with the songs of Saadi and the troubadors and minnesingers, along with the madrigals of the seventeenth and eighteenth centuries and the lyric effusions of Schiller's contemporaries, there existed the cultural customs of the harem and of marriage according to the will of the suzerain or of parents or for business reasons, and when the ideas of marriage and love suggested ideas of perpetual obligation as well.

So long as [in the patriarchal family] a woman was inferior to a man both by cultural custom and in level of intellectual development, lovers' moral ideals differed and consequently the idealization of their mutual attraction bore no trace of equality. A woman sought in a man the moral ideal of strength, intelligence, energy of character, social influence, and civic activity. But for her this was not an ideal but an idol, because *she* forsook its fulfillment in life. A man sought in a woman merely an aesthetic ideal of beauty and grace, while regarding this same ideal as degrading to himself and even allowing coarseness to be a virtue for *him*. Thus on the woman's part correct idealization of the sexual impulse was out of the question. Condemned to worshipping an idol, which nevertheless included a legitimate attraction to moral strength, she bore the whole burden of the *obligatory* cultural forms of the family. All the labor of thought in constructing an idealization through the legitimate attraction to beauty redounded to the benefit of the man, upon whom culture conferred the right of *free choice*.

The true idealization of mutual love becomes possible only when a woman commands respect in the name of the same ideal of moral dignity that has been established for the man. Then a union of love represents the reciprocal free choice of two beings who are mutually attracted physiologically, and who join together because each respects the human dignity of the other in all its manifestations. Physiological attraction remains the rightful basis of their union, but it is subject to legitimate and humane idealization. Their union is strengthened by the fact that through it, in aspiring toward the same moral ideals, they mutually perfect and develop each other.

It is this, too, which transforms a casual attraction into an enduring moral union which is not cemented from without, is not obligatory in the name of cultural customs and traditions, but is created by the individuals themselves. External obligation ceases to have any meaning in the face of this stronger tie. Mutual respect sanctifies the tie, while freedom of association eliminates all hypocrisy; and mutual trust makes the individuals who join together best fit to assist one another in the economic struggle, in intellectual work, in social affairs, and in educational duties toward the younger generation.

Given its proper, scientific idealization, the task of the family today has two aspects, each of which takes into account the inescapable conditions of natural needs, is grounded upon the sincerity of free affection, and poses an obligatory goal of human activity in the name of justice. The sexual impulse as the inescapable source; personal sympathy as the intimate bond freely determining choice; the mutual development of two equal beings for participation in the progressive activity of society as the obligatory social goal—this is one aspect of the family ideal of today. Education of the child by the adult as the inescapable source; preparation of the adult for the work of education as a personal inclination, the free choice of an enjoyed occupation; development in the future man of a mind which is fit for critical work and of conviction which is ready for a selfless cause, as the social duty—this is the other side of the same ideal.]

Thus, sincere regard to a natural impulse, by eliminating cultural forms which are illusory and false, presents the family [(if this name is to be retained)] with a new ideal, produced by thought—an ideal which has all the merits of the former ideals of the family but which safeguards the stability of the family in a higher degree since it is grounded upon scientific facts, upon the demands of justice, and upon the dignity of the human person.

Let us take another need which made its appearance in the earliest stages of human culture—the need for economic security, which has created the various institutions of property, inheritance, usufruct, the economic interdependence of capital and labor, and so forth.[12]

[As soon as the broad kinship association broke up into family groups which competed with one another economically under the protection of custom or law, of necessity there rapidly developed, out of the elementary methods for the temporary and more or less prolonged appropriation of goods, a concern for building up and safeguarding monopolistic personal and family stockpiles.] With societies so little developed, the individual's chance to earn a living was very insecure. Today hunting, pillage, or favorable weather enabled a man to acquire a great deal, but on the other hand these gains might not be repeated for a long time. And one had to live not only today but tomorrow and the next day. Furthermore there were old people and children in the family who could not obtain their own food, and one had to think about providing for them, too.

The simplest and most rational solution was to lay in a surplus on a successful day against possible failure on other days. The skillful hunter, the lucky thief appropriated everything he could seize, for the future maintenance of himself and his family. The thing he seized became his exclusive, monopolistic property, even when neither he nor his family could use it. Children likewise became monopolistic owners of what the father had procured, even when they would have been able to earn their own living. So long as society was at such a low level that no one could be guaranteed against starvation for even a few days, such monopolization of goods by the individual far beyond the bounds of his own and his family's immediate needs was almost inevitable. Each had to defend himself and those dear to him by every means at his disposal.[13] For man the struggle for existence was, if not the only, at least the prevailing law.

But conditions in society began to improve. Stockbreeding and agriculture reached the point where the likelihood of subsisting for some time exceeded the likelihood of perishing from hazards of every sort. Monopolization of *everything* seized or inherited lost the sense of urgency that had justified it in a more difficult age. But though it had lost its legitimate meaning, it remained a tradition going back to time immemorial, a cultural custom which led—with the aid of an improved technology, the labor of slaves and hirelings, and perfected methods of plundering—to the monopolization of vast holdings in the hands of a single class, a single circle, a single family, a single person. Hence the form of economic system of a society [based on monopolistic private property,] where a minority of hereditary proprietors is surrounded by a majority of slaves, hirelings, and beggars.*

And now we see the poetic, religious, and metaphysical idealization of this system. Wealth, luxury, plundering, conquest, the hereditary aristocracy, the fat bourgeoisie have had their rhapsodists, their eulogizing theoreticians, their commandments to protect them, and their *te deums* to glorify them. Similarly, here again asceticism renounced all possessions and all economic labor and cultivated the parasitism of mendicancy [in the name of God].

In this case the operation of critical thought was preceded and aided by the natural evolution of such a system. The practice of rapacity and monopolization, carried over from a more savage system to a more civilized society, was bound to bring with it elements of the primitive savages' form of life: the struggle of all against all and the precariousness of the very thing they were trying to make secure by such efforts. The aristocracy of proprietors went into physical and moral decline. Personal and family attachments parceled out property, while the members of the family wasted in senseless extravagance the wealth accumulated by plundering, and robbed and ruined each other in order to get a fatter portion for themselves. The state seized as much of the sacred private property as it could. Hungry hirelings and beggars stole what they could successfully steal. The social order became so unsteady that a vigorous push from without or an explosion within swept away the minority's tinseled civilization. Added to that, the mutual strife of the proprietors ruined them one after the other. In recent periods the monopolistic proprietors, in order to strengthen the social order, have been obliged to sacrifice an ever-increasing portion of their property on the army, the police, prisons, the poor, the fortuities of economic crises, and so on.

In view of these facts of history, the economic critique [of socialism] develops and strikes equally at the monopolists who live in the lap of luxury and at the ascetics who live as parasites.

---

* This would require extensive development, which was impossible in the edition published in Russia. I leave the text of 1870 almost without alteration. (1891)

Critical thought organizes the campaign of united labor against monopolistic capital and poses a new economic ideal. It acknowledges the need for economic security, but demands a social order in which the individual will be secure without at the same time being obliged to monopolize goods beyond his immediate needs.

Here again the idealization corresponding to the need is not new. It is the idealization of labor. But before, labor was idealized as a humble instrument of capital; as a subordination [of the worker] inherent in the laws of the world and the decrees of Providence; as a mystical punishment for original sin. Socialism offers the worker another ideal: [14] the ideal of the struggle of productive, useful labor against unearned capital; the ideal of labor as giving the worker security and winning him humane development and political significance; the ideal of labor as enjoying all the comforts and even the luxuries of life without having to resort to the devices of savages, to monopolization of goods by the individual, because the comforts and luxuries of life become available to all.

From the elementary needs which we have examined in their false and true idealization, let us now proceed to the more complex principles which the history of man has produced.

ELEVENTH LETTER

Nations in History

OVER A LONG PERIOD, the descendants of kinship associations of different ancestry are drawn together by a wide variety of regional and climatic conditions and historical circumstances. For the most part all these associations adopt the same language, differing only in nuances of dialect, and take on more or less similar psychological traits and certain similar customs and traditions. History distinguishes the group thus formed from other, similar groups, as transitional stages disappear. The result is a historical product of birth and culture, a particular *nation*.

As soon as it has been isolated, a nation, like everything living, begins the struggle for existence. It hands down from one generation to the next a very simple ambition: do what you can to defend your existence, to extend your influence and dominate everything around you, and to devour other nations physically, politically, or intellectually. The more vigorous the nation, the more successfully it carries out the first demand. The more humane it is, the less significance it attaches to the last. Its *historical* role is determined by its capacity to influence other nations while preserving their distinctive features as well as its own.[1]

As a product of nature and history, nationality is a perfectly legitimate principle. But false idealization has been quick to effect its own transformation of even this great principle. Since at any given moment in history some nation or other, inevitably, is becoming a true representative of mankind's progressive march, a theory has arisen which identifies different social ideas produced by the common thinking of mankind with different nations. Since the greater part of the history of nations has passed in mutual slaughter and devouring, a doctrine of false patriotism has arisen according to which the citizen makes a virtue of the desire that his nation devour all others. Since the principle of nationality has played a role of no small importance in political history, a political theory has arisen which divides the earth into states according to nationality.

Let us take a close look at these theories.

Time and again in historical works and discussions we encounter the idea that some nation or other is in some respect the chief agent of progress; that it is pursuing a definite idea in the over-all forward march of mankind; that with its victory is linked man's development, and with its defeat his stagnation or long delay on the path of progress. There are even historical thinkers—including some quite remarkable intellects—who identify the general historical significance of the principal nations with different ideas of human reason, or with different psychological phenomena in an individual mind. What rational meaning can we give to these historical constructs?

If we consider it a historical fact that in a given age all the leading representatives of a certain nation were imbued with a single ruling idea, and that the most remarkable features of the literature and life of this nation served to express this idea—if, in a word, we see in the idea of a particular nation a general formula for one phase of its civilization, then we may accept the foregoing statements and grant them a historical meaning of no small importance. As a matter of fact, in every age the civilization of a society which is at all developed does have its own characteristic features and its own guiding ideas. Depending upon the health of the society, the success with which its institutions promote the all-round development of the individual, and the degree to which its civilization is integrated, this civilization expresses its idea more fully and determinately. It is clear that in such a case the nation's civilization has an influence, as an ideal center, on other contemporary nations and on succeeding ages of mankind. This influence is the more progressive the more the nation's guiding idea in the period in question promotes the development of individuals and imbues the forms of social life with justice. To the extent that these latter conditions are fulfilled we may also say that the nation is a representative of progress in this period, and that man's advance or delay on the path of development is bound up with its historical fate.

But ordinarily something more is meant by a national idea. It is supposed that the idea is not restricted to a particular age but links all the ages of national life—that it sums up the whole history of the nation. One can conceive of such a fact in three ways.

First, the civilization of a particular social system may have become so much a matter of national custom that it has turned into culture—into an anthropological feature—so that individual thought is no longer capable of devising improvements in social life, or is immediately stifled by social institutions as soon as it arises. Generation succeeds generation, but the forms of life and the guiding ideas remain the same. In other words, complete stagnation reigns and the history of the society has become a zoological function. But it is a little strange to call "progressive" a civilization which serves to embody an idea in *this* fashion. Nations which have sunk to such a state no longer influence the development of mankind. No one desires their triumph; no one regrets their destruction. Upon collision with something living they are doomed to [historical] death, unless they are able to awaken living elements within themselves.

Or, second, the idea that guides the entire history of a particular nation is to be regarded as something *innate* in all individual members of the nation—as an anthropological element which is inherent in their brain structure and which conditions the development of a whole series of generations, however diverse the forms of their culture and however extensive the development, or fantastic the fights, of their thought. In such a case, nationality must be regarded as one of the specific differences within humankind.[2] [The causes of the likeness in individuals' cerebral or psychical systems must be sought in their common origin.] In other words, from this point of view a national idea exists only in nations which have been formed by *birth*. Apart from members of the same race it is unthinkable.

But where are there such nations in history? In modern Europe only the Germans might be able to lay claim to racial unity, since for all other nations intermingling of races is a historical fact. But even among the Germans it is easy to find racial diversity; to see this we have only to glance at Riehl's well-known work *Land und Leute,* for example. In ancient history, Rome was a hybrid nation, and many scholars believe on very good grounds that the same is true of Greece. Persian civilization was properly speaking Medo-Persian. To more ancient ages we may as well not appeal, since they offer science no firm support for any substantial conclusions [on this score]. If, then, unity of origin cannot be considered likely for a single historical nation, the proposed conception of a national idea is not admissible either.

Finally, we may imagine the matter thus. Individuals of the same race or of different races, under the influence of identical conditions of climate, soil, economy, and culture, develop certain common psychological traits—while they differ greatly in everything else. These psychological traits common to all, however they may have been acquired, are also what distinguish the nation. So long as they do not exist, the nation does not exist; as soon as they have been acquired, they can be formulated in a special idea, which is continuously manifested in the entire subsequent life of the nation. As the nation influences the history of mankind, the corresponding idea also enters this history. The triumph or destruction of the nation entails also the rise or decline of its idea.

We can, of course, accept the initial premises of this theory, and some thinkers have already undertaken the task of investigating phenomena of national psychology. But the question is to what extent one can admit something progressive in the distinctive national traits while at the same time taking them to be constant elements.

If comparing a nation's life with an individual's had any significance beyond the superficial likening of two diverse processes, one might acknowledge that the unity in the life of a historical nation corresponds to the unity in the life of a thinking human being. There are moments when a [cultivated] individual interprets his existence, weighs his strength, becomes imbued with a definite conviction, sets himself a general goal of life, and lives in accordance with this goal—deviating from it at times as a result of external influences or internal inclinations, but finding in this goal the unity and meaning of his entire development. If something analogous to this could exist for society, one might imagine that in a certain age the national consciousness awakens; that it formulates a conscious goal of national development; that individuals strive toward this goal, transmitting their aspirations to their descendants, who thus, inspired by the same idea, pursue the same conscious national goal in a new phase. And so it goes from generation to generation, until the nation's power to develop is exhausted like a senile individual's, or until a historical catastrophe shatters the nation as disease or violence destroys an individual.

Such a comparison, however, is a fantasy. The only thing common to the life of an individual and the life of a nation is that for every shattered nation there was a moment when it appeared on the historical scene, a period of historical existence, an age of life and an age of agony. Beyond that, everything is different. For the individual, the physiologist can show how the very same processes which develop an embryo into an infant also develop the infant into a mature being, and subsequently lead the old man to inevitable death. For society, all attempts made thus far to give anything resembling such an explanation can only be regarded as unscientific. Furthermore, in the historical life of a society, phenomena which by strict analogy can only be regarded as ages of youth and senility are sometimes repeated several times over. As for the death of societies, history does not know their natural death but only a series of murders of some nations by others, and thus even the question of whether a historical nation *can* die a natural death cannot be considered decided. Consequently, it would be more accurate to compare nations with an individual who is born, sometimes becomes senile and grows young again several times over, and is subject, in most cases, to being murdered whenever a convenient opportunity arises. Such an individual belongs to the realm of fantasy.

Still more fantastic is the assumption that the national idea is handed down from generation to generation as a conscious tradition. No one has ever shown, with confirmation by anything resembling scientific fact, so much as the shadow of a conscious tradition of any idea for any historical nation. As we saw at the beginning of this letter, the generations of a given nation hand down only one ambition, which is in no way ideal. Its demands are common to all nations, and they contain no *idea*. It is nothing but the natural struggle for existence. Wild animals, people in their clashes with them, and primitive people in their clashes with each other have all been governed by its demands, and nations in their clashes are governed by them now. There is nothing progressive in these demands. Of course, without conflict among individuals, there would [probably] have been no subsequent progress. Without conflict among nations, the advances of civilization would hardly have been generalized and disseminated. But necessary conditions for the commencement of progress are not yet progress, and the tradition of conflict among nations merely *precedes* an understanding of their just relationships—an understanding with which conflict ceases and the common progress of nations begins.

Aside from a *conscious* tradition of a national idea, it remains for us to assume an *unconscious* transmission of some constant ideal aspiration from generation to generation. But is there any possibility of actually proving the existence of such an aspiration? By way of example let us take two unquestionably historical nations, for the first of which there is even a possibility of assuming racial unity—though the antiquity of this nation's origin prevents a completely scientific resolution of the question.

The Jews, despite their small numbers, played a historical role in antiquity and in medieval Europe, and they are not lacking in historical significance even in our time: some writers have linked the revolutionary disturbances in Germany at the end of the 'forties with the influence on German society of its many Jews. [The names of Jewish socialists are so indelibly inscribed both in the annals of science and in the annals of the social agitation of the whole period following 1848 that it would be impossible to deny their influence, which it is hardly legitimate to separate completely from their nationality. The anti-Semitic movement of the last decade itself represents, in a pathological form, the recognition by their enemies that the Jews as a distinct group constitute a social force which in one way or another influences the most vital functions of contemporary society.]

But can one really for a moment suppose that the prophets of the time of the first fall of Jerusalem, the medieval cabalists, talmudists, and translators of Averroes, and the contemporaries of Heine, Rothschild, Meyerbeer, [Marx, and Lassalle] have all represented one and the same idea in history? Yet there is hardly a nation in which distinct identity and the power of tradition have been more important than among the Jews.

As another example let us take France, and here for convenience let us simply look for a few salient features in its history. In recent times, of course, the tendency toward administrative centralization can apparently be regarded as such a feature. On this point the Convention, the doctrinaires, and Napoleon III were in agreement. The politicians centralized the government; the university professors centralized education; Auguste Comte wanted to centralize, by means of his positive religion, all manifestations of thought and life. If a feature common to such diverse parties in a recent period is not an element of the "national idea," we shall hardly find anything more characteristic. But who has ever looked for this feature in feudal France? Yet one cannot but assume that the French nation was already defined in the feudal period.

Let us take some periods when French literature unquestionably influenced Europe. In the twelfth century we meet the medieval French epic, which was imitated everywhere. The scholastics of the University of Paris in the thirteenth and fourteenth centuries were the teachers of Europe. The court poets of the seventeenth century likewise found imitators. The Encyclopedia of the eighteenth century, in its turn, ruled European thought. Let us compare these four periods; let us add, perhaps, the less influential period of the new French romanticism and eclecticism. What common idea will we find in all these phases of French thought, which in greater or lesser degree influenced mankind's development? If we reject interpretations which are completely artificial and strained, we shall also have to reject any idea common to the whole historical course of French thought.

The same may be said for all other outstanding features of whatever sort, with respect both to France and to other nations. There proves to be no common idea running through the entire history of any nation.

Thus it seems that one may grant a national idea only the significance of a *temporary* general formula for the civilization of a certain people or a certain state. Through shared psychological traits and the events of history, a particular nation in some period of its existence *can* become, by virtue of the character of its civilization, an outstanding representative of one or another idea, and consequently can occupy, in the name of this idea, a definite place among the promoters of progress or of reaction in some period of the history of mankind.

Having destroyed the false idealization which identifies ideas with nations, criticism should proceed to the true idealization of the principle of nationality. We have just seen that a nation is not *by its very nature* a representative of a progressive idea or an organ of progress, but merely can become one. This being the case, the true idealization of the principle of nationality should consist in indicating how this *possibility* can be actualized.

On the basis of what has been said in the Ninth Letter, we can easily infer that if a nation—whatever the idea which permeates its civilization in a particular age—remains too long a representative of the same idea, it will almost inevitably pass from the progressive ranks to the reactionary or vice versa, because no idea can be granted an eternal monopoly on progress. On the other hand, we have now seen that the same nation can in the course of its history become successively a representative of various ideas. Sometimes it will stand at the head of the movement for a progressive idea. In another period, another idea, which has the most reactionary influence on mankind, will be inscribed upon its banner.

Hence it turns out that a particular nation can cease to promote progress both by stubbornly clinging to an idea once acquired and by changing its guiding principles. In the sphere of thought neither conservatism nor revolution is in itself a guarantee of progress. To continue to play a progressive role in history, a nation which has once acquired such significance must adhere to its guiding idea provisionally, while constantly testing—in the light of new circumstances, new demands, and new thought—the extent to which its idea remains progressive. In changing its guiding idea with the same end in view, a nation should again draw only upon a critical examination of the contemporary demands and contemporary thinking of mankind for the principles which it should inscribe upon its banner in the name of progress, as promising the best development for individuals and the broadest extension of justice in social institutions.

Hence it also follows that under favorable circumstances any nation can become an agent of historical progress. The better it understands mankind's contemporary demands, and the more fully it embodies them in the forms of its culture and the expressions of its thought, the more likely it is to attain this historical status. Of course, at the same time certain conditions—which I discussed in the Third Letter—must be present in the social order: The social environment must allow and encourage the development of independent conviction in individuals. It must be possible for the scientist and the thinker to assert propositions which they regard as expressions of truth and justice. The social institutions must permit of change as soon as it turns out that they have ceased to embody truth and justice. Apart from these conditions a nation has progressive historical significance purely by accident, since in itself a nation is an abstraction and one may say only metaphorically that it "understands" or "embodies" something. In reality only individuals—who, as has been said in the foregoing letters, are the sole agents of progress—can understand and embody things. They alone can make the nation to which they belong a progressive factor in mankind, or give it a reactionary character.

Thus true [national] patriotism for the individual consists in attempting to understand the natural requirements of his nation through a critical understanding of what is required for the progress of all mankind. At the beginning of this letter I indicated the three natural ambitions of a nation, but in the face of rational criticism they differ in significance.

The demand to maintain one's nation as an independent and distinct unit is perfectly legitimate, since it corresponds to the aspiration that the ideas in which a man believes, the language he speaks, and the vital goals he sets himself should be transmitted to the future as living elements and be regenerated in accordance with the demands of human progress, rather than becoming extinct. The only person who can legitimately refuse to support his nation is one who has become convinced that it harbors a principle of stagnation or reaction which it cannot throw off. But what nation cannot throw off such principles?

The ambition to devour foreign nations, destroying their distinctive features, is an antiprogressive phenomenon. A man who has set himself such an ideal has little right to the name of patriot, just as a man who advocates the assimilation of human social culture to the customs of a wolf pack or a herd of sheep has little right to the name of humane thinker. Such "patriots" defile the nation's banner and strive, consciously or unconsciously, to abase their own people by laying the stigma of brutality upon them and preventing them from being reckoned among the promoters of progress. Such a "patriot" was Cato the Censor with his celebrated refrain, "Carthage must be destroyed!" And the subsequent history of Rome showed how little the majority of Roman citizens benefitted morally and politically from the destruction of Carthage, and how, shortly thereafter, the venality of the Romans surprised even Jugurtha, while their civic consciousness was expressed in a number of local civil wars and bloody proscriptions, and in Caesarism. In Russia the same sort of "patriotism" is represented by the "Katkov press" which became its organ in the 'sixties and has multiplied and flourished in recent years.[3] As a denial of progress, the ambition of some nations to devour others is also a denial of true patriotism.

Maximize the truth in your nation's thought; maximize the justice in its system of social institutions. Then it can stand fearlessly beside other nations whose thought contains less truth and whose social institutions are less imbued with justice. It will influence them; it will dominate them morally without having need to devour them—that is, to deprive them of [independent] historical life. Such influence and such preeminence, every true patriot is entitled to desire. He has a rational right to seek such significance for his native land. He has a right to promote this historical ascendency of his nation over others with all his strength, because in so doing he is also promoting the progress of mankind.

Progress is not an impersonal process. Someone must be its organ. Some nation must, before others, and can, better and more fully than others, become the representative of progress in a given age. The true patriot can and must desire that it be *his* nation and thus that he be a contributor to its historical significance. [Precisely because the culture of his own people is more familiar and customary to him, and his own countrymen's modes of thought and action easier for him to master, he can more readily remain a patriot while pursuing the common goals of all mankind.] Rational patriotism consists in striving to make one's nation the most influential agent of human progress [with the least possible effacement of its distinctive features].

To this end the true patriot will strive, first, to provide his country with those social conditions, discussed above, without which the progressive development of society is unlikely. [He will strive for the greatest possible dissemination of hygienic and material comforts among his countrymen. In his native environment he will propagate critical understanding, a scientific outlook, and those social theories which are most imbued with the demands of justice. He will take an active part in the reformist or revolutionary movements which seek to introduce into the political and economic order of his country greater opportunity for the individual to develop and to defend firm convictions. He will support freedom of thought, freedom of speech, and forms of social contract which facilitate the replacement of obsolete laws and institutions by more perfect ones.] Next, he will strive for a better understanding of the contemporary problems of science and justice. Finally, he will strive, [to the limits of his ability,] to make his country the supreme representative of science and justice among contemporary nations. Apart from these aspirations there is no patriotism. There is only its mask, assumed by obtuse prattlers, self-loving publicists, or calculating exploiters of the animal passions of mankind.

If at the same time nations did not come into conflict in the name of the incidental interests of their rulers or in the name of the animal principle of devouring one another, this would be an end to the question of the significance of the national factor in progress. But the circumstances just indicated give historical significance to the stability and material strength of the national organization. The national question, in practice, gives rise to the question of the state.

TWELFTH LETTER

Contract and Law

IT HAS BEEN MUCH DEBATED whether the state is founded upon contract or precedes it. The historical school has made much sport of the theorists who imagined that semibeasts having no intercourse with one another suddenly got the idea that it would be better for them to enter into a contract and live in a state, and that thereupon they assembled, discussed the best course of action to take, made their decision, and became a state. The historical school has made it abundantly clear that such a deliberate contract presupposses everything that was supposed to have resulted from it. But however evident this is, the characteristic feature of the state has been equally evident: the legal obligation of its members to support the system it establishes and to compel those to support it who will not voluntarily fulfill this obligation. Thus there is here presupposed a genuine or fictitious *contract* linking all the members of the state. *Law* serves as the expression of this contract. These two principles are intrinsically so important and are subjected to false idealization so often that I think it best to examine them first separately before proceeding to the question of the state.

One of the first and simplest manifestations of thought is con-

cern for the future. An individual's infancy ends when he begins
to reflect about means of securing himself a better future. If it is
permissible [in any sense] to apply to society the much used but
highly inexact comparison of social with individual development,
one might say that society's infancy ends when the principle of
contract is established. By this means men attempt to secure
themselves against hazards in advance. For the changeable will
of the individual, for the unforseeable calculation of the better,
the more convenient, the more useful which will be made *tomorrow*, for the necessity of resorting to force or persuasion at the
actual moment of need—there is substituted an obligation, more
or less voluntarily assumed. Man himself binds his future.

The dread, invisible gods guard the contract with penalties in
this life and in the life to come. The penalties of law guard it
more tangibly. Inner self-respect—the honor of a man who has
given his word—guards it.

We must assume that this device has proved highly efficacious,
because thinkers have attempted to apply the principle of contract, really or fictitiously, to the majority of social institutions.
The physiological attraction of two lovers has been brought under this principle, just as has the relationship of citizens to the
state. The Jews have even found it convenient to represent the
religious life, the worship of Jehovah, in the form of a contract
between the god of the Jews and his chosen people.

In essence contract is exclusively an *economic* principle, since a
purely quantitative comparison of services is possible only in an
area in which there are mathematical quantities, and among social phenomena only the economic have found a standard of
measurement, in *cost*. Only things that can be given a set value
can be equal in value; but where it is impossible to determine
equality contract is [always] fictitious, because it is unjust.

Contract assumes a service rendered for another, equal service.
Thus in everything which can be given a set value it is perfectly
applicable. The exchange of goods for goods and of work for a set
price are the simplest cases, but even in these cases retrogressive
phenomena may be present along with progressive. Even here
there may be exploitation of man by man, the draining of the
strength and resources of one individual to permit monopolization of strength and resources by another. Contract is just, in

these cases, only when the two individuals equally understand the value of the goods and [the role] of labor and capital, when both equally need to make the exchange, and when both approach it with equal integrity.

But such a case is exceptional, and when it is encountered there is scarcely need of a formal contract. Contract must be viewed as a weapon against fraud and oppression. But a weapon of such a sort is required, in a progressive sense, only for the protection of the weak against the strong, because the strong are already protected against fraud and oppression by their strength. When a lawyer makes a contract with a man unversed in law, it is not the latter whom we should expect to introduce clauses which subsequently will embarrass the other party by some unforeseen legal point. When a capitalist manufacturer enters into agreements with a proletarian worker, oppression can come only from the side of capital.

Thus contract is a progressive principle only when it protects the weaker against arbitrary alteration of value by the stronger. When a more clever, more knowledgeable, wealthier man concludes a contract with the less clever, the less knowledgeable, the less wealthy, then the moral obligation of the contract should lie with all its force upon the former. The latter could not have understood or appreciated the conditions they took upon themselves, could not have had a chance to reject these conditions. Each such circumstance, by destroying the justice of the contract, also destroys its moral force. Executing it may be important in the eyes of society for the preservation of social order, the law of the state, and sacred custom, but certainly not for the preservation of justice.

Contract departs still further from the conditions of progressive development—that is, from the conditions of justice—when it demands of both parties to the contract, or of one of them, such services as can in no way be given a set value or are unrecompensable by any set value. The first case occurs wherever the economic element does not embrace the whole range of actions covered by the contract, or has no connection with these actions at all. [Actions which, given normal relationships among men, depend upon love, friendship, trust, and respect, cannot take place on an obligatory basis among people who preserve their human dignity, and consequently cannot be subjects of contract.] The second case occurs when the contract covers the entire life of one of the parties, or such a considerable part of it that no rational calculation can predict all possible combinations of circumstances that may arise during that time. In this case he who obligates himself to render an unrecompensable service acts just as wrongly as he who accepts such an obligation. It is undertaken under the influence of fantastic notions: that what I desire today I shall still desire tomorrow; that what I am today I shall continue to be all my life.

For economic obligations such long-range calculation presents no insuperable difficulties. The value of a service changes, but the value of the monetary unit also changes. For a person who assumes a great many such obligations, a loss in one is [often] balanced by a gain in another, which, together with the enormous economic importance of rendering services at the right time, [sometimes] compensates for any risk.

But for services which cannot be given a set value, such is not the case. Since there are no objective units of measurement for them, and consequently no possibility of their being compensated for by other equivalent services, these unpriceable services are based, in their moral signification, only upon the inner conviction of the individual. Only an action which accords with conviction is moral; only an action which is performed in accordance with conviction can be regarded as contributing to the individual's development. But a contract may demand of me actions which were in accord with my convictions when I signed the contract but have become discordant with them by the time I have to execute it.

Honesty demands the execution of the contract. And I shall execute it, but my actions will be venal and hypocritical. [Venal and hypocritical are the endearments of love, the sacrifices of friendship, the declarations of respect for authority and law, and the performance of a religious rite, when there is still no love or no longer any love, when pity or scorn have replaced friendship, when authority has become an outrageous yoke and law an acknowledged injustice, when belief in the magical or mystical power of the rite has vanished. These actions are venal because by them] I simply purchase the right to escape reproach from others and from myself for violating the obligation. They are hypocritical because in all such contracts it is assumed as an un-stated condition that I shall fulfill the obligation *in the same way* in which I contracted it, that is, voluntarily. But I shall fulfill it against my conscience.

I shall be told that I can avoid this hypocrisy be declaring that I cannot execute the contract voluntarily and am compelled to do so against my will, and that in such a case the responsibility for the immoral act falls upon him who demands its execution and not upon me. But this can only be regarded as a fiction. True, he who demands fulfillment of a noneconomic obligation when he knows that there is no desire to fulfill it, may and should be con-sidered a criminal. He is demanding an immoral and degrading act, and consequently he is himself immoral and base. But a crim-inal act performed by someone else in no way diminishes my guilt, when I know that I am committing a crime and still commit it, when I know that I am selling something which is not to be sold. A man who lays upon another the moral responsibility for his own actions is reducing himself to the level of a machine: only a machine is not responsible for its actions. But to reduce oneself to the level of a machine is no less degrading than to sell one's *self* through an action performed contrary to conviction.

The crime here is already incorporated in the contract itself. Any contract which demands the future performance of a service which by its very nature must be sincere and cannot be compen-sated for, is in itself morally culpable. Only through self-delusion do people commit themselves to friendship or to love (and to the actions corresponding to them) in the rather remote future, when the object of today's friendship or love may no longer merit either, and when they themselves also may have changed. The same actions which friendship and love call forth are profoundly immoral if performed without sincere feeling, purely out of obli-gation. Similarly it is criminal to assume an obligation to obey the orders of an absolute state power when you do not know what these orders will be, when you do not control them and are in no position to influence them.[1]

It goes without saying that a contract concluded for a lifetime, or for the indefinitely remote future, represents this same im-morality, multiplied by as many times as the continued repetition of an evil act is worse than committing it once. The latter may serve the individual as a stimulus to development, since he may wish to redress by useful activity the immoral act he once performed. But the former makes evil habitual, blunts a man's moral sensibility, and not only reduces him to the level of a machine but sets up mechanical activity as the ideal of all or part of his life.

This is particularly applicable to both of the areas from which the previous examples were drawn. [The sale of the endearments of love for a lifetime is still a degrading sale, though it be sanctified by Church and law. Voluntary support of an absolute and uncontrollable power is still an immoral and pernicious act. Performance of a religious rite by someone who does not believe in it is still a symptom of moral decay.] Actual and moral slavery [in all their forms] are natural manifestations of such an abasement of human dignity. For a society which envelops the greater part of individuals' lives in obligatory contracts, the more assiduously it regiments itself, the more it creates within itself the elements of reaction and of its own destruction.

Thus contract, one of the most important elements of social life, one of the simplest and to all appearances most beneficent of its discoveries, becomes a terrible, corrosive evil if it is extended beyond its legitimate sphere. There are periods in the life of a society when contract is its sole salvation. There are others when it becomes the most oppressive yoke.

[An analogy can be found in the career of an individual.] A young man must pass through a period in which he accustoms himself to consider the present in the light of the future, to weigh his words and his actions. But this acquired habit should not become the sole basis of the activity of the mature man; it is only an element in this activity. He who is *only* cautious becomes a coward. From absence of resolution he misses good opportunities. Sometimes he harms himself more by cowardice than by risk. He ends by completely losing the capacity for resolute action in any situation, even the most urgent for him personally. Caution and deliberation become potent instruments of vital advance only as aids to resolute action, as one element in bold and forceful thinking.

Similarly, society arrives at the idea of contract in its youth. [Elementary instincts, cultural habits, ancestral customs, or] an immediate community of interests unite people for a time. Their association is [convenient, habitual, or] advantageous to them all, and they realize this. But they have already become aware of the mutability of their desires and of their susceptibility to temptation. This awareness makes them apprehensive about the future execution of what they recognize as convenient or advantageous to themselves. They conclude a contract, which obliges them to do what is in fact most beneficial to them.

[Then comes another period.] In the society there are stronger men and weaker men, exploiters and exploited. The latter suffer at the hands of the former and distrust them. But there are moments when the former, for all their power, cannot achieve their objectives without the cooperation of the latter. This cooperation they purchase by guaranteeing the exploited against their power in the future, to a greater or lesser extent. A contract is concluded between the strong and the weak at a moment when the strong happen to be weaker and the weak happen to be stronger. Consequently this contract gives the social order more justice than it had before.

Gradually the advantage of such contracts becomes so evident that people cannot fail to notice the improvement in social life which comes as their direct result. Contract is idealized. [A contract is sealed by magical rites which threaten its infringer with inevitable retribution. A host of invisible spirits is called to witness it and, as it were, take part in it.] Subterranean and celestial gods come forth as guardians of the oaths, and these almighty and all-knowing witnesses, who punish both on earth and beyond the grave, impart objective sanctity to the contract. Honor becomes part of the ideal of the moral man, in the broadest and simplest meaning of this designation, and this internal judge demands the fulfillment of contracts more insistently than all the Olympians. Contract thus takes on subjective sanctity. The ideal of the honest man is generalized in the images of poets and in the world views of thinkers. Honesty becomes a social custom. He who breaks contracts sees his condemnation in the sneer of an acquaintance, in the cool greeting of a friend, in the insinuation of a society scandalmonger. From the fantasy world of myths and the subjective world of convictions, honesty passes into the real world as the most sacred of social bonds.

But the dread Olympians, the guardians of the oaths, can be

propitiated by sacrificial offerings, and the [Christian] confessor absolves the perjurer of the sin which threatens punishment in the future life. A man's inner world is concealed from view, and he who to all appearances is a man of the utmost integrity may covertly be only biding his time for an act of gross dishonesty. As for the verdict of public opinion, the proprieties of social life form such a counterweight to the disapproval of dishonest acts that those who infringe contracts do not fare badly at all. What is more, in the eyes of the majority conspicuous success imparts a certain grandeur even to a dishonest act, and between *dupes* and *coquins* contempt is divided rather evenly. Perhaps it even falls more to the lot of the former.

Hence to safeguard contract it is found necessary to resort to an additional power, independent of the Olympians, the conscience of the contracting parties, and society's treatment of perjurers. Contract is placed under the protection of *law*, and law itself becomes a social contract guarded by all the power of the state.

Here at once two elements are added to contract which are completely foreign to its moral principle. Law itself (as we shall see in the next letter) is a fictitious contract, because not all subjects of the state who are obliged to fulfill this contract are asked for an expression of voluntary consent to it; and even if we assume that they were asked, the majority of them would be unable to assess the advantages and disadvantages of accepting the contract. Hence the term "honesty" cannot even be applied here, and we find ourselves in a completely different sphere of actions. On the other hand, the legal contract always tends to become more and more formal. The obligation of a legal contract depends least of all upon the inner conviction of the contracting parties and mostly upon various points of law, concerning, for example, the dates for submitting documents, the number and character of the witnesses, a word written in this fashion rather than that, and so on. The most eminently legal contract can be in fact the most dishonest act, just as the most honest agreement can be illegal.

Law becomes an element of progress and a moral force only when legislation takes account of the two fundamental points mentioned above. The first is that any contract which demands a service that presupposes sincerity, and similarly any contract which binds a man's will for life or for a considerable period of time, is in itself criminal. The second is that a contract, even one relating to services which can be given a set value, is just only when the contracting parties are on an equal footing with regard to understanding the contract [and with regard to the possibility of declining it]. Thus legislation, to be moral, must prohibit all absolute contracts of the former sort; as for conditional contracts, it must guarantee the contracting party the chance to declare his sincerity before the actual execution of the contract, or else refrain from executing it. Similarly, legislation must not only protect contracts already concluded, but in the conclusion of contracts must defend the weak against the strong, the less clever and knowledgeable against the more clever and knowledgeable, by giving the former the chance to acquire a good understanding of the provisions which might subsequently harm them. Law is an instrument of morality, an instrument of progress, only when it safeguards the sanctity of the fair contract and becomes a bar to the unfair.

But if legislation has not had this in view, but is in fact based upon the fiction that most actions can be subjects of contract and that the parties to a contract equally understand its meaning and its force [and have had an equal chance to decline it], then contract becomes a snare for the weak in the hands of the strong and fosters one-sided development in society—fosters deliberation and cautiousness, as consequences of universal mutual distrust. Then the gods who guard oaths turn into a metaphysical god, the state, wherein the volumes of the code take the place of morality. Honesty pales before legality, and there appears a breed of moral monsters who imagine that by having fulfilled the letter of the law they are men of integrity. As for condemnation by society, it loses all meaning, both because expressions of public opinion prove inconsequential in the face of acquittal and conviction by law, and because formal correctness, becoming habitual in society, gradually replaces the habits of honest understanding and honest execution of a given obligation.

Naturally in such a state of affairs two social institutions are particularly exalted. Since by its very nature contract is the extension of commercial relationships to all relationships of life, the entire benefit of the legality which sanctifies complete freedom of contract accrues to the commercial element. Business competition becomes the model of social relationships. The family bond, social life, and public service take on the coloring of commercial transactions. Literature, science, and art become trades. Individuals who are better off than others, having a better opportunity than others to assess the force of a contract and to enter into it at an opportune moment, acquire great capacity to develop. The wealth and splendor of society increase. Industrial technology makes enormous advances, and attempts to turn science and art into mere instruments for its own betterment. By contrast, individuals who are less well off acquire less and less capacity to develop or even to hold their own. Not only are they oppressed by men of power, they are in addition oppressed by the invincible power of points of law. The stock exchange and the factory swallow up more and more elements of society.

On the other hand, since the law is upheld only by state power, the state also acquires more and more significance in life and in thought. In some cases, under the guise of better legal supervision of social affairs, administrative centralization is increased and the administrative network expands. In other cases, the honor and glory of the state in the abstract become an idol demanding incessant sacrifices of inanimate property and animate personnel. In the realm of thought the theory develops that the state is divine and that all man's highest ideals are identified with it. Thinkers seek social progress in the strengthening of precisely that element which, as society progressively develops, should be subjected to quite a different process, as we shall see.

But in such a state of affairs the strengthening of commercial and state elements in society gives rise to a further phenomenon. Since stronger individuals can easily fight their way into the ranks of the more fortunate minority when circumstances are at all favorable, the most vigorous intellects do not suffer the discomforts of the social order to any great extent. They look at it critically from a theoretical point of view only. Not only do they quickly become reconciled to its discomforts, but for the most part, through the very force of circumstances, they join the ranks of the defenders of the *status quo*. As for malcontents, they are all ensnared so tightly in the administrative and juridical network that criticism of what exists either cannot be expressed or is expressed too feebly. As a result the state approaches the celebrated ideal of the completely stable social system—which, expressing it more accurately and graphically, should be called the ideal of stagnation. The cultural element of custom and tradition becomes more and more firmly entrenched in society. Thought labors with increasing difficulty under the conditions of commercial profit and legal restraint. It sinks deeper and deeper into the rut of customary opinions and traditional forms. Life in the society begins to wane. Its humanity diminishes. The likelihood of progress decreases.

Of course even in this situation elements are ordinarily encountered [in society] which can support thought in its work of criticism. Sometimes the state element comes into collision with the economic.[2] Or within the class which is concerned with economic matters the more far-sighted begin to note the danger threatening society both from the suppression of majority interests and from the possibility of stagnation. Or science, which both industry and the state need, becomes an instrument of social criticism and progress. Or, finally, thought operates within the downtrodden majority and generates an explosion which in turn awakens the society to new life.

[The past one hundred years have presented a number of examples of how, with increased participation of the business and state elements in social life, social discontent has led to more or less major reform movements and, in the event that there were no legal avenues to reform, to revolutionary outbursts. At the end of the eighteenth century, the French bourgeoisie had sufficient economic and intellectual strength so that with the support of the downtrodden masses exploited by the state it could, in the absence of any legal concessions on the part of the *ancien régime,* carry out a purely political revolution in its own behalf. In the 'thirties, again with the support of the discontented masses, who did not recognize their class antagonism to the bourgeoisie, the latter made itself out to represent a constitutional state (*pravovoye gosudarstvo*) against the police state, but in fact was only consolidating its own legal and economic ascendancy.

[At present, consciousness of the class struggle is penetrating more and more into both the theoretical writings of sociologists and the stirring masses of the working class. The latter continue to organize, and their organization inevitably promotes the very capitalistic economic process which tends to centralize property and gives rise to an inevitable succession of industrial, commercial, and stock exchange crises. The governments and ruling classes of Europe and America are doing their utmost to avert the impending catastrophe, which must envelop every sphere of social life as a result of the economic revolution. Even here there is still a chance that timely concessions by the ruling classes through legal means will facilitate the transition to the new order. But with each day this chance diminishes, and at the same time the likelihood of a more acute and bloody catastrophe increases.*

[But I have already had occasion here to discuss those modes of solving social problems which lie outside the legal sphere.] ³ In connection with the foregoing I should like to call special attention to the fact that the transformation of the moral principle of contract into a formal principle of law is not a progressive phenomenon, just as the substitution of legality for integrity is anti-progressive. In the Ninth Letter I have already discussed the fact that in itself law, like all great principles, can be both an instrument of progress and an instrument of reaction. From all that has gone before it can be concluded that the true idealization of law—as also of contract, which gradually changes into law—must have its source in *other* principles. Only these auxiliary principles, by supplementing and regulating the principles of contract and law, can eliminate the tendency toward stagnation which lies at the heart of legal formalism.

A contract is sanctified by the individual's conviction at the mo-

---

* In our country, with its archaic political institutions, the struggle for the elementary requisites of a constitutional state still goes on side by side with the universal modern struggle for a better economic order. The social evils resulting from the present demoralizing influence of uncontrollable power and from the threat of future social catastrophes can be mitigated only by the firm and broad-scale organization of the socialist elements in society, with the support of the harried advocates of a constitutional state, who ought to realize that in the present day a constitutional state is no longer conceivable apart from the victory of labor in its struggle against capital.

But can those forces which, alone and with frightful losses, have led the struggle for a better future in Russia for eighteen years, again succeed in organizing? Will the Russian liberals finally understand the only role which both their principles, properly understood, and their vital interests permit them to adopt? On this hinges the form in which Russia will participate in the worldwide economic and political revolution which is inevitably approaching for all the nations which take part in modern civilization. (1891)

ment he enters into it—and similarly by his sincerity at the moment he executes it. A law is sanctified by the individual's conviction that it is a good law, whether in the sense that it protects fair contracts and prosecutes unfair, or in the sense that greater evil will spring from opposing the law than from observing it.

Faced with a contract which demands sincere actions in the remote future, the individual finds himself faced with the possibility of moral crime. He who has assumed such an obligation can only be pitied, because the dilemma of violating the obligation or selling the unsaleable is for him practically unavoidable.

Faced with a law which is opposed to personal conviction, the individual's situation is morally less difficult. In many states, law itself shows the individual ways of criticizing it and of contributing to the elimination of obsolete legal forms. This is the legal course. If it is not available, [the individual must join the ranks of those who are combatting the law which he cannot acknowledge and the system which prohibits his criticism. Whatever the consequences,] the man of conviction can always say to himself: I am acting in accord with my conviction; let the law punish me. This is the moral course.

There is another course, the so-called utilitarian, in which the individual, with an eye to the greatest good, subordinates his conviction to a law [which this conviction cannot justify]. But here there will always remain a question which is difficult to answer: is the evil morally worse than an act against conviction? The progress of society depends infinitely more upon the strength and clarity of the convictions of the individuals who make up society than upon the preservation of any cultural forms whatever.[4]

THIRTEENTH LETTER

The "State"

THOUGH IT CANNOT BE SAID of a single great social principle that it has not been abused by idealization, in recent times scarcely any principle has been subjected to this operation so extensively as the principle of the *state.**

There was, of course, a logical reason for this. Against feudal license, against the theocratic ambitions of Catholicism, and against the despotic ambitions of individual rulers, the principle of the state was an excellent weapon. The progressive party of modern Europe, combatting each of these ambitions in turn, was quick to display this principle upon its banner. During the transition from medieval to modern times, the representatives of the state principle—the jurists—acted in league with European sovereigns, helping them defeat the feudalists and the clerical party. It was a struggle between predatory forces, but in the name of the principle of the state, idealization embellished the activity of Louis XI, Ferdinand the Catholic, [Ivan the Terrible,] and so on, investing their enterprises with the halo of rationality and of an affinity for the common good. By the end of the seventeenth century, by which time Louis XIV and the Stuarts already held sway over the other forces, the progressive party had countered the slogan, "The state—it is I," with another slogan, "The state—it is the common good," and had declared war against arbitrary rule in the name of legality.

* The two letters which follow would require considerable emendation. The reader who is interested in this subject can find much that relates to what is said here in my work *The Element of the State in Future Society,* which appeared in London in 1876 as the first (and only) number of Volume IV of the irregular miscellany, *Forward!* (*Vperyod!*) [1] I plan also to say something on this subject in the last chapter of Part II, Book II, of my *Essay in the History of Thought in Modern Times.* Here I have confined myself almost entirely to expressing more clearly, in a number of places, ideas which Russian censorship compelled me to veil in various ways. (1891)

But here a phenomenon I have mentioned made its appearance. The word "state" proved flexible enough to admit of extremely diverse meanings. Some took it to mean strengthening the government, others to mean limiting the government through the broadest possible participation of society in political affairs. Some stressed increase in the size of the state and its external influence. Others emphasized the mechanical linkage of its parts through skillful administration, uniform laws, and uniform modes of life throughout its territory. Still others argued that only the organic connection of vital and sufficiently independent centers, united by a community of clearly recognized interests, constitutes a state. It proved necessary to carry on polemics not *for* the state or *against* it, but in order to come to an understanding of *what* precisely constitutes the true ideal state.

That the *state* is the chief social principle, there seemed to be no need even to argue. Except for benumbed feudalists and clericalists everyone agreed, and the victories gained by the principle of the state over medieval principles and over the arbitrary rule of individuals were fresh in everyone's memory. Thus, conservatives and progressives, monarchists and republicans, men of order and men of revolution, practical men and philosophers—all agreed on one thing: recognition of the state as the supreme principle, the law of which cannot be put on a level with other laws but is supreme, and admits of certain limitations more from a spirit of humanity than from acknowledgement of others laws. Around the 'thirties of this century the deification of the state reached its apogee, and the last great representative of German idealism, Hegel, was at the same time the thinker who expressed this deification most baldly.

But history moved on, and the critical inquiry which was elucidating the true meaning of the state did its work. Political economy discovered in social life elements which have nothing to do with politics but have an incomparably more profound influence on the general welfare or misery than politics does. The influence of the stock exchange on political affairs translated the theoretical reflections of political economists into the realm of practice. The principle of nationality, which the idealists had overlooked, declared its right to govern the decisions of diplomats concerning territorial boundaries, and in many cases its declarations proved so effective that the principle of the state was obliged to yield to this new [(but in fact very old)] principle. Finally, it was found that the modern social order is threatened not so much by political revolutions as by social revolutions; that political parties blend into one another and that their significance pales before the antagonism of economic classes.[2]

Furthermore, among the theorists of the state one conservative party rendered it the dubious service of arguing that the state, properly speaking, is not a product of reason and reflection but is a natural, cultural phenomenon in social life. By this they intended, of course, to give the state greater stability; but in fact they destroyed its idealistic significance: everything that is necessary and purely natural, man strives to understand and to refashion. Consequently the question arose: should we not refashion the natural phenomenon of the state into a superior product, such that the quantity of human reason it contains will exceed the quantity of natural material?

All this compels us today to deal much more critically with a principle which only recently was deified—compels us to expose its false idealization and replace it with true: that is, by penetrating to the natural basis of the state in its simplest form, to show in what way this principle is open to progress—to show how it can satisfy the conditions of individual development and of the embodiment of truth and justice in social institutions.

As long as people live together pursuing economic, moral, and intellectual aims which each may freely modify or even renounce without fear of constraint, they constitute a *social* association to which everything juridical and political is alien. As soon as they enter into a contract which is binding upon the contracting parties, their society enters a new phase of its existence. It is bound together only *juridically* if the compulsory power which supervises the execution of the contract is vested in persons who are not parties to the contract. It becomes *political* when the authority which obliges the members of society to execute the contract is set up within the society itself. A political society becomes a *state* when it causes the contract which is binding upon the members who have entered into it, to be binding also upon persons who have never been asked to give their consent to it, or who consent only because they fear personal harm should they oppose it. Examples of the first three forms are a scientific society, a legal trade association, and a secret political organization.

It is clear from the foregoing that the state is as old as the forcible subjection of individuals to conditions which are not of their own choosing. Since there has always been an immense number of persons in society who, through lack of intellectual cultivation, knowledge, or energy, have needed other persons who are more intelligent, knowledgeable, and energetic to choose a mode of life for them, so the state system had its root in the first pre-clan groups and clans, in the first nomadic tribes, and is still by no means limited to the so-called *political* organs of society. Wherever a man, without deliberation, submits to conditions of life which are not of his own choosing, he is submitting to the principle of the state.

The foregoing also clarifies the two opposing views of the state which I discussed at the beginning of the Twelfth Letter. The principle of state obligation is, of course, a perfectly natural product dating from remote antiquity, and in fact the further we go into antiquity the more extensive is its application. Initially it appears as the physical domination of some men by others, subsequently it turns into economic dependence, and finally—now by way of idealization—it becomes a moral force.

But in the earliest stages of state development the principle of contract also appears, distinguishing the state from the simple subjection of one person to another. The head of the family, adult and strong, rules over the young children and the weaker women not on the basis of the state principle of compulsion but on the basis of personal preeminence. Similarly, the prophet commands the faithful through his personal influence. The state principle makes its appearance in the family when there are adult members who *could* disobey the head but who instead help him govern the others; in the religious sect, when the prophet is surrounded not only by followers but by aides. And in general the state arises whenever a group of people, in the name of their own interests, well or poorly understood, voluntarily *upholds* the obligatory character of certain decisions issuing from a person, an institution, or an elected council—an obligatory character which extends to others who have *not* entered this union voluntarily. Thus to the principle of *compulsion* is joined the principle of *contract* —with this peculiarity, that the contract is concluded by a smaller

number of people while the compulsion extends to a larger number.

Of course this extension of the principle of contract changes it
materially. The whole moral and legal meaning of contract resides, as we have seen, in the obligation of the *honest* man to fulfill a condition he has deliberately *accepted*. But here the contract
is actually concluded by *some* persons, while the fiction of a contract is extended to *others* as well. The conclusion of a contract
by one person in the name of others who have not the slightest
comprehension of the contract but are nonetheless obliged to fulfill it, violates the most elementary demands of justice and thus
contradicts the idea of progress.

What would a jurist think of a contract which is binding upon
hundreds, thousands, even millions of people, but which is known
with certainty to have been drawn up, ratified, and made obligatory by a few persons in no way authorized to sign it? How just
can we consider a contract which is concluded by one generation
and is binding upon all succeeding generations until they finally
decide to break it by force or drown it in blood? There is, of
course, no justice in such contracts, and they presuppose one
thing only: the existence of a powerful organization, or of a considerable majority of persons, for whom the contract is advantageous and who, thanks to their organization or their numbers,
forcibly compel all those who are dissatisfied with the state contract to submit to it. Leave the state or fulfill the state contract—
such is the dilemma confronting every subject.

If the number of dissidents is small, they alone feel the force of
this dilemma. They must either endure the painful yoke of laws
which are odious to them or resign themselves to sacrificing the
most elementary comforts of life, to imprisonment, banishment,
or execution, for failing to observe these laws [or for combatting
them]. They can, in the end, emigrate. As long as the malcontents
are scattered, they will always be suppressed. [The more prolonged the suppression and the more perverted the legal order
under which it takes place, the more completely does such an environment demoralize its inhabitants, by atrophying their clarity
of thought, their strength of character, their capacity to have convictions and fight for them, and finally their sense of social solidarity.]

But as the malcontents join together in a growing social force [and organize], it is no longer possible to ignore them, and the state system itself is threatened. The threats are of two sorts. If the malcontents are spread over the entire state territory or are concentrated in its chief centers, the state is threatened with alteration of its fundamental laws through reform or revolution. If, on the other hand, they are concentrated in one part of the state, it is threatened with dissolution. In both cases the state's cohesion is precarious, and this because its laws represent a fictitious rather than a genuine contract: a considerable number of persons are obliged to submit to the state contract who have never been consulted about it, have never consented to it, and submit to it only through weakness, want of energy, or inability to recognize their own rights and powers.

As participation of individuals in the state contract increases, the contract becomes more firm. First, because its discomforts are more readily recognized, more properly discussed, and can more easily be eliminated through reform instead of revolution. Second, because a greater number of individuals accept the law of the state as a contract binding upon them, while its opponents feel increasingly powerless and more readily submit to it. It is clear that the ideal state system is a society all members of which view the law as a mutual contract, consciously accepted by all, which permits of alteration by general consent of the contracting parties, and which is compulsory only for those who have consented to it, precisely because they *have* consented to it and are subject to a penalty for violating it.

But the reader will see at once that the ideal thus derived from the very essence of the state principle works to negate this same principle. The state is distinguished from other social institutions by the fact that its contract is adopted by a *smaller* number of persons and is maintained by them as binding upon a *greater* number. The two sources of state cohesion—the natural principle of compulsion and the deliberative principle of contract—come into conflict because the latter, in the name of justice, strives to diminish the former. Hence the inescapable conclusion that political progress has had to consist in the reduction of the role of the state principle in social life. And thus it is in reality.

Political evolution manifests itself in two tendencies. First, the state element distinguishes itself from all social institutions which have sprung from inherent (*nalichnyye*) social needs, so as to create for itself special organs. Second, the forcible subjection of the majority of individuals to the state contract is confined to an ever-diminishing number of individuals. In this latter process the fictitious state contract takes on greater reality and state cohesion is strengthened, but at the same time it approaches purely social cohesion. Both these tendencies may be called progressive, because the first looks to the theoretical truth in the idea of the state and the second to the introduction of justice into state institutions. Yet in the course of their realization both tendencies must reduce the state element in the life of mankind to a minimum.

When in more civilized societies the authority of the husband, the father, and the patriarch had lost almost all its coercive force in the family; when economic obligations, in the event of nonfulfillment, came under the jurisdiction of disinterested parties; when the judicial element was separated from the ecclesiastical and the administrative—then the proportion of human activity subject to legal constraint was not [particularly] large. A great many persons could live their entire lives almost without feeling the pressure of the state.

The roles of various social institutions were then revised in the theories of thinkers. The ideal of the family became a free union of lovers and rational education of the younger generation by the older. The ideal of [a dominating and intolerant] Church was replaced by the demand for freedom of individual conscience, for the free association of believers in pursuit of the practical aims of their faith. The ideal of economic association became [the conception of a free and solidary society in which there are no social parasites. In this society competition has disappeared, having been replaced by universal cooperation. Everyone labors for the welfare and development of all, while at the same time labor, by becoming varied and combining elements of both manual and intellectual work, not only is no longer onerous and stultifying but is itself enjoyable and conducive to development. Each receives from the solidary society everything he needs for subsistence and for all-round development according to his personal needs, while to the extent of his abilities he works for society, the development of which he recognizes as at the same time his own development.][3] Thus the element of compulsion, which extended originally to the family, to the economic relationship of slave owner and slave, landlord and serf, proprietor and proletarian, and to the court in its patrimonial, ecclesiastical, and bureaucratic forms, gradually loses its force in all these areas.

Cultural customs still sustain despotism in the family, it is true. Capital continues to rule the proletariat. The irremovable elective judge and the independent juror, out of personal interest, still bow at times to administrative orders; [these representatives of the "public conscience" are too often simply representatives of class interests. In some of these cases we are dealing simply with particular abuses which are inevitable in a society where only the most highly developed but inconsiderable minority is guided by principle, while the majority acts under the influence of personal and group interests. In other cases we have the result of a class struggle which becomes more and more acute as it is waged more consciously. Here the evil can be eliminated only with cessation of the struggle itself, and its appearance is no longer a function of compulsion in particular cases but hinges simply on the compulsorily disadvantageous position of one class relative to another in present-day society.

[All forms of compulsion are now being combatted and will continue to be combatted in the name of ideals which are already in part acknowledged, and which in the natural course of events tend to be actualized more and more fully. Some of these ideals are already being realized in the contemporary social order in the name of free individual competition—quite apart from the other consequences of this principle. Others should be realized when this competition is replaced by universal cooperation, and many thinkers consider it legitimate to hope that then the last traces of compulsion can disappear from society.] [4]

But the more the ideal of social institutions excludes compulsion and demands freedom, the more it must be protected from incidental abuses by individuals. Even if we admit that the individual who acts morally and rationally in all these areas will not permit himself to employ compulsion, we must remember what was said in the Tenth Letter: namely, that moral, rational activity is only *one* sort of human activity. A man may also act mechanically, under the influence of animal impulses, routine, or passion. It may be hoped that progress in humanity will decrease the proportion of actions of these sorts; but as long as they are present, as long as the intellectual and moral development of individuals remains highly inadequate, weaker men must be protected from the actions of the stronger. Such protection unavoidably assumes the character of compulsion, and hence embodies the state element. Of course even here this element tends toward a minimum, but it exists nonetheless, until progress significantly alters the inclinations and the habits of men. In eliminating individual and administrative arbitrariness, society strives at the same time to transform state organs into mere executors of impersonal law and to confine the state's role to superintending the absence of coercion, to protecting the weaker against constraint by the stronger. As a family man, as a believer, as a participant in an economic enterprise, a man seeks to confine the state system which he obeys to merely an impersonal form of law, interpreted and applied by a judge who is free from every state interest.

Here ends the progressive development of the political elements in society in its first aspect—that is, the differentiation of the state function from others. The false idealization of submission to authority in all spheres of society is destroyed by the principle of free association. The true idealization of the state demands justice from it: protection of the weak, protection of the fair contract and prevention of the unfair. It reduces the state's role in this connection to a minimum, and depicts its natural further reduction in the future as a result of the perfection of individuals themselves. The obstacles to progress here lie more in the old customs of society than in the actual nature of the case. [Primarily they consist in the insufficiently rapid decrease in the number of individuals who are forcibly subjected to the state contract.] [5]

This second political tendency encounters obstacles incomparably more substantial; nevertheless it is closely bound up with the first. The whole foregoing evolution of social ideals is based, just as is the protective role of the state, upon the assumption that the law accords with the vital needs of society. But this is one form of false idealization of this great principle. Law in itself, as we have seen, not only has no inherent reason for developing as society develops, but is inclined rather to shackle society in cultural forms and lead it into stagnation. Potentiality for development on the part of legislation resides only in other, supplementary principles [—namely, in altruistic sentiments, in the better-understood interests of individuals and groups, in moral convictions]. Law can be developed, but it cannot develop of itself.

Justice demands that law, in its origin, operation, and repeal, increasingly lose its compulsory character. This comes about through increased participation of society in legislation. As legislation is transferred to society and to its freely elected representatives, law itself provides the means for correcting laws. [That form of government which completely demoralizes society, and the authority of which is limited only by custom, is transformed into class and police states of various sorts, in which a certain portion of the population first acquires the right to influence the course of affairs. Subsequently it becomes imbued with the aims of the constitutional state, in which only the economic conditions of the class struggle limit such influence for the masses. State union comes closer and closer to social union.] The state [increasingly] assumes the character of an association of persons who have entered into a free contract and can freely change it. The compulsory character of the state contract diminishes, and tends to diminish still further. The ideal of the state, as I have already said, becomes the conception of a union in which he alone is subject to the contract who had the means and the opportunity to discuss it, did discuss it, acknowledged it freely, and can just as freely decline to execute it by declining all of its consequences as well.

But can such an ideal be realized? In general, is significant progressive advance in society possible in such a direction? Are there not insuperable natural or historical obstacles in its path? These questions force themselves upon us when we compare the present condition of civilized nations with the ideals we have posed, and when we note how far these ideals are from realization.

Knowledge and energy of character are necessary if the individual is to be able to defend his freedom and to exercise it without violating the freedom of others. But dissemination of knowledge and development of character are so insignificant in mankind that nothing can be expected from the present order but obligatory subjection of the majority to conditions established by a minority. Everywhere the state still shows us a mass of persons who from their very birth are subjected to a given code of laws and are pronounced criminals or traitors if subsequently they declare their disagreement with political institutions about which they have not been consulted. Of this mass, a small minority attains sufficient development to enable it to point out clearly just what it is that is especially onerous in these institutions which burden the masses, and with what exactly it is desirable to replace it, so as through reform to improve the condition of society without impairing state cohesion. Of this political intelligentsia, only a small minority attain a position in which they can put their views into action through legislation, [or at east attempt to do so.

[Nevertheless the work of this minority leaves its mark in history. There is a continual reduction in the number of countries which, though they have become part of this history, continue to preserve the archaic institutions of completely unlimited power, as in our country.] In the most advanced countries the government which rules over the state contract is formed by electing fiduciary representatives from the masses who are subject to the law, and the number of electors is enlarged as much as possible. The right to participate in revising the contract is increasingly extended: the patricians accept the political equality of the plebeians; the third estate merges with the nobility and the clergy; parliamentary reform bills lower the qualifications; generally, manhood suffrage becomes the law; champions of the political rights of women appear.

But however broad the suffrage and however great the difference between the political system of the United States of America and the system of an Asiatic khanate [or of the Russian empire], in both of these [extreme] forms, as also in all intermediate forms, there is still a common feature: the subjection of a considerable number of individuals to a [juridical] contract [or to a class domination] which these individuals have not discussed or concerning which they declare their disagreement. The state everywhere remains a forced obligation for a more or less considerable portion of the population.

Just in this last point lies the confining character of the state contract for the individual. A man is born in a particular locality. This locality is part of a particular territory, inasmuch as a series of events in the more or less remote past has partitioned the entire habitable land into [political] territories. By being born here, he is also subject to the local laws, which he has not discussed, has not accepted, and in the great majority of cases will never even have an opportunity to discuss. Yet they crush him, hamper his development, contradict his sincere convictions, and throw him into the ranks of the discontented. To leave his native land —this is a painful solution, sometimes in fact impossible to adopt, and in any event difficult. To submit against his convictions—this is an abasement of personal dignity. One course remains: struggle, with all its uncertainties and grievous consequences for the individual; [entry into the ranks of the parties of reform or revolution].

I have already discussed the path which parties inevitably follow here in their formation. But now we must take note of another circumstance [—namely, the danger to the state organism from the presence within it of contending political parties, and the disorder which this contention introduces into social life in general]. The presence of malcontents within its territory compels the state to expend a disproportionate amount of its energies on preventing violation of the laws and maintaining its own influence in society. This diverts society's energies from productive, developmental activity in other spheres of social life to activity which, in accordance with the demands of progress, should be reduced to a minimum, as we have seen. This creates irritation and mutual distrust in society, and consequently becomes a constant obstacle to healthy social cooperation.

A conservative assembly votes against an excellent and well-qualified lawyer proposed for a judicial post, because he has a different opinion about the best form of government. A liberal editor cannot buy the novel of a declared conservative. A professor of botany is replaced because a minister finds his views on economic questions dangerous. Friends are ready to fight a duel over the condemnation of a half-wit to death.

The broader the territory of the state, the more likely it is that, given some particular ground for dissatisfaction, there will be more malcontents in the state, it will be more difficult to keep track of them, and there will be greater expenditure of energies on the socially unproductive activity of protecting what should itself be confined simply to the role of protector. But intensifying such measures ordinarily increases the discontent still more, and the durability of the social system becomes more and more doubtful. The system is afflicted with the disease of chronic distrust and agitation, attacks of which are brought on by the most trifling events. Even if matters do not come to revolt, all normal physiological processes of the social organism are disrupted, [society becomes demoralized, and its solidarity vanishes].[6]

But the state which covers a broad territory is threatened by infinitely greater dangers if its laws generate discontent which is not individual but local: if they constitute a more or less willingly acknowledged contract in one part of the territory, but provoke the enmity of the population of another part.

In the whole course of history the demarcation of [political] territories has very rarely proceeded from a clear understanding of the needs of the population.[7] But even in those cases in which boundaries were established by the clearly understood needs of a particular age, there is no further guarantee that the rational linking of the territory's parts will remain firm and rational for long. The needs of a population in one age do not remain its needs forever, and while a society, as it develops, may strengthen the bond among its members, it may also generate divergent interests which separate regions that formerly had no cause for separation.

Separatism can spring from very absurd motives as well as from very rational foundations. But whatever its source, it is always a principle that weakens society. This is by no means to say that, to a state which had ruled over a territory of 100,000 square miles, its reduction by some 20,000 square miles, along with a reduction of income by a few million francs, constitutes a threat. The secession of the American colonies did not weaken England, just as the independence of India and Australia probably would not weaken her significantly. Separatism weakens society in that it is a principle of social discord and distrust. It makes one part of the citizenry indifferent to the common cause. It compels the other part to spend [—for the most part unproductively—] enormous capital in money and in men on protecting the unity of the state, when this capital is needed for social development.

If separatist ventures are unsuccessful, suspicion and enmity long persist in the memory of the victors and the vanquished.

Even if separation is effected, it takes time for the tradition of enmity to cool and for yesterday's enemies, who recently were *unwilling* allies, to establish the peaceful relationships of neighbors, of partners in a common human cause, of *willing* allies for some specific purpose. Only the convulsions of the first French revolution [and the more capacious political ideals it established] smoothed over the disaffection of Brittany and southern France for the Paris which dominated them. The memory of their eighteenth-century conflict still has not disappeared between John Bull and Brother Jonathan, their present mutual courtesies notwithstanding. The trees above the graves surrounding Richmond will yet bloom and fade many times over before the descendants of the Yankees and the copperheads [8] again [fully] feel themselves citizens of a single state.*

Thus, to states, the rise of separatist tendencies is incomparably more dangerous than separation itself. To forestall these tendencies is the aim of progress in the state, where a difference in economic conditions, a difference in political importance between the centers of authority and the rest of the country, a difference in the scope of the political activity of individuals and [political] parties, can always arouse discontent.

Violence conceals and [temporarily] averts the danger, but the danger continues to mount as the state's use of force increases. In the first place, there is increase in the mutual irritation of the citizens, which is exactly what constitutes the worst evil of separatism. In the second place, the use of force debases human dignity and puts a stop to all development in a society which becomes accustomed to it. But heightening of irritation in society and debasement of the human dignity of its citizens are phenomena which greatly weaken the state and place it in an unfavorable

* Only their community of socialist convictions and their international mission were able to smooth over the traditional distrust within the ranks of the socialists which the predatory partitions of Poland at the end of the eighteenth century bequeathed to the Poles, the Russians, and the Germans.

Unjust laws relating to Jews heve created animosity toward the political system of the Russian empire among whole groups of individuals who in fact had no grounds for political opposition, either in tradition or in their economic interests; while in countries where such laws have already been abolished, the memory of actual injustice in the past, by generating mistrust, has led to the shocking rise in "anti-Semitism" which we observe around us as one symptom of the present age of social reaction. (1891)

position with respect to its neighbors—whereas the whole object of the state's struggle against separatism can be nothing other than its external strength.

In fact, if we retrace the phases of history we shall find that size of states and firm cohesion of their parts have not been particularly important except from the standpoint of foreign relations. Economic prosperity, the scientific and artistic development of society, extension of the rights of individuals and establishment of more just relationships among them—these phenomena have been present in small states as well as large. Even if we were to imagine the world as a collection of separate, autonomous communes (*obshchiny*) we would have no reason to think that in all the respects mentioned we would encounter a reduction in progress, since broad economic, scientific, and similar undertakings could be carried out through intercommunal associations expressly formed for specific purposes.

But foreign relations are quite another matter. A state with a firmly organized dominion has an enormous advantage in war and diplomacy in a clash with a confederation of states, even one materially surpassing the former in strength, provided the difference in level of civilization is not too great (as it was in the Persians' struggle against the Greeks). Secrecy of combat preparations and vigorous pursuit of diplomatic objectives are infinitely easier for a single state than for a confederation of independent powers. Not to mention that the confederation can be fragile and fictitious: in such an event a small member can easily be crushed by a larger one, become a victim of its rapacity, or be placed in the position of having to follow the policies of the larger state, thus remaining sovereign in name only.

In any event, the foreign relations of states pose the question of small and large states on quite a different ground. The smaller the state, the looser the connection of its parts, or the more its geographical situation permits a predatory posture on the part of its neighbors—the greater are the dangers to which its independence is exposed. Consequently, the less stable is the internal development of society within it, the greater are the energies which it must expend unproductively in preparing for possible danger from without, and the more heavily do these disproportionate expenditures weigh upon its population. In such a situation it is quite understandable that false idealization sees every expansion as strengthening the state and every contraction as weakening it.

Of course, sometimes the loss of part of a state does weaken it, but this occurs when the part is a truly organic element of the body politic and is wrenched away by the rapacity of a neighbor, [as was the case, for example, in the predatory seizure of Alsace and Lorraine from France by the new German empire. Such seizures, of course, have a very unhealthy effect upon the country which suffers them, but again not so much in the sense that the country is really weakened as that a thirst for restitution and reprisal long remains in the forefront of all state and social concerns. But these acts of rapacity have a still more pathological effect upon the country which performs them. The partitions of Poland have testified to this: their demoralizing influence on all European powers has not ceased to this day. Alsace and Lorraine with their persistent separatist tendencies testify to it now.] The loss of parts which are infected with deeprooted separatist tendencies can more often strengthen the state than promote its decline.

Nevertheless, since it is very difficult to determine accurately to what extent the separatist aspirations of a given part of a territory have become deeply rooted, since it is quite easy to make mistakes on this score, and since it often happens that separatist aspirations are in the interests of one class of the population and contrary to the interests of another, it is perfectly natural that in doubtful cases every state combats separatism in its parts and that society is obliged to expend on this struggle an enormous quantity of resources, sometimes completely uselessly. Confronted by other powerful states with predatory inclinations, no society wishes to be weak. And the relations of states with each other have still retained in large measure their primitive predatory character.

All this has its inevitable consequences. Since the existence of large [historical] states is an historical fact it must be taken into account, and as long as the map of the world shows a number of large states it will be perfectly natural for all societies to strive to join together into large and powerful states so as to safeguard their *independent* development. And when a state is already united, it is perfectly natural for it to strive to defend its integrity with all its might.

Thus we are faced with a dilemma. The smaller the state, and consequently the weaker it is in external combat, the more it is menaced by the external danger of losing its independence. It can safeguard its independence only by becoming more powerful and growing in size. But as it does so, the interests of its parts become more diverse and the difference between the political influence of the centers and that of the rest of the country becomes greater. Dissatisfaction mounts, and consequently the state, weakened by separatism, is exposed to greater internal dangers.

Progress in state organization consists, of course, in striving to resolve this dilemma, that is, striving to eliminate gradually both of the difficulties it presents. This can be achieved theoretically in one way only: by the state's maintaining its external significance with the least possible constraint upon the individuals within it and with tolerance of the broadest possible political life in the smaller centers of population.

In the United States of America an attempt has been made— thus far the most extensive in history—to combine a sufficiently powerful state union, capable of being enlarged to any desirable limit, with the fullest possible independence of the major centers. But the United States is a federation of units which are still too large to permit general popular participation in the most important functions of the political life [of the units], and which thus offer no guarantee that the whole population of each State will consider itself genuinely at one with the state contract, that is, with the constitution of the State. Similarly, it is evident both in theory and in practice that the federal constitution still contains too many powers, which in course of time can be transferred to the local centers without its becoming impossible for the whole union to act as a single state in relation to other states. [The Paris Commune movement of 1871 advanced a program for a federal system in which the smaller centers had a more significant share of self-government, but hostilities prevented this program from being developed even to the point where it might have been called a political experiment.]

Thus the above dilemma has not yet been resolved anywhere,

but it can be resolved by more rigorous separation of the two aspects of state life: the internal and the external. [This, perhaps, could be achieved through creation of more perfect forms of federal system, whether with the permanent establishment of an over-all territory according to the plan of the United States of America, or with free, temporary federations for specific purposes, which is more likely in the future system toward which socialists are striving. In the first case,] the external aspect of state life—the state as a unitary force in the world system of states—in remaining the property of the central authority which unites the territory, may have a natural tendency to extend this territory. But this function must become less and less important as history makes the relationships among states less predatory and clashes among them less likely.

As for the internal side of state life—that is, precisely the side which can prove to be more or less confining for separate localities and individuals and can generate [the most] discontent—it should be transferred more and more completely to the smaller centers which permit real participation in political activity by almost all adults. The differences in local systems should reflect all the diversity of local needs and local culture. The citizen who is cramped by the political system of one local center can move to another which has equal rights politically but is more suited to his ideal of life. In this case extensiveness of territory not only cannot be confining, but rather makes things easier for the citizen, since the broader the territory the more likely it becomes that he will find a local center which accords with his desires. And at the same time he retains the sense that, while exchanging certain political surroundings for others, he is remaining loyal to his over-all political homeland.

As for the central authority, it can retain custody only of those laws, common for the entire territory, which represent not historically produced cultural conditions, not the result of local demands or temporary enthusiasms, but unalterable conclusions of science concerning universal human truth and universal human justice—concerning, namely, what constitutes the conditions of progress, mentioned in the previous letters, and their direct and common consequences. The very fact that these laws are scientific and universally humane must have as a consequence their applicability to all individuals, regardless of the cultural diversity within the society. The fact that they are obligatory and compulsory can mean only that it is obligatory to safeguard the conditions of progress for the whole society against the private passions of individuals. But as society develops, this obligation can be transferred more and more from state law to personal conviction, and consequently it will increasingly lose its compulsory character: that is, the feature which distinguishes the state system from other political associations will be increasingly mitigated.

In such a state of affairs the attitude of individuals toward the compulsory character of law would be completely different from what all ages of history show us. Individuals who are less highly developed have always adapted to a culture more easily, and, their intellects working less vigorously, have suffered less from the defects of the system. It is the individuals who are most highly developed and who have most vigorously exercised their minds who have most felt the constraint of law. In the social system just examined, thinking individuals will encounter the fewest obstacles of a political nature, since the possibility of moving to some distant place without leaving the political homeland permits them to live in a culture they have chosen, while the scientific character of the over-all laws of the state permits them to direct their energies not to the alteration of political conditions but to the more vital interests of personal and social development.

In this way, as has already been said, the role of the state in human life would tend toward a minimum as society progressively develops. A reduction in the clashes among states would lessen the significance of the state element in foreign relations, and the growth of consciousness in individuals and of the realization of truth and justice in social institutions would reduce the internal constraint which emanates from the central state authority. As for those state functions which would be transferred to the small particular centers, they would lose their compulsory character as a consequence of the diversity of local political systems and their correspondence with local cultures, and as a consequence of the full opportunity which individuals would have to select the most commodious political system without leaving the boundaries of the homeland. In this way the local centers would tend to become free social unions, and the state would tend to base its existence and its unity upon the obligatory character of reason rather than upon historical constraint. The state contract would become, on the one hand, a free contract among individuals, and on the other, a product of science. [The state bond would be transformed almost entirely into the bond of a free society. Even this form of state system, however, would have to be regarded as transitional to the future, more perfect, and more free federation of small centers and groups envisaged by contemporary socialism.]

"But all this nowhere exists," the reader will say. "States today stand watch over each other, continually strengthening their armaments and jealously guarding their integrity through laws and penalties. The state contract is binding upon the subject who has never been asked whether he consents to it; here, too, obedience is secured through fear of punishment. Science remains in professorial chairs and in books, without passing into the law codes."

It is certainly true that states as they exist today contain immeasurably more traces of past history than marked tendencies toward progress. False idealization of the mechanism of the state still has many adherents. The true idealization of the state as the protective organ of society and as having an inherent tendency always to reduce itself to a minimum, not only has nowhere been translated into reality, but is not yet even recognized by very many people. But let us not reprove the present, since it is the inevitable product of the past. In the present, however, there is potentiality for progress, and progress for the state is possible on one path only. [Everyone who understands progress and desires to serve it must strive to guide existing states onto this path, through reform or through revolution.] If it should prove impossible to take this path, then progress for the political system is unthinkable and political history will remain the annals of social pathology.[9]

[To another reader, does it seem a direct contradiction to make reduction of the role of the state principle in society a requirement for political progress? Does it seem to him that by weakening this principle, in the name of demands for progress in general, the party of progress is depriving itself of its best weapon for combatting opponents?

[The idea that the role of the state decreases with the progress

of society is by no means new. It was already expressed, incidentally, by the elder Fichte in a work which appeared in 1813, and
it has been expressed repeatedly since that time. The anarchists
made elimination of the state element fundamental to their doctrine, denying the need for it even in a time of stubborn struggle
against powerful opponents of progress—but with this view it is
now difficult to agree.

[Reduction of the role of the state depends, of course, upon
abatement of the need to defend the weak, to protect freedom of
thought, and so on, with *state* force. As long as there are men
who monopolize capital under the protection of the laws, and as
long as the majority does not possess even the elementary means
of development, state power is an indispensable weapon, which a
party fighting for progress or for reaction strives to appropriate.
Given these conditions, critically thinking individuals should regard it simply as a weapon in this fight, and can bend every effort
to gain possession of this indispensable weapon and direct it toward the cultivation of progress and the suppression of reactionary parties.[10]

[But in using this weapon, those who fight for progress must
remember that it has its peculiarities, which oblige the agent of
progress to treat it with extreme caution. In a battle it is perfectly
natural to concern oneself with strengthening the weapon one is
employing; but strengthening the authority of the state can, by
the very nature of this authority, be detrimental to social progress
the moment it goes a little beyond what is absolutely necessary in
the case at hand. It always coincides with an increase in the
obligatory, compulsory element in social life, always stifles the
moral development of the individual and the freedom of critical
thought. This is also what constitutes the chief obstacle to progressive activity through state means. It has been responsible for
the failure or the harmful influence of the eminent reformers who
have decreed progress in a society unprepared for it.

[It is difficult to define in each particular case the limit to the
use of state power in the struggle for progress, but it seems most
correct to assume that this power can be used to advantage only
negatively—that is, only to overcome the obstacles to the free development of society posed by existing cultural forms. But this is
an extremely debatable question.

[As long as the state is a powerful factor in the struggle for progress and for reaction, the critically thinking individual is justified in using it as a weapon to protect the weak; to extend truth and justice; to provide individuals with the means of developing physically, intellectually, and morally; to provide the majority with the minimum of comforts required to enter upon the path of progress; to provide the thinker with the means of expressing his ideas, and society with the opportunity of appraising them; to give social institutions the flexibility which will prevent them from ossifying and open them to changes which promote a broader understanding of truth and justice. This is true not only for the state *since it exists* in a particular age, but also for all social institutions encountered by the individual in his cultural environment, as was said above in the Eighth Letter.

[But, in working *with the aid* of the state element for the scientific satisfaction of human needs in other social institutions, the agent of progress must remember that in itself the institution of the state does not correspond to any separate real need. Consequently it can never be an *end* of progressive activity but is in all cases nothing more than a *means* to such activity, and thus must be modified in conformity with other *ruling* ends.

[When vital functions are extremely unsound, very vigorous treatment may be needed. When the patient's condition is improving the medication should be milder. A physician knows that his patient is not well until proper hygiene is sufficient and therapeutic measures can be eliminated entirely.

[Can human societies really aim at perpetual political therapy rather than a healthy life in accordance with the precepts of sociological hygiene?]

The Natural Boundaries of the State

IN THE LAST LETTER I DISCUSSED political progress in society and concluded that it consists in diminishing the state element in social life. I was obliged to point out that the present social order has yet made very little progress in this direction, and that the state principle of the forcible subjection of one segment of a territory's population to conditions of life concerning which this segment has not been consulted is the general rule for present-day societies.

For individuals this situation is made all the more oppressive by the fact that states strive to expand in order to gain greater assurance of success in the event of a conflict among them, and as they expand they seize regions which differ more and more in the economic and moral needs of their inhabitants. Isolated individuals are, of course, in no position to combat the state, which annexes their homes and imposes the duties of subjects upon them.

To safeguard individuals against continual eventualities of this sort, thinkers have advanced various principles designed to indicate the natural limits of the expansion of states. If such principles were established, one could determine scientifically, for every state, the legitimacy or illegitimacy of its existence, the justice or injustice of its wars of conquest—in short, the ideal system of dividing the earth's surface into territories. Then every state would have a precisely defined terminus for its territorial expansion, and each time it strayed beyond this terminus it would know that it was bequeathing to succeeding generations an onerous struggle, which would nevertheless end in the state's being reduced some day to its natural boundaries. Such a consideration would perhaps eliminate from human history many bloody conflicts and much personal suffering and grief, since it must be supposed that at least some of the leaders of the fates of nations would realize how absurd it is to shed blood and waste resources on undertakings which, by their very nature, run counter to the natural course of events.

Thus far, however, not a single principle which is in any way rational has been advanced in this connection. In the majority of cases the "natural boundaries of the state" have proved to be nothing more than a mask for predatory inclinations to seize some patch of ground. If we examine carefully the activity of the various aggrandizers whom history had exalted, the boundaries they sought for their states will indeed prove to be natural, but in a quite different sense. These men have been guided by a very simple principle, which unites man with his lesser zoological brothers: take what you can. Under this principle the natural limits of the state have been determined by the natural limits of power. The ideal of such aggrandizers has always been a universal state. Neither the form of government nor the conquerors' race nor the level of their civilization makes the slightest difference here. Tamerlane, Louis XIV, Alexander the Great, Napoleon I, the Roman republic, the Venetian aristocracy, and the North American democracy have all had the very same objective.

If our transatlantic friends confine their political program to the continent of the New World, this is nothing but temporary diffidence. In the first place, the program of conquering the American continent is extensive enough in itself to provide several successive generations with a good deal of work. In the second place, a state which embraces the entire American continent will inevitably dominate all the states of the world, and consequently their independence will be only seeming. Finally, in the third place, what would prevent drawing up a second, broader program when the first has been fulfilled?

Of the various principles which have thus far been advanced for determining the natural boundaries of states, only two deserve special attention: these are the principle of strategic boundaries and the principle of national boundaries.

If conflict is the essential relationship among states, then it is perfectly logical to take as the natural boundaries of each state the lines behind which it is most secure against attack—the lines behind which it can at the least cost defend its territory against seizure. But such lines prove effective only in cases where the state is prepared for defense and possesses sufficient energy for defense, and, what is more, where the defenders' forces are not inordinately inferior to the attackers'. In other words, strategic boundaries are effective only when the country's defense can be very strong even without them. And if the conditions mentioned are not present, strategic boundaries have never helped. Broad rivers and oceans have no more halted clever and energetic generals than have mountain ranges, Chinese walls, or the celebrated polygons of fortresses. For the state which is strong materially and morally, there is an adequate strategic boundary everywhere; at moments of political debilitation such boundaries exist only on maps.

In recent times the principle of nationality has acquired more and more influence on the course of historical events. In the Eleventh Letter, I discussed the individual's attitude toward this principle and the conditions under which nationality can be a progressive principle. But at that point it was not convenient to analyze a circumstance which complicates the question—namely, the case of a conflict between nations. It was impossible to examine this case without having considered the principle of the state, since a conflict between nations arises either in the form of a conflict between states or in the form of a struggle for unity or for secession within a state.

Although history has repeatedly shown that wars occur just as frequently between different nations as between societies which belong to the same nation, recently many people have come to believe that applying the principle of nationality to the determination of the natural boundaries of a state is the most likely means of preventing future international and civil wars. In this connection the principle of nationality expresses a two-fold aspiration: the first or *positive* side is the unification of persons of the same nation in a single state, and the second or *negative* side is the liberation of individuals from a state formed by an alien nation. Let us see to what extent these two sides of the principle of nationality can be considered progressive.

The first may be reduced to the following proposition: it is natural and just that the same state contract should be binding upon all individuals whom culture has bound together by language, traditions, and way of life. It is quite evident, however, that a cultural bond can exist even for individuals whose economic, political, and intellectual needs are highly diverse. Two groups of people who speak the very same language can have entirely different surroundings. Industrial and commercial centers can be common for people who have different ways of life, and different for people who have similar ways of life. For one segment of a nation, the need to defend its existence against the rapacity of its neighbors can require greater administrative centralization and greater discretionary powers on the part of the authorities, while another segment of the same nation, protected from external attacks by the character of the locality it inhabits, has no need for such centralization and can strive to reduce the compulsory character of the state contract to a minimum. What, then, can be regarded as progressive in the unification of these diverse groups under a single state contract?

Can it really be called progress when political arrangements which have been worked out by the population of one part of a territory as a result of its particular interests and needs, become binding upon the population of another part, which is linked to the first only by a common language and a few other cultural traits? Such artificial unification, by a single compulsory contract, of people who have very little in common can promote neither understanding of the true needs of separate individuals nor understanding of the most just relationships among them; least of all can one see in such unification the introduction of justice into social institutions. Such unification creates for the population of the state nothing but mutual irritation, which is the source of separatist tendencies and which, as has already been said, is more pernicious than the actual disintegration of the state. Such unification increasingly transforms the state into an abstract whole rather than a living unity; it becomes increasingly evident that unification is based not upon a community of interests, cultural customs, and intellectual issues but upon the compulsion of a contract backed by the administrative organization and the force of arms.

Thus the merging of societies of the same nation into a single state contains no guarantee that their progress will be furthered. And the more spread out the nation, thus the broader the territory of the state which it forms, the more likely it is that constraint of the population by the state contract will be intensified and will be a greater obstacle to social progress.

But there is still another reason for supposing that unification of a nation in a single state is more likely to impede than to promote social progress. In previous letters I discussed the fact that through the idealization of one or another principle in society, a minority develops which reaps the benefits of this idealization; and that, if the society is to endure, it is the obligation of the minority to extend these benefits to the majority. But this task, though it is a moral obligation as well as being demanded by the minority's own interests, has been carried out only on the most limited scale, as is well known from history. On the contrary, the minority enjoying the blessings of a given civilization has for the most part desired—in consequence of ill-considered egoism—to arrogate to itself a monopoly of civilization's benefits while leaving the majority nothing but its burdens. Ordinarily what could and did serve as the best instrument for such ambitions was the state organization. With its help the monopolizing minority endeavored to strengthen its hold on the benefits of civilization and to crush every attempt at alteration of the established social order—alteration which would have as its goal the introduction into society of more just relationships among individuals.

But such attempts, provoked by social miseries, were made by individuals nonetheless. [Opponents of antiquated laws and forms of government appeared. Reformists carried on propaganda. More or less energetic parties of opposition to the existing order were formed.] This has been, as we have already seen, society's only route to progressive development. Consequently, social progress demanded that it be *possible* for private individuals to attempt to view the existing social order critically, to disseminate their ideas, to gather like-minded people around them, and to form a party which would take up the fight for a better understanding and a more just fulfillment of social tasks. [Where this was not possible, demand for legal reforms became preparation for revolution. The dissidents were turned into insurgents; under favorable conditions, into revolutionaries.]

Naturally, the chief weapon individuals had in such a struggle for social progress was propaganda [or agitation], either oral or written, in the language of the society to whose system their criti-

cism was directed and upon which they had to act for their reformist [or revolutionary] ends. But, just as naturally, it was
against these individuals that the blows of the state organization,
which aimed to protect the minority's monopoly on the benefits of
civilization, were particularly directed. Thus if all persons who
spoke the given language lived in the *same* state, their influence
on its population was very much impeded. Critical thought grew
weaker. The formation of reformist [and revolutionary] parties
encountered significant obstacles. Most of the individuals who
had tried to lead the society onto a more progressive path
perished in the fight, and the society's progress was retarded.

On the other hand, when several independent states used the
same language, rivalry very quickly sprang up among them, not
only in the sphere of political influence but in the realm of
thought in general. Individuals whose critical aspirations could
and did expose them to persecution in one state found refuge in
another. In freedom their thought grew stronger. The community
of cultural conditions in the two states allowed words and ideas
to flow easily from one to the other, despite all obstacles. The
party of progress grew stronger, and the likelihood of progressive
social reform increased.

History presents a multitude of examples to support this. The
division of the Greek world into independent centers promoted
the development of Greek thought, not only in the age of the free
republics but even under the despotic Diadochi. The unity of the
Roman state crushed the development of critical thought. The
feudal world of Europe, despite the savagery of its civilization
and the extreme poverty of its culture, produced a satirical and
polemical literature the boldness of which is scarcely imaginable
in that age of the horrors of the Inquisition and the absolute
arbitrariness of the lords, who cared nothing for the life and freedom of the individual. The critical thought of Bourbon France
was made possible and became influential only because neither
Louis XIV nor Louis XV could prevent the existence of French
literature among the French-speaking population outside their
state. German philosophical thought could hardly have received
such brilliant development and acquired such an independent approach to its subject if the German universities had not been scattered among independent states which vied with one another in

the intellectual arena, like the ancient Diadochi, despite their tendency toward absolutism. Even with respect to ancient Rus it may be noted that the ascendancy of northern Rus over southern, and subsequently of Moscow over Rus' with the fall of the independent democracies, was accompanied by the weakening of intellectual activity. By the time of Muscovite Rus criticism could manifest itself only in the form of Stenka Razin and the schism.

All this leads to the conclusion that the division of nations into independent states contributes much more to the progress of the societies making up a nation than does the unification, under the laws of a single state, of all people who speak a given language. With this in mind, progressive parties should concern themselves more with the independence of territories which lie outside their political homeland but share their language, than with incorporating them into a single state. Sober-minded French progressives [in the period of the Second Empire] were of course bound to see that it was more to their advantage for Belgium and Geneva to remain independent than for them to become part of the Bonapartes' domain. Where there are no such independent territories, the progressive party should bend every effort to creating them, since they are an important aid to free individual criticism, to the spread of independent thought, and to the strengthening of the progressive party.

All in all one may say that the *positive* aspect of the national principle in the division of territories should not be considered progressive, and that the nation which strives to achieve state boundaries which are natural in the sense that they include all individuals who speak its language, is very much mistaken if it sees progress in this ambition.

The *negative* side of the principle of nationality has greater significance. A difference in language and cultural customs usually creates sufficient disparity in economic, political, and intellectual needs to make state union under these conditions extremely difficult. When different nations are joined in a single state, ordinarily the contract which binds them together is advantageous to one and disadvantageous to the other, and generates mutual hostility. The outcome of this friction may be either that the stronger nation devours the weaker by gradually destroying its distinctive features, or that state union tends more and more to become a federative union of separate states. In this situation it is perfectly natural for the weaker nation, in defending its existence with all its strength, to strive to form a separate state, since otherwise it is threatened with destruction.

The fight of the weaker nation for its own existence is completely legitimate, and the desire to set up a separate state is in this case entirely natural. Equally natural, in view of the conflict that exists among large states, as I said in the last letter, is the desire of the state's rulers to preserve its unity. Here two natural ambitions come into collision, but justice and progress are by no means inseparably connected with either one of them. Like all other social party banners, both separatism (in the name of the principle of nationality) and the desire to maintain state unity can be progressive in one case and reactionary in another. The answer depends upon the whole complex of circumstances and not upon any of them taken in isolation.

In a given period of its history a nation is entitled to a thinker's sympathy only insofar as it has translated the aspiration for truth and justice into reality in the institutions of its civilization. In the clash of nations on the question of state unity versus separatism, victory in the name of progress is desirable for the nation which has cultivated a more critical approach to intellectual issues and a more vital desire for the practical realization of greater justice. The nation which bases its demands upon the brute force of numbers, upon traditions alien to scientific criticism, upon long-outlived periods of history, upon treaties which formerly protected the rights of plunderers under the form of a contract— such a nation is signing its own death warrant in the historical clash of peoples.

History is distinguished from the other processes of nature precisely by the fact that in it phenomena do not repeat themselves and for it the past is nothing but a memory. If one could remodel the present by looking to the past, such remodeling would have no end: beyond the past of fifty years ago would rise the past of a century ago, and beyond that the past of two centuries ago, and so on and on, each with *its own* lengendary conflicts and desires, *its own* heroes and villains. What is past is past, and it cannot be the judge of the present. The judge of the present is the still-unrealized future, in its ideals of truth and justice as they live in the minds of the thinkers of the present.

The thinker has before him, as the foundation of everything, the immutable law of nature—a law which no aspirations for the highest good, truth, and justice can suspend. He has before him the actual distribution of the material, intellectual, and moral forces of the present—a distribution determined by past history, which again cannot be ignored because of new ideals, since it is an accomplished fact. He has before him the ideals of truth and justice which have been developed around him and within him by history. In them lie the motive forces of the future, the operation of which is limited by immutable laws of nature and by the given fund of historical facts. By reference to these ideals, and only by reference to them, can the present distribution of forces be declared legitimate. No other law can be recognized before the bar of ongoing history.

The nation which desires to defend itself in the struggle for existence under conditions unfavorable to it must declare itself a representative of the best aspirations of the future, without appealing to the irretrievable past. The nation which desires to reign supreme over others must repudiate everything which chains men's lives to obsolete principles; it must engage in critical inquiry as vigorously as possible in the realm of thought and implement justice as fully as possible in the realm of life. Aside from these practices there are no firm bases for the political development of nations. If nations inscribe phantoms of the past upon their banners, their existence will always be precarious and phantom, despite the heroism of individuals, despite the sympathy always aroused in a spectator by the valor of the weak in a desperate struggle against the strong. If a nation chains itself to a mummy of lifeless principles, neither vastness of territory nor wealth of material resources will warrant it firm dominion among men: its thought will remain barren, its highest aspirations will be defeated by debility, and it will have to submit intellectually and morally to nations incomparably weaker than itself. The strength of nations lies only in truth and justice.

Thus, too, for the struggle between state unity and separatism: whichever of these principles is inscribed upon the banner of a nation that has fully renounced the phantoms of the past and is introducing critical inquiry into thought and justice into life—this is the principle which has right on its side. The state is an abstract concept, and if this concept contains no real content it becomes an idol to which bloody sacrifices are made, senselessly [and immorally]. Only the individual, as he develops, gives real content to the concept. By investing the concept of the state with the demand for truth and justice, the individual transforms an irrational idol into an inseparable element of the supreme social ideal, and for this ideal all sacrifices are rational and just.

The nationality distinction is eliminated as immaterial wherever the state, if only remotely, is approaching the ideal requirements. An example of this is furnished by the United States of America, where immigrants from all over the world are becoming simply Americans, as early as the second generation and sometimes even in the first. The separatism shown by the Southern states was illegitimate, given a constitution which is better than any other history has yet produced and given the establishment of equal rights among the races, which could be countered only by an apology for slavery. On the other hand, the numerous separatist tendencies manifested in Europe and South America have often been legitimate, because the states against whose integrity the separatists took arms were very far from tolerating free critical inquiry in thought and embodying justice in social institutions. Here right inclined all the more to the side of the separatists the more progressive was the political ideal which they pursued through secession.

But where separatists and defenders of state unity alike argue over opinions and over the phantoms of the past, investing their demands with contemporary ideals only to a very negligible extent, there the battle is not waged for progress or humane aspirations. There the thinking man averts his gaze, lamenting the waste of strength and blood. There only the lover of historical melodramas can avidly follow the gladiators' bloody struggle, the fanatical selflessness of the knights of old with their assorted mottos. The Homeridae will always celebrate the Achilles and the Hectors, but what sense did the contest for Helen of Troy have for Aristotle?

When a nation has become imbued with demands for truth and justice, when it has resolved to break with the past and to serve progress, then it has the right to defend its secession from a political union which is confining its aspirations. Or if it has already achieved political ascendancy, it has the right to take the most energetic steps to defend its integrity and the material strength of its political organization, to defend its place beside its neighbors who occupy a lower level of civilization. A progressive nation has the right to disjoin itself from a less progressive state. A progressive nation has the right to suppress the separatist ambitions of less progressive nations that are bound to it historically by a state contract.

But there is never an occasion to apply this last, *abstract* right in practice, since a progressive nation never has occasion to combat separatism in the whole population of a part of its territory, but only in one class of the latter's inhabitants. Thus the Northern states fought not against the entire population of the Southern, but against a minority which was striving to retain its power over the majority. Under such circumstances the contest is legitimate only in the event that the nation defending the integrity of the state actually intends to improve the situation of the oppressed majority and can *actually* offer it social principles superior to those which the nation seeking separation can offer. Thus it was in America.

Here a question which has already been examined above arises in a new form: if in its progressive development the state principle must be reduced to a minimum, should not progressive parties avoid questions of [international] politics entirely and apply themselves exclusively to other aspects of social activity? Since we have already said that historical conditions determine what is *possible* for every activity, it is in them that we must seek an answer to this question as well. Now because the most progressive parties still constitute a minority of mankind, and because the nations which are most progressive are exposed to the danger of predatory violence on the part of their neighbors, they must prepare themselves to fight and must defend progress even by supplying it with greater material force. Hence the provisional duty of progressive parties not only to defend their ideas through critical thinking and personify them through conviction, but also to employ existing state organizations to combat the hostile parties in control of other states.

Of course this is only a provisional duty, necessitated by the rapacity which prevails in the intercourse among states and by the danger of political wars. We have seen that political progress consists in the reduction of the state element in society to a minimum—in the elimination from the political contract of every form of compulsion over individuals who are not in agreement with it. Since progress of this sort destroys separatist ambitions at their very source, the grounds for conflict between nations and the grounds for the oppression of some nations by others in the name of state unity will also disappear.

And at the same time the question of the natural boundaries of states loses its significance. Temporary economic, cultural, or scientific interests should bring societies together and define, provisionally, the territory of a federation having a specific purpose. This purpose modifies, extends, and narrows the federation's boundaries, which remain natural throughout. As for unity on a higher level, such unity, as we have seen in the last letter, must be cemented by the science which is common to all men and for which it is impossible to draw natural boundaries on any map.

Whether or not the reader agrees with me that such is the possible future toward which we must strive, as for the past he is very well aware, of course, that the situation has been otherwise. The ruling principle within states has been compulsion, and between states, rapacity. Quite naturally it is this state of affairs that has caused the greatest distress to a minority distinguished from the masses by its strength of intellect and energy of character. Understandably, then, it is political questions that have most often and most noticeably absorbed the minds and the energies of forward-looking individuals in the past. When the power to compel was in the hands of men having a personal interest in the very matters that occasioned compulsion, it was only natural to expect abuses of power. These abuses, in their turn, more often than not gave rise to opposition, the formation of parties, and a contest of strength, and it is precisely for this reason that the most noticeable side of history has been the history of political strife.

Who in fact shall have the right to frame the state contract? To what extent can separate individuals and societies influence its composition, speak out against its defects, and demand its alteration? Who shall have to submit to the state contract without being consulted? Controversy on these issues forms the entire immediate basis of the struggle of individuals for crowns, vizierates, and portfolios; the struggle of political parties in the press, in parliaments, in the public squares, and on the battlefields; the struggle of nations for independence or for the subjugation of others; the struggle of states for supremacy; the struggle of the best people for political progress.[1]

But this is the most *visible* aspect of history—its dramatic exterior, its gaudy apparel. The thinking historian is interested in seeking the more substantial principles beneath the surface. Sometimes the most dramatic epochs testify only to a waste of resources on matters of little importance. The most gifted individuals have sometimes applied their minds and energies to highly insignificant objectives. Successful, brilliant exploits are not in themselves evidence of lofty humanity in the individual. The perspective in which the facts of history are viewed should correspond to the significance of these facts for human progress. If the growth of some factor has the greatest importance for progress, even its scarcely noticeable manifestations can be significant. On the other hand a factor which is bound to lose its significance as society progresses has least right to the historian's attention.

As society progresses the role of the state is reduced to a minimum. Consequently, for anyone who wishes to find some meaning in human history, political history is the least interesting. For every external clash between states, as for every disturbance within them, the historian should first of all ask himself: what extrapolitical elements played a role in this clash or this disturbance? From every leading figure an account should be demanded: what has he done to diminish the operation of the compulsory, state element upon society? To what extent has he promoted or opposed the progress of extrapolitical elements?

From this point of view the expansion and collapse of states, vast conquests, bloody battles, diplomatic stratagems, and administrative decrees take on new interest, completely different from the interest they had for the historians of the past. In themselves these phenomena have no importance: they are the meteorological processes of history. Violent hurricanes, earthquakes, epidemics, exceptionally beautiful displays of the aurora borealis, and the uncommon birth of twins or monsters are facts of exactly the same significance as the processes mentioned above. In both cases the fact is important to the scientist not in itself, but in virtue of its consequences or its causes. It arouses interest and is carefully studied in an attempt either to find a new general law of basic physical and psychical phenomena or to bring about advantageous states of affairs, and eliminate harmful ones, in the future.

What needs and ideas gave rise to this or that political phenomenon? How far did it promote the appearance of new needs and the modification of old? To what extent did it weaken or strengthen the old culture? How much impetus did it give to new intellectual development? These are the chief questions which history must ask concerning every political phenomenon. Other questions follow: from this phenomenon how much can be learned about the individual's psychical processes, his intellectual resourcefulness, his desire for personal development and for justice? How much can be learned about the influence of social culture on the psychical life of the individual?

The answer to the former questions indicates the strictly historical significance of political events. The answer to the latter shows their importance as material for individual psychology and for sociology. In both cases it is the tasks of the higher natural sciences or the tasks of the history of civilization which give significance to political history.[2]

FIFTEENTH LETTER

Faith and Critical Inquiry

IN SOME OF THE FOREGOING LETTERS I have examined the principal mottos commonly inscribed upon the banners of social parties. For each of these mottos, a general proposition stated earlier has proved correct: none is in itself an expression of progress. Depending upon the circumstances, each may represent reaction or advance, may take on vital significance or become an empty word. False idealization is continually operating upon these mottos, using them to mask impulses completely alien to them and by no means ideal, and neglecting those natural needs which admit of true, humane idealization. Thus great ideas, the motive forces of history, are in fact *great* ideas only in their concrete significa- tion, as banners of particular individuals under particular circum- stances. Only constant critical examination of their historical, con- crete content can assure the individual that, in enrolling under the banner upon which the high-sounding word is inscribed, he is not pursuing an illusion or becoming the tool of calculating and self-seeking intriguers.

But the reader, continually encountering such expressions as "critical examination" and "critical inquiry" in these pages, is justified in asking this question: If the individual always has criti- cal inquiry and nothing but critical inquiry in mind, will he not rob himself of the energy to act? Critical inquiry assumes uncer- tainty, hesitation, sufficient time to weigh arguments pro and con. But does life always provide leisure? When a man is perishing be- fore our eyes, is there time to discuss the advantages and dis- advantages of saving him? When some chance political tempest has aroused society, and the masses, lacking leaders, may rush onto a false path, mistake enemies for friends and friends for enemies, or lose all the benefits of their strength and enthusiasm through indecision, does the true citizen who understands the state of affairs really have the right to hesitate, and miss the mo- ment? What is commendable in the study may be inappropriate in the public square; what is essential to the scholar may be detri- mental to the man of social action.

This is true. But the fact is that critical inquiry is a lifelong affair, a habit which a man must acquire and master in order to merit being called a cultivated person. Sorry is he who, until the moment he sees a man perishing, has not reflected and come to a decision concerning whether a man perishing under the circum- stances at hand should be saved. A citizen has no right to con- sider himself a man of social action if he has remained such a stranger to the course of history that a popular outburst takes him by surprise and he must still hesitate and ponder what to say, what to do, which way to turn, where the truth lies, and which banner is the banner of the hour.

Moments which summon a man to decisive action are uncom- mon, and all life serves as preparation for them. No one can pre- dict when personal or social circumstances will confront him with the stern commandment: Go and do your duty. Consequently each individual must constantly prepare himself. In cultivating his individuality, a man arrives at answers to vital questions of every sort. In following the shifting tide of history, he acquires the training necessary for doing battle at the moment he is needed. He needs critical inquiry *for* his action, but not *in initiating* it.

The moment arrives. A brother's voice calls out to him for help. Society has awakened indignantly from its long slumber. Here and there the banners of hostile parties are unfurled. Critical inquiry has done its job. Taking stock of his physical, intellectual, and moral capital, a man flings this capital into his undertakings. The more rigorous, circumspect, cool, and extensive was his critical inquiry, the more mighty and ardent is now his *faith*.

Yes, faith—and only faith—can move mountains. At the moment of action it must possess a man or he will prove powerless, at the very instant when he must summon up all his strength. It is not their enemies that imperil militant parties: they are most imperiled by the disbelievers and indifferentists who find themselves in their ranks, rally to their banners, and proclaim their slogans sometimes louder than the most dedicated leaders. They are imperiled by those who spurn critical examination of these slogans while there is still time for it, but who, just when the moment has come and action is necessary, begin criticizing, hesitate, and are ready to quit the battle as soon as it has begun.

The weightiest words have usually been open to the most diverse interpretations. The word "faith" is surely one of those which have occasioned the greatest controversy, as an express result of misunderstanding: the disputants, while employing the identical word, have been talking about entirely different things.

It is by no means necessary to connect the word "faith" with the idea of various religious cults, myths, dogmas, or philosophical world views. As a *consequence* of their faith men have defended and preached myths and dogmas and performed the rituals of different cults, but this has been only *one* of the applications of faith. Similarly it is by no means necessary to connect the term "faith" only with the idea of the supernatural. Everyday life, nature, and history in all their diversity offer abundant material for the operation of faith; and a person who has acquired the habit of taking a sceptical view of everything that has no analogy in the world of observation can be strongly disposed to faith.

Faith is a psychical or overt activity in which consciousness is present but critical inquiry is absent. When an idea has taken possession of me which I no longer analyze but which is basic to my analysis of other ideas and concepts, I have faith in that idea. When I act on the word of another person, considering *how* it may be implemented but no longer considering whether it *need* be implemented, I have faith in that person. When I have set myself a goal and I examine critically the means of attaining it but not the goal itself, I have faith in my goal.

Thus one can say that faith is opposed to critical inquiry, but only in a limited sense. That in which a man has faith he *no longer* subjects to critical inquiry. But this in no way rules out the case in which the object of today's faith was *yesterday* examined critically. On the contrary, such is the strongest faith and the only rational and enduring faith. The proof of faith is the action one takes at a moment when there are grounds for acting both in accord with it and against it; but if my faith is not a product of critical inquiry, if it has never been exposed to objections, who can guarantee that at the moment of action, the grounds prompting me to act contrary to this faith will not shake it?

Only critical inquiry creates firm convictions. Only a man who has cultivated firm convictions can find in his convictions sufficient strength of faith for vigorous action. In this respect faith is opposed to critical inquiry not in essence but in time: they are two different moments in the development of thought. Critical inquiry paves the way for activity, and faith generates the action.

An image takes shape in an artist's imagination. The artist subjects it to rigorous critical examination, both scientific and aesthetic, in every detail. This critical examination discloses to him finished forms of greater and greater artistry. And then the integral, living image arises before the artist's mind. He takes brush or chisel and incarnates his ideal, because he has *faith* in its vitality and beauty. Otherwise his activity is hesitant and uninspired. When the painting or statue has become objective, critical examination of it may begin anew, and the artist, dissatisfied with his work, may destroy it. But in the process of artistic creation critical inquiry plays no part; what does play a part is faith in the vitality of the image.

A scientist carefully specifies and weighs his facts. Independently of his will they arrange themselves in his mind into a law, more or less hypothetical. Other facts known to him spring up in his memory, as confirming, supplementing, and extending the discovered scientific parallel (*analogiya*). He checks himself again and again. Critical inquiry has done its job. He is convinced of the truth of his discovery. And then he mounts the rostrum to inform students of the new acquisition of science. He summarizes the experiment, anticipates objections, sets forth the parallel, and points to likely new discoveries. At this stage he no longer criticizes or hesitates; he has *faith* in the force and completeness of his critical investigation, and he is propounding a new truth. So long as he did not *trust* it, he did not announce it, precisely because he values critical inquiry above all.

A man becomes acquainted with another person and sees the latter's virtues and faults. He knows to what extent his friend can be swayed by emotion and to what extent he can deal rationally with various subjects. At a particular moment, on his friend's word he must act in one way or in another. The critical examination carried out earlier will yield the result. The man has faith in his friend, or does not have faith in him. He makes his decision, and acts on the basis of his faith.

Life and social history confront man with just such questions. A man has worked out certain ideals of truth and justice. He himself has developed under the influence of these ideals, and he has developed them under the influence of both his accumulating experience of life and the critical operation of his intellect. He has studied the culture of the society around him, the work of intellect which goes on within it, and the concrete meaning of the different slogans of contemporary parties. He has come to see, not an ideally perfect, but a historically better situation *here*, and a worse one *there*.

He knows that there is no *complete* truth and justice here, and no *absolute* evil and falsehood there. But he has come to realize that under the given historical circumstances struggle is possible, with any hope of success, only in alliance with the existing parties and that only the existing parties can dispute the victory. One of them is *better* than the others and at the moment progress is possible only through its victory. It contains the *most* truth and the *most* justice. Of course a thinking, sincere person, recognizing the party's faults, should try to use his own influence to mitigate and eliminate these faults, to increase the proportion of truth and justice embodied in the aspirations of the best of the contemporary parties. If the party is adamant he can declare his disagreement, speak out against its leaders, and set up his own banner apart.

But the historical moment of clash arrives. All forces of society are summoned to the battle for progress or for reaction. To stand aloof is to weaken the *better* party. He has *faith* in its superiority, and he sides with it in the name of this faith. The time for critical inquiry and division has passed. All the best men must unite to fight for what progress is *possible*. All must side with the party that promises the *best* future. The more severely critical a man has been in investigating the merits and faults of the different parties and the more truly convinced he has become, on the basis of his critical investigation, that the best resides *here*, the more absolute is the faith with which he devotes his activity to the chosen party, combats its enemies, rejoices in its victories, and grieves over its defeats. The critical activity of thought has not lost its force, but its time has passed; it can begin again as soon as there is an opportune moment.

The faith which inspires an individual to action is manifested with still greater force and fullness when there can be no concessions, when one must unfurl a new banner and fling mankind a new message. Social misery and critical thinking have produced conviction in the individual. He stands alone, or has very few sympathizers. Only recently, perhaps, the tide of history has scattered and swept away the men who were fighting for what he regards as truth and justice. Age-old cultural customs and traditions press in upon him from all sides. The ideas of hostile parties have powerful, clever, and highly placed spokesmen. Why, then, does not the individual lose heart? Why, recognizing his weakness, does he not abandon his senseless undertaking? What induces him to fling himself into the fray—despite the obstacles, the indifference of the majority, the cowardice of some, the baseness of others, the sneers of enemies?

This is the work of *faith*. Critical inquiry has led the individual to the conviction that truth and justice reside *here*. He has faith that the truth and justice which are obvious to him will be evident to others as well; he has faith that the thinking which inspires him to action will conquer the indifference and hostility that surround him. Reverses do not discourage him, because he has faith in tomorrow. To age-old custom he opposes his personal thought, because history has taught him that the most tenacious social customs have fallen before a truth in which individuals had faith. To the law which is armed with all the power of the state he opposes his personal conviction, because neither codes nor state power can falsify or make unjust in his eyes what he believes to be true and just. Expiring under the blows of enemies or the weight of circumstances, he still exhorts those who share his convictions to fight and die as he did—if only he has faith in what he is dying for.

A supernatural element is by no means required here. Assorted myths, incomprehensible dogmas, and solemn cult rituals in no way impart greater strength and inflexibility to this determination to live and die for what one believes. True, the past history of the human race has preserved many more legends about people who fought and died for the illusions of religion and metaphysics than for convictions devoid of fantasy.[1] Faith in illusions is just as possible as faith in progressive ideas. People whose thinking is weak and who give little place in their lives to critical inquiry can achieve heroism only through the operation of [religious] faith, and this characteristic, which constitutes their only distinctive feature, will naturally carry them into history, too, as heroes of [religious] faith. Thinking, critical people present the biographer with such versatility in their intellectual and civic careers that he sometimes pays scant attention to the heroism of faith which critical inquiry produced in them and which filled their lives with onerous, unceasing strife and caused them to renounce a great many goods, sometimes including life itself. Giordano Bruno's pyre was not inferior to that of St. Laurence or Jan Hus.[2] Spinoza, Feuerbach, and Strauss [3] were no less capable of enduring poverty and ostracism than ancient and modern [religious] visionaries. Republicans have perished under the swords and bullets of royalists with just as much determination as royalists perished on the scaffold of the Convention.

The faith which makes a man willing to sacrifice unhesitatingly his time, the comforts of life, the affection of others, and life itself, for what he regards as truth and justice, has appeared in all parties in the hour of strife. It has even animated men who had no other virtues. It has animated agents of reaction, who have shed rivers of blood and strained every nerve to arrest the course of history, which they could not arrest. And it is faith which has inspired, too, the martyrs of thought and the heroes of progress.

Thus faith is indifferently the motive force of truth and falsehood, of progress and reaction. Without it progress is impossible, because all vigorous selfless action is impossible. But faith is not a *sufficient* condition for progress. Where we see heroism and selflessness, we are not yet entitled to infer the existence of progressive aspirations. Only faith grounded upon vigorous critical inquiry can lead to progress; only critical inquiry can define the life goal in which a cultivated human being is justified in having faith.

Thinking people have worked out notions of the useful, the proper, the true, and the just.[4] Believers have fought for what they believed in, as being useful to them and proper for them; the best of them have fought for what they considered true and just. The more ardent their faith and the faith of others—the more bitter was the strife. The weaker their thinking and the more inadequate their critical investigation—the more diverse were their notions of the useful and the proper, the true and the just, the greater was the division among parties, and the greater were the human resources wasted in futile strife. The variety of illusions is endless, and the further they are from reality the more various they can be.

The frightful cost of progress which I discussed in the Fourth Letter has sprung chiefly from illusory notions insufficiently exposed to critical examination. The more firmly men believed that their own interests were inimical to the interests of others, the more prodigious was the waste of resources in the open struggle among exploiters and in the hidden struggle among mutually malevolent and mistrustful people. The more firmly men believed that what is *proper* consists in the magical rites of religion, in its fantastic dogmas and myths, and in the proprieties dividing castes and classes, the more they frittered away their already brief lives, allowing themselves less time for genuine development and enjoyment. The more falsehood their truth contained, and the more immoral was their justice—the more inferior was their thought and the more onerous their lives. Profound faith and selfless heroism for the most part went for nought, because they were not sufficiently grounded in critical investigation.

Only as illusions were dispersed through the work of thought and thought moved closer to reality was it possible to mitigate the strife and the waste of resources—possible because a new faith, grounded upon superior critical investigation, led to conciliation rather than enmity. Faith in a common scientific truth, by purifying this truth of the creations of fantasy, banished enmity in the sphere of thought. Faith in the equal dignity of individuals, in a common justice, eliminated the clash of thousands of diverse national, juridical, class, and economic justices and eliminated all strife on behalf of these idols. Faith in individual development and in justice, as the sole duty, reconciled all personal aspirations in a common effort to extend truth and justice, and eliminated the waste of resources in observing fantastic obligations. Faith in the identity of the greatest good of each [cultivated person] with the good of the greatest number is *the* principle which must minimize the waste of humanity's resources on the road to progress.

And the salutary influence of these articles of faith flows precisely from the fact that they [are not products of religious thinking, that they] contain nothing of the supernatural and require neither myths nor mysteries. They are grounded upon rigorous critical inquiry, upon the study of real human beings in nature and in history, and they become articles of faith only at the moment the individual is summoned to action. Their fundamental dogma is man. Their cult is life. But they are capable, no less than religious faith, of inspiring the individual to selfless action, to the sacrifice of all life's blessings and of life itself upon the altar of his sanctities.[5]

It may be objected that these articles of faith are far from common, that they belong, in fact, to a scarcely noticeable minority.

This is true. On the other hand there has also been very little progress in mankind, and its cost has been great. Besides, history will not end today, or tomorrow, and a progressive future belongs nonetheless to a faith grounded upon critical inquiry.

[But is a progressive future possible? Is true historical progress possible in the sense here given to the word? [6]

[Thus far it has been absolutely impossible to make predictions in history. Meteorology, with less complexity and without the element of evolving personal convictions to deal with, cannot predict the phases of the weather in Europe for November, 1872, with any degree of probability. Even attempts at predicting the general meteorological changes accompanying the peopling of continents, variations in quantity of vegetation, and so on, belong mostly to the realm of fantasy. So much the less can one affirm the likelihood of a definite course of progress in history, where the most important element, the distribution of personal convictions among individuals, is still not amenable to statistical treatment, much less prediction.

[Perhaps at some time in the far distant future science will have progressed to the point where we can predict changes in the distribution of star clusters for billions of centuries, or forms of organisms which will be observed after hundreds of thousands of years. Then, or a little sooner, it will also be possible, perhaps, to predict the true course of history with sufficient probability, and hence to test the theory of progress against the possibility of its realization. At present such an undertaking is visionary.

[No one should think that by talking about progress he is resolving the question of how *in fact* the course of events takes place and what is the natural law of history. The theory of progress is the application of the natural laws of moral evolution to the problems of sociology as they arise in their historical evolution. The theory of progress makes a moral appraisal of the events of history which have taken place, and points out the moral goal toward which the critically thinking individual must move if he wishes to be an agent of progress.

[The moral development of the individual is possible on *one* path only. Morally progressive activity on the part of an individual is possible in a *certain* direction only. Whether or not the ultimate tasks of progress will be fulfilled is not known, just as it was not known to Buckle whether he would complete his history, or to Comte whether he would complete his "Course of Positive Philosophy." One died at the beginning of his work, while the other not only completed his but lived to see the phase of positive religion. These are contingencies, accidents, having not the slightest significance for the thinker as he begins his work. He begins it as if it were bound to be completed, and as if he will never have to lay it down.

[This is precisely the attitude of critical individuals toward the theory of progress. The individual has developed morally; he has applied his moral demands to existing cultural forms and to the existing distribution of goods among mankind. He has said to himself: these demands are realizable in *this* way only; here are the ideas which can be preached today; here are the enemies who must be fought today; here is the attack which must be readied for tomorrow; here is the ultimate goal which will not be achieved today or tomorrow but which nevertheless is and must be the goal. As soon as the road has been determined, the individual must set out upon it.

[I have attempted to point out some landmarks upon this road, nothing more. Whether or not there is a law of nature which leads to moral progress does not concern the individual, who in any case cannot know this at the present moment. Everything which takes place independently of his will is for him simply an instrument, a medium, an object of objective knowledge, and should have no influence upon his moral aspirations. It is useless for him to hope that the Olympians are seconding his aspirations, or to fear that they regard his independent activity with jealousy; it is useless to turn to the conscious Olympians of providentialism or the unconscious Olympians of fatalism when the question is one of implementing convictions.

[Develop your convictions and implement them—this is all you need to know. Progress is not a necessary, uninterrupted movement. What is necessary is only the evaluation of the course of history from the point of view of progress as the ultimate goal. From this point of view actual history presents both progressive and retrogressive phases. The critically thinking individual must be fully conscious of this and must direct his activity toward furthering the progressive phases and curtailing the retrogressive.

The resources for this he must seek within the depths of his conviction, within the depths of his faith.]

The Theory and Practice of Progress

1. The Dual Character of the Problem of Progress

LET US EXAMINE THE RESULTS of what has gone before concerning the real conception of progress which the evolution of thought has produced in mankind and which must be distinguished from the illusions that surround it.*

Ever since thinkers first came to view historical problems as among the most complex and important subjects of human study, they have labored ceaselessly to elucidate the concept of progress and to analyze the process it embraces. Ever since men first ceased to believe in the inviolability of the social order bequeathed them by their fathers, ever since individuals arose among them whose thought was no longer confined to exploiting existing social institutions and social conditions for personal ends but was directed toward discovering and actualizing forms of society which promised a better life for all—since that time the world has never lacked men who fight for progress.

* This letter was not included among the *Historical Letters* either in *Week* or in the first edition of this book. It was first published, with minor omissions and alterations necessitated by censorship, in one of the major legal Russian journals in 1881.[1] I add it now to these letters written at the end of the 'sixties because it deals with the same questions from a somewhat different point of view and can give the reader some indication of the lines along which the *Historical Letters* as a whole would have been constructed had I begun them at the beginning of the 'eighties instead of the end of the 'sixties. Minor repetitions were inevitable, but they are not numerous and I did not consider it necessary to eliminate them. The reader will not, I think, find anything that contradicts what has gone before; but some aspects of my position which are, perhaps, insufficiently clear in the earlier work may take on greater definition here. No important changes have been made here in the text of 1881, but everything which before was intentionally expressed without complete clarity, owing to the unavoidable circumstances of the Russian legal press, has been corrected. (1891)

Yet the majority of thinkers and practical men alike have fallen into error. Into the elucidation of the theoretical concept have crept, first, the unexpressed and sometimes even entirely unconscious desire on the thinker's part to promote his personal interests and the interests of those close to him, and second, a traditionalist worship of some conventional conception. Even in cases where the thinker was completely sincere and fully desired to treat the question critically, too often his conception of progress has suffered from lack of observation and experience in the realm of sociological facts.

Still more frequent and still more grievous have been the errors of the practical champions of progress. Some, exasperated by the defects of the existing social order, have not allowed themselves time to reflect and to come to an understanding of the conditions governing its *possible* improvement, but have flung themselves into the fight without calculating either their own strength or that of their adversaries. They have destroyed themselves, have destroyed whatever their fanatical rush toward progress touched, and have left behind them in history nothing but a halo of heroism. And this halo, by blinding some and terrifying others, more often than not has served as a ground for fresh illusions concerning the conditions of historical progress and has engendered fresh disasters in the future. Others, by attempting to master in thought all the conditions of a complex process, by fearing that their actions might provoke more suffering than necessary, by dealing irresolutely with antiquated tradition, by wavering in doubt before an uncertain future, have prevented themselves and their friends from fighting for progress with appropriate means. They have dampened the ardor of their allies, allowed less sincere and less knowledgeable men to take the lead, and allowed calculating opponents to circumvent them. And they have finally been compelled to throw up their hands in despair when they discovered that the tide of history—to the rise of which they, too, had contributed—was by no means taking the course for which they had been working and to which they were prepared selflessly to sacrifice their lives and their personal happiness.

Sad have been the consequences of these theoretical and practical mistakes. Too often the men who fight for progress have proved to be sources of social distress and even real agents of reaction—obstacles on the only avenues which could lead human societies to a better future. The voluminous literature defining the best and most commodious social order has left the new generation as bewildered as their fathers and grandfathers were regarding the true meaning of these terms. The fight for progress has led to results which in no way resemble what one could call progress. Finally, what is best and most commodious for the descendants has sometimes been found in a direction which the majority of "progressive" intellects among the ancestors would never have dreamed of, in a direction which filled them with loathing and aroused the vigorous opposition of those among them who fought most sincerely for a better social order.

Primitive sages argued that society's only salvation consisted in preserving the sanctity of ancient custom. But their descendants considered such preservation to be the greatest social evil, and found that the only healthy historical process consists in the reconstruction of social institutions under the influence of the rational and ever-expanding needs of man.

The development of distinct and opposing nations with strong internal bonds was an ideal of the Greeks and Romans—an ideal in the fight for which they gave their own lives and destroyed other outstanding representatives of that age in the life of mankind. But centuries passed, and within these same nations the conviction has arisen that the ideal of distinct nations is a principle which is most detrimental to the progress of mankind, and that the economic, political, intellectual, and moral solidarity of all mankind—both the developed and the developing—constitutes the only possible aim of progress.

Throughout a long period of history the best minds regarded religious beliefs as the foundation of social life, as the spiritual bond of society, as the nerve center of literature, art, and philosophy, which themselves served only to embellish or to ground this supreme manifestation of human thought. But a different age has come, an age of *secular* civilization, in which men of theory and men of practical affairs alike have, as far as possible, eliminated religion from all spheres of thought and life, and have recognized that the only truth man can win lies outside the sphere of religion, that the only morality consonant with his dignity is that grounded solely on natural needs, logical criticism, and man's rational convictions.

The political objectives pursued by the great statesmen of the seventeenth and eighteenth centuries proved to be only shadows of economic realities for the generation of the nineteenth century. The economic ideal of the affluent state, posed still later, is proving today to be a nebulous and narrow ideal so long as the problem of the rational *distribution* of a country's wealth is not resolved and so long as the ulcer of a degenerating or fermenting proletariat continues to spread along with this wealth.

Finally, even the isolated empirical science of recent centuries —the science which has stood aloof from life and life's burning questions and has carried out its colossal conquest of the inorganic and organic world in calm indifference—even this science is proving to be, for the foremost minds of our time, merely an elementary exercise in scientific thought, the lesson of an intellectual period which a more highly developed mankind must and will rapidly outlive. This more highly developed mankind sets itself the task of constructing a science of society as the crown of contemporary knowledge—a science which not only does not require the scientist to be isolated from life with its burning questions but which is completely permeated by life, is itself life in all the fullness of these burning questions. This science by its very nature not only sets its adepts the task of understanding it, but poses more extensive demands: Understand me, it says, in order to embody me in life; translate my demands into reality, or you have not understood me!

If the history of unriddling the idea of progress and fighting for progress is a history of human errors, self-delusions, and fatal blunders, it becomes all the more imperative to work toward eliminating these errors and self-delusions, preventing these blunders. If the goals our ancestors posed for social life and social development have continually proved inadequate to their descendants, so much the less can the present generation rest content with the established formulas and inherited tasks of life and development. The present generation must ask itself again and again: Given all the former conquests and errors of thought, how are we to understand the theoretical task of progress? Given all the victories our ancestors have gained and all the defeats they have suffered, how are we to fight more effectively for progress as we understand it? We, too, shall make mistakes in our understanding of progress; this is quite likely. But we shall strive to reduce our errors to the smallest possible minimum by carefully studying the errors of our predecessors. Perhaps we, too, shall be defeated; yes, this is possible. But even in such a case we shall strive to do everything in our power to gain the victory, or in our very defeat to show our successors the conditions of possible victory.

Most important to remember here is that the problem of progress is unavoidably twofold—theoretical and practical. It is impossible to fight for progress without striving to understand its objective as clearly as possible, and it is equally impossible to acquire a thorough understanding of its objective so long as we shrink from fighting for it with all the strength that is in us and by every means at our disposal. In rushing impulsively into the fight for the ideal without attempting to understand this ideal critically, we constantly run the risk of repeating the numerous mistakes of former times and, perhaps, of fighting for the triumph of reaction or stagnation while we think we are fighting for progress; history provides abundant examples of this. In limiting ourselves to theoretical understanding and renouncing the concrete battle for progress, either we have not understood the nature of progress or we are consciously acting *contrary* to what we ourselves have recognized as the ideal.

An essential element in the understanding of progress is the recognition that it never has and never could have taken place of itself, unconsciously. Apart from the efforts of past individuals to understand and implement the ideal, nothing could have occurred but repetition of what had gone before, nothing could have ruled but custom and routine, nothing could have resulted but stagnation. Only the vigorous work of individual thought could again and again have introduced critical inquiry into social outlooks, which by themselves turn naturally into frozen tradition. Only the unceasing efforts of individuals with convictions (even if their efforts were only moderately successful) could have molded the fighters for progress into an organized social force capable of defending their banner in the struggle against other social tendencies, of overcoming these tendencies, and of wresting from stagnation and from indifferentism at least a little ground for subsequent progress.

If this is the case, if everyone who has come to understand the nature of the process by which progress is won in history must also understand *this*, then he must realize that by remaining indifferent in the constant struggle men wage over different conceptions of real progress—or, still more frequently, over *any* conception of progress as against stagnation and routine—we are not only debilitating our supporters but are actually joining the ranks of the supporters of routine and stagnation. For the natural inertia of everything that exists—in sociology as well as mechanics—allows motion to begin, or allows already existing motion to change its character, only when forces are present to counteract the inertia. In *social* life these forces—which create social motion where none exists, accelerate it where it has slackened, and give it a new civilized character in epochs of renewal for mankind—are nothing other, and can be nothing other, than personal thought and personal energy which embody the needs of the age and the intellectual labor of all past time. Anyone who does not strive with all his strength to actualize progress as he understands it, is fighting *against* it.

Thus the need to participate in the fight for progress is the moral duty of the individual who has become alive to the meaning of this concept. But how are we to participate? How are we to strive effectively to actualize progress as we understand it?

The moral duty of the agent of progress, if he examines it attentively, is self-explanatory. First of all, in the name of his conviction, if it is sincere, he must strive to explain to others the conception of progress he has acquired; he must strive to gain supporters for it. But if his is the voice of one man, it is, as the proverb states, the voice of no one, and he is just as powerless as any isolated individual, however strong and sincere his conviction. Only a collective force can have historical significance. And so it becomes the duty of the fighter for progress to strengthen his ties with those who share his ideas, to join an organized group of people who are working in a certain direction by word and deed.

Parallel to this there arises another area of morally obligatory activity. The fighter for progress has become aware of the need for progress in a certain direction, and consequently of the need for a certain alteration in the social order or in social thought. He has developed this awareness only thanks to favorable circumstances of some sort, which have allowed him to adopt a sound critical attitude toward the defects of the system within which he lives and has developed. But he must not succumb to the illusion that acquiring this awareness has all at once distinguished him from his environment. No, he is bound to it by thousands of habits of thought and life, and all these habits have become tightly interwoven with the very defects in the social order or in social thought which he means to eliminate in his quest for progress. Thus he finds in himself the same elements which he, as an agent of progress, is combatting in the whole. To conquer these elements in their various social manifestations he must combat them within himself as well, must reeducate himself and recast his habits of thought and life. The fighter for progress must spread an understanding of progress in the realm of thought, become a member of a collective organism, and organize a social force to fight for progress in society. But he must further, at least in some degree, present in his own thinking and in his own life a practical example of the way in which progress in a particular direction should affect the thought and life of individuals in general.

Thus it is essential to have a firmly fixed plan of personal life, conforming to the progressive ideal that has become an inseparable element of the individual's conviction. Along with this must go the determination to put this plan into practice as far as circumstances permit. These circumstances are the environment, which from all sides presses the individual in the direction of old routine and old habits, and his own weaknesses and fancies, all of which have sprung from the same soil that must now be retilled and reconstituted by the progress which he has undertaken to serve and for which he is obliged to fight, on pain of betraying his own understanding and his own conviction.

It is essential, further, to adopt a clear plan of action for an organized social force, without which future progress cannot be effected. It is essential to have a clear understanding of the obstacles that must be encountered in effecting such progress, and of the conditions conducive to effecting it; an understanding of the strength and resources of the adversaries who must be combatted, and of the resources which must be employed in combatting them; an understanding of the distribution in society of actual and potential friends and allies in the impending struggle for progress. And along with this it is essential to have the firm determination to employ the organized collective force in the most effective manner to execute the plan once it is adopted, to eliminate the obstacles to progress, to crush its opponents, to employ all requisite means, of whatever sort, to do this—so long as they do not contradict the ideal of progress toward which we are striving—and to organize the final victory of progress after the social force has been organized to effect it.

It is essential, finally, to have a rationally thought-out set of arguments, so that my conviction as to the meaning of progress may become the conviction of those to whom I appeal. I must have a logical argument for the minority who will yield to nothing but critical thought. I must have graphic, striking facts for those who find it difficult to generalize but who demand concrete, empirical proofs. I must have an argument from the sphere of feeling for people who are strongly swayed by their emotions. And I must have the broadest utilitarian support in the sphere of vital, tangible interests which everyone can understand, for the vast majority who are moved only by immediate, positive interest. Progress can have reliable and numerous supporters only when it is grounded with equal force on the methods of science, the sentiments of the imagination, and the calculation of personal interest.

Such are the conditions of the practical program which alone can bring about progress.

But all these conditions themselves require theoretical support. To disseminate an idea in all the various spheres of society, to organize a social force to work toward progress and subsequently toward its victory, and effectively to remake one's own personality in a direction that accords with the ideal of progress one has adopted—for all these things an understanding of much theoretical material is required. The agent of progress must understand the environment in which circumstances of birth and education have placed him. He must understand the historical process which, on the one hand, has produced this environment and, on the other, has made it possible for thought to view it critically and to discover in this very environment the objectives of the progress which must rework it. But as a foundation for both there must be an understanding of progress as a natural process in the social order, but a process which takes place under definite conditions, in accordance with definite laws, under the influence of definite forces—however miscellaneous and chaotic the picture of historical movement, in all its complexity and change, may seem.

Thus, as groundwork for the practice of progress there is the theory of progress as a natural process and a real historical phenomenon, and there is the application of this theory to that social order and that social environment which rouse the agent of progress to practical action.

2. The Doctrinal Debate

In the present age, what are the results of our understanding of progress? What bearing have the facts of contemporary social life on the problem of progress?

We are confronted with a number of completely contradictory and to all appearances irreconcilable views of this problem. If we examine them carefully, we shall find that they agree on one point only: that the age in which we live presents a most mournful picture of the disintegration of all firm social ties, a picture of class hostility and increasingly bitter conflict among individuals. As to the outcome of this struggle of nearly all against all, and as to the means of treating this social disease which all acknowledge, the views are diametrically opposed.

Let us disregard the providentialists and, in general, all those who openly resort to a religious factor to explain the all-too-real social cancers of the present and the equally real martyrology of the majority of mankind—the martyrology which is called the chronicle of historical events. Their teachings belong to a system of thought that is alien to modern science. And we have more than enough interpreters of the social process who remain—or think that they remain—on a realistic foundation.

Before us, first of all, come the *pessimists*. What is called progress in history, they tell us, is a fatal tendency toward the augmentation of mankind's miseries. All roads lead to this end. Everything in existence, to be better understood, can be understood only as a source of calamities; and the clearer our understanding becomes, the more we become convinced of the inevitable increase of these calamities.

Beside them we hear the calm, consoling voice of the *optimists*. Progress is inevitable, they say. The improvement and elevation of human existence in all its aspects and of human community in all its forms is inevitable. All evils and disharmonies are unreal and transitory. The errors and sufferings of individuals and all apparent reactions and digressions from progress are simply ripples on the surface of the ancient "river of time"; these ripples are raised by ever-shifting winds, but no wind can halt the over-all flow of this vast river. The power of human thought is increasing, revealing truth after truth and illuminating previously unknown paths to progress. Even the well-being of those classes which ordinarily are represented as stepchildren of modern civilization is increasing. At the same time the various instruments of the human symphony are tuning up, so as in due course to blend into one ordered harmony.

Both these antithetical world views are completely rejected by those who may be called *naturalists* in history. Progress, say the latter, is one of that multitude of illusions which one after another divert and entertain mankind in the fatal succession of events which constitute its life. Everything "best" and "supreme," every personal or social ideal is an illusion and nothing but an illusion. The only reality is the mechanico-chemical process which, in its diverse and eternally recurring cycles, generates here and there in the universe the phenomenon of organic life and the phenomenon of consciousness. Wherever organic life appears, a struggle for existence begins, and it ends only with the cessation of life itself. Wherever consciousness develops, there spring up various illusions of truth, beauty, moral duty, social bonds—illusions through whose billowing clouds the sober but mournful truth is visible only rarely. The happiness of some and the sufferings of others are fortuities with no more significance in the over-all process than a bubble dancing on the surface of a boiling liquid. There is in nature neither change for the better nor change for the worse, neither rise nor fall; there is only a succession of phenomena, all of which have identical significance and to which any sort of moral evaluation is completely inapplicable. And in history, too, the only reality is the struggle for existence, the struggle among the forces at hand. All the ideas and ideals which crowd history's surface are simply self-delusions which consciousness produces to conceal from itself the monotony of the real process which is taking place, and to prolong it.

To these metaphysicians of various persuasions the historical *realists* take exception, completely changing the very formulation of the question.

We cannot know the essence of things, they say, and there is no use troubling ourselves about it. Even if we assume that the whole intellectual world of our aspirations toward theoretical and practical truth is nothing but a world of illusion enveloping the monotonous process of the struggle for existence, still we cannot strip this wrapping from the essence of things, and in real life we shall go on setting goals and seeking means of achieving them, all the same. We shall continue to suffer and to enjoy—however insignificant, perhaps, are our sufferings and joys for "the whole." We shall continue to seek truth, or what seems *to us* to be truth. We shall continue to rebel against injustice, or what *to us* is injustice. Consequently, the question of progress and of what is "best" will always have vital significance *to us*, whatever may be the essence of things. And we raise it for the intellectual world which constitutes *our* science, *our* morality, and *our* philosophy.

From this point of view the ideas of the pessimists or optimists make little difference to us, the realists continue. What takes place in history of itself, inevitably, is beyond our power and beyond the scope of our activity. Perhaps the quantity of evil and misery in the world as a "whole" is relentlessly increasing. Perhaps it is relentlessly diminishing. But before us is the aching humanity of *our* day, its sufferings the result of past historical processes, in the development of which people such as ourselves have taken part. Before us is the potential future of *this* suffering humanity, a future in the construction of which we, too, must take part. We stand at the junction of this past and this future, with our opinions and convictions, our scientific investigations, and the determination to act, whatever these intellectual and moral data of ours may be. In the name of these data we inevitably say to ourselves: *here* is evil and falsehood, *there* is truth and the good. *This* past event was a phenomenon of progress and *that* a fact of regression, because the former is *for us* an approximation to the good and the true, while the latter is a departure from them. And in the immediate future, which we must help to build, *here* are the phenomena which promise the greatest truth and the greatest good; *here* is what we must fight for, so that the sufferings of mankind will be relieved.

Fresh sufferings inevitably will come, say some. Perhaps; but *our* task is to combat *these* sufferings which we know and understand, leaving it to future generations to devise means of combatting the evil of which we have no clear conception. Man's sufferings are immaterial, say others. This, too, is possible; but his *present* sufferings are palpable to him, and we are obliged to seek in the past for their explanation, and in the future for their cure.

For us progress is a *potential* direction of the historical course of events toward what is "best" as *we* understand it, for that period of time which *we* can encompass intellectually. For us the struggle for progress is the obligatory promotion of this potential direction of events. Being merely *potential,* it may, for all we know, give way to some other course of events, even one completely antithetical to it; consequently it stands in need of the assistance of all who view it in this way rather than in that. Pessimism and optimism with their general considerations are completely irrelevant to the theory of progress we need for practical action.

On this realistic foundation we find various groups of opinions, which can and should now be discussed from the standpoint of framing a true theory of progress.

Here again we shall eliminate those spokesmen for mysticism (not numerous in our time) who seek mankind's progress in the replacement of one religion by another, who see the principal evil of the present day in the absence of religious faith, and who seek man's salvation in the creation of new dogmas and a new cult. If the religious element must be disregarded in the metaphysics of history, it is surely better not to resort to it for an understanding of the real process of history, either—much less for the treatment of social maladies.

But even realistic accounts of the contemporary social predicament and a possible way out of its perplexities are extremely diverse, and I shall have to confine myself here to a few principal doctrines only.

Only a small minority of thinkers today find the source of social evil exclusively in the realm of *ideas* and rely for its cure upon the establishment of a sounder world view among highly developed intellects and the extension of rational education in all classes of society. For them it is still sufficient to formulate progress in the words "ideas move the world." For them the growth of science and the elucidation of a world view constitute the *whole* of progress, since in their opinion this element determines all the rest. For them the fight for progress consists in self-development and the propagation of science and rational philosophy, since the evil in all other spheres of human existence will, they believe, be eliminated through cultivation of this ruling sphere.

The majority go further—into the realm of vital *interests*.

Some say that progress has consisted and still consists in introducing the principle of law (*pravo*) into the social order—in establishing a constitutional state (*pravovoye gosudarstvo*) which will eliminate violence and inequality in all its forms, protect the weak, restrain the strong, invest life with freedom and equality, and through collective force eliminate the excesses of the struggle for existence, the excesses of competition for profit and for power. The constitutional state will itself be governed by the principles of freedom and equality which it will establish for its subjects, and will join with all its sisters, the other constitutional states, in an equitable federation of harmonious political units.

For these worshipers of law, progress in the past has consisted in the approach to the constitutional state, and this progress, which comes about gradually through peaceful reforms and bloody revolutions, is bound to proceed further in the future, in the same way and by the same means. All other phenomena can be subsumed under the phases of this evolution, and apart from it there is only the world of pernicious social illusions. Men who fight for progress must enrol under the banner of the constitutional state, under the principle of political freedom and political equality. To the struggle for these supreme social principles, highly cultivated people should devote all their energies. Everything else will come as a consequence of establishing a constitutional state, the concept of which embraces the entire ideal of historical progress.

No, reply others—legal relationships and the whole of political life are only the outward manifestation of a more fundamental social process—the process of economic growth. A country's progress consists in its enrichment, which determines both its external significance and its internal cultural development. The difference in political form between monarchies and republics and between more liberal and less liberal constitutions disappears in the vast process of world production and the international transactions of the exchange, in the indestructible bond of economic interests among all countries, all peoples, and all social classes.

Civilization is the product of wealth, they say, and the progress of mankind consists in the gradual growth of human industry, in the broadening of economic ties among men, and in the closer interweaving of all groups of men in the name of their economic interests. Wealth brings independence and power, cultivates human dignity, and is the condition under which freedom and equality can be established. To attain the goal of economic progress—the only real progress—a country may make any sacrifice and may view all sufferings with equanimity, because in this case both sacrifices and sufferings are temporary and will be requited a hundredfold when the intimate connection of all economic interests infuses the social order with a consciousness of their harmony and solidarity. The struggle for human progress, these thinkers assert, consists in the natural quest for enrichment —in competition, by means of which the most clever and skillful person, in enriching himself, thereby shows mankind the best means of enrichment and hence the truest path to progress. By devoting all his energies to this struggle, eliminating all the emotional and moral illusions which distract a man from the rational path, judging everything from the standpoint of economic interests and putting a market price on everything, the individual can best cultivate his individuality, develop his capacities, and fight most rationally for progress—for the most rapid establishment of a harmony and solidarity of the interests of all individuals in the course of enriching mankind.

In recent times there are even more outspoken writers—who in this case, however, are simply presenting a very ancient doctrine in a new form. They regard the ideas of freedom and equality and the dreams of a harmony of economic interests as equally illusory. They find an inner contradiction in the very concept of a constitutional state. Progress, they say, has been and can be attained only by the domination and direction of the majority by a minority. Not law but the state is supreme. The state may institute legal relationships and a certain amount of freedom and equality among its subjects, but it itself remains the unalloyed supreme authority even in regard to these elements.

But political domination is impossible without economic domination, they say, and for this reason the dominant class politically, which is the ruling power in the state, should also be the dominant class economically, which concentrates property in its own hands at the expense of others. An economic monopoly of property is a necessary condition of the existence of state power, without which both civilization and progress are impossible. Progress can consist only in the following: the state's ascendency will grow firmer and firmer, the condition of its existence—the economic and political inequality of social groups—will be acknowledged more and more universally, and furthermore the ruling classes, in consequence of the greater firmness of their sway, will treat the subject classes in a more humanitarian manner and provide them with a more humane existence. Under these conditions the fight for progress amounts to promoting the inevitable concentration of property and political power in one class at the expense of others, and morally exhorting the world's sovereigns to leave a certain share of human dignity and well-being to the subject masses.

In opposition to the foregoing sociological doctrines, a group of socialist thinkers and men of action adopt some of the principles of each school enumerated, but adopt them in quite a different combination and arrive at quite different conclusions. Yes, say those who support this view, human progress does consist in introducing freedom and equality into the social order, in introducing law in the form of justice into social life. But it is not for the state to do this. The state, by its very nature, is domination, inequality, constraint of freedom. And with strengthening and consolidation of the ascendency of one class over others, not only is it impossible to count on a more humane existence for the subject classes—their material, intellectual, and moral degeneration must ever increase. A constitutional state is an unrealizable dream.

For this reason progress requires that the state, as the domination of one class over others, must tend toward a minimum in respect to power and historical significance. As an external force the state may have been a historical necessity over a long period, because society was insufficiently developed. But as social development increases the state yields one after another of its functions to other elements of society, and its role in history inevitably diminishes. At present it is already aware of its complete dependence upon the economic forces which govern the forms of social development. Thus in seeking social justice and the social realization of freedom and equality we must look first not to the establishment of better juridical relationships among individuals and groups, but to the establishment of a sounder economic order. If the latter is sound, unsound political institutions cannot long endure.

But the present economic order is unsound. It *inevitably* generates inequality and limits the freedom of the majority. It *inevitably* gives rise to the domination of some classes by others. In economic competition it evokes, strengthens, and legitimizes elements of hostility among individuals and conflict among and within groups. It stifles individual development in millions of people, permitting only a few to develop—and even here perverting their development by engulfing them in this same war of all against all. Progress is possible today only through radically altering this unsound economic order and providing it with new foundations which permit every individual to develop in a comprehensive way, permit the greatest possible introduction of freedom and equality into life, and permit justice in social life.

In the past, too, progress has consisted and could consist only in the development of those forms of thought which made clear to men the real interconnections of things and the real requirements of personal human development and a sound social order. It could consist only in strengthening those factors in social relationships which cement the bond between individuals and groups and broaden this bond to embrace all thinking humanity. In other words, progress has consisted and could consist only in the growing awareness of truth through the ever-increasing development of critical thought, and in the growing embodiment of solidarity in social life—a solidarity ultimately spreading to all thinking humanity in its cooperation for universal development. This solidarity can be established, of course, not on the basis of competition for wealth and struggle for existence, but on the basis of the common interests of all men who work productively with their muscles and their brains. On the basis of the availability, to all and to each, of the means of personal development and the means of productive labor. On a basis which eliminates every material or intellectual monopoly. On the basis of collective labor for the common good.

Elements inimical to progress here are, first, the routine of existing social relationships and, second, the interests of the individuals and groups making up the current ruling minority, which would lose its ascendency with the cessation of competition—the competition which goes on among some for the right to live on the verge of starvation, and among others for the greatest profits and the greatest appropriation of superfluous luxuries. Inimical to progress, too, are many current trends of thought. Some fail to recognize the supremacy of economic interests over other interests in the social order and the need for establishing solidarity among these economic interests as the only sound foundation for solidarity among men in general. Some see competition rather than cooperation among personal interests as the principal instrument of progress. Some regard the domination of one class by another as a necessary condition of progress. Some, finally, view progress and reaction as inevitable historical processes which take place through the operation of metaphysical forces, there being no need to take into account the personal efforts of individuals. All these views are inimical to progress.

In the teachings of socialism, those who fight for progress are called upon to forge, from the present actual relationships among men, new relationships which will permit the solidarity of all thinking and toiling human groups. They are called upon to make clear to themselves and to others what existing factors are contributing to this reconstruction and what are impeding it. They are called upon to form a collective force which can utilize what is favorable to change and can remove or shatter the obstacles that arise in its path. They are called upon to cultivate, in themselves and in those who share their convictions, a personal force of mind and a personal energy which is fit both for the fight for progress against its enemies and, still more, for the establishment of that social order which alone can make solidarity among individuals and groups possible and strong.

I shall limit myself to the foregoing. In addition to the doctrines mentioned, which express the different trends of thought about progress most sharply and determinately, other, less significant doctrines are encountered which serve as transitional and mediating stages between those I have indicated. For the purposes of this letter, however, there is no need to enumerate these compromise doctrines of progress. It is sufficient to point to the extreme differences in views.

Each of these views has its partisans and its history. Each had its reason for arising and enduring. Weighty arguments have been and are advanced for each of them. Thus some questions arise: Given the various conflicting doctrines of progress which have been expounded, how are we to go about weighing the arguments for and against each of them? How are we consciously to settle upon one or another practical program of progress which is the inevitable consequence of one or another theory of progress?

I shall confine myself here to outlining the issues which must be resolved in this connection, and the order in which it seems to me most convenient to raise them for effective solution. But to raise them is unavoidable, since it is not the arbitrary will of the individual which raises them but the fatal course of history. And to resolve them in one way or another is obligatory, because—as has already been said above—he who does not wish to seek an avenue to progress and, to the limit of his ability, to set out upon this avenue as a fighter for progress, is by that very fact fighting *against* progress.

3. The Order of Posing the Questions

In what has progress consisted and in what might it have consisted in the history of mankind?

For answering this question we have material of three sorts. We have, first, the society we can observe around us, as it now exists—with its virtues and its defects, its elements of solidarity and its elements of hostility, its healthy processes and is pathological processes. We have, second, the historical process which has produced the present from the past, and through historical criticism we can reconstruct more or less accurately the actual course of this process. We have, finally, particular scientific works —far from definitive but in some cases quite remarkable—on questions of sociology and its sister disciplines of psychology and biology. In these works the diverse elements of the social order in its various historical phases are examined and analyzed and their dependence shown, with the aid of the above-mentioned descriptive material and the material established by historical criticism, and with the aid of methods of induction and deduction no less accurate than those which permit us to draw inferences in other fields of science.

Thus a solution to the question just raised can be approached in three different ways.

What is closest and best known is the society around us. It would seem, then, that it is easiest to begin directly with it: not without reason have we been taught that in an investigation one must always proceed from the known to the unknown. So let us provide ourselves with descriptive material, statistical data, and comparative tables, and let us attempt to answer these questions: In our society, what can be a source of progress and what is an element of reaction or stagnation? What must be promoted and what opposed in the name of the goal of human development? What constitutes a fatal necessity, against which it is as foolish to argue as against the law of gravitation, and what is a result created with the help of personal conviction and personal energy, and capable, therefore, of being altered by clarifying convictions and redirecting energy?

But can we really answer these questions *solely* by observing present-day society? We see only the gross results of a long process; this process must be analyzed, by other methods.

Here is a catalogue of human ills; here is a list of criminals and suicides by categories; here is a ledger of bloody wars and revolutions; here are the figures on a worker's income—an income which cannot possibly equal the sum of his *essential* expenditures. All this is indisputably evil, and all this, in the name of an involuntary sentiment, in the name of simple sympathy, we wish to eliminate. Very good. But how?

Alongside the foregoing picture is a completely different one: The ever-increasing power of technology burrows across continents and permits communication between the antipodes; it surrounds daily life with unprecedented comforts. Science wearies the observer with the quantity of its conquests, and through popularization it makes accessible to the weakest mind what only recently could scarcely be understood by intellects of exceptional cultivation. Feats of philanthropy are performed amid the universal struggle for gain. Feats of heroism and abnegation are performed amid the bloody scenes of mutual slaughter. Feats of solidarity are performed among beings whom statistics doom to chronic hunger, to a daily struggle for existence in which victory is impossible, to competition for a scrap of bread. We involuntarily pride ourselves on these achievements of the present day. We should like to expand and generalize them. Here are the elements of progress, we say, and we must cultivate these elements at the expense of others. Let us grant this, too. But again, how is it to be done?

What if the list of criminals and suicides turns out to be no more subject to sociological alteration than the average annual rainfall or hail damage? What if the evil we mean to combat can only be replaced by other, still worse evil? And what if the glowing pictures in which we thought we discerned elements of human prosperity and growth are so intimately bound up with the disturbing pictures of social sufferings that as the beauties dear to us increase these same outrageous sufferings will inevitably grow —and what is more, will perhaps grow in greater measure? Besides, the bloody wars and revolutions—like the achievements of science and technology—and the budget sheet of the chronically starving workers—like the feats of solidarity amid these same workers—have appeared not at the wave of a wand but as results of the historical process. And the one set of phenomena can be eliminated, and the other extended, only in the subsequent course of this same process, through the same forces which are at work in it and effect it, and alone *can* work in it and effect it.

Observation of contemporary society can show us an appropriate practical program of progress only after we have come to understand as *natural* or as *historical* the phenomena which take place around us. We must know which of these phenomena depend upon natural causes, upon other phenomena which continually recur (such as the need for food, for example), or upon processes which operate in all historical generations of man (such as, for example, the climatic and topographical features of a country). We must know which of them are inseparably linked through conditions of coexistence and logical dependence. And we must know which of them are products of the historical past, have arisen in specific circumstances and under the influence of specific social forces, and can disappear or change in other circumstances and under the influence of other forces. A theory of progress cannot be derived from even the most painstaking observation of the contemporary social order until we have come to understand this order as the product of all past history, in which specific historical forces were at work—some constant, determined by the very processes of nature, and others produced by history itself but, once produced, capable of joining battle, sometimes victoriously, with the elementary historical motives supplied by nature.

To understand the present as the product of history we must turn to the second type of data mentioned above, to historical material. In it we must consider the following: Which phenomena repeat themselves under all cultural conditions and which are linked only with particular forms of civilization? What groups of social phenomena are always observed as wholes, their elements necessarily coexisting, and what elements can be present in various combinations? What historical forces have arisen independently of the personal convictions and the personal energy of individuals, and in what historical forces have such convictions and energy been inseparable elements? What motives are the real basis of history, which everyone who fights for progress, as well as everyone who opposes it, must take into account? In what combinations have these motives served as a real basis for progress, and when have the *same* motives given rise to reaction? And what forces, though substantial, offer only temporary assistance to the agent of progress, since one cannot count upon either their duration or their constancy?

History can, to be sure, provide answers to these questions—

but under two conditions: that both the scope of its material and the statement of its problems are sufficiently broad.

The material at the disposal of exact historical criticism covers a fairly limited period of time. For the preceding period our pictures of society are somewhat dim, and in peering at them the historian is too prone to reconstruct ancient ages on the analogy of more modern ones—an analogy which is always rather dangerous. Still more distant lies the semihistorical and prehistorical period, which at least in part must be re-created in the imagination simply by a series of constructs, and once again it is very easy for the investigator to introduce his own habits of thought and life into these constructs. Given such methods, a historical institution which arose for good reason in a particular age, and by the same token may wither and die for good reason in another age, is sometimes pictured by the historian as an unchanging, constant, natural element of the social order. The ancient Greeks viewed slavery as an institution without which society of any sort was inconceivable. The modern jurist generally sees in the present institutions of the family, property, the police, and the law court something which does not admit of alteration. The modern politician can hardly help but look for the state element in every age as something distinct and predominant; he cannot admit that in the present order economic forces determine domestic and foreign politics, and that in the future other social elements will reduce the state's role in life to a rather inconsiderable minimum.

The problems of history are gradually being broadened, but it is still far from being the case that all investigators pose them with equal breadth. If the era of biographical history has passed, there is still not a single work, in any way complete, in which the role of economic forces in all periods of mankind's life is elaborated in adequate detail and on adequate grounds. In existing historical works, the evolution of philosophical world views and particularly of scientific works is far from satisfactorily interwoven with the course of political events. Still less, perhaps, are the following taken into account: the coexistence in a given period and society of several groups within the minority occupying different levels of intellectual and moral development and participating differently in the work of thought; the presence beside them of a majority occupying still another and quite different level of development; the interaction of all these groups, which are linked by a common life; and the completely different course which history takes for each of them, each course constituting an element in the over-all picture of the period's historical life.

At present, of course, these problems cannot yet be resolved properly for all periods of history. Of course one cannot demand of contemporary writers in this field that they handle all these difficulties in an entirely satisfactory manner—difficulties which can be overcome only through the most rigorous investigation of historical material which hitherto has been in part completely neglected—or even unknown—and in part very inadequately exploited. But it is essential, nonetheless, for every historical work which is abreast with the contemporary tasks of thought, that the investigator have in mind all these aspects of the problem; that he be armed, insofar as possible, with both the capacity to discern the facts relevant to these aspects of historical life and the capacity to understand their significance.

But are there many historians today who are so familiar with economic phenomena that they can properly appraise the economic significance of a fact? Are there many who are capable, I shall not say of tracing the connection between particular scientific works and the general state of culture, but even of understanding the role of a particular scientific work without assistance? Are there many who can so familiarize themselves with the concurrent historical development of different social groups that they can reconstruct in their imagination the diverse operation of a given event on each of these groups? Unfortunately all these questions must be answered in the negative.

But without a clear conception of the economic processes of the production, exchange, and distribution of wealth, the historian can never become an historian of the popular masses, who are governed primarily by the conditions of economic security. Without a definite view of the scientific significance of a given idea, can the historian understand the true character of intellectual evolution in a given period? Having confined his investigation to a few social groups only, or having failed to raise the question of the potential and actual interaction of these groups, can he possibly form anything like an exact notion of the progress of the entire society in that period?

Thus to answer the questions which, as has been shown above, arise out of a consideration of the historical material available for a theory of progress, the investigator must be armed with an understanding of sociological problems in their interdependence. And he must illuminate the facts before him by a definite view of their relative importance and essential connection—a connection rooted partly in constant laws of natural human needs, and partly in temporary laws of historical needs generated by the actual course of events and conditioned not merely by social life in general but by life in particular forms of culture.

The historical material becomes clear only in the light of the laws of biology, psychology, and sociology—which themselves contain, along with elements that repeat themselves indefinitely, a large share of historical elements, elements produced and destroyed by history. Becoming accustomed to cooked food cannot but change in some degree the physiological and pathological conditions of man's digestive process, just as neural processes in the central organ of consciousness were bound to change under the influence of different forms of social life. The proportion of psychological processes which depend directly upon biological conditions is quite negligible in comparison with the psychological processes which have developed under the direct influence of social association and social needs. As for sociology, today the truth is scarcely even worth repeating that all functions of social life change quantitatively and qualitatively with the course of history, and that all organs for performing these functions are created by history as man's various social needs arise, change, and disappear. Thus historical material serves for inferring the laws of psychology and sociology at the same time that these laws, once established, serve for ordering and explaining additional historical material.

We cannot even begin to analyze the bearing of given historical material on the theory of progress until we have accepted as a point of departure some antecedently established theory of human needs and some definite view of the role of society in the life of man; some definite view of the relation between individual and society in the process of social change; some definite view of the basic social forces which (according to some doctrines) inevitably create human progress or (according to others) may in some cases promote and in others retard it; and finally, some definite view of the fundamental processes of history which provide a schema for appraising the essential, the more or less important, and the subsidiary facts of history. More extensive and painstaking study of historical facts can modify the point of departure; this is what constitutes progress in psychology and sociology, and this progress in its turn occasions new advance in the understanding of history. But at any given moment one must appraise and order historical material only on the basis of those findings in sociology and its sister disciplines of psychology and biology which in the present state of knowledge are considered most plausible.

The question posed above concerning the theory of progress resolves itself, then, into three questions, which must be raised in the following order:

On the basis of the present findings of biology, psychology, and sociology, in what *might* progress in human society have consisted?

On the basis of the historical material which has been analyzed and investigated, in what *have* the various phases of historical progress consisted?

On the basis of the social order we observe around us and of the intellectual work taking place within its various groups, and taking into account the historical origin of this order and the principal phenomena of progress in history, in what does the social progress which is *possible in our time* consist?

The practical program of progress which is obligatory for the highly developed individual hinges upon the answers given to these questions by the theory of progress.

4. An Outline of the Theory of Progress

Into what particular inquiries, then, do the three new general questions just raised resolve in their turn? Let us try to find out in very general outline.

To answer the question of what progress *might* have consisted in, we must first define its elements and find, among the various processes which can be included under the term "development," the processes which *for us* constitute a tendency toward what is best.

We shall find here two types of development which from the

first glance we cannot but regard as progressive, but which seem to differ so greatly that they may appear contradictory. And in fact they have come into conflict in the actual course of history. One is the growth of individual thought, with its technical inventions, scientific achievements, philosophical constructs, artistic creations, and moral heroism. The other is social solidarity, with its cardinal dictates of "one for all and all for one," "to each everything needed for life and development, from each all his energy for social utility, social welfare, social development."

The growth of conscious processes in the individual, his development in the sphere of thought, is unquestionably a phenomenon of progress for us. Consequently the conditions which ensure the greatest and most rapid growth of individual thought in mankind are conditions of progress. On the other hand, firm social cohesion is a necessary condition of a healthy society and of the well-being of the individuals comprising it. Thus everything that strengthens this cohesion is for us a beneficial, progressive element; everything that weakens it, everything that generates hostility and creates inequality in society is for us a pathological, retrograde element. In this regard our social ideal is a society of individuals who are equal, who have a solidarity of interests and convictions, who live under the same cultural conditions, and who have, as far as possible, eliminated from their environment all feelings of mutual hostility and every form of struggle for existence.

But these two conceptions of progress can and have come into conflict in the course of history.

The ideal of a stable society of equals is satisfied in high degree by the primitive empire of custom, in which all intellectual activity and all individual development are stifled by the prevailing routine of life, and where social equality means only that all are equally devoid of more cultivated needs and it is equally impossible for all to win themselves a more human existence. Can this primitive, semimythical, human-herd condition really be something desirable, something ideal?

The ideal of the higher development of individual thought can be satisfied by a system in which a small minority makes substantial intellectual achievements through sucking the lifeblood of the vast majority which is subject to its rule and is deprived of all chance to participate in its intellectual life. Great flights of individual thought can be bought at the price of enslaving the masses, at the price of incalculable suffering. Can a social environment which gives rise to the vigorous development of conscious processes in a few individuals, under such circumstances, really be called without reservation a progressive environment?

No, we say, the primitive human herd, under the sway of custom as much as the ant heap or the beehive is under the sway of instinct, is not the ideal of progress. Given what stability is possible, a society is progressive only when consciousness and new, higher needs are developing in it; when the fullest possible equality among individuals serves only as a basis for the greatest possible personal development of each of them; when the customary order and customary life are continually being reworked under the influence of expanding thought; when the social bond which is the foundation of the society's stability is not an identical inherited custom but an identical conviction animating all.

No, we continue, development of individual thought bought at the price of the suffering and enslavement of the majority does not satisfy the requirements of progress. It is a narrow and one-sided development. An indisputable indication of this is the fact that the minority thus produced at the expense of the sufferings of others, for all its intellectual advances, must be very undeveloped morally if it *allows* itself to develop under such circumstances, if it is not revolted by the conditions which produce it. A truly progressive development of individual thought takes place only when this development is directed toward a consciousness of solidarity between the more highly developed individual and the less highly developed groups, toward the reconstruction of social relationships in this spirit, and toward the reduction of inequality in the development of the members of the solidary society. The true development of the individual can take place only within a highly developed group, where there is cooperation among social elements within which the difference in the level of development of individuals has been reduced to the smallest possible minimum, and where there is a common aspiration to reduce this minimum still further. In the healthy community individuals develop not at the expense of others but through the most active cooperation of all.

But is this not an impossible ideal? Must we not choose between a society which is firm and solidary, but has renounced the development of individual thought, and a society in which thought is vigorously at work, but at the price of continual dissension, endless strife among individuals and groups, repeated internal and external disasters? Must we not choose between a minority which is developing its own thinking thanks to the suffering and enslavement of the majority, and the absence of intellectual development? Can we ever establish a social system which is bound together by the convictions of the members of society, which is solidary in the name of these convictions, and in which individuals cooperate for their common development? Do not personal interests forever set one individual against another? Do they not forever set the individual against the social system, making him either an exploiter of society or a martyr at its hands? Can personal needs be identified with social goals? Can personal interest become a binding force in social life to the same extent that it is an incentive to personal intellectual activity?

At this stage in the development of our understanding of progress we must compare the interests of the *individual* and the interests of *society,* and see to what extent they can be reconciled.

The facts of history show that there is no irreconcilable contradiction between firm social cohesion and the vigorous operation of thought within a society. They show that individual thought can operate effectively not only to set the interests of the individual against the interests of society, or to help the individual exploit society, but also to promote solidarity between the highly developed individual and his society. Thought can arouse in the individual a love for his kinsmen, his countrymen, for men in general; can arouse the urge to strengthen their solidarity with one another and his solidarity with them; can arouse the individual to selfless activity for the common good, to which personal well-being, personal attachments, and life itself are sacrificed. Along with its struggle against social customs, thought has worked in history for the development of progressive social civilization. Along with the struggle of interests for existence, for wealth, and for a monopoly on pleasure, we see, counteracting this struggle, feats of conscious service to the common cause, entire lives dedicated to the strengthening of solidarity among men.

It is not only in the name of submission to prevailing custom that the individual can take a sympathetic attitude toward the social association in which he lives, just as his personal interest need not consist only in exploiting the social environment for such of his own ends as are opposed to the ends of a majority of society's other members. The individual, at a certain level of development, can recognize that his interests are *identical* with the interests of this majority; he can recognize that firmer social cohesion would be *advantageous* to him. Thus his thought can work to *strengthen* social cohesion, to *reinforce* social solidarity. Then the power of the developing thought of individuals *coincides* with the power of the increasingly unified society. Then the harmonious progressive development of both elements considered will become possible, and in such a case both processes, aiding one another, will become truly progressive.

It remains only to examine the motives which move the individual to action. They are the authority of custom, the force of interest, the impulses of emotion, and the moral power of conviction.

The rule of custom and routine, as absolutely contradicting the healthy operation of thought, should be considered an absolutely retrogressive phenomenon. Progressive thought must constantly rework inherited customs in conformity with its developing ideals. It must become increasingly critical in its treatment and ordering of the existing material. In scope it must become the thought of an increasingly broad, consistent, and harmonious world view, the thought of an increasingly well-ordered and comprehensive philosophy.

Emotion as an independent motive to action cannot be regarded as a progressive force in social life any more than the rule of custom can, because of the extreme irregularity and inconstancy of emotional expression. It is progressive only when it imparts greater energy to interests and convictions which are already progressive in themselves; in all other cases it can just as readily be an instrument of stagnation and reaction as an instrument of progress.

There remain interests and convictions. When these contradict each other within the breast of a single individual, we may have a fanatic, a hero, or a solitary sage—but in each such case we have

an isolated fact which is incapable of becoming the basis of a social force and a historical influence. When the convictions or interests of the minority contradict the convictions or interests of
the majority, there is no solidarity in society, no firm cohesion; it is
the eve of disaster, and no brilliance of civilization, no vast a-
chievements of superficial culture or individual thought can conceal the gaping wounds in the body politic. The social order is
doomed to destruction or radical alteration.

Progress is possible only when the highly developed minority
has become firmly convinced that, in the name of a sound social
order, its interests are identical with the interests of the majority;
when in highly developed individuals the desire to bind the society into a more solidary whole in the name of their own interests
has become a moral conviction; when the individual can become
part of a growing social force in the name of the unity of interests
of all the elements which compose it. When in becoming part of
this force, the individual brings to it a clearer awareness of the
community of interests binding society, and in so doing trans-
mutes these interests into moral conviction. Then the task of
progress is set in a determinate manner. Progress is the growth of
social consciousness, insofar as it leads to the strengthening and
broadening of social solidarity; it is the strengthening and broadening of social solidarity, insofar as it is based upon growing consciousness in society. The organ of progress is the developing
individual: apart from his activity progress is impossible. As his
thought develops he discovers the laws of social solidarity—the
laws of sociology—and applies these laws to his present environment. And as his energy develops he discovers avenues of practical activity—specifically, ways of reconstructing the present environment in accordance with his confirmed ideals and his factual
knowledge.

If the interests of thought and the interests of social solidarity
—the interests of the individual and the interests of his society—
can be reconciled, and if this is the road to a true understanding
of progress and a true practical program of progress, we must examine more carefully and classify the needs the individual seeks
to satisfy in social life—the needs for the satisfaction of which society creates different organs corresponding to different functions,
and which constitute the basic schema of historical development.

There are, first, basic and permanent needs; second, needs produced by the development of thought and life, which in turn they condition; third, needs generated by passing phases of history and thus transitory; and fourth, pathological needs.

The presence of pathological needs imparts a pathological direction to the course of history as well; their elimination is one form of the struggle for progress. But the establishment of the proper hierarchy of basic and transitory needs, the elucidation of their mutual dependence and rational connection is one of the principal departments of the work of critical thought in preparing a sound practical program of progress. The goal of proper historical development can be nothing but the fullest possible satisfaction of the healthy needs of man, in that hierarchy in which he views them as lower or higher according to the degree of his personal development.

In the interaction of man's basic needs and his healthy acquired needs arise the fundamental processes of history.

All the basic needs are needs of a purely material character and are connected with the most elementary processes of life. The transitory needs produced by history are much more complex. Man ordinarily places the latter higher, but beneath them is concealed, in fact, the urge to satisfy all of those same elementary needs in the best way; everything else which has been added in the course of time is for the most part a pathological excrescence. The elementary needs first appear in an unconscious form and create the world of custom. When there is a narrow aspiration to satisfy some single need, social life becomes encumbered with a quantity of purely pathological excrescences which prevent other sides of individual and social development from appearing and which thought must combat in its pursuit of progress. In a later phase of development the same needs are embodied in religious beliefs, philosophical world views, and artistic images; and as mystical or metaphysical ideas, as ideals of art or morality, in the form of asceticism or a superior wisdom they join battle, as it were, with their own elementary forms. But this battle is again a pathological phenomenon. The basic needs *must be satisfied,* and man's proper intellectual labors are directed to the question of satisfying them in the fullest and best way.

At the same time the work of thought itself creates new needs, which are inseparable from the growth of thought and are for that reason healthy, but are produced by man in the course of his development, as needs for the creation of historical progress. They are at once forces which accelerate progress and man's most powerful instruments for the proper satisfaction of his basic needs. The need for critical thinking discloses the pathological element in custom and in transitory needs, and frees the real content of basic needs from accumulated layers of cultural customs and religious, metaphysical, and artistic constructs and images. Science poses the problem of the hierarchy of man's healthy needs in a determinate manner. The need for philosophical thinking integrates the various particular attempts to solve this problem, and successively rebuilds the system of thought until it embraces all the conquests of science and until the hypothetical element in it is reduced to the smallest possible minimum. The need for artistic creation incarnates man's ever-clearer understanding of his basic and historical needs in integral and moving images. The need for moral action creates heroes and martyrs who personify and implement this understanding, who lay down stone after stone to construct a society in which it will be possible to satisfy basic needs and eliminate pathological, and who frequently cement these stones with the sacrifice of their own happiness.

But beneath this varied fight for progress the basic process of history is still going on—the attempt to satisfy man's basic and very elementary needs in the best manner.

Upon closer examination these basic needs reduce to a very few: the need for food, clothing, shelter, instruments of labor, and so on—the so-called *economic needs*— and the need for *security*. The former create the economic system with its various functions and organs; the latter creates political relationships, both internal and external. All basic needs of man which do not fall under these two categories have no direct bearing on the strengthening or weakening of social solidarity, and consequently they need not be examined here. All other needs which are relevant here are developed in the course of history, under the influence of historical processes, and consequently are either transitory needs, pathological needs, or needs which, as has been said above, are products of the healthy development of society and are the principal instruments for accelerating social progress.

And thus, in the rich and varied scene of historical and contemporary social phenomena, beneath the humble forms of custom and the sumptuous trappings of the religious, scientific, philosophical, artistic, and moral products of human activity, we must first of all discern the economic interests of the individual and of society and the interests of personal and social security. For *these* interests must be satisfied first of all. Without satisfaction of these interests society can possess neither stability nor solidarity, and the individual cannot develop morally.

But even among these basic needs it is necessary to establish in thought an order of dependence, since upon this hinges a true understanding of the conditions of progress. Which take precedence in social problems and in social development—political interests or economic interests? Can we achieve economic progress through proper reconstruction of the state, or must we see beneath political conflicts and the struggle for power nothing but economic problems?

Must we call upon the ancient, sagacious Solon or the more modern, fictional Utopus to establish proper economic systems by legislation? Must we seek, in the Houses of Commons and Lords, in the Convention under the banner of "liberty, equality, and fraternity," in the federal Congress in Washington, in the *zemskiye sobory* of Ivan the Terrible, Alexis "the Meek," or Catherine "the Great," laws to resolve the whole social question? [2] Must we agitate for universal suffrage and fight on the barricades, as they did in Paris, Vienna, Berlin, and Rome, in order to win political progress, and with it economic progress as well?

Or perhaps on this path mankind has been chasing illusions. The sagacious solons have simply given juridical form to the economic domination which really existed beforehand. Men such as Utopus have never existed; and if they were to exist they would be powerless before the economic forces which ruled around them until they had found means to undermine these forces. Is it not true that constitutions, codes, and charters have everywhere been written by the social groups in whose hands economic dominion was actually located? That all political revolutions have been pitiful fiascos, for all the heroism and abnegation of the individuals who took part in them, if they failed to alter the distribution of wealth in society, and that those alone have remained durable which signified economic reconstruction? That the only plans for the redistribution of wealth which have proved realizable are those which were based on changes already effected in the form of production and exchange? That the only truly realistic and truly radical demands of contending parties have been those which had to do with the satisfaction of economic needs and which corresponded to the real conditions of the economic life of society in the given age?

Upon examination of the interaction of economic and political needs in history, the scientific resolution of the question inclines toward the supremacy of the former over the latter. Wherever the historical material permits us to discern the true tenor of the facts in greatest detail, we are obliged to say that the political conflict in all its phases was grounded in the economic conflict; that the resolution of the political problem in this or that direction was determined by economic forces; that in each case these economic forces created the political institutions which suited them and then sought a theoretical idealization in appropriate religious beliefs and philosophical world views, an aesthetic idealization in appropriate artistic forms, and a moral idealization in the glorification of the heroes who defended their principles.

But once these political institutions, abstract ideas, and concrete ideals, created by economic forces, have been established and have become elements in the cultural system, time and again they have turned into independent social forces. Forgetting or repudiating their origin, they have joined battle for supremacy with the same economic forces which created them, by summoning to the historical arena new forms of economic needs and new economic forces. The feudal property system was undermined largely by the system of state administration which it itself had created for its own protection, and by the idea of contract which it itself had advanced as a defense against the abuses of the central state organ. The state militarism of the present day, which protects the sacred property of the financial and industrial lords from the hungry proletariat, repeatedly has been, in the hands of the Louis Napoleons, the Bismarcks, and their imitators, an instrument of designs far from identical with the economic interests of these lords. The ideal of equality, in the name of which the bourgeoisie consolidated its dominion over the feudal proprietors in a former period, is becoming a two-edged sword for the bourgeoisie in the present social conflict, when the fermenting proletariat is emphasizing the element of *economic* equality in this ideal.

Thus, the conflict of economic forces is complicated by the part played in it by the political institutions and ideas which it engenders and which demand supremacy for themselves in the name of their independent right to historical existence. But however varied the forms of this conflict, essentially it is not a particularly complex process.

The conditions of production and exchange in a particular period, in combination with the existing political institutions and inherited cultural customs, inevitably determine the distribution of wealth in society, and consequently determine the distribution of labor and leisure and the distribution of the *opportunity* for intellectual activity. A ruling minority is formed which concentrates the major share of wealth in its own hands, thus monopolizing the major share of social influence and political power and inevitably gaining an almost exclusive monopoly on both the leisure for intellectual activity and on this activity itself. It strives to fortify its ascendency through customs, laws, religious beliefs, philosophical and scientific ideas, and works of art. The lot of the subject majority becomes worse and worse. Habits of thought and life increasingly divorce the ruling minority from the subject majority. The history of the former, with its more or less brilliant exterior of cultural forms and its more or less mighty conquests of leisure thought, becomes more and more alien to the social life of the majority which labors to create this minority civilization. But their very coexistence side by side generates pathological phenomena. The need to keep the exploited majority in subjection distorts the intellectual work of the minority. The existence of material and intellectual enjoyments inaccessible to it increasingly irritates the majority and makes it hostile to the ruling classes and to the whole existing social order. The class struggle grows and intensifies. Social solidarity becomes a fiction and the existence of the society is threatened.

Given the acute form in which this social discord quite often existed in the ancient world with the emergence of distinct nations, disaster came rapidly and decisively. A poorer, predatory neighbor came with the intention of appropriating in the simplest fashion the wealth amassed by the minority. The majority was more or less indifferent to the impending danger. The minority was despoiled, or it perished. The civilization with all its glitter disappeared, and after thousands of years amazed archeologists read on papyruses and clay tablets the evidence of unprecedented intellectual achievements, bemoaned the catastrophe which destroyed this "forgotten civilization," and ordinarily forgot to bemoan the fate of the majority millions who lived beside it, created it with their own sweat and blood, never shared in its enjoyments, and suffered sufficiently during the centuries or millennia of its existence to view its fall with indifference.

There was also another outcome. Intellectual activity and the creation of political institutions called into being, in the interests of the ruling minority, new social groups which won economic independence, and consequently social influence as well, by seizing an opportunity or profiting by the inevitable development of the techniques of production and exchange and the techniques of political life. Between the absolutely sovereign minority and the absolutely subject masses there arose certain intermediate strata which had a share in the rule as well as a share in the subjection, and naturally strove to increase the former and decrease the latter. Sometimes intellectual labor was transferred almost entirely to these intermediate strata. Progress in technology and in exchange strengthened some of them. Literary, scientific, philosophical, and artistic creation fell to the lot of others. Diverse ideals and world views were created and came into collision in the intellectual arena. Diverse forces joined issue for social supremacy. The force which knew how to connect its interests—genuinely or fictitiously—with the interests of the absolutely subject and suffering masses became the prevailing force, because it succeeded in directing the real or illusory "growth of social consciousness" toward the "strengthening of social solidarity" for its own advantage. This prevailing force demoralized the social organs of its opponents and grew up on the ruins which, as it were, collapsed of themselves (as the Church organization grew up on the disintegrating Roman empire). Or it gave rise to a more or less bloody revolution and rose to absolute economic and juridical supremacy on the shoulders of the subject classes, creating new social forms in which its aides in the struggle ordinarily occupied just as subordinate a position as in the former system. A new period of history began, conditioned essentially by the economic supremacy of the new social stratum, which accordingly created new political institutions and new intellectual products to idealize the existing reality, and thereby gave rise to new intermediate strata which could grow into new social forces.

But if this basic process repeats itself, the terrain on which it has taken place has constantly changed, and for that reason the same phenomena have never been repeated, nor could they have been repeated. The new economically dominant class was by no means in the same position as its predecessors, since it was supported by other forms of production and exchange. Surrounded by another combination of social forces, it had to take into account other ideal products of thought and other social customs, and for that reason it was threatened by other catastrophes.

And accordingly, in each age those who fight for progress have been faced with different tasks—different with respect to the possibility of disseminating their conception of progress, different with respect to the means of organizing a social force to fight for it, and finally different with respect to forming, in themselves and around them, new habits of thought and life which harmonize with the new conception of progress. But these tasks, correctly understood, have always and everywhere been the same in essence. Their essence has consisted in the following: First, in altering the forms of the distribution of social power—primarily the forms of the distribution of wealth—in accordance with existing conditions of production and exchange, by utilizing existing customary and juridical forms of social organization and taking into account the various existing products of thought: scientific achievements, philosophical theories, artistic patterns, and moral ideals. Second, in directing these changes toward the greatest strengthening and the greatest extension of social solidarity and the greatest increase in social consciousness. And finally, in consolidating the changes through political institutions which are most in harmony with the effected revolution, through ideal products of science, philosophy, and art which best justify this change, and through the embodiment in life of the moral ideals which best accord with the healthy needs of man.

This is all that progress *might* have been in human society, and only after we have acknowledged this as a point of departure can we rightly pose the next question: In what have the real phases of historical progress *actually consisted?*

Here we must first of all bear in mind the tasks of the history of civilization, and on that basis come to an understanding of the phases of historical progress as a whole. I have already indicated these tasks in the First Letter, but they can now be formulated in a somewhat different way.[3]

The history of civilization should show: How the first culture arose out of natural needs; how it quickly added artificial needs in the form of customs and traditions; how thought operated on this soil, augmenting knowledge, elucidating justice, developing philosophy, embodying its acquisitions in life; how in this way there arose a series of cultures, succeeding one another; how their forms gave greater or less scope to the work of thought; how the civilizations which arose in this fashion either developed through the critical efforts of individuals, grew weak and destroyed themselves through an inadequate understanding of the demands of justice, sank into stagnation through the inadequate operation of critical thought within them, or fell victim to external historical catastrophes; how periods of the intensified operation of critical thought accelerated and vivified the progressive march of mankind; how they were succeeded by periods of the reign of tradition, still strong in the masses, who had been insufficiently developed by the advanced minority; how critical thought again set to work, under what seemed to be the most unfavorable institutions and the most inappropriate slogans; how parties grew up and came into conflict; how the meaning of the great principles inscribed on their banners changed; how critical inquiry and critical inquiry alone led mankind forward; how false idealizations little by little gave way to true; how the province of truth was extended; how justice was elucidated and embodied in the life of individuals and in social institutions; how the most entrenched traditions fell before them, the most deep-rooted habits disappeared, the most prodigious forces proved feeble; how individuals, nations, and states inscribed their names in the drama of history, becoming alternately organs of progress and organs of reaction; and how there grew up in present-day humanity that ideal of progressive action which is struggling today against all the false idealizations and patently reactionary tendencies which surround it, against the accumulated crust of cultural customs and traditions of the past, and against the apathy of the majority.

Still more briefly, the task of the history of civilization may be expressed thus: To show how the critical thought of individuals has remade the culture of societies by striving to invest their civilizations with greater truth and justice.

On the basis of the foregoing, resolving the question of the actual course of historical progress takes the following form. The investigator must first examine the transition from the anthropological empire of custom to the emergence of distinct nations. Then he will encounter, as a consequence of the increased exchange of material and ideal products and the increased economic and intellectual interdependence among nations, the idea of a universal human wisdom, a universal juridical state, and a universal fraternal religion. But because these universal principles were not firmly linked with the basic needs of man, they did not succeed in establishing solidarity among men. Modern European civilization, which had become a *secular* civilization, reverted to the contradictory notions of distinct state organisms, despite the existence of a universal scientific truth preached in every language and every school; despite the continued—though weakening—survival of a universal religious dogma; despite the existence and the ever-increasing growth of a universal, worldwide industry which envelops all of civilized or semicivilized mankind in its system of production, exchange, circulation, credit, speculation, and inevitable crises.

It goes without saying that the contradictory social ideals here created could not endure. The ideal of social solidarity in the form of political absolutism did not last two centuries. Scarcely had it been replaced by the ideal of political democracy when alongside the latter arose the ideas of political economy, corrupting political ideals and demanding primacy for economic principles.

But political economy, which had come forward as the ally and the ideal vindication of the economic and political supremacy of the bourgeoisie, as a scientific element in a constitutional state, very soon encountered new problems, which the bourgeoisie was powerless to resolve. The capitalist economy inevitably gave rise to an ever-growing proletariat which is either degenerating or in a state of ferment. With the political institutions this economy engendered and the ideal products which developed under the influence of its struggle against medieval feudalism and modern absolutism, this economy gave the bourgeoisie no chance either to eliminate the proletariat or to prevent it from growing in social strength.

In the name of the democratic ideals developed earlier, demands for the economic reconstruction of society arose again and again under different forms. First the utopians presented the world their pictures of a new organic period in the life of mankind, a reign of harmony among capital, skill, and labor, an ordered world of universal cooperative labor and development. But the conflict among social forces could never end so peacefully. Those who toiled to sustain contemporary civilization were separated by an ever-widening gulf from those who enjoyed this civilization, and with the growth of modern thought the world could no longer lack numerous intermediate classes between the undisputed lords of the exchange and the proletariat which marketed its hands and its brains. In the ranks of those who rebelled against the capitalistic system there soon appeared men who were guided by all the intellectual achievements of previous ages, and inevitably their thinking, as it developed, set increasingly pointed and categorical tasks.

It set the task of constructing sociology as an integral science and the queen of the sciences. It advanced the law of universal evolution and proclaimed that all social phenomena and forms are transitory, are "historical categories." It even allowed perception of the irreconcilable opposition of capital and labor, the inevitable creation of a proletariat through the very growth of capitalism, and the unavoidable catastrophe which threatens capitalism. To the bourgeois ideals of progress through universal competition and of world-wide speculation for the accumulation of incalculable wealth in the hands of the lords of the exchange, there was opposed the ideal of the solidarity of those who work and *only* of those who work. To the ideal of the omnipotent state protecting the sacred property of the speculators, there was opposed the ideal of political anarchy based upon the mutual exchange of services.

The idea of creating a new social force to conquer the old

forces was expressed in the call, "unite!" addressed to the chronically starving classes of all countries and races. The first attempt to organize this force, which terrified all ruling elements of the old world, lasted for eight long years.[4] It fell, not under their blows, but because of defects in its own organization—defects inevitable in any initial attempt of such a sort.

The sound and fury of political rivalry among states, the strategems of diplomats, the transient fireworks of the *kulturkampf* of secular thought against expiring clericalism—these could not and cannot now conceal from an attentive observer either the economic bases of the present discord, which give rise to most of the ills of our time, or the economic problems which urgently demand solution since upon *their* solution hinges the solution of all other problems.

And now, on the basis of this understanding of the general content of progress and its different phases, there arises the third and most urgent—because it is the closest to practice—of the questions posed above: In what does the social progress which is *possible in our time* consist?

If the present order is unsound, if it contains irresolvable discord, if past history has destroyed the solidarity of religious, national, family, and state ties, if all the old ideals have withered and grown barren, and if the general laws of the sociological connection of phenomena convince us that failure to satisfy economic needs is the basis of every social disease and that economic reconstruction is the first and most essential step in any social therapy —in what, then, should the reconstruction which is needed today consist? Do not the existing conditions of production and exchange contain direct indications of how distribution, too, must be altered? Have not science and literature, philosophy and life already clearly enough placed before every candid mind the truths which must be embodied in practice and the ideals which must be realized on a broader scale? Can we not now map quite incontestably the road along which competition inevitably prevents us from conceiving of a harmony of interests or the establishment of solidarity among individuals and groups, and the road along which solidarity is not only possible but has already appeared, under the most unfavorable conditions and in the most dismal surroundings? Can we not, on the basis of the previous growth of thought, determine with sufficient certainty the next phase in the progressive development of social consciousness?

If the question of the required economic reconstruction is for us resolved, if we have adopted a definite plan for restoring and strengthening the solidarity which is now destroyed in society, a definite plan for the growth of social consciousness, then what political forms will best correspond to the new economic forms of production, exchange, and distribution, will best correspond to the need for the comprehensive development of the individual and for general cooperation for collective social development, and will make this progress most secure? What system of scientific knowledge, what philosophical outlook, what artistic types will best fortify the new order in the realm of ideas? How must he who fights for progress live today, so that his life will accord with his determination to champion progress?

We simply pose the questions. But the reader we are addressing, the reader who has not cast aside the foregoing pages because they disturbed the tranquillity of his thinking and the routine of his life, the reader who has reflected upon the problems raised in these pages, will already have found definite answers to these questions himself. Nor should these answers be learned from a book and taken on faith. They should be drawn from life; they must form the basis of a living conviction.

It is precisely these answers, once obtained, which in their combination answer the question posed above: In what does the social progress which is *possible in our time* consist? In what does it consist for the society which wishes to represent the best aspirations of contemporary man? In what does it consist for the individual who craves not the tranquillity of a routine life, and not the pleasures of a cultured sensusal animal, but the pleasures of a conscious life of principle, a life of solidarity with everything in mankind that seeks development, a historical life which promises mankind an ever fuller future?

At this stage the theory of progress merges with practice. One cannot understand progress without taking an active part in it; the action itself clarifies one's understanding. This understanding is not easy, demanding as it does both internal disruption and a multitude of vital sacrifices. Nor is the action easy, since it very often severs a man's ties with his intimates, destroys his illusions, and at times forcibly tears him from family, from country, from everything that comforts and consoles a man but can at the same time diminish his desire for progress, from everything that can drag him into the mire of social stagnation. History demands sacrifices. And sacrifices both internal and external are made by him who assumes the great but formidable task of fighting for his own development and the development of others.

The problems of development *must* be resolved. A better historical future *must* be won. Before each individual who has come to recognize the need for development there arises the stern question: Will you be one of those who is ready for any sacrifice and any pain, if only he can succeed in becoming a conscious and knowing agent of progress? Or will you stand aside, a passive spectator of the frightful mass of evil being perpetrated around you, conscious of your defection from the path of development, the need for which you once felt? Choose.*

SEVENTEENTH LETTER

The Author's Aim

IN PERUSING THESE LETTERS, the reader may have wondered why they are called "historical." What is historical in them? I have considered neither personalities, nor periods, nor events, but rather some general principles which may easily have struck the reader as somewhat abstract and sometimes even as foreign to the interest he finds in a historical narrative.

But let us take a closer look at the matter. I shall try to draw together here some ideas which have been expressed in various

---

* Censorship forced the journal which published this article to omit its conclusion, and apparently the manuscript has been lost. After ten years it is difficult to recall with any exactness the line of thinking which that conclusion expressed. Thus if the manuscript of 1881 has somewhere been preserved, it may in this case differ significantly from what is printed here. (1891)

places in these letters, as well as ideas which I wished to arouse in the reader but may not have expressed with sufficient clarity. Perhaps at the same time some ground for vindicating me will be found.

What is it we seek in history? A motley narrative of events? By now few will venture this answer, but those who do seek nothing more are entirely right in complaining about the abstractness of the letters which have been presented to them. Approaching history with more serious demands, we may seek in it either, first, the struggles of individuals and societies for truly human interests, men's clashes over beliefs, and the growth and decline of men's various particular ideals; or, second, a general natural law embracing the whole course of historical events, past, present, and future. The first point of view distinguishes the interest of history from the interests of the natural sciences; the second brings history under the general principles of the investigation of nature. But in fact, for a rigorous study these two points of view do not differ greatly, because knowledge of any object is determined not only by what we would *like* to know about it but by what we *can* know about it.

Thus the question of what we can look for in history reduces to another question: How, in accordance with the invariable laws of his psychical functions, can man treat history? What inevitably eludes his scientific appraisal and can be only a phantom element in a historical construction? Only after this basis for scientific investigation has been more or less established can man, with some confidence, put to history questions concerning what he would *like* to learn from it.

Now I attempted at the very outset to develop the thesis that man inevitably introduces his *personal* moral construct, his own moral ideal, into the appraisal of historical events. In conflicts among individuals, what is most important to the investigator are the personal qualities he views as elements of moral virtue— intelligence, skill, energy, resourcefulness, strength of conviction, faith in the ideas he finds important, and conscious or unconscious contribution to the strengthening or weakening of these ideas in society. In conflicts among societies and parties, what is most important to the investigator is again the strengthening or weakening of those trends of thought which he as a human being finds best or worst, most true or most false. In embracing in an over-all world view the entire historical process, both past and future, man is prevented by the laws of his thinking from seeking in history anything but phases of the progressive development of his own moral ideal.

Consequently, in attempting to understand history and to bring to it a serious intellectual interest, man inevitably looks at personalities, events, ideas, and social revolutions according to the standard of his own cultivation. If his cultivation has been narrow and shallow, history presents him with a lifeless series of facts, which he will find uninteresting and lacking in humanity. If his cultivation has been one-sided, the most painstaking study of history will not save him from a one-sided conception of historical events. If he has become imbued with a distorted, fantastic creed, he will inevitably distort history, strive as he may to understand it objectively.

In each case, assuming adequate factual knowledge, the individual's understanding of history is determined by his level of development—by his moral stature. The particular historical interest aroused by one or another personality and one or another event reduces to the general interest aroused by the part they play in the progressive cultivation of mankind. The general scientific interest aroused by the search for a law of history as a whole is nothing other than the interest we take in the realization of our moral ideal in the progressive course of history.

If this is so, then all we seek and all we can seek in history is the different phases of progress, and to understand history means to understand clearly the ways in which our moral ideal is being realized in the historical context. Our ideal is subjective, but the more fully we test it through critical examination, the greater is the likelihood that it is the highest moral ideal possible in the present age. We apply this ideal to the objective facts of history, and this does not prevent the facts from remaining objectively true: here again, their truth is a function of our knowledge and our critical inquiry. The subjective ideal puts them in perspective, and there is *no* way of constructing this perspective other than with the aid of a moral ideal.

I may be told that there is another way, and a surer one: namely, to construct a perspective for the events of an age according to their inner connection and according to the moral ideal of the age itself. But what is meant by inner connection? What is meant by the moral ideal of an age? Out of a thousand miscellaneous facts known to us about a particular age, we construct the connection which seems most plausible *to us* on the basis of what *we* have come to recognize as the truest psychical functions of the individual and the most general sociological phenomena in the group. This is the "inner connection" for us. The historian who has cultivated an understanding of the economic problems of society will not find the same inner connection among events as the historian who has concentrated on understanding the influence of political intrigues. The writer who recognizes the force of convictions, enthusiasms, and unconscious self-delusions in the individual will not connect events in the same way as the writer who has become accustomed to attribute everything to guile and calculation.

And the "moral ideal of the age"! Why do we gather its features from *these* events, rather than others which paralleled them? Why do we draw evidence primarily from *this* author, rather than his contemporary? Because *these* events are more coherent and consistent; because *this* author is more intelligent, more logical, more honest, more candid than his contemporary. But are we not hereby expressing *our* moral ideal concerning the most important events and persons?

It is perfectly true that historical events must be expounded in their "inner connection" and assessed in accordance with "the moral ideal of the age." But in the first place, this same inner connection and this moral ideal must and can be discovered through the development in *us* of an ideal of impartial truth and historical justice. In the second place, the connection of historical periods and successive ideals is subject to further judgment by another criterion, namely the criterion of historical progress, that is, of *our* moral ideal in its totality. That is why we attach greater importance to one age than to another; why we analyze some events in their inner connection in greater detail than others. I repeat: a moral ideal of history is the only beacon which can impart perspective to history as a whole and in its particulars.

Consequently, to understand history today means to understand clearly the moral ideal developed by the best thinkers of today, and, since history is not an abstract but a concrete process, to understand the historical conditions of the realization of this ideal. History can utilize instruments of a certain kind only. It takes place under particular circumstances which define what is possible and what is impossible. Like all other processes, it obeys unvarying laws of nature. To understand history one must constantly attend to these external circumstances in which human ideals are placed.

The *necessary* processes of physics, physiology, and psychology can be neither turned aside nor hurdled. Similarly, the *historically given* environment, with all its influences, cannot be eliminated in a particular age, any more than the foregoing necessities can *ever* be eliminated. The manifestation and the dissemination of the most luminous truth and the most exalted justice are subject to these limiting conditions. The most talented and energetic person can draw the material for his thinking and for his action only from the necessary circumstances of nature and the historically given circumstances of the environment. The first question posed for each age by a historical interest that is clearly understood is this: what was the potential for progress in that age? To what extent did the promoters of progress understand the circumstances in which they found themselves? In pursuing their ends did they take advantage of all the circumstances of the day?

But to understand clearly the ideal of the present means to strip away all the illusions which have been fastened to it by popular convention, erroneous traditions of thought, and the harmful customs of former ages. Truth and justice are inscribed more or less without question on all the banners of our time, but the parties disagree as to *where* the truth lies and *what* justice comprises. If the reader has not made an attempt to understand this, for him history will remain a dark concatenation of events, a contest in which good men fight over trifles or madmen over phantoms, or in which blind tools fight on behalf of a few calculating intriguers.

Many sonorous phrases resound on all sides. Many resplendent banners fly in all ranks. Much selfless energy is expended by the representatives of all parties. What are they quarreling about, these men whose slogans seem so similar? Why is the banner borne yesterday by the best of them, in foul hands today? Why does an excellent idea encounter such ferocious opposition when it is voiced? And why is it opposed not only by the exploiters in the given social order, but by sincere individuals as well?

We can resolve all these riddles only when we have looked closely and attentively at the process by which truth is elaborated and strengthened, at the formation and clash of parties, at the changes in the inner meaning and historical significance of the great words which move mankind, and at the operation of the thinking which remakes culture. We can resolve them only when we have studied the situation of individuals in the light of the necessary and the historically given, in the light of cultural customs and clashing ideological parties, in the light of the great words on party banners and the eternal demand for truth, justice, and progress, in the light of critical inquiry and faith. In the foregoing letters my object has been precisely to dwell on these subjects, so as to eliminate, as far as possible, the misunderstandings unwittingly brought to the study of past and present history when the diverse elements which comprise and condition historical progress are insufficiently understood.

Moreover, history is not completed. It is being made around us and will be made by generations now maturing and by generations yet unborn. The present cannot be severed from the past, but the past, too, would lose all living, real significance if it were not inseparably linked with the present, if one great process did not embrace history as a whole. The men of the past are gone. The culture of society has changed. New concrete questions have replaced the old. The slogans of the past have changed their meaning and significance. But the common human role of individuals remains the same today as it was thousands of years ago.

Under heterogeneous forms of culture, in the complex problems of modern times, under the various slogans of the victors and the vanquished, the same tasks are still concealed. Apart from truth and justice progress has never existed. Without individual criticism not a single truth has ever been acquired. Without individual energy nothing that is just has ever been accomplished. Without faith in its banner and without the skill to combat its opponents not a single progressive party has ever triumphed. Cultural forms require the work of thought for their development. just as in past millennia. The great slogans are just as little immune to the danger of losing or changing their meaning. The social conditions which make progress possible have not changed. The demands of payment for the cost of progress cannot be ignored by the cultivated individual.

All this was true for our ancestors, will be true for our descendants, and is true for us. The difference is simply that we can understand it better than our ancestors did, and that our descendants, no doubt, will understand it still better than we.

Thus the foregoing *Historical Letters*, by attempting to solve problems which have existed and must exist in every historical age, attempt also to elucidate the problems of today. They address the reader with a message concerning not only the past but the present as well. The author is acutely aware that these letters are both imperfect and incomplete. Moreover our age is not very propitious for discussions of such a sort. These letters may seem ponderous, abstract, uninteresting, and alien to the questions of the day. Another author, under other circumstances, might have been able to write them in both a better and a more interesting way. But I trust that in our society there are still a few persons, if only among the younger reading public, who are not intimidated by the need to think seriously about questions of the past, which are still questions for the present. For these readers the defects in the execution of my work will, perhaps, be less important than its content.

Perhaps these readers will understand, too, that the questions of the day derive their true, essential interest precisely from the timeless historical questions which the author has taken up in these letters. Such readers will understand that it is *they*, as individuals, who must complete the work of critical thought on contemporary culture. That it is *they* who must repay, with their thought, life, and action, their share of the enormous accumulated cost of progress. That it is *they* who must set their conviction against the falsehood and injustice existing in society. That it is *they* who must make up the growing force that speeds the march of progress.

If these letters find even a few such readers, then the author's task has been fulfilled.

NOTES

Works here cited in abbreviated form are fully identified in the bibliography. Where the bibliography contains only one title for an author, only the author's name is cited below. Lavrov's works are cited by title only. Page references refer in each case to the edition or printing listed first in the entry for the corresponding title in the bibliography.

Notes to the Introduction

[1] Rusanov, *Biografiya*, p. 23.

[2] The chief published sources of biographical information concerning Lavrov are his autobiography and the works by Rusanov, Knizhnik-Vetrov, and Vityazev cited in Section IV of the bibliography. Unless otherwise identified, the information presented in this introduction is drawn from those sources. For a more complete account of Lavrov's life, see the dissertation by Pomper listed in the bibliography. Dates are given in accordance with the Julian or Old Style calendar used in Russia during Lavrov's lifetime, unless otherwise indicated. During the nineteenth century the Julian calendar was twelve days behind the Gregorian or New Style calendar, which was not adopted in Russia until 1918.

[3] Quoted in Shtakenshneyder, p. 361.

[4] *Ibid.*, pp. 146–148.

[5] "Pis'mo k izdatelyu," p. 111.

[6] Chernyshevsky, *Selected Philosophical Essays*, p. 70.

[7] Pisarev, *Selected Philosophical, Social, and Political Essays*, p. 107.

[8] Shtakenshneyder, p. 272.

[9] *Ibid.*, p. 275.

[10] Quoted in *Izbrannyye sochineniya*, Vol. I, p. 27.

[11] Nikitenko, Vol. II, pp. 166–167.

[12] Quoted in *Izbrannyye sochineniya*, Vol. I, p. 32. During this period Lavrov also edited a Russian translation of John Stuart Mill's *A System of Logic*, published in St. Petersburg in two volumes in 1865 and 1867.

[13] Nikitenko, Vol. II, p. 166.

[14] *Ibid.*, p. 188.

[15] "Mekhanicheskaya teoriya mira," p. 465.

[16] See Antonovich, pp. 61–62.

[17] "Mekhanicheskaya teoriya mira," p. 466.

[18] *Ibid.*, p. 480.

[19] *Ibid.*, pp. 483–484.

[20] *Ibid.*, p. 465.

[21] *Ibid.*, p. 483.

[22] *Ibid.*, p. 491.

[23] *Ibid.*, p. 492.

[24] *Ibid.*

[25] *Tri besedy,* pp. 16–26.

[26] "Mekhanicheskaya teoriya mira," p. 487.

[27] "Moim kritikam," pp. 66 ff.

[28] "Mekhanicheskaya teoriya mira," p. 485.

[29] *Ibid.*, p. 486.

[30] *Ibid.*, p. 492.

[31] *Ocherki,* p. 12. Here as in the *Historical Letters* Lavrov employs the Russian word *lichnost'* to refer both to an individual (plural *lichnosti,* individuals) and to individuality. It has been translated either "individual" or "individuality" depending on the context.

[32] *Ibid.*, p. 14.

[33] *Ibid.*, p. 28.

[34] *Ibid.*, pp. 19–20.

[35] *Ibid.*, p. 19.

[36] "Otvet g. Strakhovu," p. 107.

[37] "Chto takoye antropologiya?" pp. 68–70.

[38] "Otvet g. Strakhovu," p. 107.

[39] *Ocherki,* p. 30.

[40] *Ibid.*, p. 31.

[41] *Ibid.*, p. 58.

[42] *Ibid.*, p. 60.

[43] *Ibid.*, p. 68.

[44] *Ibid.*, pp. 69–81.

[45] *Ibid.*, p. 32.

[46] *Ibid.*, p. 91.

[47] *Ibid.*, p. 31.

[48] *Ibid.*, pp. 34–35.

[49] *Ibid.*, p. 63.

[50] *Ibid.*, p. 93.

[51] "Chto takoye antropologiya?" p. 72.

[52] *Ibid.*, p. 73.

[53] *Ibid.*, p. 62.

[54] *Ibid.*, p. 72.

[55] *Ibid.*, p. 74.

[56] *Ibid.*

[57] *Tri besedy*, pp. 63–64.

[58] *Ibid.*, p. 66.

[59] *Ibid.*, p. 64.

[60] *Ibid.*, p. 68. Italics added.

[61] Rusanov, "P. L. Lavrov," p. 254.

[62] See Lavrov's *Zadachi pozitivizma i ikh resheniye*, published in 1868.

[63] "Predisloviye," p. 14.

[64] Vityazev, *Vperyod!*, p. 25.

[65] *Tri besedy*, p. 67.

[66] *Ibid.*, p. 63; *Ocherki*, p. 39.

[67] *Ocherki*, pp. 7–8.

[68] Vityazev, *Materialy*, p. 86.

[69] Shtakenshneyder, p. 364.

[70] "Biografiya-ispoved' " p. 103.

[71] Vityazev, *Materialy*, p. 85.

[72] See *Izbrannyye sochineniya*, Vol. I, p. 33.

[73] See Rusanov, *Biografiya*, p. 21; Vityazev, *Materialy*, p. 87.

[74] Nikitenko, Vol. II, pp. 181.

[75] Vityazev, *Materialy*, p. 78.

[76] Quoted in Rusanov, *Biografiya*, p. 20.

[77] Vityazev, *Materialy*, p. 89.

[78] *Ibid.* For an account of Lavrov's trial see Nechayev, *op. cit.*

[79] Quoted in *Izbrannyye sochineniya*, Vol. I, pp. 56–57.

[80] Quoted in *Izbrannyye sochineniya*, Vol. I, p. 45.

[81] Vityazev, "P. L. Lavrov v vospominaniyakh sovremennikov," p. 119.

[82] Rusanov, "P. L. Lavrov," p. 261.

[83] Pereselenkov, p. 37.

[84] *Ibid.*, p. 38.

[85] *Ibid.*, p. 40.

[86] *Ibid.*, p. 38.

[87] Utechin, p. 128.

[88] Venturi, p. xix.

[89] Chernyshevsky, *What Is to Be Done?*, trans. Benjamin R. Tucker, revised and abridged by Ludmilla B. Turkevich (New York, 1961), pp. 114–115.

[90] *Zadachi pozitivizma i ikh resheniye,* p. 43.

[91] *Ibid.,* p. 44. See also "Po povodu kritiki na 'Istoricheskiye pis'ma,'" pp. 314–315.

[92] Alexander Herzen, *From the Other Shore,* ed. Isaiah Berlin (New York, 1956), p. 114.

[93] Pereselenkov, p. 38.

[94] See *Izbrannyye sochineniya,* Vol. I, p. 47.

[95] Lukashevich, p. 5.

[96] Rusanov, *Biografiya,* pp. 23–24.

[97] Lavrov's motives for escape remain a disputed issue. See Venediktov-Bezyuk, *op. cit.*

[98] Rusanov, "P. L. Lavrov," p. 264. In the Soviet period there has been much debate as to whether Lavrov may properly be called a revolutionary. For the extreme positions see Koz'min, *op. cit.,* and Knizhnik-Vetrov, *Pyotr Lavrovich Lavrov,* especially pp. 121–124. See also Ostrogorsky, *op. cit.*

[99] From an unheaded note at the beginning of the first volume of *Vperyod!,* reprinted in *Izbrannyye sochineniya,* Vol. II, p. 22.

[100] Quoted in *Izbrannyye sochineniya,* Vol. III, p. 388.

[101] "Nasha programma" (Our Program), *ibid.,* Vol. II, p. 38.

[102] Quoted in *Izbrannyye sochineniya,* Vol. I, p. 62.

[103] Rusanov, *Biografiya,* p. 30.

[104] Rusanov, "P. L. Lavrov," p. 275.

[105] "Biografiya-ispoved'" p. 106.

[106] *Pamyati P. L. Lavrova,* p. 31.

[107] Lavrov explains in the preface to his *Perezhivaniya doistoricheskovo perioda* (Survivals from the Prehistoric Period) that he decided to discontinue the *Essay* because he despaired of completing it. He decided to replace it with a more condensed work, to be called *Ocherk evolyutsii chelovecheskoy mysli* (An Outline of the Evolution of Human Thought). The *Perezhivaniya* was the only portion of this second work which Lavrov succeeded in completing before his death.

[108] "Biografiya-ispoved'" p. 95.

[109] Rusanov, "P. L. Lavrov," pp. 276–278.

[110] Quoted in *Izbrannyye sochineniya,* Vol. I, p. iv.

[111] Ostrogorsky, p. 204.

[112] "Biografiya-ispoved'" p. 89.

[113] *Ibid.,* pp. 103–104.

[114] "Biografiya-ispoved'" pp. 106–107.

[115] *Ibid.,* pp. 90–91.

[116] Rusanov, "P. L. Lavrov," p. 270.

[117] *Zadachi ponimaniya istorii,* p. 130.

[118] *Ibid.,* pp. 86–103, 112.

[119] See, for example, Rusanov, "P. L. Lavrov," p. 270.

[120] *Perezhivaniya doistoricheskovo perioda,* p. 160.

[121] G. Shpet, "Filosofiya Lavrova" (The Philosophy of Lavrov), in Vityazev, *Vperyod!,* p. 27.

Notes to the Historical Letters

PREFACE TO THE SECOND EDITION

[1] "Forgotten Words" (*Zabytyye slova*) is the title of a posthumous work (published not long before Lavrov wrote this preface) by M. E. Saltykov-Shchedrin (1826–1889), a leading Russian satirist. The expression, taken in the sense of "forgotten ideals" or "forgotten sanctities," became widely used.

[2] Vera Zasulich (1849–1919) was a member of the revolutionary "Land and Liberty" society who in 1878 attempted to assassinate a high-ranking St. Petersburg official. Her acquittal in the same year caused great jubilation in radical and liberal circles.

[3] G. Z. Yeliseyev (1821–1891) and N. V. Shelgunov (1824–1891) were leading socialist journalists. All four of the writers mentioned had died within two years of the time Lavrov wrote this preface.

[4] V. G. Belinsky (1811–1848) and N. A. Dobrolyubov (1836–1861) were major early proponents of the view that literature must serve a progressive social function.

[5] See Lavrov's "Po povodu kritiki na 'Istoricheskiye pis'ma'" and "Formula progressa g. Mikhailovskovo." The criticisms to which Lavrov replied in the former article were published by N. V. Shelgunov (*Delo,* 1870, No. 11, pp. 1–30) and A. A. Kozlov (*Znaniye,* 1871, No. 3, pp. 169–197). Numerous passages from this article are incorporated verbatim in the 1891 edition of the *Historical Letters;* they are identified in the notes which follow. Contrary to Lavrov's statement, no passages from the latter article, a critique of Mikhailovsky's conception of progress, were directly used in revising the *Historical Letters.*

FIRST LETTER. *The Natural Sciences and History*

[1] The *byliny* (sing. *bylina*) are Russian epic folk songs or chants, many of which recount the exploits of legendary heroes of the tenth to thirteenth centuries. *Russkaya pravda* (Russian Justice) is the name given to a Russian legal code dating from the eleventh century. The *oprichnina* (or *oprichina*) was a cruel and extreme program intro-

duced by Ivan the Terrible in 1565; it produced a radical upheaval in land ownership in Russia and a reduction of the political power of the old landed aristocracy.

2 For "so many" the 1870 edition has "all." Similar softenings and qualifications in the 1891 edition are indicated below only where they have some special significance for Lavrov's views.

SECOND LETTER. *The Historical Process*

1 The 1870 edition has the following: "In our day, of course, the theory of the transformation of animal species permits us to extend questions about the alteration of these species even to species other than man. But here the naturalist has before him events which are instances of the general process of the transition of some organic forms into others, and his immediate objective is always to study the *laws* of this general process.

2 There are minor errors in the factual information Lavrov presents in this note. When found in Nuremberg, Caspar Hauser bore not one but two notes: one, supposedly by his mother, said that he had been born April 30, 1812; the other, supposedly by the person who had raised him, said that the infant had been left at his house on October 7, 1812. Hauser was stabbed on December 14, 1833, not December 17; he died on December 17. Except for the dated parenthetical addition at the end, this note appeared in its entirety in the 1870 edition.

3 Beginning with this sentence, this long addition is drawn verbatim (with a few modifications) from Lavrov's "Po povodu kritiki na 'Istoricheskiye pis'ma,'" pp. 300–306.

4 In 1858 Ferdinand Lassalle published a book on Heraclitus in which he compared the views of Heraclitus with Hegel's philosophy.

5 The 1870 edition has the following: "First of all, in order to find some sort of guiding thread in the motley kaleidoscope of events, it is desirable to distinguish the more important from the less important. For the natural scientist this is easy: what is repeated in unchanging connection is more important, because here there is a law; what pertains to chance variation is of little importance, and is merely kept in mind for possible future consideration. Probably no investigator has found two human hearts which are entirely identical in form and size. But discarding individual variations as unimportant, he incorporates in science only the unchanging features of the heart's over-all structure. In history this criterion is impossible because phenomena are not repeated. But this is the only criterion of the importance of phenomena which an observer can draw from the phenomena themselves, the only *objective* method of judging the importance of phenomena. Since it is

not applicable in history, the importance of historical phenomena cannot be evaluated objectively. They are evaluated by the individual in accordance with the same standard which the individual applies to the actions of men in general. They are subject to evaluation according to their *moral* influence."

[6] The 1870 edition has "and the ultimate triumph of progress."

[7] A fashionable main boulevard in St. Petersburg.

[8] For this quotation and those following, the original texts of Proudhon and Spencer have been used, rather than Lavrov's (generally faithful) Russian translations.

THIRD LETTER. *The Extent of Human Progress*

[1] The objection was made by A. A. Kozlov in his critical review of the *Historical Letters*. The subsequent paragraphs in this long added passage in the 1891 edition are drawn almost verbatim from Lavrov's reply to Kozlov in his "Po povodu kritiki na 'Istoricheskiye pis'ma,'" pp. 306–310.

[2] The 1870 edition has the following: "We constantly see people who perform just actions from a momentary mood, a habit, or an inner inclination of character. But on the other hand no less frequently, if not more so, do we see the very same persons perform unjust actions as well. Inconsistency in such cases proceeds much more often from a poor understanding of personal interest than from evil intentions, and can diminish only with the realization that justice and egoistic calculation, when it has taken all the circumstances into account, are identical. But this progress, if it is ever to take place, still lies entirely in the future." Elimination of this passage in the 1891 edition is symptomatic of Lavrov's shift from the view that the true interests of all social classes are harmonious to the view that in a society based on economic competition there are irreconcilable conflicts of interest.

[3] For "Europe and America," the 1870 edition has "the civilized world." Similar specifications are made throughout the 1891 edition.

[4] The 1870 edition has the following: "is to a certain degree realized in some places, namely, where a legal organ of public opinion exists invested with legislative power. But the progressive significance of this institution is to a considerable degree diminished by two causes, rooted in the inadequate realization of the conditions of physical development for the masses, and of intellectual and moral development for almost all."

[5] The 1870 edition has the following: "With a more critical attitude toward *its* interests, it influences more beneficially the whole social system as well. But lack of critical thinking in society is expressed here in

another way also, which hitherto has limited still more the possibility of beneficial alterations through legislation."

[6] The 1870 edition has "or of a dynasty by a president elected for a limited term could not take place."

[7] For "essence" the 1870 edition has "moral basis."

[8] For "not by peaceful legislative reforms but by violent revolution" the 1870 edition has the following: "not by regular change but by revolution, which ordinarily creates the greatest calamities for the masses who are overwhelmed by daily cares, and particularly for that part of the masses which has not taken part in the revolution and has not profit from it even by a temporary alleviation of its lot."

[9] The 1870 edition has the following: "He is dangerous only in a time of famine, when his sufferings become unbearable. He serves as a firm support only when he believes that the minority is concerned about him; when he is linked with this minority either by a practical creed or by a community of material interests; when for the particularly gifted and energetic individuals from his environment there is a chance to fight their way into the secure minority."

[10] This paragraph and the three which follow are drawn verbatim, with some modifications, from Lavrov's "Po povodu kritiki na 'Istoricheskiye pis'ma,' " pp. 326–327.

FOURTH LETTER. *The Cost of Progress*

[1] The 1870 edition continues with the following: "the protection of the pregnant female, in view of the future pleasure or the future aid to be gained from her in time of sleep. This was the first utilitarian *bond* among men and the first lesson showing how advantageous an association of individuals is for each of them. This was bound to lead, sooner or later, to the safeguarding of infants, the formation of the family, the traditional transmission of skill and thought, the origin of nations." Between the 1870 edition of the *Historical Letters* and the writing of these revisions Lavrov changed his view of primitive society, perhaps under the influence of such writers as Lewis Morgan and J. J. Bachofen. In his revised view he centers his attention not on the family but on the broader kinship group or clan (*rodovoy soyuz*), and holds that the first significant social union was a matriarchate, which was superseded by patriarchal forms. A number of subsequent revisions also show these changes.

[2] Lavrov uses the English word "steeplechase," printed in Latin characters.

[3] The 1870 edition has the following: "Your interest demands improvement of the lot of the majority. The goods you sacrifice today

with this aim will return to you in the form of the greater security of the remaining goods, greater tranquillity in their enjoyment, and a greater influence on the majority, which despite its unhappy lot is still a force. Consult your own *true* interest; strive to improve the lot of others: this is what is most useful to you."

⁴ The Russian is *Zlo nado zazhit'*. *Zazhit'*, meaning "to heal" (as a wound) and also "to begin to live," is formed from the root *zhit'*, "to live.

⁵ The 1870 edition has "to provide themselves *tranquillity in enjoyment,* that is, exactly what they are striving for."

FIFTH LETTER. *The Action of Individuals*

¹ For "forty years" the 1870 edition has "twenty years."

² For "the institutions of censorship" the 1870 edition has "an organization which stifles speech."

³ The 1870 edition has the following: "which embrace man in his unexplored past, which permit him to look more soberly into the distant future, and which clarify for him the distinction between the necessary zoological element in the historical process and the potential element of human progress."

⁴ For "the teachings of the Christian churches" the 1870 edition has "the present day."

SIXTH LETTER. *Culture and Thought*

¹ The 1870 edition adds "in the name of pleasure or calculation."

² For "justice" the 1870 edition has "harmony."

³ The 1870 edition adds: "Society is animated by religion." In the following sentence, "religion" is listed as a fourth factor after "morality" in the 1870 edition.

⁴ The 1870 edition has "and divests society of order and tranquillity."

SEVENTH LETTER. *Individuals and Social Institutions*

¹ The *Stoglav* (literally, "one hundred chapters") is a set of enactments concerning ecclesiastical and civil affairs produced by a council convened in Moscow in 1551 by Ivan the Terrible. The *Domostroy* is a book of precepts concerning household management and family relationships, dating from the sixteenth century, which emphasizes strict paternal authority. The *veche* was an ancient Russian urban popular assembly, first known in Novgorod and Kiev in the eleventh century;

townspeople were summoned to meetings by a bell. Vladimir I, Grand Prince of Kiev from 980 to 1015, married the sister of the Byzantine emperor and is responsible for the mass introduction of Christianity into Russia; Lavrov's text uses an untranslatable endearing nickname, "Vladimir krasnoye solnyshko" ("Vladimir the dear bright sun"). Svyatogor is a hero of superhuman strength in the Novgorod cycle of Russian *byliny*. Michael Speransky (1772–1839) was one of the principal advisers of Alexander I; at Alexander's request he drafted a system of constitutional government for Russia, but the plan was largely rejected.

2 For "some even at 1889" the 1870 edition has "or 1866." In citing these years Lavrov is no doubt referring to the following events: 1854—the height of the Crimean War; 1861—emancipation of the serfs; 1863—the Polish uprising; 1866—Karakozov's attempt to assassinate Alexander II; 1889—establishment of the post of "land captain" (*zemsky nachal'nik*), a rural official having a large degree of more or less arbitrary power over the peasants in his township.

EIGHTH LETTER. *The Growing Social Force*

1 The 1870 edition has "and stand at the head of the party and direct the others."

2 For "conscious workmen," the 1870 edition has "leaders."

3 After "organize the party," the 1870 edition adds "and direct it."

NINTH LETTER. *The Banners of Social Parties*

1 For "Katkov," the 1870 edition has "Mr. Askochensky." Michael Katkov (1818–1887) was an influential publisher and writer who from the early 'sixties became a notorious nationalist. V. I. Askochensky (1820–1879) was a reactionary writer best known through his journal *Home Talk* (*Domashnyaya beseda*) in the 'sixties.

2 For "French clergy" the 1870 edition has "Belgian clergy."

3 The 1870 edition has the following: "There was for mankind an age in which the family was the cardinal progressive principle of association—an age in which the economic, political, religious, and scientific requirements of mankind were best met by a system in which the patriarch had absolute sway over his descendants and there was the firmest ancestral tie between generations. Even then, of course, this principle led to personal despotism, xenophobia, petty genealogical pride, superstitious trafficking with deceased ancestors, tribal hostility—all of which brought much suffering. Yet by comparison this

form reduced suffering in society to a minimum, and consequently at that time the patriarchal system constituted progress."

⁴ Here as in many passages, for "kinship group" or a similarly broad expression, the 1870 edition has "family."

⁵ For "the government or of an influential minority" the 1870 edition has "persons."

TENTH LETTER. *Idealization*

¹ In this sentence and those following, the 1870 edition uses not the words "religious," "deity," and "God" but rather expressions such as "supernatural force" and "a higher power."

² For "conspirator" the 1870 edition has "person who talks imprudently.

³ The 1870 edition has the following: "As I have already said, we encounter idealization in the inmost depths of the human soul. The first manifestation of it is in fact so deeply intertwined with the psychic life of man that it is impossible to rid human thinking of this idealization. One can only arrive by analogy and strict deduction at the intellectual conviction that this is in fact an idealization, but nonetheless it remains the basis of all our practical activity and of all our moral theories. I am speaking of the idealization of *free will,* which invariably presents the individual to himself as a being who is responsible for his acts, as the only source of his activity of which he is *aware.* Theoretical *knowledge* analyzes this source further and shows that the free will is simply a necessary consequence of the preceding series of events, and at the same time a necessary instrument in the overall process of world events."

⁴ For "This makes it possible" the 1870 edition has "The anthropological point of view in philosophy permits us to compare." In the 1891 edition there are no such explicit references to "the anthropological point of view."

⁵ Here the 1870 edition adds the following: "All these matters have significance and validity only in the realm of practical philosophy. For theoretical philosophy they are objects of valid psychical observation, but not objects of the real world. But since both the real world and valid psychical observation, which is ineradicable from human nature, have *for man* identical significance, from the *anthropological* point of view I was fully justified in basing myself on the principle of responsibility in one's own eyes as a psychic fact underlying practical philosophy. For persons who adopt another philosophical point of view, such reasoning would be inconsistent—though almost everyone resorts to it. Let the reader excuse this dissertation on a point which in essence is

somewhat abstract. It was necessary for two reasons: the reader who goes somewhat deeper into the matter receives here an explanation of the basic views which there is no opportunity to discuss in these letters; further, from this example it can be seen how deeply rooted in mankind is the tendency toward idealization—toward singling oneself out from the unchanging connection of phenomena, and toward rationalizing within oneself even what in reality represents only submission to necessity."

[6] The 1870 edition has the following: "Finally, third, phenomena have presented themselves to man as the *actions* of a complex of real *beings* who are endowed with consciousness, reason, and will and who constitute the world. Since the first two methods of idealization do not come from direct observation but result from complex considerations which do not admit of verification through observation or experiment, we may leave them aside. As for the last method of idealization, we may note that in primitive mankind it was widespread and in lower races is still present even now. It is precisely in these cases that consciousness, reason, and will have been attributed to most of the objects in the world."

[7] This added paragraph is drawn almost verbatim from Lavrov's "Po povodu kritiki na 'Istoricheskiye pis'ma,' " pp. 315–316.

[8] The 1870 edition has the following: "The sexual impulse gave rise to the first firm social form—the family." This substitution is one of the clearest indications of the change in Lavrov's view of primitive society.

[9] For "because kinship ties gave them a certain position in their tribe" the 1870 edition has "because he had intercourse with a fertile woman."

[10] For "monks and nuns" the 1870 edition has "ascetics, male and female."

[11] For "less involved" the 1870 edition has "not involved."

[12] For "economic interdependence of capital and labor" the 1870 edition has "economic union of capital and labor."

[13] The 1870 edition adds "A society of men was in no way superior to a society of animals."

[14] For "Socialism" the 1870 edition has "A new time."

ELEVENTH LETTER. *Nations in History*

[1] For "by its capacity to influence other nations while preserving their distinctive features as well as its own" the 1870 edition has "by the second."

[2] The 1870 edition continues with the following: "and cannot but be identified with national character (*narodnost'*) by seeking the

causes of the likeness in individuals' cerebral or psychical systems in their common origin.

[3] For "by the 'Katkov press' which became its organ in the 'sixties and has multiplied and flourished in recent years" the 1870 edition has "in our time by the *Moscow Gazette* (*Moskovskiye vedomosti*)." The *Moscow Gazette* was a conservative, nationalistic newspaper edited in the late 'sixties by Michael Katkov and P. M. Leont'yev.

TWELFTH LETTER. *Contract and Law*

[1] For "the orders of an absolute state power" the 1870 edition has "someone's orders."

[2] For "economic," in this and the following sentence, the 1870 edition has "commercial."

[3] The 1870 edition has the following: "The last case presented itself in the political sphere in France at the end of the eighteenth century, and at the present time all of western Europe is employing gigantic efforts to avert the danger of a similar explosion in the socioeconomic sphere. The 'thirties gave us an example of the first case, when the industrial class of the bourgeoisie, in the name of its own interests, halted the growing administrative arbitrariness of state power. The possibility of uninterrupted progress for mankind and of averting the social explosions which threaten present-day Europe resides precisely in present-day science: its critique of the theoretical bases and the practical forms of modern culture can save mankind from numerous miseries and much economic waste, if the conclusions of this critique are in good time embodied in life through legal means. But these are paths which lie in spheres other than the juridical."

[4] For "preservation" the 1870 edition has "violation."

THIRTEENTH LETTER. *The "State"*

[1] In Lavrov's text the date is erroneously given as 1875.

[2] For "economic classes" the 1870 edition has "social parties."

[3] The 1870 edition has "the free and rational distribution of labor and profits according to the free and rational evaluation of the capacities and needs of the persons who make up the association."

[4] The 1870 edition has the following: "But these abuses always long remain as traces of the former legal order, while new ideals are assimilated only gradually. Nevertheless the new ideals have already been posed, are to a significant degree acknowledged, and are striving to realize themselves fully. One can hardly doubt that they will succeed,

and that the coercive element of the state will play a smaller and smaller role in them, until it completely disappears."

[5] The 1870 edition has the following: "Primarily they consist in the small advances of the other departments of political progress."

[6] For "revolt," the 1870 edition has "a crisis."

[7] Here the 1870 edition adds the following: "And for the most part it has been determined by the rapacity of highly placed individuals, by historical accidents, and by the irrational passions of a part of the population."

[8] Evidently Lavrov took "copperhead" (a Northerner who sympathized with the South's cause in the American Civil War) to refer to Southern secessionists.

[9] In the 1870 edition the Thirteenth Letter ended here with the additional sentence: "Let us believe in progress for the political order."

[10] This paragraph and the three which follow are drawn almost verbatim from Lavrov's "Po povodu kritiki na 'Istoricheskiye pis'ma,' " pp. 319–320.

FOURTEENTH LETTER. *The Natural Boundaries of the State*

[1] For "immediate basis of the struggle" the 1870 edition has "essence of the struggle."

[2] In the 1870 edition, this letter concluded with two additional paragraphs; in the 1891 edition, these paragraphs were incorporated in the Sixteenth Letter. See below, note 3 to the Sixteenth Letter.

FIFTEENTH LETTER. *Faith and Critical Inquiry*

[1] For "the illusions of religion and metaphysics" the 1870 edition has "illusions unexamined by criticism."

[2] After "Giordano Bruno's" the 1870 edition adds "or Serve's," evidently in reference to Michael Servet or Servetus (1511–1553), a Spanish physician who was burned at the stake for his heretical beliefs.

[3] David Friedrich Strauss (1808–1874), German theologian and philosopher, whose *Life of Jesus* (1835–1836) created a storm of controversy. Both he and his countryman Ludwig Feuerbach (1804–1872) were kept from academic posts by public opposition to their antisupernaturalistic views.

[4] The expression "the proper" was omitted from this sentence in the 1891 edition, evidently inadvertently.

[5] For "religious faith" the 1870 edition has "other fantastic beliefs."

[6] The following seven paragraphs are drawn verbatim from Lavrov's "Po povodu kritiki na 'Istoricheskiye pis'ma,' " pp. 321–323.

SIXTEENTH LETTER. *The Theory and Practice of Progress*

[1] In editions of the *Historical Letters* after 1891, the word "major" was omitted and the passage "(*Slovo*, No. 4), under the pseudonym P. Shchukin" was added to this sentence.

[2] The *zemskiye sobory* (sing. *zemsky sobor*) were representative councils, the first of which was convened by Ivan the Terrible in 1549. Alexis "the Meek" (*tishayshi*) was Alexis Mikhailovich (1629–1676), the father of Peter the Great.

[3] In the 1870 edition this sentence plus the two following paragraphs formed the conclusion of the Fourteenth Letter.

[4] Lavrov refers to the first International, founded in 1864. Apparently he considered 1872, the year it broke into Marxist and Bakuninist factions, its last year of existence; it was officially dissolved in 1876.

BIBLIOGRAPHY

BIBLIOGRAPHY

BIBLIOGRAPHY

I
Collected Editions of Lavrov's Works

Sobraniye sochineni Petra Lavrovicha Lavrova (Collected Works of Peter Lavrovich Lavrov), ed. P. Vityazev and A. Gizetti. Petrograd, 1917–1920. Published serially. Of a proposed 54 numbers in nine series, 11 numbers in five series were published: Series I: *Stat'i po filosofii* (Articles on Philosophy), Nos. 2 and 6; Series III: *Stat'i nauchnovo kharaktera* (Articles of a Scientific Nature), Nos. 1, 2, 5, and 8: Series IV: *Stat'i istoriko-filosofskiye* (Historico-Philosophical Articles), Nos. 1, 7, and 9; Series V: *Stat'i po istorii religii* (Articles on the History of Religion), No. 1; Series VI: *Stat'i sotsial'no-politicheskiye* (Socio-Political Articles), No. 7. Cited hereafter as *Sobraniye sochineni.*

Izbrannyye sochineniya na sotsial'no-politicheskiye temy v vos'mi tomakh (Selected Works on Socio-Political Themes in Eight Volumes). Edited with an introductory article by I. A. Teodorovich. Prepared for the press with commentary, notes, and biographical and bibliographical essays by I. S. Knizhnik-Vetrov. Vol. I: 1857–1871; Moscow, 1934. Vol. II: 1873–1874; Moscow, 1934. Vol. III: 1873–1874; Moscow, 1934. Vol. IV: 1875–1876; Moscow, 1935. No more published. For the years covered, these volumes contain the most complete and most detailed bibliographies of Lavrov's works available; the entries are annotated. Cited hereafter as *Izbrannyye sochineniya.*

Filosofiya i sotsiologiya: Izbrannyye proizvedeniya v dvukh tomakh (Philosophy and Sociology: Selected Works in Two Volumes), ed. I. S. Knizhnik-Vetrov and A. F. Okulov. 2 vols., Moscow, 1965. A collection of some of Lavrov's chief works on philosophical and social questions, including the *Historical Letters*, with an introductory article and notes. Cited hereafter as *Filosofiya i sotsiologiya.*

Etyudy o zapadnoy literature (Studies in Western Literature), ed. A. A. Gizetti and P. Vityazev. Petrograd, 1923. xxxii, 218 pp. A collection of Lavrov's chief articles on literature and aesthetics.

Sistematicheskaya khrestomatiya (Systematic Chrestomathy), Berlin, 1923. 170 pp. Short passages from Lavrov's works ranged under various philosophical and social topics.

II
Editions of the Historical Letters

First publication: *Nedelya* (Week), 1868: No. 1, pp. 13–19; No. 4, pp. 103–108; No. 7, pp. 197–203; No. 8, pp. 233–239; No. 13, pp. 391–395; No. 15, pp. 455–460; No. 16, pp. 481–486; No. 28, pp. 887–892; No. 35, pp. 1103–1109; No. 38, pp. 1217–1222; No. 41, pp. 1361–1366; No. 47, pp. 1651–1655. 1869: No. 6, pp. 182–187; No. 11, pp. 343–346; No. 14, pp. 441–445.

First collected edition: St. Petersburg, 1870. iv, 265 pp. Pseudonym: "P. L. Mirtov." A revised and expanded version of the first publication, including an additional letter, the tenth, "Idealization."

"Second edition, supplemented and corrected." Geneva, 1891, xvi, 319 pp. Author listed as "P. L. Mirtov (P. Lavrov)." A revised and expanded version of the first collected edition. Includes a second preface by the author, many additions to the text, a number of new footnotes, dated by the author with the year in which they were written, and an additional letter not included in previous editions— the Sixteenth Letter, "The Theory and Practice of Progress." Called the "Paris edition" in reference to Lavrov's place of residence at the time of its preparation. Reprinted in *Izbrannyye sochineniya*, Vol. I, pp. 163–396; and in *Filosofiya i sotsiologiya*, Vol. II, pp. 7–295. Cited hereafter as "1891 edition."

"Second edition." St. Petersburg, 1905. iv, 265 pp. Pseudonym: "S. S. Arnol'di." An exact reprint of the first collected edition of 1870.

"Second edition." St. Petersburg, 1905. 368 pp. No author indicated. Contents the same as the 1891 edition except that Lavrov's second preface and many of the added footnotes are excluded.

"Third edition, unchanged." St. Petersburg, 1906. 379 pp. Author listed as "P. L. Lavrov (P. Mirtov)." Contents and pagination identical to that of the "Second edition" in 368 pp. listed above, except that Lavrov's second preface is appended.

"Fourth edition, unchanged." St. Petersburg, 1906. 379 pp. Contents and pagination identical to the "Third edition, unchanged."

"Fifth edition, unchanged." Petrograd, 1917. 299 pp. Contents identical to the "Third edition, unchanged."

Polish translation: *Listy historyczne P. L. Mirtowa.* Lwow, 1885. 193 pp.

French translation: *Lettres Historiques*, translated and with a biographical and bibliographical notice by Marie Goldsmith. Paris, 1903. xxiii, 329 pp. A translation of the 1891 edition which is complete except for Lavrov's two prefaces, which are omitted entirely, and some minor deletions from footnotes. Contains a nine-page bibliography of works by Lavrov (all titles are given in French translation only)

German translation: *Historische Briefe,* translated by S. Dawidow with an introduction by C. Rappoport. Berlin, 1901. xxxxi, 368 pp. A complete translation of the 1891 edition. The introduction is a somewhat condensed version of Rappoport's book listed below.

English translation (selections): Translated by James P. Scanlan in James M. Edie, *et al.,* eds., *Russian Philosophy* (3 vols.; Chicago, 1965), Vol. II, pp. 123–169.

III
Other Chief Works of Lavrov

"Antropologicheskaya tochka zreniya v filosofii" (The Anthropological Point of View in Philosophy), *Entsiklopedichesky slovar'* (Encyclopedic Dictionary), Vol. V, St. Petersburg, 1862, pp. 6–12. Reprinted in *Sobraniye sochineni,* Series I, No. 2, pp. 197–206.

"Biografiya-ispoved'" (Biography Confession), *Izbrannyye sochineniya,* Vol. I, pp. 77–107. Lavrov's "autobiography," thought to have been dictated by him to someone; written in the third person. First circulated as a hectographed brochure in 1885 in connection with a literary festival in Lavrov's honor. Expanded and brought up to date by Lavrov in 1889. First published as "P. L. Lavrov o sebe samom" (P. L. Lavrov on Himself) in *Vestnik Yevropy* (Herald of Europe), 1910, No. 10, pp. 92–108; No. 11, pp. 83–103. Reprinted in *Filosofiya i sotsiologiya,* Vol. II, pp. 617–654.

"Chto takoye antropologiya?" (What is Anthropology?), *Russkoye slovo* (Russian Word), St. Petersburg, 1860, No. 10, pp. 53–76. Reprinted in *Sobraniye sochineni,* Series I, No. 2; and in *Filosofiya i sotsiologiya,* Vol. I, pp. 465–491.

"Formula progressa g. Mikhailovskovo" (Mr. Mikhailovsky's Formula of Progress), *Otechestvennyye zapiski* (Annals of the Fatherland), 1870, No. 2, pp. 228–255. Reprinted in *Sobraniye sochineni,* Series III, No. 8; and in *Izbrannyye sochineniya,* Vol. I, pp. 397–424.

"Gegelizm" (Hegelianism), *Biblioteka dlya chteniya* (The Readers' Library), 1858, No. 5, pp. 29–72; No. 9, pp. 1–72. Reprinted in *Filosofiya i sotsiologiya,* Vol. I, pp. 45–175.

Gosudarstvenny element v budushchem obshchestve (The Element of the State in Future Society), London, 1876. viii, 199 pages. Published as Vol. IV, No. 1 of *Vperyod!* (Forward!). Reprinted in *Sobraniye sochineni,* Series VI, No. 7; and in *Izbrannyye sochineniya,* Vol. IV, pp. 207–395.

Istoriya, sotsializm, i russkoye dvizheniye (History, Socialism, and the Russian Movement), Geneva, 1893. iv, 42 pp.

Iz istorii sotsial'nykh ucheni (From the History of Social Doctrines), Petrograd, 1919. 132 pp. First published in *Vperyod!* (Forward!), 1873, Vol. I, Section I, pp. 60–109; 1874, Vol. III, Section I, pp. 45–119. Reprinted in *Izbrannyye sochineniya,* Vol. II, pp. 143–249.

"Komu prinadlezhit budushcheye?" (To Whom Does the Future Belong?), *Vperyod!* (Forward!), 1874, Vol. II, Section I, pp. 1–73. Reprinted in *Izbrannyye sochineniya,* Vol. III, pp. 79–144.

"Kriticheskaya istoriya filosofii" (A Critical History of Philosophy), *Znaniye* (Knowledge), 1873, No. 6, pp. 9–28. Reprinted in *Filosofiya i sotsiologiya,* Vol. II, pp. 331–352.

"Mekhanicheskaya teoriya mira" (The Mechanistic Theory of the World), *Otechestvennyye zapiski* (Annals of the Fatherland), 1859, No. 4, pp. 451–492. Reprinted in *Sobraniye sochineni,* Series I, No. 2.

"Moim kritikam" (To My Critics [Antonovich and Pisarev]), *Russkoye slovo* (Russian Word), 1861, No. 6, pp. 48–69. Reprinted in *Sobraniye sochineni,* Series I, No. 2.

Narodniki-propagandisty 1873–1878 godov (The Populist Propagandists of 1873–1878), 2 vols., Geneva, 1895–1896. 292 pp. Republished in St. Petersburg in 1907 and in Leningrad in 1925.

"Neskol'ko mysley ob istorii mysli" (Some Thoughts on the History of Thought), *Nevsky sbornik* (Nevsky Miscellany), 1867, Vol. I, pp. 546–575. Reprinted in *Sobraniye sochineni,* Series IV, No. 1.

Ocherk evolyutsii chelovecheskoy mysli (see *Perezhivaniya doistoricheskovo perioda*).

Ocherki voprosov prakticheskoy filosofii: I. Lichnost' (Outlines of Problems of Practical Philosophy: I. Individuality), St. Petersburg, 1860. 94 pp. First published as "Ocherk teorii lichnosti" (An Outline of the Theory of Individuality), *Otechestvennyye zapiski* (Annals of the Fatherland), 1859, No. 11, pp. 207–242; No. 12, pp. 555–610. Reprinted in *Filosofiya i sotsiologiya,* Vol. I, pp. 341–461. Cited hereafter as *Ocherki.*

Opyt istorii mysli (An Essay in the History of Thought), St. Petersburg, 1875. 162 pp. Originally published, in part, under the title "Vvedeniye v istoriyu mysli" (An Introduction to the History of Thought) in *Znaniye* (Knowledge), 1874, No. 1, pp. 1–42; No. 2, pp. 43–98.

Opyt istorii mysli novovo vremeni (An Essay in the History of Thought in Modern Times), Geneva, 1894. 2 vols., 1568 pp. The two volumes together make up "Book I—Prehistory" of the contemplated longer work. No more published. Originally appeared serially in Geneva between 1888 and 1894.

"Otvet g. Strakhovu" (A Reply to Mr. Strakhov), *Otechestvennyye zapiski* (Annals of the Fatherland), 1860, No. 12, pp. 101–112. Reprinted in *Filosofiya i sotsiologiya*, Vol. 1, pp. 495–507.

Parizhskaya kommuna 18 marta 1871 g. (The Paris Commune of 18 March 1871), Geneva, 1880. x, 232 pp. Other editions: Petrograd, 1919; Leningrad, 1925.

Perezhivaniya doistoricheskovo perioda (Survivals from the Prehistoric Period), Paris, 1897. xii, 160 pp. Also published in Geneva in 1898. Reprinted in *Sobraniye sochineni*, Series III, No. 5. Identified as "Book VI" of a projected longer work, *Ocherk evolyutsii chelovecheskoy mysli* (An Outline of the Evolution of Human Thought); no more published. (See above, note 107 to the introduction).

"Pis'ma o raznykh sovremennykh voprosakh" (Letters on Various Contemporary Questions), *Obshchezanimatel'ny vestnik* (General Herald), 1857, No. 1, pp. 43–50; No. 20, pp. 722–726. Only two letters—Letter I and Letter III—were published in this series. Letter II, rejected by the censors, was published in 1858 in another journal under the title "Vrednyye nachala" (Harmful Principles).

"Pis'mo k izdatelyu" (Letter to the Editor [Alexander Herzen]), *Izbrannyye sochineniya*, Vol. I, pp. 108–117. First published in *Golosa iz Rossii* (Voices from Russia), ed. Alexander Herzen, Bk. IV, London, 1857, pp. 5–29. A second edition was published in 1858.

"Po povodu kritiki na 'Istoricheskiye pis'ma'" (Apropos of Criticism of the *Historical Letters*), *Filosofiya i sotsiologiya*, Vol. II, pp. 299–328. First published in *Znaniye* (Knowledge), 1871, No. 10, pp. 1–27. Reprinted in *Izbrannyye sochineniya*, Vol. I, pp. 425–448.

Po povodu Samarskovo goloda (Apropos of the Famine in Samara), London, 1874. 174 pp. A considerably altered and expanded version of material first published in *Vperyod!* (Forward!), 1874, Vol. II, Section II, pp. 1–74; Vol. III, Section II, pp. 1–81. Reprinted in *Izbrannyye sochineniya*, Vol. III, pp. 173–331.

"Postepenno" (Little by Little), *Kniga i revolyutsiya* (Book and Revolution), 1922, No. 6 (18), pp. 16–18. Seized in proof sheets upon Lavrov's arrest in 1866. Reprinted in *Izbrannyye sochineniya*, Vol. I, pp. 128–133.

"Prakticheskaya filosofiya Gegelya" (The Practical Philosophy of Hegel), *Biblioteka dlya chteniya* (The Readers' Library), 1859,

No. 4, pp. 1–66; No. 5, pp. 1–61. Reprinted in *Filosofiya i sotsiologiya*, Vol. I, pp. 179–338.

"Predisloviye" (Foreword), in Karl Marx, *Vvedeniye k kritike filosofii prava Gegelya* (Introduction to a Critique of Hegel's Philosophy of Right), Geneva, 1887. Reprinted in *Filosofiya i sotsiologiya*, Vol. II, pp. 583–613.

Russkoy sotsial'no-revolyutsionnoy molodyozhi (To the Russian Social Revolutionary Youth), London, 1874. 60 pp. Reprinted in *Izbrannyye sochineniya*, Vol. III, pp. 335–372.

"Sotsializm i bor'ba za sushchestvovaniye" (Socialism and the Struggle for Existence), *Vperyod!* (Forward!), 1875, No. 17, pp. 513–526. Reprinted in *Izbrannyye sochineniya*, Vol. IV, pp. 99–110; and in *Filosofiya i sotsiologiya*, Vol. II, pp. 365–381.

"Sotsial'naya revolyutsiya i zadachi nravstvennosti" (The Social Revolution and the Problems of Morality), *Vestnik narodnoy voli* (Herald of the People's Will), 1884, Vol. III, pp. 1–76; Vol. IV, pp. 1–84. Reprinted in *Filosofiya i sotsiologiya*, Vol. II, pp. 385–504.

"Sovremennyye germanskiye teisty" (The Contemporary German Theists), *Russkoye slovo* (Russian Word), 1859, No. 7, pp. 141–212.

Sovremennyye ucheniya o nravstvennosti i yeyo istoriya (Contemporary Doctrines of Morality and the History of Morality), St. Petersburg, 1903–1904. 216 pp. Originally published in *Otechestvennyye zapiski* (Annals of the Fatherland), 1870, No. 3, pp. 76–105; No. 4, pp. 437–468; No. 5, pp. 126–148; No. 6, pp. 225–270; No. 8, pp. 341–378.

"Staryye voprosy. Ucheniye grafa L. N. Tolstovo" (Old Questions. The Teachings of Count L. N. Tolstoy), *Vestnik narodnoy voli* (Herald of the People's Will), 1884, Vol. V, pp. 137–214. Reprinted in *Filosofiya i sotsiologiya*, Vol. II, pp. 507–580.

"Teoriya i praktika progressa" (The Theory and Practice of Progress), *Slovo* (Word), 1881, No. 4, pp. 25–62. Added to the *Historical Letters* for the 1891 edition, forming the Sixteenth Letter.

Tri besedy o sovremennom znachenii filosofii (Three Talks on the Contemporary Significance of Philosophy), St. Petersburg, 1861. 69 pp. First published as "O sovremennom znachenii filosofii" (On the Contemporary Significance of Philosophy), *Otechestvennyye zapiski* (Annals of the Fatherland), 1861, No. 1, pp. 91–142. Republished in Kazan in 1904 and 1907. Reprinted in *Sobraniye sochineni*, Series I, No. 2; and in *Filosofiya i sotsiologiya*, Vol. I, pp. 511–573. Cited hereafter as *Tri besedy*.

Tsivilizatsiya i dikiye plemena (Civilization and Savage Tribes), St. Petersburg, 1903. 264 pp. First published in *Otechestvennyye zapiski* (Annals of the Fatherland), 1869, No. 5, pp. 107–169; No. 6, pp. 359–414; No. 8, pp. 253–311; No. 9, pp. 93–128.

Vazhneyshiye momenty v istorii mysli (Paramount Moments in the History of Thought), Pseudonym: "A. Dolengi." Moscow, 1903. xvi, 998 pp. Completed, except for the conclusion, by Lavrov before his death. Prepared for the press by N. S. Rusanov.

"Vrednyye nachala" (Harmful Principles), *Illyustratsiya* (Illustration), 1858, No. 39, pp. 222 ff. (See "Pis'ma o raznykh sovremennykh voprosakh" above.) Reprinted in *Izbrannyye sochineniya*, Vol. I, pp. 118–127

Zadachi ponimaniya istorii: proyekt vvedeniya v izucheniye evolyutsii chelovecheskoy mysli (The Problems of Understanding History: A Draft of an Introduction to the Study of the Evolution of Human Thought), Moscow, 1898. xii, 371 pp. Pseudonym: "Arnol'di." 2nd ed., St. Petersburg, 1903.

Zadachi positivizma i ikh resheniye (The Problems of Positivism and Their Solution), St. Petersburg, 1906. 78 pp. Printed in one cover with *Teoretiki sorokovykh godov v nauke o verovaniyakh* (The Theorists of the 'Forties in the Science of Religion). First published in *Sovremennoye obozreniye* (Contemporary Review), 1868), No. 5, pp. 117–154. Reprinted in *Filosofiya i sotsiologiya*, Vol. I, pp. 577–634.

IV
Selected Works on Lavrov

Antonovich, M. A. "Dva tipa sovremennykh filosofov" (Two Types of Contemporary Philosophers), in *Izbrannyye filosofskiye sochineniya* (Selected Philosophical Works), Moscow, 1945, pp. 18–91. First published in *Sovremennik* (The Contemporary), 1861, Vol. 86, No. 4. A critique of Lavrov's *Tri besedy.*

Chernyshevsky, N. G. "Antropologichesky printsip v filosofii" (The Anthropological Principle in Philosophy), in *Sovremennik* (The Contemporary), 1860, Vol. 80, No. 4, pp. 329–366; Vol. 81, No. 5, pp. 1–46. A review of Lavrov's *Ocherki.* Available in English translation in Chernyshevsky, *Selected Philosophical Essays*, Moscow, 1953, pp. 49–135.

Ivanov-Razumnik, R. V. *Istoriya russkoy obshchestvennoy mysli* (A History of Russian Social Thought). 2 vols. 4th ed. St. Petersburg, 1914. Vol. II, pp. 96–131.

Kareyev, Nikolay U. *Teoriya lichnosti P. L. Lavrova* (P. L. Lavrov's Theory of Individuality). St. Petersburg, 1907, 64 pp.

358 BIBLIOGRAPHY

Knizhnik-Vetrov, I. "P. L. Lavrov ot pervykh publitsisticheskikh vys-tupleni do izdaniya 'Vperyod' (1857—mart 1872)" (P. L. Lavrov from his First Journalistic Publications to the Editorship of "Forward" [1857—March, 1872]), in Lavrov, *Izbrannyye sochineniya*, Vol. I, pp. 14–74.

Knizhnik-Vetrov, I. *Pyotr Lavrovich Lavrov*. 2nd ed., revised and supplemented. Moscow, 1930. 142 pp. Annotated bibliographies, pp. 113–134. The chief study in print of Lavrov's life and socio-political ideas. The first edition, entitled *Pyotr Lavrovich Lavrov: Yevo zhizn' i trudy* (Peter Lavrovich Lavrov: His Life and Works), was published in Leningrad in 1925.

Koz'min, B. "Tkachov i Lavrov" (Tkachov and Lavrov), in *Voinst-vuyushchi materialist* (The Militant Materialist), Moscow, 1924, pp. 291–337.

Kulyabko-Koretsky, N. G. *Iz davnykh let: Bospominaniya Lavrista* (From Years Gone by: Memoirs of a Lavrovist). Moscow, 1931. 311 pp.

Lukashevich, A. O. " 'V narod!' " ("To the People!"), in *Byloye* (The Past), 1907, No. 3/15, pp. 1–44.

Masaryk, T. G. *The Spirit of Russia: Studies in History, Literature, and Philosophy.* Trans. Eden and Cedar Paul. 2 vols. London, New York, 1961. Vol. II, pp. 115–135.

Nechayev, V. N. "Protsess P. L. Lavrova 1866 g." (The Trial of P. L. Lavrov in 1866), in *Sbornik materialov i statey* (Collected Material and Articles), ed. *Istorichesky arkhiv* (Historical Archive), 1921, No. 1, pp. 45 ff.

Nikitenko, A. V. *Moya povest' o samom sebe* (My Story of Myself). 2nd ed. 2 vols. St. Petersburg, 1905. Vol. II, *passim*.

Ostrogorsky, M. "Perly sovremennovo 'lavrizma' " (Pearls of Modern-day "Lavrovism"), in *Katorga i ssylka* (Penal Servitude and Exile), 1932, No. 1, pp. 175–219. A severe critique of Knizhnik-Vetrov, *Pyotr Lavrovich Lavrov.*

Pamyati P. L. Lavrova (In Memory of P. L. Lavrov). Geneva, 1900. 90 pp. Contains articles by N. S. Rusanov, N. E. Kudrin, J. Kolub-ovsky. Bibliography, pp. 81–86.

Pereselenkov, S. A. "Ofitsial'nyye komentarii k 'Istoricheskim pis'mam' P. L. Lavrova" (Official Commentaries on P. L. Lavrov's "Histori-cal Letters"), in *Byloye* (The Past), 1925, No. 30, pp. 37–40. Con-tains the texts of the censors' reports on the *Historical Letters.*

Pisarev, D. I. "Skholastika XIX Veka" (Nineteenth Century Scholas-ticism), in *Russkoye slovo* (Russian Word), 1861, No. 5, pp. 74–82. These pages of Pisarev's articles contain a critique of Lavrov's

Tri besedy. Available in English translation in Pisarev, *Selected Philosophical, Social and Political Essays,* Moscow, 1958, pp. 106–114.

P. L. Lavrov: Sbornik statey. Stat'i, vospominaniya, materialy (P. L. Lavrov: Collected Articles. Articles, Memoirs, Material). Petrograd, 1922. vi, 522 pp. Contains reminiscences and articles on various aspects of Lavrov's thought by Shpet, Radlov, Kropotkin, Ovsyaniko-Kulikovsky, and others.

Pomper, Philip. "Peter Lavrov: His Life and Thought." Unpublished dissertation. University of Chicago, 1965. This work, which draws on archival material as well as published sources, is the most comprehensive and trustworthy study of Lavrov in any language.

Rappoport, Charles. *La Philosophie Sociale de Pierre Lavroff.* Paris, 1900. 64 pp. Russian translation as *Sotsial'naya filosofiya Petra Lavrova* (The Social Philosophy of Peter Lavrov), St. Petersburg, 1906.

[Rusanov, N. S.] *Biografiya Petra Lavrovicha Lavrova* (Biography of Peter Lavrovich Lavrov). N.p., 1899. 36 pp. Cited hereafter as *Biografiya.*

Rusanov, N. S. "P. L. Lavrov: Ocherk yevo zhizni i deyatel'nosti" (P. L. Lavrov: Sketch of His Life and Activity), in *Byloye* (The Past), 1907, No. 2, pp. 243–286. An expanded version of the same author's *Biografiya.* Cited hereafter as "P. L. Lavrov."

Shtakenshneyder, E. A. *Dnevnik i zapiski (1854–1886)* (Diary and Memoirs [1854–1886]). Ed. I. N. Rozanov. Moscow, Leningrad, 1934.

Utechin, S. V. *Russian Political Thought: A Concise History.* New York, London, 1963. Pp. 128–143.

Vartanyants, V. *Antropologicheskaya filosofiya: P. Mirtov i sub'yektivny metod v sotsiologii* (The Anthropological Philosophy: P. Mirtov [Lavrov] and the Subjective Method in Sociology), Tiflis, 1901. 38 pp.

Venediktov-Bezyuk, D. G. "Pobeg P. L. Lavrova iz ssylki" (P. L. Lavrov's Escape from Exile), in *Katorga i ssylka* (Penal Servitude and Exile), 1931, No. 5 (78), pp. 183–197.

Venturi, Franco. *Roots of Revolution: A History of the Populist and Socialist Movements in Nineteenth-Century Russia.* Trans. Francis Haskell. New York, 1960. Pp. 445–468.

Vityazev, P. "Chem obyazana russkaya obshchestvennost' P. L. Lavrovu?" (How is the Russian Intellectual Community Indebted to P. L. Lavrov?), in *Yezhemesyachny zhurnal* (Monthly Journal), 1915, No. 2, pp. 79–85; No. 3, pp. 81–88.

Vityazev, P. (ed.). *Materialy dlya biografii P. L. Lavrova* (Material for a Biography of P. L. Lavrov). Petrograd, 1921. 89 pp. Cited hereafter as *Materialy*.

Vityazev, P. (ed.). "P. L. Lavrov v vospominaniyakh sovremennikov" (P. L. Lavrov in the Recollections of Contemporaries), in *Golos minuvshevo* (Voice of the Past), 1915, No. 9, pp. 131–145; No. 10, pp. 112–148. Recollections by Antonovich, Lopatin, Negreskul, and Sazhin.

Vityazev, P. (ed.). *Vperyod! Sbornik statey, posvyashchennykh pamyati P. L. Lavrova* (Forward! A Collection of Articles Dedicated to the Memory of P. L. Lavrov). Petrograd, Moscow, 1920. 64 pp. Articles by P. Vityazev, V. Trutovsky, P. Sorokin, G. Shpet, A. Gizetti, E. Radlov, A. Shteynberg, Ivanov-Razumnik, B. Stoyanov, and P. Stolpyansky. Cited hereafter as *Vperyod!*

Zenkovsky, V. V. *A History of Russian Philosophy*. Trans. George L. Kline. 2 vols. New York, London, 1953. Vol. I, pp. 348–362.

INDEX

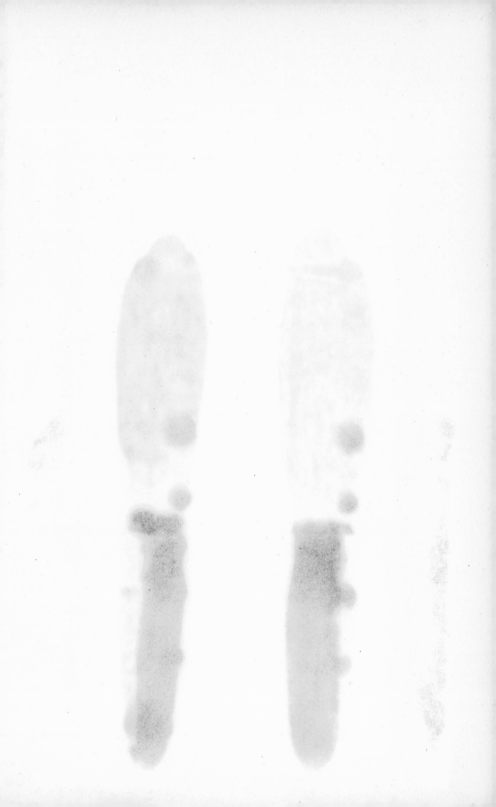

DATE DUE

GAYLORD   PRINTED IN U.S.A.